THE RIGHTS AND RESPONSIBILITIES OF THE MODERN UNIVERSITY

The Rights and Responsibilities of the Modern University

The Rise of the Facilitator University

SECOND EDITION

Peter F. Lake

Carolina Academic Press
Durham, North Carolina

Library of Congress Cataloging-in-Publication Data

Lake, Peter F.
The rights and responsibilities of the modern university : the rise of the facilitator university / Peter F. Lake. -- Second edition.
pages cm
Includes bibliographical references and index.
ISBN 978-1-59460-898-8 (alk. paper)
1. Universities and colleges--United States--Safety measures. 2. Universities and colleges--Law and legislation--United States. 3. College students--United States. I. Title.

LB2866.B52 2013
378.00973--dc23

2012038571

Carolina Academic Press
700 Kent Street
Durham, North Carolina 27701
Telephone (919) 489-7486
Fax (919) 493-5668
www.cap-press.com

Printed in the United States of America

For Jennifer

Table of Contents

Preface

This is the first time I have done a second edition of anything. It's exciting—a bit like opening a time capsule.

What amazes me the most looking in the rearview mirror at *Rights and Responsibilities of the Modern University: Who Assumes the Risks of College Life?* (R&R1) is seeing the convergence of ideas at the millennium. The first edition was published in 1999, and I do not think I had even heard the term "millennial student." Strauss & Howe's famous first book on millennial students came out shortly after R&R1. I was also destined to meet Bill Dejong and learn about environmental management strategies in alcohol and drug prevention. The Texas A&M bonfire collapse timed out right after the publication of the first edition, and a connection to risk management was off and running. And in short order top courts in Nebraska, Florida, and Idaho would release cases that supported key themes in the book. Law, generational theory, risk management, and prevention congealed in a very mutually supportive way. The need for a second edition became more apparent as the 2000s unfolded—particularly to draw attention to an interdisciplinary convergence of similar and mutually supporting ideas.

Since the publication of R&R1, I also have had the opportunity to tackle the related issues of student discipline systems and the role of a student in a facilitator university in *Beyond Discipline—Managing the Modern Higher Education Environment* (Hierophant Enterprises 2009). *Beyond Discipline* is very much a companion to *Rights and Responsibilities*, even more so to this second edition.

Readers of both editions of *Rights and Responsibilities* will notice immediately that the second edition is a substantial update from the first. The second edition addresses modern alcohol prevention efforts, new risk management strategies, generational theory (particularly related to millennials), new research on community efficacy, and a decade plus of rapid evolution of safety law on campus. Legally, a great deal has come into better focus since the first edition; there have been as many key cases since 1999 as there were in the 50 years prior. Moreover, regulators are more involved in college safety than ever. There has also been an explosion of research and writing on college safety issues, and new issues like suicide and active shooter risk have emerged to priority levels of concern. Finally, R&R1 had an impact in the courts, litigation, student affairs practice, risk management, and even prevention. The second edition is not a chronicle of the impact of the first edition, but the new edition draws attention to many of the ways R&R1 has interacted with various disciplines in the field of higher education.

I have tried to be as respectful of the first edition—"old blue"—as possible. Nonetheless, the facilitator model was designed to be organic and evolutionary and so it is here. In many ways this edition is the product of speaking at several hundred events. The field has helped *Rights and Responsibilities* grow and mature into a second edition. I also credit R&R1 for helping me see America, and England for the first time—and for introducing me to my future wife. Working on the second edition I also remember my pal Coyote napping next to me on the white carpet in my office at home on sabbatical—two sabbaticals ago—and I can tell that the younger man writing that manuscript had only a dim idea of the great adventures, and challenges, that lay ahead.

I want to thank Stetson University College of Law for providing generous support for this book in the form of a long-term research grant. Special thanks to Dianne Oeste for deciphering my scribbles and whipping this into form. The invaluable Mark St. Louis provided critical assistance as did my research assistants Aaron Swift, Christie Letarte and Mercy Roberg. Most importantly of all, my wife, Jennifer, gave this book the loving and diligent attention it needed to come to form.

Peter Lake
Bradenton, Florida
January 2013

The Rights and Responsibilities of the Modern University

I

Introduction

Toward a Balancing of Rights and Responsibilities on Campus

"The premise of modern post-secondary education is that students have both rights and responsibilities . . ."

—*Pawlowski v. Delta Sigma Phi*
(Connecticut Superior Court, January 23, 2009)

American universities once evoked images of laureled sanctuaries where higher learning is facilitated in a unique and particularly safe environment. Yet, college education is filled with potential safety risks for students. College can be a dangerous experience and modern universities, unlike their ancient counterparts, struggle to strike a balance between creating a safe learning environment and holding students accountable for their own risky decisions.

The media has increasingly drawn attention to the dark side of the college experience and reports regularly about criminal attacks on students on campus, injuries to students on field trips and in study abroad programs, injuries from defective premises or other unsafe conditions, Greek life incidents, and alcohol problems on and off campus.[1] The incidents reported by the major media are

1. *See, e.g.*, Peter F. Lake, *Beyond Discipline—Managing the Modern Higher Education Environment* 5–7 (Hierophant Enterprises 2009). *See also* Amy Gajda, *The Trials of Academe: The New Era of Campus Litigation* (Harvard Univ. Press 2009); Peter F. Lake, *Still Waiting: The Slow Evolution of the Law in Light of the Ongoing Student Suicide Crisis*, 34 J.C. & U.L. 253 (2008); Susan H. Duncan, *College Bullies—Precursors to Campus Violence: What Should Universities and College Administrators Know About the Law?*, 55 Vill. L. Rev. 269 (2010).

only a fraction of the risk management problems. Student safety has become a core issue for modern universities—indeed integral to core mission delivery. An unsafe campus is not a responsible or effective learning environment and will be plagued with non-safety risks, such as poor retention rates, diminished academic success, and the potential for tarnished reputations, *inter alia.* A college that does not strike the right balance of safety and responsibility faces enterprise risks and compromises core mission delivery. Higher learning requires a reasonably safe learning environment. A reasonably safe learning environment requires a constant balancing of respective rights and responsibilities.

There are four central causes of danger on college and university campuses.

First, college campuses were not designed with safety as the first goal. Colleges house students in densely populated living arrangements. Some of these living arrangements are decades old and were first designed and occupied in an era when crime on campus was not a major concern to administrators, students, or parents (indeed the very notion of an open campus, growing organically over long periods of time, is at odds with most modern commercial safety design). College campuses in general may feature a hodgepodge of buildings constructed over decades, even centuries. Retrofitting older facilities can only do so much. Colleges have a tendency to allocate resources to educational and other endeavors first, not to facility maintenance or to proactive risk management efforts. Campuses are vulnerable to criminality.

Second, and related, most universities are *open* campuses. The campus is often an amalgam of buildings, put to a variety of uses—e.g., science laboratories, sport and recreational facilities, art studios, residences, parking garages and lots, arenas, etc. Operation of each facility brings with it standard risks that other similar operations face. However, campuses are virtually unique in the variety of facilities and operations that work simultaneously. The risk signature of a modern campus is unique in American business, particularly in the combination of services offered. From a safety point of view, the business of higher education is more challenging than running a theme park, cruise ship, casino, or even an assisted living facility. Colleges often offer whole-life living/learning experiences longitudinally.

Third, for many college students campus life seems safer than it is. Many students were raised in a culture that has emphasized child safety, sometimes almost to an extreme. The illusion of safety is its own kind of danger. Many of our students are *millennial* students, who were highly sheltered, protected, and mentored in high school and at home. The shift to a higher learning environment is challenging because many students were raised to believe that their environment is always reasonably safe and someone is in charge of their safety.

Fourth, American college campuses have experienced persistent dangers associated with high-risk alcohol use, the drug of choice for college populations. In combination with the other risk factors, alcohol use by college students enhances other risks. Alcohol risk is the primary risk for modern colleges on a wide range of indicators, especially safety.

The four central causes of college risk, therefore, are *generational* and *structural.* The structure (and structures) of the college experience, in combination with the populations who learn in these structures, give college its unique risk signature. Modern efforts to combat risk on campus often focus—after a crisis—on immediate causes of risk, such as the presence of guns on campus, or the proliferation of prescription medications and their misuse, etc. However, whatever the risk du jour, danger on campus ultimately arises from the structure of the college experience and the populations who learn in those structures.

Unfortunately, the dangers of college and university life have not decreased. Indeed, it seems that some risks have become more prominent, such as the risk of active shooter violence, bullying, and mental health related risk. Insurance statistics have shown steady rates of growth in college student injury claims. The growth may continue: students have experienced a culture of violence, incivility, and intoxicants in K-12 education and are on their way to college bringing risk with them. The rise in travel abroad and externship programs, for instance, also has generated risk.[2] With danger rising and mutating in colleges, we seek answers on how to make college life reasonably safe and how we should fairly and reasonably allocate the rights and responsibilities of students and universities to make campuses safe.

Paradoxically, at a time of great need, the law of higher education relating to the allocation of rights and responsibilities remains complex and confusing. Obviously, there is much more to creating safe and productive learning environments than legal rules. However, university law has had, and will have, a major impact on university safety and ultimately on the effectiveness of a college's educational program. Higher education law co-creates the foundations of the university environment and apportions the rights and responsibilities of the participants in university life. Legal archetypes and images, as we shall see, serve to focus the imagination of university culture. That imagination is remarkably powerful. Legal images and rules can radically alter parameters of risk and can foster a range of effects on university culture from dictatorial-style

2. *See, e.g.*, Kathleen M. Busch, *Going Global: Managing Liability in International Externship Programs—A Case Study*, 36 J.C. & U.L. 455 (2010).

control of student life, to disorder, danger, or administrative disempowerment. For example, if courts tell students that they are consumers completely free of university control and are destined to drink, they may begin to believe and act on those messages. Messages—implicit or explicit—are powerful forces influencing behavior.[3] Even seemingly harmless ideas like treating a university as a business can be troubling. Radical consumerism can disserve safety and fracture any sense of shared responsibility for safety on campus. Ultimately, the university is both a creator and mirror of society itself. The law can help to make the image in the mirror brighter or darker.

There are conflicting messages on how responsibility for student safety should be allocated, and just how dangerous college life is. Parents and prospective students often see college promotional materials filled with serene, almost monastic pictures of campus life; pictures of scholarly faculty and diligent students in libraries, laboratories, and office settings; and visual images of sophisticated extracurricular activities and a high quality of life. University lawyers and administrators, however, are well aware of the dangers of student injury and the (potential) litigation that comes from it.[4] University administrators exercise responsibility for student affairs—but may be criticized if they have inappropriately "assumed duties" to students. Their jobs are on the line with each decision they make. They often live in a world with classic "catch 22s": the typical college administrator may feel both frustrated and disempowered by law and parental/student expectations. The law of student safety itself is often a complex, confusing maze, especially in an era of increasing regulatory accountability.

The complexity and confusion in university law is the natural and direct result of the revolutions in university law and culture in the post World War II era. Since World War II, and particularly since the 1960s, university law has changed dramatically from emphasizing images of university *authority* to images emphasizing student *freedom.*

Most commentators and courts believe that the American university stood (for the most part) *in loco parentis*[5]—in the place of a parent—to its students before 1960 (being somewhat arbitrary in the dates). The basic idea

---

3. *See* Marc Edelman & David Rosenthal, *A Sobering Conflict: The Call for Consistency in the Message Colleges Send About Alcohol,* 20 Fordham Intell. Prop. Media & Ent. L.J. 1389 (2010).

4. *See, e.g.,* Nancy Tribbensee, *Tort Litigation in Higher Education: A Review of Cases Decided in Year 2001,* 29 J.C. & U.L. 249 (2003).

5. *See* Chapter II for a more thorough definition and discussion of the concept.

of a university *in loco parentis* is easy to grasp—simply imagine parental, sometimes even paramilitary-style, *control* of student life and affairs. Dean Wormer, of fictional Faber College in the movie *Animal House*,[6] comically portrays the legal archetype of the (almost) limitless power a university had, or at least asserted, over its students. In this era a university was rarely, if ever, subject to a lawsuit. It was a time of insularity[7] from legal scrutiny, and like governments, charities, and families of that era, the college was considered to be another institution outside the safety rules of the legal system and, in a sense, above the law. University law tracked the law of interpersonal family relations, governmental/citizen relations, and charitable organizations regarding liability in civil courts. Disputes were kept and settled within the university, as within a family (or a church).[8] If a matter involved a public university, the matter was considered "governmental" and not subject to private civil lawsuits seeking reparations for injuries.

Then in the 1960s and early 1970s, as Professor Charles A. Wright observed, the Constitution (and a great deal of public civil rights cases) came to campus. This period, detailed in Chapter III, witnessed student challenges to university control and to the idea that college life was insulated from legal scrutiny. Students argued that *in loco parentis* authority had been used on them in extreme and unfair ways by colleges that disciplined and/or expelled students for participation in the civil rights movement and even for asserting basic constitutional rights of free speech and association. Beginning with the landmark decision in *Dixon v. Alabama State Board of Education*[9] (discussed in Chapter III), students succeeded in challenging abuses of university power and won basic constitutional rights on campus. To some courts students were no longer children; they became *constitutional* adults.

As a result of the rapid fall of a long period of legal insularity, student *freedom* ascended over university *authority* and *control*. The university was no longer insulated from legal scrutiny. So much changed in American society in this period in similar ways—rights of women against husbands, children against parents, the disgrace of Nixon and the presidency, lowering of respect for military and police activities, Vietnam, etc.—that the profound shift in *campus* law was a footnote in a chapter of social change and upheaval in America. But the shift

6. Universal Pictures 1978.

7. Alternatively, the era can be viewed as an era of power and prerogative. *See* Lake, *Beyond Discipline*, *supra* note 1 at 27–61.

8. *See id.*

9. 294 F.2d 150 (5th Cir. 1961), *cert. denied*, 368 U.S. 930 (1961).

was a groundbreaking one. The American college was no longer insular: colleges entered a new era of accountability in the law and in the eyes of the public.[10] The fall of legal insularity and the new role of the legal system on campus facilitated important developments in legal relations between students and administrators (and others) on campus. These developments have had important student safety implications, many felt even to this day.

In 1987, Ernest L. Boyer, former U.S. Commissioner of Education, published *College: The Undergraduate Experience in America,* in association with the Carnegie Foundation for the Advancement of Teaching. Boyer's book is a widely celebrated resource on post-1960s college education in America.[11] The book is a comprehensive survey of college experience including college application issues; academic, curricular, and faculty concerns; campus life; and governance of a university. It is noteworthy that Boyer makes only oblique, indirect, or passing references to university law and the profound *legal* changes which occurred. Commenting upon the gap between academic and social life, Boyer found:

> [A] *great separation*, sometimes to the point of isolation, between academic and social life on campus. Colleges like to speak of the campus as *community*, and yet what is being learned in most residence halls today has little connection to the classrooms; indeed it may undermine the educational purposes of the college. The idea that a college stands in for parents, *in loco parentis,* is today a faded memory. But on many campuses there is great uncertainty about what should replace it.[12]

Admittedly, Boyer was focused more on policy and academic administration than college law and the effects of change(s) in college law.

Nevertheless, from his lens, Boyer observed the central perplexing problems that university law has faced and helped to create since the fall of university insularity began in the 1960s. Boyer commented upon the *distance* created between faculty and administration on the one hand and student life on the other.

---

10. This trend has accelerated. *See* Beckie Supiano & Elyse Ashburn (Eric Hoover, contributing), *With New Lists, Federal Government Moves to Help Consumers and Prod Colleges to Limit Price Increases*, Chron. Higher Educ. (June 30, 2011), *available at* http://chronicle.com/article/Governments-New-Lists-on/128092/. "Colleges have stumbled into an age of accountability. The government and the public are evermore interested in holding them responsible . . . ." *Id.*

11. *See* Ernest L. Boyer, *College: The Undergraduate Experience in America* (Harper & Row 1987).

12. *Id.* at 5 (some emphasis added).

He also recognized the inherent need to make the connection between educational goals and non-academic student life.[13]

Importantly, Boyer stated the principal question presented in modern American university law and policy regarding student safety: "How should tension between student freedom and institutional authority be resolved?"[14] An entire epoch of the *legal* understanding of the university and its relationships to students abruptly ended. Long standing day-to-day relations among students and universities changed almost instantly as if a meteor struck.

In place of a community ordered by plenary university authority, students and colleges began to grow increasingly distant. The profound and sudden shift from an authoritarian and legally insularized university model to a student rights/freedom model where students had basic constitutional and other civil rights soon ushered in a new period in the courts reflecting this distancing. It was the birth of what this book refers to as the "bystander" era.[15] In the 1970s and early to mid 1980s (again, somewhat arbitrarily), American courts began hearing lawsuits involving student physical injuries arising from the risks of campus life, not just student constitutional rights style cases. These cases—detailed, described, and critiqued in Chapter IV—were different. The focus in the student civil rights cases was on positive aspects of student freedom from autocratic university control. The new cases were oriented to the negative side of student freedom. Namely, if students were free from autocratic control, what, if any, *duties* were owed to them regarding their physical

---

13. As Boyer wrote:

> We were especially impressed that many faculty and academic administrators distance themselves from student life and appear to be confused about their obligations in non-academic matters. How can life outside the classroom support the educational mission of the college? How should tension between student freedom and institutional authority be resolved?

Id.

14. *Id.*

15. Many commentators now adopt this parlance. *See, e.g.*, Judith Areen, *Higher Education and the Law: Cases and Materials* (Foundation Press 2009) (adopting this description to organize a section of her book). Since the publication of the first edition of this book, modern college alcohol, other drug, and violence prevention efforts have focused increasingly on "bystander" intervention strategies. These strategies seek to empower bystanders to reduce the risks of high-risk alcohol use, violence, etc. Prevention efforts use the term "bystander" in a slightly different way. This book describes bystanderism as a negative and dangerous phenomenon: prevention efforts view bystanderism as a potential positive source of proactive intervention. Ultimately, the goal is the same.

safety? Who now assumed the risks of student life? A prominent group of decided cases (but relatively few in number, and mostly in less prominent jurisdictions) defined a brief, but critical, post-*in loco parentis* period in university law. Several courts of this period reacted to newly won student constitutional rights by rejecting student injury claims. These courts recreated a new form of insularity for colleges. The new legal protections were not due to a college being family-like, charity-like, or government-like. The logic of the new bystander[16] cases was that new student constitutional rights and freedoms had created a caste of *uncontrollable* students (legally and socially) and some *insolvable* safety problems.

The conclusions of the bystander era cases were harsh and reminiscent of the worker's rights cases of the late 19th century—cases which left workers with little protection at work from injuries arising from work.[17] Some leading cases stated that students injured in the course of higher education now were in a milieu of student freedom and that their institutions owed them little or no responsibility to protect them from harm. The courts implied that the attainment of constitutional rights on campus made students adults for all purposes and beyond the control of the university. It was an important leap of logic, particularly because the kinds of constitutional freedoms and rights students sought to vindicate in the 1960s were very different from the "freedoms" that courts of the bystander era believed students possessed.

Many of the bystander era courts used highly technical tools of legal reasoning (most of the legalese was over the heads of parents and media, and often even confused administrators). Invariably, these courts made reference

16. A bystander university is like a stranger who has no power or responsibility to step in to "assist" the endangered students. As with a bystander to a serious injury or crime, there is a disquieting sense of forcing someone legally to assist, and an equally disquieting sense of the immorality of those who would just stand by. By casting a university into this image, the university gained the advantages and disadvantages of this morally and legally ambiguous archetype. The major advantage was insulation from financial responsibility for much student injury. The major disadvantage was a burgeoning sense of hypocrisy or failure: universities were supposed to be places of moral development, yet they sometimes opted for the low road or tacitly admitted their inability to meet expectations and goals set for and even by them.

17. In the late 19th century, workers were perceived to have freedom of contract, *inter alia*. Courts often reasoned that a typical worker who had not bargained for specific safety protection with her employer basically assumed all risks at work. Most workers who were maimed at work did not so bargain and were—along with their families—left destitute. In the early 20th century, the progressive era saw a shift in favor of worker's compensation, now embodied almost universally in America.

to a technical legal concept in denying university responsibility for student safety—"duty." These courts said *no* "duty" was owed to students because students owed duties to protect themselves as free and uncontrollable beings.

"Duty" thus became the central focus of university safety law. It was the principal legal rule of the bystander era and the replacement legal archetype for *in loco parentis*—out with legal insularity based on *in loco parentis*, charitable immunity, and governmental immunity, *inter alia*, in with "duty."

For most people, the word "duty" has a straightforward meaning. It is a commonly used word with common usages in English. Lawyers and courts at times use this word in ways that are similar to common usages and, at other times, in highly technical ways. Not only is the legal concept of "duty" complex, but its meaning has been rapidly changing in recent times. Making sense of legal "duty" is a special task of Chapter V. And making "duty" work for universities who want to facilitate safety and education is the basic theme of Chapter VI. No one interested in or affected by university law can fail to deal with "duty."

Thus, university law swung from legal insularity to more precarious, sometimes obtuse, footing on the new concept of "duty." "Duty" has become the central legal safety concept since the 1970s. The uncertainty surrounding the application of "duty" rules is by no means merely legal or theoretical. College administrators and officials need day-to-day practical answers to questions which run the gamut from admissions to graduation and even beyond. Shall we admit this student with a history of violence? If this person is denied the opportunity to graduate, what are the ramifications? How shall I write this letter of recommendation—can I omit reference to disciplinary records? What do I do with this student who has harassed women on campus? American courts, by electing to reconceptualize the relationships between universities and students, have ushered in—perhaps without so intending—a new era of *uncertainty* in university law.

A major goal of this book is to speak simultaneously to the legal *and* university community to overcome what has become a crisis in practical university affairs *and* archetypal legal vision. Uncertainty breeds at least two problems: it is disempowering for college administrators, and it undermines safety initiatives by working against the sharing of responsibility for campus safety. Legal uncertainty leads to more distancing and to "cover your rear quarters" strategies.

For a brief time following the fall of legal insularity, many "bystander era" courts used critical, if nebulous, "duty" concepts to reach fairly predictable results. These courts often held that *no* "duty" was owed by a university to a student to protect that student from injury. For at least some purposes, the university thus still was in a no-legal-liability-for-student-safety situation—same as it ever was, almost. Because of these bystander cases, for a brief interval, the university law situation *seemed* clear in consequence if not in theory—a time to which many university attorneys and some courts still cling tenaciously. In some cases, the university was now a "bystander" to student injury claims and not legally responsible. The "bystander" message was that it was better not to get too involved or to "assume" duties to students. This message, however, was unappealing to most college administrators and almost all campus law enforcement administrators. Both student affairs administrators and campus law enforcement had embarked on their careers because of their interest in proactive safety initiatives, the desire to mentor students, and the hope of co-creating better college communities. The courts—and university lawyers—sent them powerful admonitions, however, that literally redefined and minimized the roles of student affairs administrators and security officers. What might have become civil war among personnel on campus was ameliorated by the dominant student development theory of the 1970s and 1980s, which stressed independence and individualism. However, the "bystander" messages were largely negative, disempowering, and served to break down the bonds of shared responsibility for safety on campus. With distance came danger and frustration—particularly as student development theory evolved and alcohol risk peaked.

But "duty" can be an elusive legal concept. Thus, even in the heyday of the "bystander" university, some cases imposed "duty" *and* legal responsibility on the university. These crosscurrent cases often cast the college in business terms and saw students as consumers/victims. In the university legal community these cases were typically dismissed as wrongheaded, anomalous, minority jurisdiction cases or, by some, as a feared return of *in loco parentis*. Yet, these crosscurrent cases were paradigmatic of the legal shift from insularity to "duty." Those who thought that a shift to a "duty" paradigm would simplify the law and protect university interests simpliciter were missing the larger picture that "duty" was casting. It was not possible for a modern college to be a complete stranger to student safety and to be a total bystander to dangers on campus.

From the mid 1980s or so to the present, courts have continued to use the concept of "duty" to organize analysis of student safety law. However, simultaneously, a shift in the legal use of "duty" has been under way in the courts, and the results courts reach are no longer strongly no-"duty" or no-liability oriented. Universities have lost prominent student injury cases; the language that the courts use is no longer unqualifiedly deferential to the university. Indeed, in some instances, courts have been highly critical of university conduct and litigation tactics. The brief perceived "halcyon" period of the bystander decisions is clearly over (if it ever really existed, as examined in Chapter IV).

This recent legal phenomenon—the consolidation of university safety law around the duty concept—has intensified the uncertainty described by Boyer. Chapter V discusses the most recent phase of the "duty" era in university law—a phase that is anything but a recreated period of insularity. Courts today are in an implicit search for the Aristotelian mean and middle ground—a fair balance between the need for university supervision, structure, and guidance and students' need for the freedom to develop and express themselves. Courts today continue to seek this balance through the legal vehicle of "duty." Understanding "duty" requires expert guidance in the law of torts generally, and some contract law. By no means is the legal state of affairs simple to grasp: courts have used a variety of technical legal tools to solve university law problems and have looked for answers in places that were once foreign to university affairs.

Moreover, American law today still lacks a well defined and appropriate overall legal vision of the university in the post-insularity era. The law needs such an image badly. Chapter V illustrates and discusses this complex situation in ways that those with legal training will follow easily and non-lawyers interested or involved in university affairs can also understand. It is good to remember that any time an industry moves out from under the roof of legal protection, the law will likely be confusing and transitory for a period of time. Perhaps *decades.*

Current confusion, then, is a product of uncertainty over legal results *and* legal concepts in times of social and political change, changing higher education populations, and transition. Moreover, communication between university officials and the legal system leaves much to be desired. Courts send messages, but what is received? How is it communicated? University officials and administrators have strong views on legal rules, but can courts hear them? Courts need guidance from the university community and vice versa. In the end, universities need guidance on how to manage student affairs in the new era of university law just as courts need to clarify their vision of higher education law. The narrow issue of student safety on campus raises much broader theoretical and practical social questions.

Chapter VI offers the image of the university as *facilitator*—the appropriate legal and cultural balance between university authority/control and student freedom.[18] This image is manifest in much of the recent case law. The facilitator model is a model of balance and is thus naturally beige, not black and white. Neither *in loco parentis* nor stranger/bystander archetypes are adequate or appropriate for the modern university environment. In essence, both are extreme

---

18. A facilitator university views students as *visitors*, a companion concept developed in *Beyond Discipline*, *supra* note 1. That book offers a vision on how to empower students to make the most of their higher education experience and links safety to core mission delivery.

images. The one is strongly authoritarian, the other is absurdly and unnecessarily libertarian and laissez-faire. Following the lead of American courts, the vision of a facilitator university builds upon the elusive concept of "duty" and offers concrete ways to conceptualize the relationships between universities and students to strike the right balance. Students can enjoy substantial freedoms in an environment that provides structure and emphasizes shared responsibility for safety. The core idea, explained in detail in Chapter VI, is that a university can provide a reasonably safe place to live and learn, and can guide and assist its students and channel their activities and energies without exercising draconian control over all aspects of student relations. Students need to experience some risks to grow and mature and need to have some responsibility for their own safety and growth as well. There is a middle ground. There exists a place of shared, balanced responsibilities among students and their universities. The facilitator university model is a model of an environment of *shared* values, risks, and responsibilities. The facilitator does not accept autocracy or abdication.

The facilitator model is also a shared *legal* and *university affairs* vision. Courts, university officials, and students should be in partnership, not in conflict. There is an important opportunity at hand to craft a truly interdisciplinary vision of modern higher education law. University administrators and officials should be empowered to do their jobs effectively. They should be able to turn to law for positive reinforcement of their jobs and for tools to be even more effective. Particularly in the bystander era, the law disempowered campus officials who came to fear that doing their jobs could cost them dearly in courts of law. New legal rules—and images—can re-empower campus officials and promote greater levels of safety.

This book is not merely about a shift in imaginings and paradigms, but also offers specific proposals for ways to rebuild the safety of our universities. Not so long ago, Americans had written off their big cities as havens of crime and degeneration, destined to remain this way because of social forces greater than any government and the powers of the police. However, a minor revolution has occurred in police work—including the ideas of community policing and efficacy—that has had dramatic effects in major cities like New York City. The ideas that turned our urban centers around have application to our universities. Chapter VI explains specific proposals to re-empower the university as facilitator. Safe campuses begin with simple steps designed to institute a sense of community of shared values and meaningful responsibility.

This book aims to fill four critical needs.

First, there has been a lack of an appropriate and complete description of where the law of university/student relations and physical safety is and where it is heading. The book describes and maps the law in ways that lawyers and non-lawyers can understand.

Second, American courts and university personnel need a vision of the modern university and university student relations. What can fill the void left by the fall of an era of legal insularity? A potpourri of conflicting images only adds to uncertainty in the law and uncertainty for administrators. Legal uncertainty is both disempowering and dangerous. Many administrators and campus police who are faced with conflicting images of their respective roles with students are pushed to overly risk-averse "cover your rear quarters" postures (or fear that they will face personal and professional damage if they "guess" wrong). This dynamic is disempowering and can leave reasonable campus officials attempting to act in good faith but with the wrong incentives. Ultimately, the safety of students on campus and the productivity of an educational environment turns upon the actions of people in the university environment, not lawyers or judges. We need clarification not just in legal rules for lawyers but in *vision*—a shared legal and university perspective of student/university relationships with concrete implications.

Thus, third, and related closely, there has been insufficient guidance *from* the courts to the university community and *to* the courts from university lawyers and their constituents. We have relational and relationship problems. University law is a classic context in which to experience the dissonance and confusion of legal rule, result, and real-world action. It is also a wonderful place to build bridges between law and university life. This book offers an ambitious, shared, interdisciplinary vision of university life. Given the rapid changes in university life and in the law, bridging these gaps is an urgent task.

Fourth, university law is not just the province of university officials, students, and the courts. The greater community needs to be engaged in the consequences of the legal decisions affecting the parameters of university law. Families often pay a heavy price for college. Families send their students off to institutions whose promotional brochures and catalogs depict serene and positive places where buildings look like cathedrals; and happy and diligent students learn in pristine laboratories, lecture halls, libraries, and play on well-manicured quads, tennis courts, and intramural fields. Colleges play into the beliefs of family and prospective students—both false *and* inappropriate—that college is, and should be, a super-safe sanctuary and will invariably be an overall positive experience. Those of us who read the cases and patrol the campuses, or know students who have been the victim of serious harm, know better. Universities are not the trenches of World War I, but neither are they risk-free utopias.[19] The way courts

19. *See, e.g.*, Lake, *Beyond Discipline*, *supra* note 1 at 3–26.

decide cases and imagine university/student relations has a profound impact on student safety *and* education. A productive learning environment is a reasonably safe learning environment. Education and safety are unavoidably interrelated. College—not the army, the workplace, or the family—is still the place where large numbers of our individuals transition into society. College is also the place where record numbers of so-called "non-traditional" students seek to improve themselves, retool, and prosper. The strength of students' overall higher education—intellectual, moral, physical, experiential, and spiritual—will determine the collective future. Society at large has a significant stake in university law–especially university safety law.

This book advances a view of the university as a facilitator of student education and development. A safe and responsible campus environment is a precondition for learning, retention, and graduation—core mission delivery itself. Modern efforts to reform higher education sometimes put safety and responsibility low on the priority list—if at all. Higher learners have their own hierarchy of needs, however. It makes little sense to push for cost saving measures, reform student lending, and apply new forms of accountability and assessment in the classrooms without first making sure that our higher learning environments are reasonably safe and responsible. The ambitious higher education agenda proposed by President Obama in the late 2000s and early 2010s will not succeed if campuses do not provide reasonably safe learning environments.

II

The Era of *In Loco Parentis* and Legal Insularity

Several American courts and most legal commentators typically have said that prior to 1960 the university stood *in loco parentis* to its students. This period—especially as it reached its nadir in the 1950s—featured powerful paradigms of university power and prerogative and almost plenary rights to discipline students.[1] Contrary to popular and some judicial belief, *in loco parentis* era case law put little to no emphasis on protecting college student safety as such. In fact, in its day, *in loco parentis* was a minor feature of a period of wide university insularity from legal scrutiny. Students enjoyed no specific legal rights to a safe campus.

As one of several operative legal doctrines in university law prior to 1960 that serves to insulate universities from legal scrutiny, *in loco parentis* performed an important, if counter-intuitive, function. In this era of insularity, university/student relations were far less "legal" than today because that doctrine, along with several others of the period, made law insignificant in college/student relations. *In loco parentis*, along with many other protective legal doctrines, protected the power and the prerogative of the university—not students. *In loco parentis* promoted the image of the parental university and contributed to a culture in which most problems were handled within the university, by the university, and often quietly.[2] That culture existed long before the first court

1. *See* Peter F. Lake, *Beyond Discipline—Managing the Modern Higher Education Environment* 27–61 (Hierophant Enterprises 2009).

2. According to most courts and commentators *in loco parentis* died hard and fast in the 1960s and 1970s. Yet it is such a powerful paradigm that even in death it has been spotted vestigially (or chimerically like Elvis). Some commentators incorrectly point to the feared

mentioned *in loco parentis.* The law placed a blanket of security and insularity around university culture. Disputes were not justiciable and university life was not predominately juridical.[3] A university was free to exercise disciplinary power and manage its student populations—or not—with wide discretion and little concern for litigation.[4]

Today it is difficult to imagine a period when serious social disputes were not perceived to have *legal* ramifications. Americans litigate almost every issue arising out of interpersonal relations. Yet, not long ago (just 60 years or less), university life enjoyed—like other major social institutions such as government, family, churches and charitable organizations, professional sports, etc.—a certain insularity from the courts and law itself.[5] The legal world, in essence, carved out space for university culture to exist without legal scrutiny, at least in most instances. When rare cases did appear as civil lawsuits, courts typically affirmed the power of the university to exercise authority and discipline over students. A curiosity of the period in which courts referenced *in loco parentis* is how little case law there was and how that doctrine fades quickly back in time to uncertain origins. To get the feel for *in loco parentis,* one must appreciate the Zen-like subtlety of what *in loco parentis* did not say and what it did not do. In today's era when interpersonal relations are generally justiciable and juridical, it is tempting to impute to the *in loco parentis* era a level of "legalism" it did not have.

The study of university law is a study of the mostly gradual evolution of the application of legal norms (particularly "duty") to university affairs, so it should be no surprise that it is hard to determine just where *in loco parentis*—the first

---

return of *in loco parentis* in cases that today impose duties upon universities to use care for student safety. *See* Cheryl McDonald Jones, *In Loco Parentis and Higher Education: Together Again?,* 1 Charleston L. Rev. 185 (2007). "The argument that *in loco* [*parentis*] is experiencing a revival in institutional tort law is unpersuasive. Courts can, and do, find tort duties of care with universities by employing traditional tort principles, not *in loco* [*parentis*]." *Id.* at 205. Protecting student safety was not a feature of *in loco parentis* doctrines as applied to universities.

3. *See also* Lake, *supra* note 1, at 27–61 (discussing the important role of visitorial power).

4. *Id.*

5. Modern university law—no longer legally infatuated with *in loco parentis*—has featured some attempts to recreate the era of *insularity* into an era of "no-duty" or other *immunity* from civil reparation for personal injury. Universities, once insulated from most legal responsibility to students, still sometimes essentially ask courts in the duty era to *immunize* them (provide special protections from responsibilities otherwise imposed by law) from liability with special "no duty" rules. Universities had some success in the 1970s in finding such shelter, but these attempts have been steadily less successful since then.

legal image of and doctrine regarding American universities—began. It turns out that the story of *in loco parentis* begins far back in time. American law looks to pre-Revolutionary War English law for its distant origins. When we look that far back, we find some references in the legal literature to the power of parents over their children, but many scholars have found the *first* reference to *in loco parentis,* in connection with teaching, in commentaries on English law by Sir William Blackstone in the mid-1700s.

Just a few years before the Revolutionary War, Blackstone commented on English law to the effect that the father: "may also delegate part of his parental authority, during his life to the tutor or schoolmaster of his child; who is then *in loco parentis,* and has such a portion of the power of the parent committed to his charge, viz. that of restraint and correction, as may be necessary to answer the purposes for which he is employed."[6] Although this has become recognized by scholars and courts as *the* seminal statement of *in loco parentis* doctrine, it is notable that Blackstone cited no English (or American) case authority for his assertion. Presumably Blackstone had most, if not all, reported cases available to him. Several English legal scholars have been unable to find any cases at all using *in loco parentis* in relation to any type of schooling.[7] This is not to say that Blackstone just made up *in loco parentis,* for he may have become aware of this rule through observations of the law or may have anticipated this position as a sensible extension of prevailing principles. Whatever the case, Blackstone is considered to be one of the greatest historical English legal commentators ever (an Oliver Wendell Holmes type), so what he said has stuck.

It is also noteworthy that Blackstone (1) equated the rights of the parent as the *father's* right (no mention of mother here), (2) saw the right as one to be "delegated" (as one might delegate a power or prerogative to another), *and* (3) conceived the right as one to discipline and to correct the child. *In loco parentis* was thus, in sum, the *delegation* of a *father's* right to *discipline.* This was all very English and pre-modern.

---

6. 1 Sir William Blackstone, *Commentaries on the Laws of England* 441 (Oxford, Clarendon Press 1765). Blackstone is one of the mighty chroniclers of English law. As a master cartographer of English law, his work guides English and American courts today. His work is not without controversy, however, and from time to time Blackstone may have had the tendency to interpolate—fill in gaps—in existing law with his own grout to make various pieces of law fit together better.

7. *See* John C. Hogan & Mortimer Schwartz, *In Loco Parentis in the United States 1765–1985*, 8 J. Legal Hist. 260, 271 n.4 (1987).

Under English family law—which became the law of America (and changed very little until after World War II)—the father was the head of the family and held power over his wife and children. Wife/mother was basically considered "one" with husband/father and the "one" was the husband/father. The father had almost limitless authority over the children of the household. Wife/mother and children were subject to discipline, deliberate corporal punishment, and even harms caused by gross negligence without much legal recourse. If father/husband overturned the cart while drinking and seriously injured the children, the children had no right to sue him—nor did the mother. The legal system viewed the parental, particularly the *paternal,* role as virtually immune from legal scrutiny and liability. Families (particularly fathers' rights) were places courts and law mostly stayed out of (unless one family hurt another family). It was as if a man/husband/father held a kind of *sovereignty* over his family affairs. The image was so strong that even today it is common for American courts to refer to the sovereign power of a state in terms of *parens patriae,* an analogy to family law. The idea that a man was king of his own castle was more than just a metaphor.

And, so it goes, the father could *delegate* his power over the children. A "delegation" is typically a feature of what we call contract or agency law today and/or a feature of law regarding governmental powers.[8] By delegation, a father paid a schoolmaster to educate his child (mostly male children, who were pre-fathers) and the schoolmaster agreed to educate the child. To make this arrangement work, the father would have to give the schoolmaster much of the nearly limitless paternal power over the child. Otherwise, if the schoolmaster harmed the student, the father could sue. Thus, to enable the schoolmaster to do his job without looking over his shoulder at every whipping, a father *delegated* his power. Children were objects of the deal and were almost always subject to a sovereign father, or his delegate.

In loco parentis power was paternal, male, often stern, disciplinary power. The father delegated the *power* to restrain, correct, even beat. As such, the delegation was not to coddle, protect, or nurture, and there was certainly no *right* of a schoolmaster to do so as such. There was a duty—a contractual duty to the father in which the child had no direct legal interest—to educate. But the very images of the day did not consider it very important to delegate traditional maternal rights, as if education had less to do with nurturing, etc. Not blankets and bears, but corporal punishment, made Johnny right and proper.

8. For example, courts today are sometimes confronted with the question of whether a sovereign power has been properly "delegated" to a regulatory agency.

This is not to say that English schooling of that period was all discipline with no nurturing and protection; it is just that the *legal* paradigm of Blackstone's era put its foremost emphasis on *discipline* and *power.* This set the tone for over two centuries of school law—including higher education law. The modern mind, which tends to equate *"parent"* with the balancing of masculine and feminine energies, also tends to impute things to the Blackstone era, which had a very different mindset.

To get some idea of how serious English law was about the absolute power of the father and his delegates, we can look to cases that actually got to court. In one case of the mid-1800s, a schoolmaster felt that he had an obstinate student who needed discipline. The schoolmaster wrote to the father asking permission to beat the youngster harshly. The father said "yes." One night thereafter the schoolmaster beat the boy for about two and one-half hours with a heavy stick. He literally beat the boy to death. You can only imagine what would happen today, legally and politically, in this scenario.

Not so back then. The schoolmaster was tried for *manslaughter* (not murder; a prosecutor felt that a murder conviction would not hold). The schoolmaster asserted a defense based on *in loco parentis*: in other words, he seriously contended he had a legal right, via delegation, to beat a child severely for hours, with substantial risk of death. Only then did the English court disagree and impose a "reasonable and moderate" standard for beatings. The schoolmaster was convicted but sentenced to only four years of penal servitude.[9] In America, people were hung for stealing horses in this period.

It is also well to remember that Blackstone wrote when there was basically no public schooling or even a concept of it. And Blackstone was talking in his *Commentaries* about school-aged children, not college-aged pupils, as such. It would take a few more years before the idea of *in loco parentis* came to college life. In fact, because the first discussions of *in loco parentis* in higher education in English case law occur well after the Revolutionary War, it is not entirely unfair to say that the United States had no particular legal doctrine whatsoever for higher education rights and responsibilities at the time it was born. This may seem unbelievable today, but recall that this was a time when education was typically considered to be a family prerogative—delegated or not—and thus not the subject of much, if any, legal interest.

Nonetheless, there is a general belief that the "system" Blackstone referred to just a few years before the Revolution did become the law of America. In a

---

9. *See Regina v. Hopley*, 2 F & F 202, 175 Eng. Rep. 1024 (1860).

prominent treatise on American law published in the 1820s, a famous American legal commentator, Chancellor James Kent, asserted that *in loco parentis* was the law of the schoolmaster.[10] After the publication(s) of Kent's treatise, American courts began to use *in loco parentis* in cases involving school children. Like the English rules, American rules were oriented first and foremost around the right to discipline students. The legal questions continued to be basically ones involving the right to employ corporal punishment and otherwise discipline students.

By the mid-1800s in America, the idea that Blackstone's whip could be used on college students entered American decisional law, if at first obliquely. In the 1866 case of *Pratt v. Wheaton College*,[11] the college forbade its students from joining secret societies. The students challenged the authority to make such rules. The court said the college had such authority under the charter from the state. That power was paternal, *in loco parentis*-like. The college could "regulate the discipline of [the college] in such manner as [the college] deem[s] proper and so long as their rules violate neither divine nor human law [the courts] have no more authority to interfere than [they] have to control the domestic discipline of a father in his family,"[12] said the court. The notion was that the university—not the law—was sovereign in this domain. This was not the only reference to an *in loco parentis*-type rule for college law in the mid-1800s.[13]

By the 20th century, higher education started to reflect *in loco parentis* law more clearly. There were several cases at the turn of the century which stated the same basic ideas of the power of universities,[14] but two stand out and have become emblematic—*Gott v. Berea College*[15] and *Stetson University v. Hunt*.[16]

Gott, a 1913 case which relied upon *Pratt v. Wheaton College* for authority, involved a college rule that prohibited students from going to certain off-cam-

10. *See* James Kent, *Commentaries on American Law* 203, 205 (2nd ed. 1832). Hogan & Schwartz indicated that they did not find any cases in America prior to the publication of that treatise. *See supra* note 7, at 271 n.9.

11. 40 Ill. 186 (1866).

12. *Id.*

13. *See Hill v. McCauley*, 3 Pa. C. 77 (Pa. County Ct. 1887), which heard, but did not accept, a particular *in loco parentis* argument.

14. *See Woods v. Simpson*, 126 A. 882, 883 (Md. 1924) (college administrators "must, of necessity, be left untrammeled in handling the problems which arise, as their judgment and discretion may dictate"); *see also Booker v. Grand Rapids Medical College*, 120 N.W. 589 (Mich. 1909); *Barker v. Trustees of Bryn Mawr College*, 122 A. 220 (Pa. 1923).

15. 161 S.W. 204 (Ky. 1913).

16. 102 So. 637 (Fla. 1924).

pus locations. *Gott* made reference to the powers explicit and implicit in a state charter. But importantly, *Gott* specifically stated these powers in terms of *in loco parentis*: colleges "stand *in loco parentis* concerning the physical and moral welfare and mental training of the pupils, and . . . to that end [may make] *any rule* or *regulation* for the government or betterment of their pupils that a parent could for the same purpose" unless *unlawful* or contrary to public policy.[17] *Gott* made it explicitly clear that as long as a university did not transgress into the prerogatives of other sovereign powers, it was free to do pretty much as it pleased with its students. Dean Wormer would be free to enforce "double-secret probation" and play host to honor council proceedings that were less than fair.

The *Hunt* case similarly held that *in loco parentis* granted wide power to a university to do with its students as it saw fit. In that case a student was suspended for "offensive behavior intruding on the comfort of others retarding the pupil's work." The offense—the student had participated in disruptive behavior in the dormitory to wit "hazing the normals, ringing cow bells and parading in the halls . . . at forbidden hours."[18] The court noted that some witnesses viewed this behavior as "bordering on insurrection,"[19] and given the climate of the day, they were not speaking metaphorically. The court noted that the power *in loco parentis* was a typical delegation of power (contract-style) from state and trustees to university officials, and in light of this delegation *judicial review was not proper.* The university rules were vague; there were little to no procedural safeguards for students, and there was ever present the potential for hidden malice in enforcement. Yet university discretion was wide and essentially non-reviewable. The court did not wish to be involved—at all—unless rules became *patently* unreasonable. It was understood that this meant almost never.

There were three indelible features of the *Gott/Hunt in loco parentis* model. First, the power *in loco parentis* was one to discipline, control, and regulate. Second, the power was imagined in paternal overtones—by analogy to the "law" of the family of that era. Third, the power came to be perceived as a *contractual delegation* of authority by parents, state, trustees, or other officials. Eventually the law came to see the delegation as contractual, but with a pre-modern twist: students were not contracting parties but were subjected to, and governed by, the "contract."

17. *Gott*, 161 S.W. at 206 (emphasis added).
18. *Hunt*, 102 So. at 639.
19. *Id.*

Except insofar as to justify indirectly the rules sought to be enforced against students, courts made no mention of responsibility for student injury and safety. In its inception, *in loco parentis* was not about university *duties* towards students but about university rights, powers, and prerogatives over students. In fact, two features of *in loco parentis* are particularly notable in addition to its proclivity to empower a university. First, prior to 1960, universities themselves were rarely held liable to a student for injuries, no matter how the student was injured. Second, university case law prior to the 1960s that raised questions of what, if any, duties were owed to protect student safety, conspicuously ignored and made no reference to *in loco parentis.* In other words the law generally did not hold universities accountable for student safety, and no one thought that *in loco parentis* required universities to be accountable. Indeed, no one even imagined that *in loco parentis* was germane to such assertions of liability. *In loco parentis* was a sword for universities but not for the students who were injured.

There were very few cases in the period of *in loco parentis* where students even attempted to sue universities—or where the issues were ever discussed—for negligently caused physical injuries unrelated to discipline and correction. The lack of case law reflects (1) the generally non-justiciable nature of student/university relations; (2) special immunity rules of the time; (3) pre-modern notions of tort duty and liability that generally left victims uncompensated except in unusual circumstances; and (4) to some extent, the safer environment of the premodern university campus. Fact patterns typically involved laboratory accidents, dormitory injuries, and medical treatment. Even though the injuries were sometimes hideous—and negligence was palpable—students rarely won these cases (which no doubt served to chill many other unreported cases from even being pursued). During the period in which *in loco parentis* was extant students typically were not winning cases establishing duties to protect their physical safety.

Hamburger v. Cornell University[20] is a classic example of a university escaping responsibility to use due care even in an on-campus curriculum-related activity. *Hamburger* is the laboratory incident case of its era. In that case, under supervision of an instructor, a college student mixed chemicals and heated them as directed. It was a bad mix and it exploded. The student was severely injured and lost an eye. The student sued the university (Cornell) and at trial succeeded in obtaining $25,000 against the university (a whopping award in 1920's dollars);

20. 148 N.E. 539 (N.Y. 1925).

but the award was reversed on appeal. The appellate courts held that the private university was immune from suit because it was a "charitable organization."

Today, it is rare to see much of what used to be called "charitable immunity." In other words, in most states today, most charitable organizations for most purposes do not receive special protection in tort law but can be sued for their negligence as any other "business" organization. Congress chose to give some protection from tort law for volunteers of charitable organizations for some torts, but blanket "charitable immunity" has largely disappeared in American law today.

Not so just a few decades ago. Until the 1970s (give or take), most courts would say that a charitable organization was generally *immune* from a private civil lawsuit. This meant that one could not sue a charity *even* if the charity were clearly negligent. This immunity was a public policy exception to general rules of responsibility based on ideas that charities—given the special nature of their work—deserved special legal protection. There were, however, numerous exceptions to the charitable immunity rules, and if you fit into an "exception" you could sue a charity. There was a great deal of litigation then over two types of issues. First, what is a "charity" (and are you a "charity" or not)? Second, is there an applicable exception to immunity that would permit a lawsuit to proceed? In most cases the private college or university would win on both issues: most often, the college was a charity and no exception applied.

Although the university came close to paying a large award to a student injured in an on-campus curricular activity, *Hamburger* ruled that the university was not subject to lawsuit by a "beneficiary" (the student) of the "charitable organization." After some discussion, the university was determined to be just such a "charitable" institution. It is particularly noteworthy that when liability was seriously considered at the lower levels of the court system, responsibility was purportedly based on ordinary rules of "duty," not *in loco parentis*. Moreover, when the higher court provided immunity to the university, that court did not say that it was based upon, or in spite of, *in loco parentis*. *In loco parentis* was not mentioned.

Similarly, in a case at Northwestern University a student lost an eye, allegedly as a result of the negligence of a dentistry professor in a laboratory. The student sued but lost on the grounds of charitable immunity.[21] No mention was made of *in loco parentis*. A federal court of this period also protected an institution of higher learning when a student operated a laboratory ma-

21. *See Parks v. Northwestern Univ.*, 75 N.E. 991 (Ill. 1905).

chine—with the protective guard twisted and removed—as ordered by the instructor.[22]

Now, if an institution were not private, it was a public university. In these cases the courts typically found another way to keep universities safe from legal liability—*governmental* immunity.

It surprises a number of people that only recently have American governments been responsible to citizens for wrongdoing in civil actions. Prior to World War II, it was good to be a sovereign political entity in America, as there were only limited avenues of relief open for citizens in the courts. This changed after World War II, at first with regard to the federal government and then more gradually with states (although some states had partially waived sovereign immunity before World War II). During the heyday of *in loco parentis,* governmental immunity was alive and well in America. Governmental immunity receded in the 1940s, 1950s, and 1960s. As will become relevant in the following chapters, governmental immunity was falling fastest just around the time of the complete demise of *in loco parentis* and legal insularity in the 1960s in higher education law.

Typically, because of governmental immunity, a person injured because of the negligence of a governmental agency would be constrained to seek reparation for his injuries in the legislature. In an early Montana case, for instance, an injured student pursued such a legislative "claims bill," and received some money this way—a typical procedure in those days—even after there was a constitutional challenge by a taxpayer.[23] The student had fallen down an elevator shaft in a negligently maintained dormitory. Without such special legislative approval, the student had no legal right to sue for basic dormitory safety: the student's sole recourse for civil reparation for personal injuries caused by a public agency's negligence was a bill seeking a special legislative appropriation. This legislative procedure could provide relief, but only in the discretion of the legislature. Otherwise, a student would bear the expense of her own injury.

Even though governmental immunity has been abated in large part, some public universities still attempt to assert governmental immunity as a defense to liability for student injury caused by university negligence. Today, however, courts regularly reject governmental immunity arguments regarding routine functions of the university such as premises and dormitory maintenance. At one time, being a king allowed you to be a slumlord; not so now (more on this later).

During the high period of plenary governmental immunity, even university-sponsored activities that resulted in medical negligence were immune. In a

22. *See Higgons v. Pratt Inst.*, 45 F.2d 698 (2d Cir. 1930).
23. *See Mills v. Stewart*, 247 P. 332 (Mont. 1926).

1920's scenario, a student at the University of California went to the infirmary for a tonsillectomy. During this operation the student was seriously and permanently injured by negligence of the physician. The student had to pay for additional hospital charges to fix the injuries caused by the negligence of the first doctor (the additional charges were not covered by the general infirmary fee). Nonetheless, the university was held immune as a governmental entity.[24] Law in other states immunized such hospitals as *both* governmental *and* charitable entities[25]—the double whammy on students.

It is worth mentioning that the negligent physician was held personally liable.[26] In practice this result—an *individual* college employee being liable—was exceedingly rare, *particularly* outside the medical context. As a leading treatise of the era explained: "[t]he natural person individually responsible for the wrong is always liable for his own tort. It is because such persons are often financially irresponsible, leaving the injured person without relief even though he wins a judgment, that the question of the liability of the institution arises."[27] The treatise overstated the legal liability of individuals somewhat, given that some immunities and defenses for certain individuals would have been recognized, but the practical point is well taken.

Thus, although rare, some cases proceeded (or at least *could* have proceeded) against persons in the university, not the institution itself. For example, if a dormitory fire forced a student to jump from an upper story window because the university neglected to provide legally required fire escapes, the university could successfully avoid liability on grounds of charitable immunity, but the individual trustees might be responsible.[28]

Prior to 1960, and despite overwhelming case law to the contrary, there were some intimations by courts that a student could sue a university or university official for duties breached and not face insurmountable immunity problems. For example, in one case in 1921 that did not involve a university defendant but another charity, a New York court stated that a college or university could be liable to a student for negligently caused injuries received at the hands of an employee of the university.[29] There was no mention of a connection to *in loco parentis*, and the court's statements were made in the context of a case that

24. *See Davie v. Bd. of Regents, Univ. of Cal.*, 227 P. 243 (Cal. Dist. Ct. App. 1924).

25. *See Robinson v. Washtenaw Circuit Judge*, 199 N.W. 618 (Mich. 1924).

26. *See Davie*, 227 P. at 247.

27. Edward Elliott & M.M. Chambers, *The Colleges and the Courts* 431 (1936).

28. *See Abston v. Waldon Acad.*, 102 S.W. 351, 355 (Tenn. 1907).

29. *See Barr v. Brooklyn Children's Aid Soc'y*, 190 N.Y.S. 296, 297 (N.Y. Sup. Ct. 1921).

did not raise questions of university liability as such. Moreover, New York historically was known to provide significantly less charitable immunity to colleges and universities than other states of the period.[30] So the "dicta" (what lawyers call court language that talks about an issue not directly presented in a case) in that case was not surprising given the legal culture of New York at that time.

In a rare, pre-modern example of university liability, a federal appellate court *upheld* a determination of liability against Brigham Young University in 1941. A student was injured in a laboratory explosion that occurred while the teacher was out of the room. The court focused in upon ideas of "duty" (discussed in Chapters IV and V) and determined that a university must adequately and reasonably supervise and instruct students in dangerous laboratory experiments. The court ruled that an appropriate baseline for consideration would be what other universities have done under like or similar circumstances.[31] Speaking in classic negligence law language, the court did *not* consider *in loco parentis* as the liability-creating rule of its decision. Instead, the court thought of university duty as arising in instructional settings that involve risk of physical injury to students. That case may be the first truly modern liability case in higher education law, and presaged changes to come.

In spite of the actual history, some academic observers have held the opinion that *in loco parentis* was a legal doctrine that placed legal *responsibility* on universities regarding student safety. A few courts, particularly those in what we refer to as the "bystander" era (starting in the 1970s, see Chapter IV), seem to believe this as well. These academics and observers have taken *in loco parentis* out of context. *In loco parentis* became a responsibility doctrine in K-12 education after WWII, but never did so in higher education law.

Gott v. Berea College, in determining that a school had plenary disciplinary *power* over students, stated: "college authorities stand *in loco parentis* concerning the physical and moral welfare and mental training of the pupils . . . ."[32] In a similar situation, the *Wheaton College* case stated that a "father"-like university may *direct* "children" students to do and not do as in a family. The *Hunt* case was another discipline *power* case; the court linked *in loco parentis*

30. Elliott & Chambers, *supra* note 27, at 425 & n.15. *See, e.g.*, *Green v. Cornell Univ.*, 184 N.Y.S. 924 (N.Y. App. Div. 4th Dept. 1920), *aff'd*, 135 N.E. 900 (N.Y. 1922) (university liable when vehicle negligently driven by university employee).

31. *Brigham Young Univ. v. Lilly White*, 118 F.2d 836 (10th Cir. 1941).

32. *Gott*, 161 S.W. at 206.

to the "physical welfare" of students.[33] *In loco parentis* was a power, not a responsibility.

Some commentators, however, have concluded that "[a]long with parental authority came an obligation to protect," and interpreted *Gott* and other cases to impose a duty to protect students on a theory of *in loco parentis*.[34] This sentiment has been persistent, particularly in certain recent cases.[35]

This belief that *in loco parentis* was a basis of tort *duty* to students to provide their safety—as opposed to merely the basis of a *right to discipline* them for misconduct—was essentially manufactured in the bystander era (the subject of Chapter IV)[36] by cases that rejected university liability for student injury. Those cases specifically linked no-duty/no-liability *results* to the rejection of *in loco parentis* on the false supposition that *in loco parentis* had created duty. They reasoned that as *in loco parentis* fell so too did responsibility for student injury. The false premise of these bystander era cases was that *in loco parentis* was a doctrine imposing *duties* on universities to protect students and that these duties were enforceable in private tort actions. *Bradshaw v. Rawlings*, one of the most important cases of this period, observed that "[a]t one time, exercising their rights *and duties in loco parentis*, colleges were able to impose strict regulations."[37] It was a subtle mistake but became magnified by later case law that has uncritically followed *Bradshaw's* misstep.

Given the broad statements of cases like *Bradshaw* and the developments of *in loco parentis* as applied to school-age children (in K-12 education today *in loco parentis* **is** the basis for imposing duties of care), it was easy for commentators and courts to fall into a subtle but important trap regarding notions of *in loco parentis*. *As a technical legal doctrine, in loco parentis was not*—**ever**—*a liability/responsibility/duty creating norm in higher education law. In loco parentis was only a legal tool of immunity for universities when they deliberately chose to discipline students.* There is a temptation to impute to a period where there is little legal history legal rules which *would* have been explanatory. In this sense, *in loco parentis* became larger in imagination than it

33. *See Pratt*, 40 Ill. at 187; *Stetson Univ.*, 102 So. at 640.

34. *See* James Szablewicz & Annette Gibbs, *Colleges' Increasing Exposure to Liability: The New In Loco Parentis*, 16 J.L. & Educ. 453, 455 (1987).

35. *See id.*; *see also Freeman v. Busch*, 349 F.3d 582 (8th Cir. 2003); *McClure v. Fairfield Univ.*, No. CV000159028, 2003 WL 21524786 (Conn. Super. Ct. 2003).

36. *See* Kristen Peters, *Protecting the Millennial College Student*, 16 S. Cal. Rev. L. & Soc. Just. 431, 438 (2007).

37. 612 F.2d 135, 139–40 (3d Cir. 1979) (emphasis added).

ever was in the reality of the time. Thus, the era of *in loco parentis* is somewhat inaptly named. As Theodore Stamatakos wrote in a well-reasoned law review article on this subject:

> The conspicuous absence of appellate court discussion of the doctrine of *in loco parentis* fully supports the conclusion that the doctrine of *in loco parentis* was never operational in the context of personal injury suits in the first place .... [T]he duty to protect students' physical well-being always has been grounded in the realm of traditional tort categories.[38]

In loco parentis was a minor doctrine in a larger era of legal *insularity.*[39] *In loco parentis* was a manifestation of a deeper legal sentiment: university affairs should generally be free from legal scrutiny. University affairs were generally *university* business and best settled there. *In loco parentis* was one tool (not the only or most significant) to protect, to *immunize,* university conduct from legal review when *deliberate* or *intentional* actions were taken to *discipline* and *regulate* students. In the era of legal insularity courts used other tools to *immunize* universities when students claimed damages for physical harm caused by *accidental* or *negligent* conduct or omissions. The tools courts used to immunize the university in those circumstances typically were governmental or charitable tort immunities. The responsibilities immunized against were responsibilities grounded in traditional tort responsibility (to exercise reasonable care for student safety). It would have been utterly incoherent from a legal doctrinal perspective to ground any potential tort liability for accidental injury responsibility in any family law doctrine because courts of this historical period knew of no such legal parental responsibilities in tort. Indeed, if *in loco parentis* had been applied it would have been a no-duty rule because *in loco parentis* was a historical device to protect parental sovereignty. Only lately, as *in loco parentis* mutated in K-12 education law, did the notion that it created legal responsibility for minors/students arise.

It remains crucial to observe *in loco parentis* first appeared in a time when wide areas of human activity existed free from legal scrutiny. As developed further in Chapter IV, it was not long ago that families, charities, governments, most business activity, and certain spheres of private inaction (like failing to

---

38. Theodore C. Stamatakos, *The Doctrine of In Loco Parentis, Tort Liability and the Student-College Relationship,* 65 Ind. L.J. 471, 484 (1990).

39. The era can also be seen as an era of power and prerogative—simply the positive way of formulating the same concept.

rescue a stranger) were subject to actual or *de facto* tort immunities. Prior to the 1950s, many social institutions had legal insularity. You did not sue your parents for neglect; or sue a church for sexual abuse; or sue a government if it wounded you with friendly fire in combat. Defective products reached consumers with very little chance for legal redress if injury were to occur, and courts hesitated to require anyone to respond to "strangers" in distress. Protecting child safety was not a huge social priority. American courts of the era of insularity saw universities simply as institutional candidates for insularity as well. In an era of insularities, universities became yet another jurisdictional island.

It would be much easier in some ways today to understand the university/student relationship if courts had specifically stated that, in addition to traditional text book legal immunities, a *university immunity* existed. They did not say so, but in practice they did effectively create such an immunity. Courts did this by viewing the university as neither fish nor fowl but as an amalgam of functions that separately and in combination deserved immunity. University was part family, charity, and/or government. But different.

Thus, in its *disciplinary* role, the university was like a family—a father—to its students. It gave students guidance and set rules and enforceable boundaries. In the family, a father had powerful, nearly plenary rights to exercise discipline. Historically, courts recognized virtually no family *responsibility* at all to care for a child, however. Care and feeding, and abuse and neglect were not justiciable. Unlike today, the legal system stayed out of family life for the most part (even where gross parental negligence directly caused injury to the child). Indeed, a father's *de facto* legal right to discipline—and even abuse and neglect—a child was one of the broadest immunities from tort responsibility that the common law ever carved out.

Because parental immunity was vast, it is not surprising then that when a university neglected to use care for student safety—as opposed to when it exercised discipline and authority deliberately—the courts were not willing to say that a university was family for all purposes. *In loco parentis* potentially could have been the rule for insularity itself: instead courts opted for other rules, in conjunction with *in loco parentis,* to create a unique legal insularity just for the university.

The university, for example, also operated like a business, albeit a special one. Businesses were typically subject to rules of contract and tort law. Some businesses were special in that they were not-for-profit and/or were charitable in nature.[40]

40. *See* Lake, *supra* note 1.

Universities were not exactly like more traditional charitable organizations, but many universities certainly had strong similarities to them in some ways. Similar to family, similar to charity, but not exactly the same.

Now, some universities were set up as *public* universities. These institutions behaved in some ways as businesses, but also like small governmental entities. Their missions were set by the people and for the people. However, public universities were not cities or towns *per se* and, given their family-like relations to students and the business-like aspects of their private counterparts, public universities were *sui generis* governmental entities. Similar to governments, but not exactly the same.

Therefore, when a court looked at a university it saw a unique hybrid legal entity entitled to significant insularity from judicial scrutiny. In some ways a university was like a family, in others like a charity, in other cases like a government or some combination thereof. Legal insularity thus was expressed predominantly through a tailoring of these patches of legal thinking. For example, while generally immune from lawsuit, charities were rarely immune from suit regarding deliberate intentional torts and also generally had to honor contracts they entered into. Charities had no special rights to discipline and thus charitable immunity rules were not useful to protect universities who disciplined and regulated students. Family immunities, however, were perfect for this. A public university could assert governmental immunity protections that were quite broad, however. Crucially, attendance at a public university was considered a *privilege*, not a right.

Nonetheless, when a student was injured through accidental or negligent means there was something inappropriate about protecting universities without *some* qualification. After all, these were institutions with tuition paid (contracts) that served public and/or private missions for the benefit of the public at large. The university was like family and like father, but it was not family or father. Similarity was not identity. Case law as a whole pointed unmistakably to the idea that most negligently caused injuries were immune to lawsuit; but eventually there were some cases imposing responsibility, and even some of the cases that did not hinted that they might under some circumstances. The courts acted (intervened) just enough to send the message that they were watching and would not allow too much latitude in terms of neglect of safety—certainly not the way they would almost completely defer to parents. A balance—detente—was struck. The balance favored the university very, very heavily and the college won in almost every instance where it acted in good faith (even if negligently).

An underlying message was that university life in the era of *in loco parentis*—truly the era of *insularity*—was subject to some very marginal scrutiny in the courts, particularly regarding physical safety of students. When negligence caused physical injuries to students, courts applied traditional tort rules—especially duty analysis—and, when appropriate, immunities relating to *charities* and *governments.* The technical legal immunity afforded by *in loco parentis* appeared in disciplinary disputes. *In loco parentis,* in this sense, was neither an *immunity* to lawsuits alleging neglect or unreasonable omissions to care for student safety, *nor* a source of any responsibility or *duty* to care for student safety.

In loco parentis was a feature of the law in this period of university legal insularity, and the era is remembered as the era of *in loco parentis.* However, overplaying the role of *in loco parentis* is nostalgia in a foggy rearview mirror. The legal rules of *in loco parentis* were just *one feature* of an overall system protecting colleges. The era in which *in loco parentis* dominated was a period where the law sought to define appropriate levels of university *insularity* from responsibility via the application of multiple legal doctrines. The law did this by drawing upon—selectively—a variety of legal paradigms from other recognized areas of legal insularity.[41] Universities were viewed variously as part family, part charity, part government, part public, part private. Underneath it all, the notion of duty—destined to become central—was immanent and growing. "Duty" would eventually grow to cover over, and even obscure, the true history of *in loco parentis.* As universities moved more and more into the public eye (recall that in *Animal House,* the final battle for the soul of Faber College spills into the streets of the town—and yet there are no lawyers in the movie), the notions of insularity came under attack. First, as we shall see in the next chapter, the fight for civil rights became directed at universities. That aspect of insularity was removed first. Later came attacks upon insularity from negligence-based tort responsibility. At first substantially rebuked in the bystander era—see Chapter IV—these attacks on that aspect of insularity eventually eroded university immunities and insularity (see Chapters IV and V).

The fall of insularity happened rather quickly in legal terms. Again, many have viewed the rise of university legal responsibility as the return of *in loco parentis.* But as powerful as this misperception is (it remains the legal vision in some cases), it is historically and conceptually misguided. *The real story of in loco parentis is instead the rise and decline of insularity from legal responsibility and the rise of justiciability of university life.* Universities, like many other social institutions (including government and charities), have increasingly been

41. The law also had other protective doctrines, like rules of proximate causation and affirmative defenses, that augmented university insularity. *See* Chapters IV and V.

asked to come to the legal system and explain and defend their conduct. In this sense, the fall of insularity is, for better or for worse, a key feature of modern university tort law and an understandable consequence of the fall of the patchwork of immunities and other doctrines that once protected the university.

The legal system, like life in general, is not beyond living out some imagined realities that never were. The pull to Avalon or the retreat to Valhalla are signals of a society in transition, uncertain of its roots and future. So it has been with *in loco parentis.* The dread of a feared return to *in loco parentis* reflects concerns over where college law is headed but is not an accurate reflection of where it has been.

III

Revolutions on University Campuses

The 1960s, Civil Rights Movement (and Beyond) and the Death of Insularity

In loco parentis flourished in an era of university legal insularity. There was a collection of legal rules and protective immunities which kept university affairs out of the courts. The law used a combination of various protections afforded to families, charities, and governmental entities to insulate university life from justiciability. Yet, in the 1960s and afterward, American law made major changes in the very legal rules that had previously insulated families, charities, and governments from significant legal responsibility for negligently and deliberately caused injuries. Major social initiatives forced changes in women's and children's rights, and charitable institutions were no longer conceived to be above the law, particularly as abuses and scandals rocked the sense of sanctity of charities and modern insurance became more available. Perhaps most importantly, in the 1960s large numbers of Americans began to challenge the government itself over fundamental issues like civil rights, the rights to make war and draft citizens to fight wars, the role of police in society, and even the nature of the presidency itself. American society and law underwent change in precisely those areas that had once protected university affairs. The fall of insularity came swiftly and in that context.

The demise of insularity was hastened by the fact that university life in the 1960s (and 1970s) became a focal point of the major social issues of the time.

"Baby boom" students increasingly became participants in a social revolution. The targets of reform in college were the improper (and sometimes racially motivated) denial of civil rights, denial of procedural due process, unequal treatment of women and individuals with disabilities, and abuses of authoritarian governmental power, etc. Students picketed, rioted, sat in, organized, marched, and *litigated.* Students asked the law and legal system to intervene in university life. Essentially for the first time, the law accepted the invitation. The era of insularity was over: university life would be increasingly justiciable.

From a lawyer's perspective, the harms that a student might suffer in college life fall into one of two very basic categories. First, students can be harmed in economic ways (like being expelled and losing tuition and future jobs) or in other intangible ways (such as being denied civil rights, or having their privacy invaded, or reputation impugned). Second, a student can be harmed physically, either in person (killed, injured, etc.) or by damage to their tangible physical property (damaged car, etc.). Although there is a great deal of legal esoterica to go along with this, it is usually safe to assume that the first type of harm became a *contract* claim or a civil rights lawsuit (or some highly specialized tort law remedy, but this has very little to do with the main theme here). The latter type of harm became tort, typically negligence, lawsuits—the stuff of personal injury lawyers and tort reform. The law divides harms up into certain somewhat arbitrary camps and then provides certain ways to remedy those harms. Economic/intangible-type harms go most often to contract or civil rights style cases; personal injury and property damage go to tort claims.

An illustration. You buy a vacuum cleaner. It does not work. You return it. The seller refuses to take it back. You sue for breach of contract or warranty. The vacuum cleaner did not live up to the promises of the bargain struck. You made a bad economic deal. Now, if the vacuum cleaner explodes and injures you, or damages your house, it is another matter. Those problems would be remedied in *tort* actions. The day after Christmas is contract day: the Fourth of July is torts day.

These distinctions have become important in university law and essential to understanding how *in loco parentis* and university insularity died. This is because the civil rights movement raised questions of basic civil rights and the bargains struck between universities and students. Students who were expelled or disciplined needed to vindicate *economic* or *intangible* rights. To do these things, students sued universities in civil rights and/or breach of contract lawsuits. *In loco parentis* had been an insulating doctrine that the university used to defend those types of lawsuits. In the 1960s (roughly speaking), the defensive power of *in loco parentis* and other doctrines of insularity came to a halt. Only later (for the most part)—see Chapters IV and V—did students begin to successfully challenge the other aspects of insularity—insularity from tort lawsuits alleging personal injury. The beginning of the fall of *in loco parentis* and legal insularity in the 1960s correlated exactly with the rise of student economic power and the rise of student civil rights.

The first court cases were cases by students at *public* universities (hence quasi-governmental entities) raising demands for basic constitutional rights. In 1969, Professor Charles A. Wright wrote that the Constitution had come to American campuses and transformed them.[1] That idea would have been novel just ten years earlier.

Most university law commentators view the landmark 1961 decision of the United States Court of Appeals (Fifth Circuit) in *Dixon v. Alabama State Board of Education*[2] as the watershed decision in this era of university law. *Dixon* ultimately presaged a radical revision of student rights, which culminated in tragic events at Kent State in May 1970.[3]

In *Dixon,* six black students were expelled for participating in civil rights demonstrations seeking the desegregation of lunch counters and other places of public accommodation.[4] The students received notice of their expulsion via a perfunctory letter from the president of Alabama State College. They were not even told what specific misconduct got them expelled. The expulsion letter was a paragon of vagueness. The letter refers to "this general problem of Alabama State College" and to several general school regulations, one of which was highlighted in the expulsion letter (and thus apparently was the rule violated). That highlighted rule empowered the college to expel for "Conduct Prejudicial to the School," "Conduct Unbecoming a Student or Future Teacher in Schools in Alabama," "Insubordination and Insurrection," or "Inciting Other Pupils to Like Conduct."[5] Like Dean Wormer's "double-secret probation," such rules could mean just about anything. The students were not given any chance to tell their side of the story—let alone given a "hearing."

---

1. *See* Charles A. Wright, *The Constitution on the Campus,* 22 Vand. L. Rev. 1027 (1969).

2. 294 F.2d 150 (5th Cir. 1961), *cert. denied,* 368 U.S. 930 (1961).

3. "There was a clear and defining moment in the law from *Dixon* to Kent State. This was the high civil rights era, which arose from abuses of power and prerogative." Peter F. Lake, *Beyond Discipline—Managing the Modern Higher Education Environment* 63 (Hierophant Enterprises 2009). *See also Scheuer v. Rhodes,* 416 U.S. 232 (1974).

4. *See* Juan Williams, *Eyes on the Prize: America's Civil Rights Years, 1954–1965* (Penguin Books 1987); David Halberstam, *The Children* (Random House 1998).

5. *Dixon,* 294 F.2d at 152.

The legal issue was whether the students had a right to a hearing or notice before expulsion.

In what would become a signature ruling in the civil rights era, the Fifth Circuit held that students at public universities were entitled to due process. Adequate prior notice and some opportunity for a hearing were essential minimums before permanent expulsion. The court reasoned that education is so basic and vital in modern society that a public, tax supported university cannot expel a student without meeting minimum constitutional due process requirements.

There was no mention of *in loco parentis* as such as a defense to the college's actions. In fact, in its defense the college reworded the *in loco parentis* doctrine into a new contract/voluntary association argument. Consider the following Board of Education regulations that read, in part:

> Attendance at any college is on the basis of a mutual decision of the student's *parents* and of the *college*. Attendance at a particular college is voluntary and is different from attendance at a public school where the pupil may be required to attend a particular school which is located in the neighborhood or district in which the pupil's family may live. Just as a student may choose to withdraw from a particular college at any time for any personally-determined reason, the college may also at any time decline to continue to accept responsibility for the supervision and service to any student with whom the relationship becomes unpleasant and difficult.[6]

The college argued that this regulation constituted—as if in a contract paradigm—a waiver of any right to notice and hearing prior to expulsion. The college in *Dixon* felt some pressure to fall back to a Dean Wormer ideal: "we may have been giving you students some rights but we retain the right to take them away."

Constitutionalizing the question, *Dixon* rejected this argument and ushered in the beginning of the end of a long era of legal insularity. *Dixon* established that a state entity—a public college—cannot condition the privilege of an education (*Dixon* did not provide a right to public post-secondary education, just a right to due process if one were attending public college) upon a waiver or renunciation of basic rights of fair play or due process. This was *critical* to the death of *in loco parentis* in particular. *Dixon* established—and other

---

6. *Dixon*, 294 F.2d at 156 (emphasis added).

courts soon followed—that whatever *contractual* relations existed in a public university, they were subject to an irreducible minimum of *constitutional* rights. Such rights were not granted to the family but to the *student*. In one fell swoop *Dixon* recreated a key feature of college law from familial to constitutional, and simultaneously ushered in the demise of "delegation" doctrines that imagined that parents or fathers gave their children over to colleges to be disciplined. *Dixon* may even be the first moment in college law where the very concept of *discipline* itself began to erode—and constitution/contract law began to rise.

As the regulation in *Dixon* suggested, education had been a primary function of the contract between *parent* and college. The court in *Dixon*, however, specifically shifted the focus to *student*: "[w]e do not read [this regulation] to clearly indicate an intent on the part of the *student* to waive notice and a hearing before expulsion."[7] To the extent that university law was contractual, the student became the party in interest. The shift was subtle but changed the nature of the contract from one involving delegation of parental prerogative to one with a kinship to consumer/service contracts at large. *Dixon* set the stage for the student consumerism and rights culture of the following decades. *Dixon* signaled a shift in the basic paradigm of post-secondary education: college was a student/university relationship primarily, not primarily the delegation of family relationship prerogatives. *Dixon* is best known for its *due process* holding, but the case *also* altered contract law and linked the contract with students to due process.[8]

Dixon did not specify exactly what procedures must be followed to protect students' rights but did provide famous guidelines for public universities to follow:

> For the guidance of the parties in the event of further proceedings, we state our views on the nature of the notice and hearing required by due process prior to expulsion from a state college or university. They should, we think, comply with the following standards. The notice should contain a statement of the specific charges and grounds which, if proven, would justify expulsion under the regulations of the Board of Education. The nature of the hearing should vary depending upon the circumstances of the particular case. The case before us requires something more than an informal interview with an administrative authority of the college. By its nature, a charge of misconduct, as op-

7. *Id.* at 158–59 (emphasis added).
8. That trend accelerated in later decades. *See* Lake, *supra* note 3, ch. 4.

> posed to a failure to meet the scholastic standards of the college, depends upon a collection of the facts concerning the charged misconduct, easily colored by the point of view of the witnesses. In such circumstances, a hearing which gives the Board or the administrative authorities of the college an opportunity to hear both sides in considerable detail is best suited to protect the rights of all involved. This is not to imply that a full-dress judicial hearing, with the right to cross-examine witnesses, is required. Such a hearing, with the attending publicity and disturbance of college activities, might be detrimental to the college's educational atmosphere and impractical to carry out. Nevertheless, the rudiments of an adversary proceeding may be preserved without encroaching upon the interests of the college. In the instant case, the student should be given the names of the witnesses against him and an oral or written report on the facts to which each witness testifies. He should also be given the opportunity to present to the Board, or at least to an administrative official of the college, his own defense against the charges and to produce either oral testimony or written affidavits of witnesses in his behalf. If the hearing is not before the Board directly, the results and findings of the hearing should be presented in a report open to the student's inspection. If these rudimentary elements of fair play are followed in a case of misconduct of this particular type, we feel that the requirements of due process of law will have been fulfilled.[9]

The watchword for these guidelines was *flexibility. Dixon* did not foresee that universities would be burdened with creating miniature court systems or arbitration boards. However, the idea that students might be owed *some* process was born.[10] Nonetheless, even when dealing with a blatantly arbitrary college administration, *Dixon* still showed significant deference to college administrators.

Dixon signaled the beginning of a college civil rights explosion, although somewhat ironically the law has prevaricated on college student due process rights.[11]

---

9. *Dixon*, 294 F.2d at 158–59.

10. It is worth noting that the right to some process was extended to K–12 education by the U.S. Supreme Court. *See, e.g.*, *Goss v. Lopez*, 419 U.S. 565 (1975) (interim suspension of high school student requires some minimal process). By that time *in loco parentis* doctrine in K-12 required duties to supervise and discipline. However, the Supreme Court has hesitated to provide the same due process protections to college students for very complex reasons. *See* Lake, *supra* note 3, ch. 3.

11. *See id.*

A new era of legal protection for a variety of student rights—contractual and constitutional—was under way.

Among others, students have won the following basic rights:[12]

- *The right to engage in political speech and to publish political messages free from censorship;*
- *The right to participate in, work for, and establish student organizations;*
- *Equal access to college funds for organizations, despite the unpopularity of religious and political viewpoints put forth by those organizations;*
- *The right to be protected against unreasonable searches and seizures;*
- *Basic rights to be free from unlawful discrimination on the basis of race, sex, and disability.*

Student civil rights typically are not absolute but are subject to balancing against the university's responsibility to provide for the orderly conduct of classes and

---

12. *See* Robert D. Bickel & Peter F. Lake, *Reconceptualizing the University's Duty to Provide a Safe Learning Environment: A Criticism of the Doctrine of In Loco Parentis and the Restatement (Second) of Torts,* 20 J.C. & U.L. 261, 268–69, n.32 (1994). The Supreme Court granted students numerous rights. *See Tinker v. Des Moines Indep. Cmty. Sch. Dist.*, 393 U.S. 503 (1969) (secondary school students have a right to engage in passive speech, including the wearing of black arm bands protesting United States political actions, so long as students do not overtly disrupt the orderly conduct of classes or related school programs or interfere with the rights of other students in the learning environment); *Healy v. James*, 408 U.S. 169 (1972) (a public university may not deny recognition to a student organization solely on the basis of its disagreement with the political views of the organization, or its undifferentiated fear that recognition of the organization will lead to disruption); *Papish v. Bd. of Curators of the Univ. of Mo.*, 410 U.S. 667 (1973) (a state university may not censor the editorial content of a student newspaper solely on the basis of its view that the editorial is "offensive" to the university's constituencies); *Rosenberger v. Rector & Visitors of Univ. of Va.*, 515 U.S. 819, 828 (1995) (a public university "may not regulate speech based on its substantive content or the message it conveys"); *Bd. of Regents of Univ. of Wis. Sys. v. Southworth*, 529 U.S. 217 (2000) (mandatory student fee systems at public university must respect students' First Amendment rights); *Christian Legal Soc'y Chapter of the Univ. of Cal., Hastings Coll. of the Law v. Martinez*, 1305 S. Ct. 2971 (2010) (requirements for membership in RSO systems at public universities must respect associational rights of students). Congress has also intervened. Congress passed landmark civil rights laws forever altering American higher education by barring discrimination based on race, sex, and disability and protecting student privacy in educational records. *See, e.g.*, Civil Rights Act of 1964, Pub. L. No. 88–352, 78 Stat. 241 (1964); Civil Rights Act of 1964, Title VI, 42 U.S.C. §2000(d)–2000(d)(1); Civil Rights Act of 1968, Pub. L. No. 90–284, 82 Stat. 73 (1968); Rehabilitation Act of 1973, Section 504, 29 U.S.C. §794 (2006); Americans with Disabilities Act, 42 U.S.C. §§ 12213 (2006); Education Amendment Acts of 1972, Title IX, 20 U.S.C. §1681; Family Educational Rights and Privacy Act (FERPA), 12 U.S.C. §1232(g) (2006).

other programs and to protect the rights of other students, particularly to a safe learning environment.[13] Moreover, many new student civil rights have become intensely controversial in some instances.[14]

Dixon challenged the unfettered powers to discipline, regulate, and expel students. Indeed, the entire parental rights paradigm was dead. Courts like *Dixon* now viewed the parties in interest as students and the rights asserted as the contractual/constitutional rights of students. Public universities looked less like parents and were now legally reconfigured to be more like governmental entities—more like cities and towns than like mom and dad.

In loco parentis specifically died, then, in two ways. First, after *Dixon* it was no longer a viable legal defense against students who challenged improper discipline. Second, and perhaps more importantly, *in loco parentis* died as an *image* in student/university relations. Students were now *constitutional* citizens and "adults" (better, non-minors) who might seek protection from government-entity universities with whom they, the students, had a "contractual" relationship. Students became citizen-consumers (not wards); universities became "the man"—commercial/governmental entities. The second shift—the shift in image—was immensely powerful and would profoundly impact *private* college students' rights and also the future of student physical safety on campus.

To preview the latter point, a crucial observation is in order. Exactly at the time that students succeeded in changing imagined student/university relationships to governmental/commercial paradigms, the law of governmental and commercial responsibility for citizen/consumer safety was in a formative stage. Governments still had few *duties* to protect citizens from harm; commercial entities were increasingly required to protect consumers, but in the early 1960s, these responsibilities were still slender. For example, strict product liability did not solidify in the courts until the late 1960s and 1970s. Tenant's rights were still forming, and women enjoyed little legal protection from stalkers or violent partners. In short, there was a hidden side effect to student civil rights victories. Students won new rights and championed a new legal image of their status and relationship to the university. However, that image had a major weakness in that it imagined the university in roles as government and business at a time when duties to provide for physical security of citizens

---

13. *See, e.g.*, *Healy*, 408 U.S.

14. *See, e.g.*, *Christian Legal Soc'y*, 1305 S. Ct. (5–4 decision on RSO membership requirements).

and consumers were only just beginning to take shape. This was a time when the police could legally ignore cries for help from endangered citizens and businesses and landowners had little responsibility to keep dangerous people away from customers and tenants. These legal rules would change, but the timing was such that students had won a paradoxical, almost perfectly star-crossed victory. Constitutional rights now won would beget a period in which universities could, like governments and businesses, stand by and not prevent even grave or readily preventable danger. The bystander era, detailed in Chapter IV, would be part backlash, but also it was the almost inevitable consequence of the precise timing of the shift in image. Had the era of insularity fallen in, say, the late 1980s, university law might have looked very different. By the late 1980s, citizen/consumer safety rights were much better established.

Now, major shifts had occurred in public universities, but what was happening with *private* universities? After all, *constitutional* protections were almost entirely the province of governmental litigation. Would *in loco parentis*, for instance, survive for private colleges? The answer would be "no." The demise of *in loco parentis*—brought on by constitutional rights cases against public universities—was a feature of the much larger movement away from university legal insularity. This movement would capture private colleges as well. When students began to assert similar rights at private colleges—process, privacy, and speech rights for example—the courts began to recognize validity to those claims as well, even if somewhat more slowly.[15]

When such issues arose at private schools, the courts typically fell back upon the "well-settled rule that the relations between a student and a private university are a matter of contract."[16] The contract theory—armed to protect economic and intangible rights—had been of little help to students in the era of insularity. For one thing, students were not typically the contracting party. For another, contracts were subject to university-favorable rules regarding interpretation and enforcement. Historically, the most notorious way to read these contracts favorably to university power would be to determine that parent/student had somehow waived rights or had never been given them in the

15. *See Slaughter v. Brigham Young Univ.*, 514 F.2d 622 (10th Cir. 1975); Hazel G. Beh, *Student Versus University: The University's Implied Obligation of Good Faith and Fair Dealing*, 59 Md. L. Rev. 183 (2000).

16. *Dixon*, 294 F.2d at 157. *See Schaer v. Brandeis Univ.*, 735 N.E.2d 373 (Mass. 2000).

first place.[17] Thus, it was not uncommon for a court to rule that rights to notice and hearing were waived—that there in essence were no rights to be heard or notified prior to expulsion, even at expensive private colleges.[18]

However, newly ordained civil rights were not waivable in the public university context, as *Dixon* held, and that idea soon had its impact in the *private* college context. In the 1960s and 1970s courts began a slow shift to a more pro-consumer contract law stance, and at the same pace retreated from the older style of contract law cases. As *Dixon* stated in regard to private college case law, "the right to notice and hearing is so fundamental to the conduct of our society that the waiver must be clear and explicit."[19] Private colleges might limit students' process rights, but only upon clearer and more explicit terms.

Over time, the contract between the student and a private college has begun to look less and less like an ordinary contract of any typical variety.[20] There have been several critical variables at work.

First, college education, even when available at private schools, is eminently connected to major features of public interest. Private colleges have always been key functionaries in the public domain in America and how they perform and what they teach have affected all of society.

Second, the college contract itself was an odd collection of printed form catalogues, applications, rules, etc., that were offered on a "take it or leave it" basis. It would seem odd for a student/applicant to write a major college and demand "renegotiation" of the contract. It would also take a non-intuitive perspective to see the college admission/acceptance process like the purchase of a car. For most students and parents, education is not a typical transaction, even if today a college education does cost the equivalent of a house or more. Every other major financial transaction in life, from buying a car or house to writing a will, is highly regulated and even regularized via standard forms and the like. Oddly, we have model codes of student discipline, followed nearly letter and verse at many institutions. But there is little to no standardization to speak of in the college "contract" itself. College law is rooted in contract in a very unusual way.

---

17. One-sided contract rules continue to show their power. *See, e.g.*, *Acosta v. Dist. Bd. of Trustees of Miami-Dade Cmty. Coll.*, 905 So. 2d 226, 228–29 (Fla. 3d Dist. Ct. App. 2005) (applying "acquiescence" doctrine requiring students to protest an alleged breach of contract in a timely manner to protect any breach of contract claims).

18. *See, e.g.*, *Anthony v. Syracuse Univ.*, 231 N.Y.S. 435 (N.Y. App. Div. 1928); *Barker v. Trustees of Bryn Mawr Coll.*, 122 A. 220 (Pa. 1923).

19. *Dixon*, 294 F.2d at 157.

20. *See* Lake, *supra* note 3, 137–58.

Third, it seems odd that state college students should routinely receive more rights than private college students. Rough parallelism in public and private makes good sense. What would justify devoting so much social resource to educate people without even minimal background guarantees of fair play in their education? What types of people would such a system produce? Public or private, most colleges survive on the government dole directly or indirectly via student loans.

Students have continued to push the line between public and private higher education. Modern universities increasingly intertwine themselves with government programs. Students have argued that large private schools are sometimes like cities in that they provide the services of small municipalities—sewer, water, police, health care, street maintenance, etc. Students have likewise argued that education serves such a fundamental function in society that it is sufficiently similar to an activity of government. Students have lost these cases, often to the consternation of commentators who have offered competing, non-contract models of university/student relations, such as quasi-corporate fiduciary models.[21]

But the attacks on the public/private distinction have had its effects, notably in the arena of contract law. Increasingly, courts began to review the college contract with more scrutiny. As one recent commentator observed:

> The contractual method, however, is also seriously flawed. Several critics of the contractual approach are quick to point out the failure of the

---

21. Brian Jackson wrote:

> Dixon v. Alabama often is hailed as a pivotal rejection of the in loco parentis doctrine. But despite the Dixon decision, thousands of students at private universities remain outside the scope of constitutional protection. Since the Dartmouth College case recognized the independent nature of private education in the United States, the courts have been nearly unanimous in holding that private colleges and universities are not instruments of the state. As a result, actions by these schools cannot be attributed to the state for constitutional purposes. The Dixon decision thus left untouched thousands of students attending private colleges and universities. These students have no substantive or procedural constitutional safeguards.

Brian Jackson, *The Lingering Legacy of In Loco Parentis: An Historical Survey and Proposal for Reform,* 44 Vand. L. Rev. 1135, 1153–54 (1991) (footnotes omitted). For writers challenging the posture of the courts *see* Melissa Weberman, *University Hate Speech Policies and the Captive Audience Doctrine*, 36 Ohio N.U. L. Rev. 553, 571–74 (2010); Robert B. McKay, *The Student as Private Citizen,* 45 Denv. L.J. 558, 560 (1968); William Cohen, *The Private-Public Legal Aspects of Institutions of Higher Education,* 45 Denv. L.J. 643, 646–47 (1968); Alvin L. Goldman, *The University and the Liberty of Its Students—A Fiduciary Theory,* 54 Ky. L.J. 643, 650 (1966); Comment, *Common Law Rights for Private University Students: Beyond the State Action Principle,* 84 Yale L.J. 120, 122–23 (1974).

> analogy: Students and colleges do not engage in an "arm's length" agreement. Without such bargaining, quasi-contracts, unconscionable contracts, and contracts of adhesion all emerge as impairments to contractual analysis. Not all potential students are free to attend the college of their choice, nor are students able to negotiate the terms contained in a college bulletin.[22]

Very recently, the U.S. Department of Education has given more attention to the cost and value of higher education. Congress has also been interested in this issue, focusing considerable attention on the for-profit sector of higher education. With student loan debt now exceeding credit card debt, an economy that is not favorable to recent college graduates and rising default rates, legal attention to core mission delivery will likely increase. As regulators and consumers become savvier, they will realize the essential connections between core mission delivery and safety. This is found to have an impact on "contract" litigation.

Many concerns—particularly the unequal bargaining power of students *vis-a-vis* universities and the cost and financial risks of higher education—have influenced the development of student legal rights and the custom and practices of private colleges.

The 1984 decision of the 8th Circuit Federal Court of Appeals in *Corso v. Creighton University*[23] provides a good example of the evolution of college contract law in modern times. In that case a medical student was expelled from a private university medical program. The student was given process but claimed that the process given was not the correct process specified by contract with the school. In considering the student's claim, the *Corso* court agreed that a student claim of this sort (economic and intangible interest) is a contract claim stating that the "relationship between a university and student is contractual in nature."[24] (The court looked principally to the student handbook.)[25]

Critically, the *Corso* court viewed the "deal" as a printed form "adhesion" contract. With an adhesion contract all ambiguities and inconsistencies are read in favor of the student. And the court decides what is "clear" and "ambiguous." This type of logic gives the contract aspects of public policy and operates to protect student interests. In *Corso* it did just that. *Corso* actually afforded *more* than min-

---

22. Theodore C. Stamatakos, *The Doctrine of In Loco Parentis, Tort Liability and the Student-College Relationship,* 65 Ind. L.J. 471, 477 (1990) (footnote omitted).

23. 731 F.2d 529 (8th Cir. 1984).

24. *Id.* at 531.

25. *See Ross v. Creighton Univ.*, 957 F.2d 410 (1992) (discussing various sources that are part of the student contract).

imum due process to the student. In essence, a private university student received greater protection through special rules of contract interpretation.

The shift in contract analysis brought about corresponding customs and practices in the private university "industry" itself. Private universities are in the habit of providing significant process today, particularly in professional schools.[26] Public universities also routinely promise, via contract, more process than is constitutionally mandated.[27] Universities have embraced legalistic systems of discipline as a way to provide fairness to students.[28] Thus, the original legal belief that private schools would provide *less* than public schools has resolved into the irony that the private law of contracts has fueled a public law-like rights explosion in private colleges.

This area of the law has evolved to the point where one major commentator, Victoria Dodd, has pronounced that contract is no longer the true (or appropriate) basis for analyzing the legal relationship of private university relations with students:

> [L]aws of contract are not in fact being applied in student-university cases. Nor should they be. Instead, theories of tort law should be applied more frequently to issues concerning the student-university relationship, as the basic conceptual premises of contract law are not truly reflective of that relationship and thus are not appropriate analytical tools in the education law area.[29]

This sentiment has been mirrored in the courts.[30] Indeed "contract" analysis had taken on an air of unreality as the results in private college cases have closely tracked those in public university contexts. Contract law in the university context had become quasi-constitutional and vice versa. Nonetheless, courts were not willing to use contract or constitutional law to guarantee students a responsibly executed case mission either in terms of academic quality or overall safety. Courts continue to reject almost all educational malpractice claims.[31] Nonetheless, treating

---

26. Some have gone too far, perhaps. *See, e.g.*, *Boehm v. Univ. of Pa. Sch. of Veterinary Med.*, 573 A.2d 575 (Pa. 1990) in which extensive procedures—nearly mimicking trial—were provided.

27. *See* Lake, *supra* note 3, at 137–58.

28. *See id.* at 176–93.

29. Victoria J. Dodd, *The Non-Contractual Nature of the Student-University Contractual Relationship*, 33 U. Kan. L. Rev. 701, 702 (1985).

30. *See, e.g.*, *Slaughter v. Brigham Young Univ.*, 514 F.2d 622 (10th Cir. 1975); *Napolitano v. Trustees of Princeton Univ.*, 453 A.2d 263 (N.J. Super. 1982).

31. *See* Judith Areen, *Higher Education and the Law: Cases and Materials* 710, n. 1 (Foundation Press 2009). And, contract law has not been used as a predicate to create tort or safety rights in any significant way in higher education law.

students as consumers/customers and the development of "business" torts would eventually come to influence private and ultimately public higher education (more on this in Chapter V). In redefining the student/university contract relationship, courts—almost as if sleepwalking—wandered into forms of analysis that would set the stage for still further inroads into the insularity of university life.

By the end of the 1960s and the early 1970s the era of *in loco parentis* and traditional legal insularity was dead—constitutionally and contractually, publicly and privately—on modern American campuses. Economic and intangible rights (civil rights, privacy, speech rights, etc.) were vindicated in new models of student/university relations that stressed student (citizen/consumer) freedom and rights over university power and authority. More significantly, a major feature of college life had ended. College life was now legally non-immunized public activity and/or commercial activity; it was no longer protected governmental activity or nonjusticiable family or charitable activity. University conduct was becoming subject to judicial review and to legal, not simply internal institutional, norms. An age of accountability was being born.

But victories in the arena of civil rights did not settle—one way or the other—the very difficult questions of apportioning risks and responsibilities regarding student physical safety on campus. The citadel of insularity fell so quickly that it seemed that Rome was sacked on the first try. But Rome did not fall in one blow, and the civil rights cases (broadly speaking) seemed to throw a system of law, once in balance, into a substantial imbalance. The reaction of the courts to this new era of university relations initially would be mixed with regard to student safety. This is the study of the next chapter, the "bystander era," in which university law explored how the student freedoms won in the civil rights dimension would translate into rights and duties regarding physical safety.[32] The law of higher education was immature and would reflect newness, variety, and even knee jerkiness in a nascent and profoundly transitional period.

---

32. This book explores the ongoing battle for student rights of safety following the initial victories in the dimension of student civil rights. In the companion book to this one, *Beyond Discipline*, *supra* note 3, I explore the next frontiers of student rights particularly in the dimension of core mission delivery. That book discusses the evolution of the law relating to student discipline and also focuses on law and power issues relating to accountability for core mission—namely, the educational component of a student's experience in higher education. In many ways the civil rights era is ongoing and incomplete as students continue to fight for basic rights in higher education.

IV

The "Bystander"[1] University in the 1970s and 1980s

The "Duty" / "No-Duty" Era

American universities of the 1960s were in a major political/legal transitional state. A crisis of identity occurred in the civil rights era. The raw numbers of students enrolled rose dramatically as did the diversity of the student body. American university campuses also became more potentially dangerous and politically divisive places. American courts soon faced a new wave of lawsuits by physically injured students against their schools. In the period ranging roughly from 1970 to the mid-1980s, American courts shifted from relying on traditional legal doctrines of insularity and began an approach to lawsuits using the legal analytical/doctrinal tools of "duty" and "no duty."

Certain well-known and oft-cited court decisions in this period cast the university in the legal and cultural role of helpless "bystander" to student life and danger. In the role of mere bystanders, colleges could argue that they had no legal duties to protect students from physical harm and hence were not legally responsible for such harm. Universities typically saw certain key cases in this period as providing protection from students' lawsuits in light of the

1. The use of the term "bystander" was coined in the first edition of this book, and has now become commonly used to describe the case law of that era. *See, e.g.*, Judith Areen, *Higher Education and the Law: Cases and Materials* 811–18 (Foundation Press 2009); William A. Kaplin & Barbara A. Lee, *The Law of Higher Education* 196 (4th ed., Jossey-Bass 2006).

reshuffling of student rights and university responsibilities.[2] However, even the "bystander" era was a period of crosscurrents and mixed messages in university law. There were cases that imposed new legal duties on colleges. Universities were more likely to avoid legal responsibility in student-caused injury cases involving alcohol use; in other areas, legal responsibility began to move onto campus quickly. The "duty" era was in a formative stage. For reasons explored in this chapter, it appeared to some for a time that bystander rules would come to dominate. It would not be so.

There are four "famous" and often cited cases (other similar cases could be used) which are emblematic of the no-duty, bystander university period—*Bradshaw v. Rawlings,*[3] a decision of a federal appellate court in 1979; *Beach v. University of Utah,*[4] a decision of the Utah Supreme Court in 1986; *Baldwin v. Zoradi,*[5] a decision of a lower California appellate court in 1981; and, *Rabel v. Illinois Wesleyan University,*[6] an intermediate Illinois appellate court decision in 1987. These courts all used duty/no-duty concepts to limit the liability of a university for student injury. No-duty rules functioned to an extent like the historical trilogy of immunities, but now on a very different basis in theory. The image these bystander decisions conveyed was that of a newly disabled university (no longer able to exercise parental discipline and control), helplessly watching hordes of "free" students suffused with alcohol (or drugs), hormones, and poor judgment. Campus disorder and danger, like urban crime, were believed to be beyond the control of universities.

---

2. As the 1980s progressed, and then into the 1990s, the thinking was that pro-university, no-liability case law was part of a larger anti-tort, anti-victim, pro-business, pro-individual responsibility movement in the law of torts. University lawyers saw tort reform as an ally and allied development. As explained in this and following chapters, several tort law developments no doubt aided universities in defending some lawsuits. However, the connections between tort reform and the demise of insularity and *in loco parentis* can be overplayed and misjudged. Any predications that conservative tort reform movements would plateau litigation rates have not been accurate in our industry.

"There is no doubt that the numbers of legal claims involving colleges and universities has ballooned significantly in recent years. According to one survey, the number tripled within the span of just five years during the mid 1990s." Amy Gajda, *The Trials of Academe: The New Era of Campus Litigation* 3, 183–87 (Harvard Univ. Press 2009) (footnotes and citations omitted). Tort reform movements have been eclipsed in higher education law by the more powerful trends of mainstreaming higher education law and the fall of insularity.

3. 612 F.2d 135 (3d Cir. 1979).

4. 726 P.2d 413 (Utah 1986).

5. 176 Cal. Rptr. 809 (Cal. Ct. App. 1981).

6. 514 N.E.2d 552 (Ill. App. Ct. 1987).

The facts of these four cases show prototypical modern campus problems—repackage these cases slightly and you have all too typical student injury scenarios.

Bradshaw, a case involving off-campus parties (and the most infamous case of the four), went like this: On April 13, 1975, an eighteen-year-old college sophomore was seriously injured in an automobile accident. He was riding as a passenger in the backseat of a vehicle driven by an intoxicated fellow student. They had just come from an off-campus sophomore class picnic. The drinking age was twenty-one in Pennsylvania: this was a *sophomore* class event where most individuals were underage.

The "picnic" was actually little more than an off-campus drinking fest. The driver, for example, drank for several hours to the point where he blacked out and was unable to recall anything from the time he left the picnic until after the accident. The "picnic," an annual event, was planned with a faculty advisor, who co-signed the check that was later used to buy beer. The case report does not indicate that the faculty advisor or any other responsible faculty member attended the "picnic." Copies of flyers for the event were made on college equipment and tacked up all over campus. The unmistakable message conveyed by the prominently featured beer symbolism on the flyers was that it was a "wet" event. The sophomore class president (underage) succeeded in purchasing six or seven half kegs of beer from a local distributor (who earned legal trouble as a result of the sale). And the city of Doylestown, Pennsylvania became a defendant because the accident resulted when the drunken student lost control of the vehicle after encountering a road hazard.

The *Bradshaw* facts portray a "system" of alcohol use broken or besieged at almost every conceivable point. Underage students engaged in irresponsible, unlawful drinking and made the inevitable drive home from the off-campus party; and vendors of liquor were willingly selling to underage drinkers. A university allowed itself to facilitate a risky student function yet refused to accept even minimal responsibility for its own actions or the potential consequences to its students. There was the student preference for an off-campus event. The university limited college drinking problems on the college "campus" strictly defined, but to what end? In addition, *Bradshaw* portrays a society that has a taste for recreation in cars and the use of alcohol. There was also a city government struggling with questions of infrastructure (a looming safety issue for colleges). And there was no sense whatsoever among the several actors and parties of shared responsibility to reduce danger and increase safety: it seems everyone acted independently and unsafely. (Scenarios like *Bradshaw* eventually led the state of Pennsylvania to confront its drunk driving issues with far stricter laws and enforcement.)

Beach, also a liquor-related case, involves not partying and picnics, but the difficult problems associated with student curricular activities that carry on off campus. Of all four cases, *Beach* may be the most reprehensible (which is no doubt why decades later the Utah Supreme Court quietly eviscerated *Beach* in the *Webb* case, discussed *infra*). In *Beach*, an underage freshman biology student at the University of Utah was rendered quadriplegic during a required field trip in the Deep Creek Mountains of Utah in 1979. The field trip—a weekend camp out/expedition at a remote location—was a required part of the course in which she was enrolled. The trip was supervised by a professor who told the students that they were to follow instructions during "class time" (whatever boundary that was), but afterwards could "do their own thing." During the trip, the student fell from a cliff into a rocky crevice in an area where she laid suffering for several hours until she was discovered and rescued.[7]

Field trips, particularly remote location camping/hiking/rappelling trips, involve risks (there is no mention of consent/release forms in the *Beach* opinion), and students can get hurt. Danger, even obvious danger, is a fact of life, and thus relevant to the planning of academically sanctioned field trips for students. Yet, the *Beach* record disclosed some facts that should have concerned university administrators and parents. On a prior trip, the same underage student had, in the risk minimizing words of *Beach's* Justice Zimmerman, "experienced only one minor problem."[8] During an earlier trip (under the same professor's control), the student drank wine and fell asleep in some bushes near camp. She was found by other students and returned to safety. As if that were not enough, the student told the professor "that the incident was unusual."[9] Yet, when an underage student drinks unlawfully and/or in violation of university regulations, *loses consciousness*, and requires assistance from others, we know that this is an indication of greater problems and often a predictor of future similar behavior. This

7. *See Beach*, 726 P.2d at 414–15.

8. *Id.* at 414. An important feature of judge-made case law is that judges in courts of last resort have tremendous control over what "facts" are reported and how they are characterized. Usually fact finding is left for a jury—a basic constitutional right—but when judges use "duty," as we shall see, the judge circumvents the jury and takes control not just of law, but of fact and image as well. Judges are understandably reluctant to exercise these powers, but activist (so called) *conservative* judges (or judges deciding cases conservatively) have sometimes taken to "duty" as a way to create a kind of judicial tort reform which can limit a plaintiff's access to a trial by jury. The power to control or limit what goes to a jury is one of the most powerful political tools in American government and for practical purposes is heavily vested in the hands of judges.

9. *Id.* at 414.

was not a minor incident: we now know that little things count in large amounts (e.g., fixing broken locks can stop intruders). Although the court in *Beach* treated the incidents as if they were functionally unrelated, there was a chilling pattern in events prognosticating danger lay ahead.

The second time, the results were serious. On the fateful Sunday, the students were taken to a cookout hosted by a local rancher. This was a *freshman* biology course in a state with a twenty-one year old drinking age; nonetheless, the professor himself stated, "that he assumed most people . . . were drinking alcohol and that he had several beers."[10] The liquor was apparently flowing quite freely because the student consumed a mixed drink, plus three or four home brewed (higher alcohol?) beers at the cookout (likely enough liquor to intoxicate an average 20-year-old female in a short period of time). *And*, the professor (who had been drinking) *drove* the student and others in a van back to the campsite. Fortunately, there was no vehicular mishap; but this van was an "alcohol wagon." While in the back of the van, the students drank whiskey from some unidentified source.[11] According to the testimony as reported by the court, when the van reached the campsite, "[the student] did not act inebriated or in any way impaired, but appeared to be well-oriented and alert."[12] Common sense (and subsequent events) suggests that either she was wrong in her reported self-assessment (also common if you are drinking), or that she was a person who had used alcohol in high-risk ways that raised her apparent tolerance for alcohol. The professor had also been drinking, which typically impairs one's judgment and particularly one's ability to assess the impairment of others. Something was certainly amiss with the student because in attempting to reach her tent—just one hundred and twenty-five feet from the van—she got lost. She called for assistance, but no one helped her. The next morning she was finally found after suffering her grievous injuries.[13] *Beach* is to field trips what *Bradshaw* is to off-campus parties, and worse.

Modern universities now conduct more field trips, externships, and study abroad as an integral part of courses, summer programs, etc. In many cases the very educational mission of the off-campus curriculum event involves inherent danger—to study huckleberries in field biology you must go where the bears and the briars are. And like *Bradshaw, Beach* involves the deliberate high-risk use of alcohol, as well as the difficulties of monitoring use by students and university officials and instructors. *Beach* is also like *Bradshaw* in

10. *Id.* at 415.

11. *See id.*

12. *See id.*

13. *See id.*

that it shocks and surprises most modern parents who learn about it. Parents may anticipate that their college-age offspring will encounter and even possibly misuse alcohol. But they do not expect universities to facilitate dangerous underage drinking on an *academic* field trip (planned and conducted by a professor), and to ignore telltale signs of high-risk alcohol use and danger. Colleges should not enhance or facilitate drinking risks in any context.

Baldwin v. Zoradi involved injuries sustained off campus stemming from on-campus drinking.[14] Because the case was dismissed on the pleadings—a technical procedural way to end litigation before facts are fully discovered or proven—the "facts" of *Baldwin* must arise by way of presumptions from allegations made in the pleadings.[15] The victim in *Baldwin* was a student at a California state university. She was injured in a car wreck that was the product of a "Fast and Furious" speeding contest, itself the byproduct of (underage) drinking at a university dorm. Students involved were underage, yet had consumed alcohol on campus in violation of university rules prohibiting their alcohol use and in violation of California law.[16]

The salient feature of *Baldwin* was the assertion (treated as fact) that not only did the university fail to enforce anti-drinking rules in *this* instance—where "mass quantities were consumed"—but that in *general,* the university "looked the other way" regarding on-campus drinking. The culture was one where rules and catalogs conveyed the image of regulated liquor consumption, but reality was exactly the opposite. The court itself related one aspect of the plaintiff's claim (again, treated as if the facts were true):

> The Trustees and dormitory advisors permitted a dangerous condition to exist at the residence hall in that consumption of alcohol by minors occurred regularly, and the said defendants knew or should have known of such occurrence and taken appropriate steps to stop the activity. "By knowingly acquiescing in the consumption of alcohol by

---

14. *See Baldwin,* 176 Cal. Rptr. at 809.

15. In *Baldwin,* the court presumed that all of the allegations of the complaint were true. *See id.* at 811. In essence, the court decides the question: "Even if everything you say is true, are you entitled to a legal remedy?" This type of inquiry *procedurally* focuses litigation upon *legal* questions, particularly legal questions of *duty.* In this way a court—not a jury—can decide to end a case, even before all facts are discovered or demonstrated. The result of this way of managing the legal questions presented is that the cases are more like epitaphs than biographies: they tend to be pithy, aphoristic distillations, or contain just snippets of information. There is no pretense that the "truth" has been elicited. However, it is possible that the "facts" stated in a complaint are erroneous, incomplete or exaggerated.

16. *See Baldwin,* 176 Cal. Rptr. at 809–13. *See also Rabel,* 514 N.E.2d at 560.

> minors on campus over an extended period of time, the Trustees, and their employees, created an unsafe condition, to wit, a safe haven or enclave where large groups of minors could, would and did gather and consume alcoholic beverages, to an excess, with complete impunity from any laws or rules and regulations."[17]

The student-victim claimed not just that university culture was dangerous. She claimed it was a sham.

Baldwin is a classic example of risks that expand into the community from inside the university culture. A culture of underage drinking and students with automobiles away from home is a dangerous mixture. Moreover, *Baldwin* illustrates a fundamental hypocrisy that can occur in drinking regulation on campus. Official rules prohibit underage and unsupervised drinking, but the college culture can actually *facilitate* drinking and its deadly combination with vehicles. What better way to sell your parents on the idea of giving you a car at college than to pursue the path of a "science nerd" at a school with "tough" regulations on drinking? *Baldwin* is to on-campus drinking what *Bradshaw* is to off-campus drinking—the results can be the same—serious injury. Alcohol danger flows over all campus boundaries freely, and injury from alcohol risk can occur on or off campus, wherever the drinking takes place. Nonetheless, in lock step with other "bystander" cases of its time, *Baldwin* determined that "no duty" was owed.

Rabel,[18] another case dismissed on the pleadings, is a consummate fraternity prank case. One afternoon in 1982, a young female college student was called upon to meet a visitor in the dormitory lobby. The visitor was a male student who was involved with a fraternity. He had just come from a fraternity sponsored liquor-friendly party. The visitor had been instructed by members of the fraternity to abduct a female student and then run a gauntlet of fraternity brothers who would strike him as he passed by (apparently a traditional activity). The good frat-soldier did just that: he forcibly grabbed the female student, threw her over his shoulder, and ran towards his task. But he was not up to the task; as he ran with her he fell and, among other things, crushed her skull in the fall.[19] She suffered permanent, life-altering head injuries. In any other location and circumstances but on a college campus, this could be kidnapping and home invasion, battery, assault, and/or assorted other crimes, torts, and wrongs.

---

17. *Baldwin*, 176 Cal. Rptr. at 812.
18. *Rabel*, 514 N.E.2d 552.
19. *See id.* at 554–55.

The fraternity member and the fraternity settled out (for relatively small sums), leaving the university faced with assertions—treated as fact—that were strikingly similar to those made in *Baldwin:*

> [The university] holds itself out to the public, prospective students and others as a University that does not allow alcoholic beverages on its campus or in its fraternity houses, and as a University whose agents stated primary concern is the general student welfare.
>
> [The university] by and through its agents and employees stated to [plaintiff and plaintiff's family], the public and prospective students by direct statement and otherwise that the University strictly controlled the activities of its students, including a ban on alcohol consumption and further, it represented and held itself out as having a strong religious background with a tradition of strong supervision and control of student activities and a premium price was charged to students as tuition to this private University in reliance upon those statements and others.
>
> ....
>
> At all times described herein, [the university] was aware of the excessive drinking occurring at the Fiji Fraternity and was aware of the lengthy and boisterous parties and activities, including the activities at Pfeiffer Hall described herein on May 1, 1982.
>
> [The university], not regarding its duty to the Plaintiff personally and as a student at Illinois Wesleyan University, and its duty to others arising out of its specific representations to [plaintiff and plaintiff's family] the public and prospective students, its stated policies, its customs and practices, its high tuition, and the special relationship between [the university] and its students, failed to take any effective action on April 30, 1982 or May 1, 1982 to discourage the excessive drinking of its students and others, or to discourage the lengthy and boisterous party and activities associated with that party, or to supervise and control said party or to provide adequate protection to the University community at large and to [plaintiff] in particular.[20]

This time a non-drinking student was victimized by intoxicated students on campus. The "look the other way" culture in this case involved Greek life—an unfortunately common source of alcohol risk and litigation on college campuses.

20. *Rabel*, 514 N.E.2d at 556–57 (citing *Bradshaw*, 612 F.2d 135).

Bradshaw, Beach, Baldwin, and *Rabel* are variations of common and dangerous themes—alcohol, college students, drunk driving, field trips, residence life, and Greek life. Implicitly, these courts sensed the common themes and reacted to them in light of a common perception of the new relational reality on campus. The dominant image in these cases was that of newly empowered students who were beyond the control of the modern university. To the courts, the university was a helpless "bystander" to such student misconduct; no "duty" was owed to the students as "adults." Nor *should* a duty be owed given the "new" role of colleges.

In each of these cases—in spite of the facts—the courts determined that *as a matter of law* (translated: no jury evaluation of the university's conduct in the matter) the university was held *not* responsible for the student's injuries. These courts looked with some dismay upon a college-aged generation with whom they had lost touch or over whom they were losing control. Previous generations of college students had accepted (or acquiesced to) the powers and prerogative of their host institutions; a new rebellious generation confounded and dismayed many in the leadership class.

These courts chose particular images and particular legal tools to create a new legal climate on university campuses. The image was that of the helpless bystander university brought about as a direct result of student freedoms won in the civil rights movements: freedom implied lack of control, lack of control implied no duty. The new legal tool—"duty"—was used to limit liability and to keep juries out of the legal process involving universities.

Bradshaw, the frequently cited and seminal case (although it was a federal court decision guessing at what the law of Pennsylvania would become),[21] portrayed the following image:

---

21. *Bradshaw,* 612 F.2d 135. In some cases, federal courts are invested with the special jurisdictional opportunity to hear what are, in essence, cases involving *state law* only. If the right mix of parties or issues is present, a single automobile accident could end up in federal court. When a federal court decides such a case, it is bound to follow state law; it is to act, at least substantially, as if it were a court in that state bound by the precedents of the state supreme court. Sometimes, as in *Bradshaw,* the state courts have not answered the questions raised in the federal case. Yet, in such an instance, the federal court is to make a *guess* (an educated guess, called by lawyers an *Erie* guess, so named after a U.S. Supreme Court case which ratified this process). *See Erie Railroad Co. v. Tompkins,* 304 U.S. 64 (1938). It is law; but it is a guess and, at least in theory, lacks the weight of a decision of the state supreme court itself. Yet it often takes years—even decades—for a state court to reach the precise issues of the federal case. In the meantime, that case stands. In the case of *Bradshaw,* it has taken on a life of its own. For instance, the *Bradshaw* case receives prominent attention in the leading casebook

Our beginning point is recognition that the modern American college is not an insurer of the safety of its students. Whatever may have been its responsibility in an earlier era, the authoritarian role of today's college administrations has been notably diluted in recent decades. Trustees, administrators, and faculties have been required to yield to the expanding rights and privileges of their students. By constitutional amendment, written and unwritten law, and through the evolution

---

on higher education law and policy, Judith Areen's *Higher Education and the Law: Cases and Materials*, *supra* note 1, (used to teach many law and master's level students). *See id.* at 811–18. In a note that mirrors typical arguments made by college attorneys in court, Areen states:

> Although many courts in recent years have been willing to hold colleges and universities liable for some student injuries, Bradshaw illustrates the dominate [sic] judicial view that they are not liable for most alcohol related injuries and deaths. See, e.g., Albano v. Colby Coll., 822F.Supp. 840 (D. Me. 1993) (college not liable for drinking related student injury on a school sponsored tennis trip); Booker v. Lehigh Univ., 800F.Supp. 234, 239 (E.D.Pa. 1992) (refusing to hold university's alcohol policy constituted an assumption of duty); Baldwin v. Zoradi, 123 Cal.App.3d 275, 176 Cal.Rptr. 809 (1981) (university not liable for student injury resulting from car race accident after drinking in a campus dormitory); University of Denver v. Whitlock, 744 P.2d 54 (Colo.1987) (overturning an imposition of liability on university for students alcohol-related injury on a trampoline); Allen v. Rutgers, 216 N.J.Super. 189, 523 A.2d 262 (App.Div.1987) (college not liable for drinking-related fall over stadium wall at school football game); Beach v. University of Utah, 726 P.2d 413 (Utah 1986) (university not liable for a student's drinking-related injury on a field trip, even though the university was aware that student had a history of similar behavior and the teacher sponsoring the trip was also drinking); Houck v. University of Wash., 60 Wash.App. 189, 803 P.2d 47 (1991) (university has no duty to prevent underage students from drinking on campus and is not liable for student's drinking related injury). Courts have also resisted holding colleges or universities liable for drug-related student injuries and deaths. See, e.g., Bash v. Clark Univ., 22 Mass. L. Rep. 84 (Mass.Super.Ct. 2006) (university not liable for student's on-campus heroin overdose).

Id. at 817, n. 1. *Bradshaw* has come to be emblematic for many chroniclers of college "alcohol" case law—even though there are a prominent series of cases, discussed *infra*, that contradict the position that there is one dominant judicial viewpoint on how to manage college alcohol risk under law. *See, e.g.*, Kaplin & Lee, *supra* note 1, at 197; Areen, *supra* note 1, at 817 n. 2. The concept of "the alcohol cases" is itself problematical for a number of reasons, explored *infra*. Moreover, *Bradshaw* is only as valid as the state law *Erie* guess that the federal court made years ago in another era, when alcohol responsibility law was primitive. Critically the law of Pennsylvania has changed dramatically since *Bradshaw* was decided—and the result in *Bradshaw* is no longer supportable under Pennsylvania law if the same facts were to occur today.

of new customs, rights formerly possessed by college administrations have been transferred to students. College students today are no longer minors; they are now regarded as adults in almost every phase of community life. For example except for purposes of purchasing alcoholic beverages, eighteen year old persons are considered adults by the Commonwealth of Pennsylvania. They may vote, marry, make a will, qualify as a personal representative, serve as a guardian of the estate of a minor, wager at racetracks, register as a public accountant, practice veterinary medicine, qualify as a practical nurse, drive trucks, ambulances and other official fire vehicles, perform general fire-fighting duties, and qualify as a private detective. Pennsylvania has set eighteen as the age at which criminal acts are no longer treated as those of a juvenile, and eighteen year old students may waive their testimonial privilege protecting confidential statements to school personnel. Moreover, a person may join the Pennsylvania militia at an even younger age than eighteen and may hunt without adult supervision at age sixteen. As a result of these and other similar developments in our society, eighteen year old students are now identified with an expansive bundle of individual and social interests and possess discrete rights not held by college students from decades past. There was a time when college administrators and faculties assumed a role *in loco parentis*. Students were committed to their charge because the students were considered minors. A special relationship was created between college and student that imposed a duty on the college to exercise control over student conduct and, reciprocally, gave the students certain rights of protection by the college. [This statement is a demonstrably false statement of tort law as we have seen—ed.] The campus revolutions of the late sixties and early seventies were a direct attack by the students on rigid controls by the colleges and were an all-pervasive affirmative demand for more student rights. In general, the students succeeded, peaceably and otherwise, in acquiring a new status at colleges throughout the country. These movements, taking place almost simultaneously with legislation and case law lowering the age of majority, produced fundamental changes in our society. A dramatic reapportionment of responsibilities and social interest of general security took place. Regulation by the college of student life on and off campus has become limited. Adult students now demand and receive expanded rights of privacy in their college life including, for example, liberal, if not unlimited, partial visiting hours. College administrators no longer control the broad arena of general morals. At one time, exercising their rights and duties *in loco parentis,* colleges were able to impose strict regulations. But today students vigorously claim the right to define and regulate their own lives. Especially have they demanded and received satisfaction of their interest in self-assertion in both physical and mental activities, and have vindicated what may be called the interest in freedom of the individual will. In 1972 Justice Douglas summarized the change:

> Students—who, by reason of the Twenty-sixth Amendment, become eligible to vote when 18 years of age—are adults who are members of the college or university community. Their interest and concerns are often quite different from those of the faculty. They often have values, views, and ideologies that are at war with the ones that the college has traditionally espoused or indoctrinated. *Healy v. James,* 408 U.S. 169, 197, 92 S.Ct. 2338, 2354, 33 L.Ed.2d 266 (1972) (Douglas, J., concurring).

Thus, for purposes of examining fundamental relationships that underlie tort liability, the competing interests of the student and of the institution of higher learning are much different today than they were in the past. At the risk of oversimplication, the change has occurred because society considers the modern college student an adult, not a child of tender years.[22]

Bradshaw—the sophomore drinking party case—saw that students had become emancipated from "minor" status and, by gaining so many freedoms, had become "adults."[23] In one magic moment, students went from being "children" to fully functioning adults, with no in-between time. Students had won freedom while responsibility as a college virtue had waned. The shift was abrupt, dramatic, and polar.

Bradshaw was cited and quoted extensively in *Beach, Baldwin,* and *Rabel.* Indeed, *Bradshaw* became the announcement of the birth of the new "adult" student body. And, *Bradshaw* birthed the bystander (helpless) university. The

---

22. *Bradshaw,* 612 F.2d at 138–41 (emphasis and editorial commentary added; footnotes and citations omitted). If a court were to survey Pennsylvania law *today,* they would come to a different conclusion.

23. The students were now not merely "constitutional" adults; they were adults to whom the university owed no duty of supervision or protection or obligation to be actively involved in risk minimization.

other three decisions amplified *Bradshaw* in the immediate moments following the fall of legal insularity.

Baldwin—the dormitory drinking/drag race case—similarly imagined that drinking on university campuses was uncontrollable. Almost unthinkably by modern standards, *Baldwin* also believed that not enforcing policies and rules prohibiting underaged drinking was actually in the best interest of society. In *Baldwin's* own words with respect to controlling college drinking:

> In respect to the burden to the defendant and the consequences to the community of imposing a duty to exercise care with resulting liability for breach, it would be difficult to so police a modern university campus as to eradicate alcoholic ingestion.
>
> ....
>
> Nor is it in the best interests of society to do so. The transfer of prerogatives and rights from college administrators to the students is salubrious when seen in the context of a proper goal of postsecondary education—the maturation of the students. Only by giving them responsibilities can students grow into responsible adulthood. Although the alleged lack of supervision had a disastrous result to this plaintiff, the overall policy of stimulating student growth is in the public interest.[24]

College anti-drinking rules were also now to have a nudge-nudge-wink-wink quality:

> Since the turbulent '60s California colleges and universities have been in the forefront of extension of student rights with a concomitant withering of faculty and administrative omnipotence. Drug use has proliferated. Although the consumption of alcoholic beverages by persons under 21 years of age is proscribed by law (Bus. & Prof. Code, § 25658), the use of alcohol by college students is not so unusual or heinous by contemporary standards as to require special efforts by college administrators to stamp it out. Although the university reserved to itself the right to take disciplinary action for drinking on campus, this merely follows state law. (Bus. & Prof. Code, § 25608.) The same may be said of the provisions of the license agreement prohibiting alcoholic beverages. We do not believe they created a mandatory duty.[25]

24. *Baldwin*, 514 N.E.2d at 818.
25. *Id.* at 817.

Baldwin believed dangerous college-age drinking did not require any unusual collegiate response and the fact that there were anti-drinking rules and regulations did not mean the college actually had to enforce them. Again, *Baldwin* tied this to the 1960s student "revolution." *Baldwin* took a final step as well in concluding that somehow this state of affairs was best for student maturation, as if to tolerate the deaths and injuries to some students as a necessary evil in service of a greater good. The *Baldwin* court lacked any vision that the freedom of which it spoke operated in an environment that should include/provide *some* structure directed toward the progression from adolescence to full adulthood. Rather, the *Baldwin* court seemed to say that students must be left free to drink themselves to death—free to be unreasonably unsafe.

Beach, also quoting *Baldwin,* emphasized "realism," and focused upon how, in its view, a university could not and should not exercise control over its students. The image again is one of university "helplessness":

> We also must consider the nature of the institution. Elementary and high schools certainly can be characterized as a mixture of custodial and educational institutions, largely because those who attend them are juveniles. However, colleges and universities are educational institutions, not custodial. *Accord Baldwin v. Zoradi,* 123 Cal. App. 3d at 281–82, 176 Cal. Rptr. at 813. Their purpose is to educate in a manner which will assist the graduate to perform well in the civic, community, family, and professional positions he or she may undertake in the future. It would be unrealistic to impose upon an institution of higher education the additional role of custodian over its adult students and to charge it with responsibility for preventing students from illegally consuming alcohol and, should they do so, with responsibility for assuring their safety and the safety of others. *Accord Bradshaw v. Rawlings,* 612 F.2d at 138; *Baldwin v. Zoradi,* 123 Cal. App. 3d at 290–91, 176 Cal. Rptr. at 818. Fulfilling this charge would require the institution to babysit each student, a task beyond the resources of any school. But more importantly, such measures would be inconsistent with the nature of the relationship between the student and the institution, for it would produce a repressive and inhospitable environment, largely inconsistent with the objectives of a modern college education.[26]

Beach envisioned a draconian choice between custodial control (like a sanitarium or jail) and merely performing *educational* functions. For *Beach,* safety

26. *Beach,* 726 P.2d at 419 (emphasis added; footnote omitted).

and responsible regulation were in zero sum relationships with education: drive up the rules, drive out the students. There is also a trace of the belief that "Animal House" culture is impossible to control. The university could try to wipe out drinking but it would ultimately fail and cause a political backlash.

Beach also hammered at the status of the student as an *adult. Beach,* like *Bradshaw* and *Baldwin,* saw a tough choice—"babysit" students as "children" in a "custodial" setting (treating them like "wards"), or treat them like "adults" and stand by and let them injure themselves. Standing by was practical *and* just, said *Beach,* because the students had demanded, and won, adult status. *Beach* turned civil rights adulthood into a much larger image of students as adults—and turned it against them. *Beach* chose particularly strong language and analogies to convey this "overnight shift" into adulthood:

> The students whose relationship to the University we are asked to characterize as "custodial" are not juveniles. Beach was twenty years of age at the time of the accident. She may have been denied the right to drink by Utah law, but in virtually all other respects she was entitled to be treated as an adult. She had a constitutional right to vote, U.S. Const. amend. XXVI, § 1, she was to be chargeable on her contracts, U.C.A., 1953, §§ 15-2-1 and 2 (1986 ed.) and if she had committed a crime, she would be tried and sentenced as an adult. U.C.A., 1953 §§78-3a-2 and 16 (1977 ed., Supp. 1986). Had she not been a college student, but an employee in industry, she could not argue realistically that her employer would be responsible for compensating her for injuries incurred by her voluntary intoxication if she violated state liquor laws during her off-hours while traveling on company business. [While defensible at the time *Beach* was decided, workers' compensation laws later changed in the United States. Such a statement is no longer generally valid today. Ed.] We do not believe that Beach should be viewed as fragile and in need of protection simply because she had the luxury of attending an institution of higher education.
>
> Not only are students such as Beach adults, but law and society have increasingly come to recognize their status as such in the past decade or two. Nowhere is this more true than in the relations between students and institutions of higher education.[27]

Beach chose to compare a student in college to a worker (and assumed the result in a factually similar worker/employee case). There is an undercurrent

27. *Id.* at 418 (footnote omitted; editorial comment inserted).

that unlike hard-working people in business and those who chose (or were drafted into) military service, the life of the college student is a rights-dripping, luxuriating experience, a position from which one is ill-suited to ask for duties of protection from a university.

Beach took this even further by determining that these adults were still subject to university authority but had lost the right to ask for correlative duties from the university. In a famous footnote (many of the most important nuggets of jurisprudence occur in footnotes), the *Beach* court stated that:

> This is not to say that an institution might not choose to require of students certain standards of behavior in their personal lives and subject them to discipline for failing to meet those standards. However, the fact that a student might accept those conditions on attendance at the institution would not change the character of their relationship; the student would still be an adult and responsible for his or her behavior. Neither attendance at college nor *agreement to submit to certain behavior standards* makes the student less an autonomous adult or the institution more a caretaker.[28]

You can almost see the "you wanted it this way—you got it" attitude in the *Beach* decision. Students won civil rights, but had left a bitter taste in the mouths of some courts. There was no hint of any possibility of shared responsibility (or meaningful intermediate definitions of the student-university relationship) outside the classroom. Students, *Beach* observed, had demanded "total" freedom as to their conduct on campus and in society, and this demand was seen as one for freedom without structure.[29]

Rabel, also quoting *Beach* extensively, seized upon the notion that higher education does not create a "custodial" relationship, but rather a merely "educational" relationship. *Rabel,* like *Beach,* feared that if the university were to have any affirmative duty regarding student conduct that threatened safety, it would become an "insurer" of student safety (blameless, but financially responsible). And, *Rabel* focused upon how "unrealistic" it would be to ask a university to pro-

---

28. *Id.* at 419 n.5 (emphasis added).

29. *Beach* and other bystander cases made many subtle mistakes in assertions of tort law. For example, a person who asks that another have some responsibility for his safety is not automatically asking for a legal custodial relationship. When you go to a shopping mall you are owed a safety duty of reasonable care, but you are not in "custody" even though that new pair of Manolo Blahniks may overpower and "control" your good judgment. Courts are people, and like people they make mistakes or may make statements with unintended implications. It is incumbent on higher education scholars and lawyers to rectify, not magnify, such errors.

tect students and prevent such events as fraternity drinking and pranks. The image is of a university community run awash in a sea of freedom and license, with the only alternative being custodial care or backbreaking strict liability (the university as "insurer" image). The causes of campus-related student injuries—particularly drinking injuries—seemed to be beyond the control of a university. The modern university was seemingly powerless.

In sum, *Bradshaw, Beach, Baldwin,* and *Rabel* painted the following images of the new, post-*in loco parentis* era on campus:

- Students are "adults." They went from being "children," in most instances *directly* into this role;
- Students are no longer in "custody" or under "university" control. Universities cannot and should not "babysit" students;
- A student's loss of a right to protection from harm is directly related to student freedoms/individual rights won in the turbulent 1960s and early 1970s. Baby boom, baby bust;
- Universities are not, cannot be, and should not be insurers or underwriters of dangerous behavior on campus;
- Universities cannot "realistically" enforce campus regulations to create a safe learning environment, especially those involving alcohol use and campus activities;
- Universities can promulgate all sorts of rules regarding the same, and even if they do and can enforce them, they are not responsible to do so or to do so responsibly;
- Students are to bear the consequences of their "adult" choices (although in some instances fraternities and alcohol vendors will share in the responsibility);
- College is a luxury and an especially luxurious lifestyle in terms of personal freedom;
- Campus police and policing are disempowered in much the way the police were disempowered in major cities in the 1960s–1980s. Crime/injury will rise on campus due to social factors beyond the control of the university and their police security forces;
- College students will resist university control regarding their physical safety. The campus drinking culture is like drug-resistant bacteria for which there is no cure;
- Society is better off letting some students drink, crash, and burn because the overall population of students will then get what they want from college and will be better citizens because of lessons learned;

- The university is the crucible for major social problems, but is helpless to do much except "educate" students in academic subjects in the classrooms;
- The university's role is educational, primarily, in the limited sense of providing courses, exams, etc. The campus is now a *limited* purpose community—the purpose is classroom education only. Henceforth, there will be two distinct classes of university employees—"academic" staff delivering core mission, classroom-related services and other staff (many destined to be called student affairs administrators) delivering non-core mission services;
- Safety and education are fundamentally inversely related variables. A safer learning environment is a babysitting, custodial environment at odds with what modern students expect;
- It is just and fair to exact a price from students who want freedom. Students forfeit rights to demand safe learning environments, reasonable alcohol use on campus, and even dormitory safety in return for other freedom (e.g., constitutional freedoms);
- College drinking, by minors especially, is an inevitable fact of campus life, with unavoidably bad consequences. As *Bradshaw* admitted: "What we know as men and women we must not forget as judges, and this panel of judges is able to bear witness to the fact that beer drinking by college students is a common experience. That this is true is not to suggest that reality always comports with state law and college rules. It does not";[30]
- Courts need to protect universities from injury claims, especially those involving alcohol;
- Implicitly, parents—especially those attempting to play the role of surrogate—should be disassociated from higher education;
- Most defendants must act reasonably, but universities are unique defendants;
- Universities are best when they act as bystanders to non-educational student pursuits.

Courts in these now famous[31] cases, concluded that the university was not legally responsible for harm caused because there was no legal "duty." The image of the disempowered bystander, non-custodial university was cemented

30. *Bradshaw*, 612 F.2d at 142.

31. These cases became famous even though they were nothing more than two intermediate appellate court decisions, a decision of a federal court making an "*Erie*" guess on state law, and a Utah Supreme Court decision (a small jurisdiction, not noted for setting or stating legal trends).

by the legal tool of "duty." The legal question in these types of cases became: "Does this type of university/student relationship create legal duty?" By crafting the question of law in terms of "duty," these courts linked American university law to a complex, changing and sometimes obtuse legal concept. The practical effect of "no-duty" rulings was to limit claims against universities at the outset of litigation and to keep cases from discovery, litigation, and jury trial.[32] The political effect of using a "no duty" benchmark was to create what was in essence a new *de facto* university *immunity*—an island in what was once a vast sea of legal insularity. By referring to legal rules of such complexity, only experts would find their way through them.

Problematically, complex and murky legal rules can be very disempowering for non-lawyers who must administer a learning environment under these rules. In the duty era university foot soldiers and lieutenants discovered that it is not easy for non-lawyers to understand what the law requires. In a sense, the bystander era should have made administration happy from a legal compliance standpoint—campus police, deans of students, Greek life advisors, etc., but instead these same administrators were often perplexed and felt disempowered. The problem was this: at the same time courts were sending a message that higher education's core mission was in the classroom, student services were rapidly expanding *outside* the classroom and expectations to deliver a broad whole-life educational experience were growing as well. Student development theory was changing; so was the science of higher learning. Populations were changing, too. In no time, the children of the baby boom would be on their way to college. Administrators increasingly felt pressure to engage *and* disengage from student life simultaneously—and the law seemed to raise more questions about compliance than it clearly answered.[33]

---

32. The practical legal effect of this "no-duty" view was to keep a court or jury from evaluating the reasonableness of university conduct.

33. Professor Areen has articulated exactly the precise questions that have faced administrators (as they have seen them) in the duty era—what to do with alcohol risk and/or law to involve parents when teaching "adults":

> A college or university that voluntarily implements measures to control underage drinking or to curb drunk driving on campus may expose itself to liability. In Coghlan v. Beta Theta Pi Fraternity, 133 Idaho 388, 987 P.2d 300 (1999), for example, the court held that the university assumed a duty to protect its students from those serving alcohol to minors when it voluntarily assigned university employees to supervise all on-campus parties. Similarly in McClure v. Fairfield University, 2003 WL 21524786 (Conn.Super.Ct. 2003), the court ruled in favor of a

The duty era has been so doctrinally complex that it has been easy to misunderstand just what was happening in the law. For one thing there were *crosscurrent* cases—cases that sent anything but a bystander message. Although *Bradshaw, Beach, Baldwin,* and *Rabel* were prominent, there were cases decided at about the same time that did not insulate university conduct from legal scrutiny. The bystander era was thus actually a complex time; some case law flew in the face of the more dominant images of the no-liability cases. Commentators have struggled to explain just what was going on—sometimes compartmentalizing the bystander cases as alcohol/drug cases when looking at them in the rearview mirror.[34] But before looking at such crosscurrent cases—cases which seem to contradict *Bradshaw, Beach, Baldwin, and Rabel*—a long look at duty and tort responsibility is in order so as to understand what these four key cases did and did not say, and what they might have said.

* * * *

In general, if someone has been injured physically by some university misconduct or omission, that person looks to the law of torts for a potential remedy.[35] A contractual relationship occasionally may form a predicate, but it is tort law

---

> student who was hit by a drunk driver late at night while walking to campus. The court held that the university assumed liability for the safe transportation of its students by offering a free shuttle service at night. Id at 8. Does this mean schools should not take any safety precautions?
>
> If a university decides to confront the problem of alcohol, what steps should it take? A growing number of universities are contacting parents when students are caught using alcohol or drugs. Elizabeth Bernstein, Colleges Move Boldly on Student Drinking, Wall St. J., Dec. 6, 2007, at Dl. Although the Family Education Rights and Privacy Act (FERPA) generally protects the privacy of students' disciplinary record, an exception created in 1998 allows universities to contact parents if a student under twenty-one commits an alcohol or drug violation. Although proponents of the measure point to the important role that parents can play in addressing the problem of alcohol abuse at universities, opponents feel that the measure violates the privacy and independence of students. What do you think?

Areen, *supra* note 1, at 817. The first question relates to the fear of "assuming duties"—discussed *infra*, and the latter relates to highly dangerous misperceptions of privacy law that came to the forefront after tragic events at Virginia Tech.

34. *See, e.g., id.* As we shall see, it was not quite that simple.

35. Since Virginia Tech, victims have increasingly turned to regulators for relief or remedies. This trend is discussed in Chapter V in more detail. The duty era may well be replaced by a regulatory compliance era.

that solves the problem. Contract rights have not been safety rights in higher education. There are three basic theories on which to proceed in tort: in other words, tort law forces someone to put his or her claim in a box that *tort* law understands. The three basic ways to sue in tort—the boxes—are negligence, intentional torts, and strict liability. For practical purposes, a university is rarely responsible under an intentional tort or true strict liability theory.[36] (For example, a university rarely intentionally injures a student physically and does not usually sell dangerous products, or engage in highly dangerous activities that call out for "strict" liability.) Negligence law—one box of tort rules—is *the* major vehicle by which people sue universities. Claims of negligence are various: negligent maintenance of premises, negligent security, negligent representations, negligent failure to give reasonable warnings, negligent failure to control or protect against dangerous persons, negligent supervision of a field trip or lab experiment, and the list goes on.

Although the ways in which people can be negligent are as numerous as sunsets, the law of negligence regulates the basic *form* that almost every negligence case must take. King-size bed sheets are a standard size, but can come in a number of colors. Negligence law is like that. To standardize cases, the law of negligence forces injury victims to fit their claims into a standard formula.

It works like this. If a person feels wronged by a negligence-based tort—a victim of negligence—that plaintiff must assert and prove four "elements." The elements are the basic building blocks of a claim. They are:

(1) Duty
(2) Breach of duty
(3) Causation ("in fact" and "proximate"), and
(4) Damage

With some limited exceptions, this formula is virtually universal in the United States.[37] If a plaintiff succeeds in asserting and proving all four of these

---

36. Universities can be liable for the torts of certain employees under what is known as vicarious liability. In some ways, some vicarious liability functions enough like some strict liability that it may seem to be so. It is not. Most often, someone in the university was at least negligent when a vicarious liability theory succeeds.

37. *See Something Borrowed* (Warner Bros. 2011). (Law students rehearse elements of negligence while falling in love. Naturally confused by "love" as lawyers, the film plays out their discovery of their feelings for each other.) *See also*, Peter F. Lake, *Common Law Duty in Negligence Law: The Recent Consolidation of a Consensus on the Expansion of the Analysis of Duty and the New Conservative Liability Limiting Use of Policy Considerations*, 34 San Diego L. Rev. 1503 (1997). There has been a movement in tort law—spurred by the latest *Restatement of Torts*—to substantially alter the role of "duty" in negligence law and reduce the role of judges in weeding out cases prior to discovery.

things, the plaintiff has established a "prima facie case" of negligence. What this means is that the plaintiff wins the lawsuit *unless* the defendant can provide a valid "affirmative defense" (more on this in a bit).

These four elements—duty, breach of duty, causation, damage—are legal ways of identifying essential aspects of a claim of negligence against any party, not just a university or its officials and administrators. University law is then, simply, the not so unusual application of general legal rules of negligence to the special circumstances of university culture. The elements also serve to apportion responsibility among the various actors in a litigation. The plaintiff—the injured party—must come forward, assert, and prove these elements.

Some elements (or more precisely, aspects thereof) are ones that a court—a judge—must rule on, while others are for juries to decide. Generally, questions of whether a duty is owed, or whether a certain *type* of damage is to be allowed, are questions for a judge to decide—no jury. Questions of breach of duty, causation, and whether a legally permissible type of damage actually occurred are usually left to a jury. Because litigation, particularly a jury trial, is expensive and time consuming—and somewhat unpredictable—defendants (including universities) often seek to end litigation by asserting that the judge-decided issues are not in favor of the plaintiff/claimant. Duty is one such question. This is principally why *Bradshaw, Beach, Baldwin,* and *Rabel* are duty cases and also why the modern law of university liability is so focused on duty questions. It is tactically sound for lawyers representing universities to raise and attack duty questions. No duty, no discovery (or very limited), no jury, no liability.

But what are these elements—duty, breach, causation, and damage—and what roles do they serve? Duty, the first element, is foremost. In American law, in order to be responsible for any consequences of negligence, you must first owe someone a duty. The concept is simple, yet also elusively complex at times and constantly changes as society does. Thus, I might be remiss and allow the railings on my stairwell to become loose, but that does not mean that I owe a duty to a stranger on the street to fix them. I am negligent, but I do not owe *that* person a duty to be responsible for my stairwell. Someone I *invite* over to my house presents a different issue—that person might fall on the stairwell. *Duty is about setting limits on responsibilities owed to others.* Duty acknowledges responsibility; no duty, or the absence of duty, creates a free space—a legally safe place to chew with your mouth open or drive a dirty car. Although nowhere in the Bill of Rights as such, legal duty is very much about freedom and responsibility, so it is natural for people to become as concerned over tort duties as many constitutional rights issues. A great deal of the heated debate about tort reform is fueled by the fundamental questions raised by tort law.

At the risk of being overly simplistic, a person interested in university law could see that duty, as a first element in a *prima facie* case, comes in three flavors—no duty, ordinary duty, and special duty. In some cases, people have no duty at all—American courts often say that there is no legal duty to come to the aid of a stranger (there are reasons to doubt whether this is or will remain true, but that is another matter). Again, if there is no duty, there is no liability, and the case is over. Judges know how important, how terminating, a no-duty rule is, so they do not say "no-duty" very often.

More often than not in negligence cases (so much so you could do pretty well just knowing this), courts say there is a duty. What is the typical, ordinary duty? When one has an ordinary duty, one then has a standard of care. If there is a standard of care, one must exercise some care for others' safety. To identify the appropriate level of care, courts postulate a *standard of care*, which, if matched or exceeded, satisfies the duty owed (because there is such similarity between *duty* and *standard of care* courts and lawyers often use these terms interchangeably, if sloppily[38]). In most instances, the standard of care that is owed is the level of care that an ordinary and prudent person would exercise in like or similar circumstances. Would someone in your shoes—being reasonable and prudent—have looked both ways when entering the intersection? It does not seem like much to ask people to act like reasonable and prudent individuals in their conduct that could injure others, so courts have historically been willing to allow this standard of care to apply in a very large range of circumstances. Owing ordinary, reasonable care is very common. It is perhaps the most common legal rule in America, and because it is so common it is almost invisible.

In a few situations, one owes a duty because of special circumstances (where otherwise no duty is owed) or owes a special duty. For instance, American courts often say that ordinarily no duty is owed to assist a stranger, but special circumstances can change this rule. For example, there is a duty to aid a stranger if your conduct or instrumentality (example, a car or truck) caused the need for aid (even if you were innocent—that is, even though you caused the peril accidentally and non-negligently).[39] No duty, because of special circumstances, transmutes into a duty owed with an ordinary standard of care. Or sometimes a duty is owed, but the duty is special because it has a special stan-

38. If you have no duty, you need exercise no care at all for another's safety. In some instances, usually only in an emergency you did not create, you may have a duty but you need do nothing for others' safety—no care at all. This is rare, but it happens.

39. *See Restatement (Second) of Torts* §§ 314, 322 (1965).

dard of care associated with it. Notable examples of this in many jurisdictions are duties owed to people who enter onto private land or properties and are injured by conditions on the property. In most states for example, a trespasser is owed a small level of care (a special, lower than reasonable care, standard) and other entrants are owed higher levels of care than that owed to trespassers. Or, professionals like doctors, lawyers, and accountants owe special professional levels of care—special professional duties. They must use a different level of care than an ordinary person due to their special expertise—special duty, special standard of care. Learning about duty under special circumstances and special duty is an important task of law students (and lawyers) and can be complex and confusing even to experienced judges. Nonetheless, the complexity is overshadowed in practical affairs by rules of ordinary duty, which are both simple and more significant in most cases. There is a definite and still progressing legal trend to continue to simplify duty law to a single ordinary standard of care—that is, a duty to exercise reasonable care under the circumstances. Such a general rule would simply say that a person is expected to do what the reasonable person would have done in the same situation.[40]

Two final words on duty are in order. First, the term "duty" technically refers to the first element in a *prima facie* case of negligence. As such, it is the foremost consideration in a negligence case because without duty there is nothing more to discuss—the case is over. Because duty is in that sense necessary for negligence, there has been a somewhat confusing tendency to use the term "duty" (perhaps another term would be better) to also mean "legal liability." Thus, sometimes courts will say or suggest that imposing a duty means imposing liability, or will say that a certain person has a duty in the sense that they are liable to another party. In fact, the existence of a legal duty is not *sufficient* for legal liability (it is a *necessary* condition) because the other aspects of the *prima facie* case must be met. The immediate post-*in loco parentis* cases had a tendency to use duty in this confusing and oversimplified "duty = liability" sense. Courts often spoke as if recognizing a legal duty would be tantamount to making universities always liable and hence "insurers" of student safety. These courts were obviously speaking loosely, even metaphorically. Technically, to say that duty mandates liability is false because an injured student must prove breach of duty (negligent conduct in a particular set of facts), causation (that the university's failure to exercise reasonable care caused the injury), and damage (and then fend off affirmative

40. Negligence is failing to do what the reasonable person would have done in the situation or doing something that the reasonable person would not have done in the same situation.

defenses if any—such as the allegation that plaintiff/student was comparatively negligent). As we shall see, these are some substantial obstacles for a plaintiff and are often the real issues in university cases. For example, a university may have done everything with reasonable care (no breach), may not be the source of injury (no causation), or face a highly irresponsible student (recovery diminished or defeated under rules of comparative fault). Technically speaking duty does not mean liability; it is a necessary precondition but not sufficient.

Second, because duty is so fundamental—so important in balancing rights and responsibilities—courts today typically make the duty element of a *prima facie* case the place in litigation at which they consider most of the social policy issues that a given case raises. Courts like *Baldwin* have openly acknowledged that student injury cases are "on the cutting edge of tort law."[41] Policy/factor analysis and the weighing of competing factors are particularly necessary in university case law. Tort law is fundamentally common law, which courts have the responsibility to assess and reevaluate as social circumstances change. You hear a great deal about "judicial activism" these days, but in most states a judge who refuses to consider major social changes would fail to meet common law and, in some cases, constitutional duties.[42]

Although there are no legal limitations on the policies and factors which courts may consider (except those imposed by a legislature, Congress, or Constitutions—but this is not typical), American courts deciding college student injury cases have settled on some fairly consistent factors and policies to balance and weigh out in determining duty. The factors and policies most often used are those that were articulated in the famous *Tarasoff*[43] case, which imposed liability upon a university when it failed to protect an off-campus nonstudent from a dangerous person on campus. Functionally restated, these factors/policies are (we will see these factors in a similar form again in Chapter VI, and add some proposed new ones specifically for higher education):[44]

---

41. *Baldwin*, 176 Cal. Rptr. at 821.

42. Fear of judicial activism has bred a new phenomenon in higher education law—the peril of judicial/legislative inactivism. Sometimes, when new issues arise, colleges need some legal guidance. This issue has come to the forefront in college student suicide law. There is so little governing law, and the pace of guidance so slow, that colleges face a painful and dangerous period of waiting for/guessing about applicable legal rules in many jurisdiction. *See* Peter F. Lake, *Still Waiting: The Slow Evolution of the Law in Light of the Ongoing Student Suicide Crisis*, 34 J.C. & U.L. 253 (2008).

43. *See Tarasoff v. Bd. of Regents of the Univ. of Cal.*, 551 P.2d 334 (Cal. 1976); Lake, *supra* note 37; *Baldwin*, 176 Cal. Rptr. at 816 (stating nearly identical factors).

44. *See Tarasoff*, 551 P.2d at 342.

(1) the foreseeability of harm/danger;
(2) the seriousness of the harm;
(3) the closeness between the defendant's conduct and the injury produced;
(4) the moral blameworthiness of the defendant's conduct;
(5) the policy of preventing future harm;
(6) the burden on, and consequences to, the defendant and the community should a duty be imposed;
(7) the cost, availability, and prevalence of insurance, if any.

No single policy or factor (or set thereof) is dispositive of duty. All the factors are to be weighed and balanced, if relevant. Most courts agree, however, that when imposing duty, foreseeability is the most important factor. Generally, if the type of harm were foreseeable when a defendant misbehaves (fails to do what the reasonable person would have done), there should be a duty owed to the victim to use reasonable care to prevent that type of harm; but if the type of harm is unforeseeable, strange, or bizarre, a presumption against duty would be appropriate.

The list of social policies and factors is so important and pervasive that courts often speak as if these concerns are dispositive not just of duty but of liability as well. As *Bradshaw* put it:

> The statement that there is or is not a duty begs the essential question, which is whether the plaintiff's interests are entitled to legal protection against the defendant's conduct. '[D]uty' is not sacrosanct in itself, but only an expression of the sum total of those considerations of policy which lead the law to say that a particular plaintiff is entitled to protection.[45]

Although a typical negligence case is permeated with these concerns, one or more of the identified factors and policies have often been used in recent times to justify conservative, liability-limiting results by limiting the scope of duty. Tort lawyers and law professors have watched and noted the developments of the law of tort duty, which has evolved in the last fifty or so years (particularly the last 25 years) in the use of policy/factor analyses.[46] This evolution has been

---

45. *Bradshaw*, 612 F.2d at 138, *quoting* William L. Prosser, *Handbook of the Law of Torts* (3d ed., West Pub. Co. 1964).

46. *See, e.g.*, John M. Adler, *Relying Upon the Reasonableness of Strangers: Some Observations About the Current State of Common Law Affirmative Duties to Aid or Protect Others,* 1991 Wis. L. Rev. 867 (1991); Gary T. Schwartz, *The Beginning and the Possible End of the Rise of Modern American Tort Law,* 26 Ga. L. Rev. 601 (1992).

particularly prominent in university law cases. Courts are increasingly willing to reexamine rules of decision in light of shifting social concerns. In areas of rapid social evolution—like university culture—the law is apt to change rapidly as well. Thus, university law and negligence/duty law in the university context have changed and should be expected to change. Of course, this is difficult for university officials because to do their jobs they must find ways to anticipate and work with legal change and indeterminacy. Without a sense of the animating policies and principles governing the law, officials can find it hard to navigate. Fear of being "wrong" can be disempowering (see Chapter VI; there are ways to work with this legal climate). The first step for administrators is to recognize the dynamic nature of duty and its underlying concerns. The law of duty works well with images of a facilitator university as it encourages a balanced model of shared responsibility for campus safety.

The second element—breach of duty—is typically a question of fact for a jury or fact finder (a judge may intercede if reasonable jurors cannot differ over a question of fact, such as breach of duty, but this type of judicial intervention is not terribly common and is procedurally discouraged). The central question is this: you have a duty and an applicable standard of care (if you did not, we would not be here)—did you use the amount of care minimally necessary to comply with that duty and standard? For example, we all have a duty to use reasonable care when we drive down the street. Usually we exercise the amount of care that is reasonable under the circumstances—we drive within the speed limit (ok, more or less), we keep a lookout, we obey traffic signals, we lay off the iPad, we keep our car in a serviceable and safe condition, etc. Sometimes, however, we do not—for example, when we fail to come to a complete stop at a stop sign or text and drive.

Observe the connection between duty and negligence: just because you have a duty does not mean that you *breached* it. Indeed, most of us, most often, do our duty. Universities often have duties these days, and most often, in our experience at least, universities do what is reasonable and more. It is worth remembering that when someone is hurt, it almost always seems—in retrospect—that more could have been done to prevent the injury, but that is not the question in a negligence case. *Breach* of duty asks the more limited question: did you do what was reasonable here? The law rarely imposes a responsibility to do extraordinary things to avoid injury. The burden on a defendant to do so would ordinarily be too great (see factor 6 on the previous page). That standard of care would be more like a strict liability standard, and there is no court decision that has ever applied true strict liability standards to a university in a situation of student injury. (However, some new regulatory standards may be inching towards heightened liability.)

The third element, causation, is actually two elements in one. Lawyers and judges divide causation questions into two parts—*factual* causation and legal or *proximate* causation. The basic idea behind both types of causation is to link a defendant to a given injury. In some cases the link is painfully obvious (many automobile accidents, for example). In other cases it is not at all clear (some environmental pollution injuries to humans, electro-magnetic field radiation cases, for example).

To link someone to an injury, there are two causal steps to take. First, did the breach of duty *actually, in fact,* cause the harm? Assume you are exceeding the speed limit in your car (negligent conduct in the sense that a duty is owed to other motorists and pedestrians, and is breached); assume further that a pedestrian crosses against the crosswalk light five blocks away and is struck by another car. She would have been struck even had you been within the speed limit. You did not hit her. There is no link, no *actual* causation. But if there is actual causation—say I drop a match at a campsite causing a fire which spreads and burns down a house three miles away—we need a second step in causal analysis. We need a relief valve to protect some defendants from some consequences of their conduct. This step is a policy-laden analysis called "proximate" causation. (Law students hate studying proximate cause; you probably will not like it much either. Try to let go of the words "proximate" and then "cause." What you have left is the essence of proximate cause.)

Lack of proximate causation is what you, the defendant, hope to escape with if you have breached a duty and, in fact, have caused legally compensable damage. It is easy to imagine a system that has no such safety valve; after all, if someone is injured by your fault, you should pay, right? In fact, most plaintiffs can successfully show proximate causation in most cases, and defendants are usually out of luck on this potentially liability-avoiding element. However, there are occasions when a jury is permitted to exonerate a defendant from liability *even* when that defendant is at fault and in fact caused harm.

A classic example of this is the famous (to lawyers) "intervening" cause analysis. Let's say you stop to get gas. You are in a hurry and overfill your tank, spilling gasoline all over the concrete. You are negligent in the sense that you have a duty to fill your tank as a reasonable person would, and a reasonable person who is aware of the various problems with gasoline will take care not to spill large quantities of gasoline on the ground (duty, breach). Now say that another person is having an argument with someone right next to your car. This bad person sees the gasoline trail and chooses a disastrous action—he throws a match into the gasoline with the purpose to cause a fire that will burn the person he is angry with. Now, your negligent conduct has in fact caused an injury.

Had you not spilled gas, this dangerous (malicious) fool would not have been able to burn someone this way. But you may be able to avoid liability. You are allowed to argue that the bad person's deliberate action (in fact a civil battery) is *so* bad that it acts as an intervening cause, cutting off your liability. You argue that it is not foreseeable to you that someone would turn your mistake into an inhumane crime and it is not fair that you should pay for this injury. In this sense, an ordinary person might say that you did not "cause" the injury. At one time not so long ago, you won this argument outright because of technical legal rules; today you still have an excellent shot at winning, but you will likely have to do so in front of a jury. Notice how the question would shift if you negligently spilled poison around young school children, and one young child ingested poison thinking it was "food." You might try to argue that the child caused his own injury. Best of luck.

Proximate cause is about saying, "Yes, my carelessness is 'connected to' this injury, but it's not fair to make me pay for this injury." (Brothers and sisters who babysit for younger siblings know this argument well and deploy it when something gets broken if parents are away.) These questions are highly fact intensive making it difficult for the law to be fair and consistent, just as it is difficult for parents to decide whom to punish. Courts and juries hearing tort cases are thrust into this very real situation. Proximate cause can be difficult and even intuitive stuff. Indeed Judge Richard Posner, one of the country's leading jurists and most brilliant writers on the subject of tort law, has observed that juries are often required to be intuitive when deciding negligence issues.

Rabel, for example, would have presented a different analytic perspective if the judges had allowed the case to go to a jury on the issue of negligence (if the court would have recognized some duty). Assume (like most courts today would) that the resident student was owed a duty of reasonable protection from dangerous persons.[47] Nonetheless, the victim in *Rabel* was abducted and assaulted by a fraternity member who used his student status as a way to perpetrate the attack. A jury could find—or might not find—that this type of deliberate intentional attack was so unforeseeable and unstoppable that it would be unfair to hold a university liable for the female student's injuries, particularly in light of how little, reasonably, can be done to stop such an incident involving a "friend." Sure, incidents occur despite reasonable cause: still others are sometimes simply the fault of one bad actor. These are all contentious points of fact/policy, but they are the types of question often reserved for a

47. *See Leonardi v. Bradley Univ.,* 625 N.E.2d 431, 434 (Ill. App. Ct. 1993).

jury of our peers in American tort litigation. *Rabel* effectively decided a proximate cause issue but did so under duty rules preempting a jury's evaluation of the university's management of its dormitories and its fraternities.

The fourth element—damage—is easiest here because we have been dealing with questions of physical security and safety on campus. American courts typically recognize that physical injury to a student creates some standard legally compensable types of damages. This element is rarely at issue in university tort litigation when a student has been seriously physically injured. Punitive damages—which get the attention of the media—are similarly rarely at issue because a plaintiff must show a very bad state of mind (for example, malicious conduct) on the part of the university to gain such damages. Most often, the claim is that a university was simply negligent, and punitive damages are not appropriate. Punitive damages are also typically prohibited in claims against public colleges.

Now that we have considered all the essential elements of negligence above, assume that a plaintiff has made out a "*prima facie* case"—meaning that the plaintiff has pled and proven duty, breach, causation (both types), and damage. Does the plaintiff win?[48] The answer depends upon the remaining aspects of the overall case, the *affirmative defenses.* A defendant (university) faced with a valid *prima facie* case of negligence can defend (and avoid liability or reduce the plaintiff's damages) by pleading and proving so-called affirmative defenses. The most popular of these defenses come in two basic flavors—that plaintiffs did not use reasonable care for their own safety ("contributory negligence") and/or the plaintiff voluntarily proceeded in the face of a known danger effectively demonstrating that the plaintiff was willing to accept the responsibility for any injury caused by the risk ("assumption of risk"). Each of those defenses seeks an evaluation of the plaintiff's (student's) own conduct to the extent that it may have contributed to the plaintiff's (student's) injury. These defenses are based on notions of shared responsibility—that is, that the student has a responsibility to exercise reasonable care for her/his own safety under the circumstances, even if a university has been negligent.

Most states once treated these defenses as virtually absolute defenses. (This is one major reason why there was not much tort litigation years ago: so few college plaintiffs are blameless in situations where they are injured.) For ex-

48. The question of whether a plaintiff who wins gets paid (and by whom) is a more complex problem. In university law, however, where universities are usually defendants with insurance, the answers are easier because plaintiffs generally recover at least some of their damage awards.

ample, this meant that if you sued someone but were yourself derelict in taking care for your own safety in the incident in question, you recovered nothing because you were not blameless. These harsh, all-or-nothing (mostly nothing) rules have changed.

Today, American courts follow rules of "comparative fault." These rules vary a bit from state to state but usually permit a faulty plaintiff to weigh in against a faulty defendant in front of a jury. The jury is asked to decide whether, for example, a plaintiff is 20% at fault and a defendant 80% at fault. In the old days that plaintiff got nothing: any plaintiff fault barred recovery completely. Today, that plaintiff recovers 80% of the total injury claim. What is compared is, in essence, the strength of the *prima facie* case versus the strength of the affirmative defenses. Although this is an oversimplified account, this is in fact what happens in most actual cases. The most technical and controversial questions are left for law school classrooms, unusually situated litigants, and the media. But, most of the time, comparative fault is easy to administer, at least in terms of what the law requires.[49] (Almost all of this *prima facie*/affirmative defense/comparative fault complexity can be avoided if a court simply says "no duty is owed." No duty means no liability. Otherwise, to establish liability a plaintiff must prove a *prima facie* case and avoid affirmative defenses.)

Pseudo-formulaically, negligence law looks something like this:

Prima Facie Case

L = D + B + C + D − ADs

(Liability) (Duty) (Breach) (Causation) (Damage) (Affirmative Defenses)

Duty is the trump card in the liability equation, and it is easy to see why courts can fall into the trap of equating "duty" with "liability." A determination of duty does not entail liability *per se,* but it almost certainly invites further litigation and often gives a case a "settlement-value." As a practical matter, a plaintiff who establishes duty typically has a case with what we call "settlement value": a defendant knows that some further litigation will occur and that there

49. Consider how *Beach*, 726 P.2d 413, might have gone differently. In *Beach,* the biology field trip case, assume that the professor/university had a duty to use reasonable care in the planning and general supervision of the field trips and that the professor breached this duty when he openly allowed the students to drink with him in the van and when he operated the van after he had been drinking. The injured student could recover, but her recovery would be significantly reduced to the extent that her own conduct was careless (a shared responsibility for careless conduct by both parties).

is always at least a statistical chance that the plaintiff will recover. There is also the nuisance value of further litigation—the cost of defending against even a frivolous claim. So a duty determination does have, practically, some monetary implications. It is against this legal backdrop that *Bradshaw, Beach, Baldwin,* and *Rabel* cast the new images of the modern university. No-duty rules protect against litigation and reduce monetary settlements with injured students.

The bystander courts chose not to see the university as a place of ordinary duty—ordinary risks and responsibility—but rather as unusual places where no duty or only special duty (or duty under special circumstances), if any, was owed. This decision to treat the university as non-ordinary was fraught with technical/conceptual legal problems, which these courts typically avoided by not addressing them—a telltale sign that policy rationales were driving these cases more than doctrinal accuracy. The lay university community and the public were, in general, in no position to assess the technical legal problems, which you, the reader, will come to see with these cases.

To find a way to protect universities from liability and litigation, bystander cases were creative. These four famous cases linked their no-duty results to one of the last vestiges of no-duty rules in America[50]—no-duty-to-rescue-a-stranger

50. At one time, many years ago, no-duty rules were very prominent in the common law. In fact they were so common that it was hard to sue anyone in many cases of otherwise negligently caused injury. For example, there was generally no duty to protect a worker at a workplace. For the most part there was no duty to protect a family member, little duty to a guest passenger in a car, no duty to protect the purchaser or victim of a product unless you sold it to them (and even then there were ways to escape liability), and no duty to act affirmatively for the benefit of a stranger. Governments and charities were only occasionally responsible for harm caused. The twentieth century has seen the steady erosion of these rules. *See* Joseph W. Little, *Erosion of No-Duty Negligence Rules in England, the United States, and Common Law Commonwealth Nations,* 20 Hous. L. Rev. 959 (1983). In fact, there has been an overwhelming trend to simplify the law of torts around the ordinary reasonable care and duty concepts. *See* Gary T. Schwartz, *The Beginning and the Possible End of the Rise of Modern American Tort Law,* 26 Ga. L. Rev. 601, 701 (1992). *See also* Peter F. Lake, *Revisiting Tarasoff,* 58 Alb. L. Rev. 97 (1994).

However, one particular strain of no-duty rules has remained resistant to modern trends—no-duty-to-rescue rules. *See* Peter F. Lake, *Recognizing the Importance of Remoteness to the Duty to Rescue,* 46 DePaul L. Rev. 315, 316 & n.1 (1997) (see citations in note 1). There is considerable reason to believe that what courts say about rescue law is based upon faulty historical reasoning, bootstrapping of case law, and academic politics (but that is another matter). *See id.* It is what it is, and has changed only incrementally in decades. This unusual crack in the law is precisely where university safety law rooted first.

rules—often known as rules of affirmative duty. In the area of rescue law, American courts continue to say that there is typically no general, non-statutory, duty to rescue or to protect someone, unless you have a "special" relationship with that person.[51] That is, absent a special relationship, a person cannot be liable for his failure to act (the law calls this "nonfeasance") but only for his affirmative conduct/acts that place another person in a position of peril or worsen that peril. For the most part, strangers are those people who are not legally special. Yet even some people with whom we are intimate are not legally special. Special relationships as defined in tort law are quite limited and not intuitive.

Practically speaking, you do have a duty to rescue, however, if your affirmative conduct injures someone or if you start to rescue someone and botch it. In these situations you owe basically reasonable care. To sum up, the law says that you can watch someone else's child drown with legal impunity unless you throw that child in the pool, or start to help but quit, or have some special relationship with that child (or the child's parent for the protection of the child). Don't cause harm, don't get involved, don't worry, be a bystander (unless there is a special relationship). The bystander cases went to this last holdout of a bygone legal era, a lost era in which duty was unusual. In rescue law, "no duty" is still the baseline.

Bradshaw, Beach, Baldwin, and *Rabel* saw the university as just such a non-acting bystander who would have a duty to students *only* if a special relationship existed. Courts typically recognize the following as "special" relationships in the absence of contract creating or causing a risk: (1) employer/employee, (2) parent/child, (3) custodians (as in a sanitarium or jail), or (4) those who have charge and control of a dangerous person, with respect to those endangered by the dangerous person, (5) landlords and tenants, and (6) some landowners/some entrants on land. A few courts recognize other relationships, but there is little consistency beyond the above list and the cases are still few in number. The only potentially applicable special relationship according to the bystander courts was (3)—custodial control. This was a curious oversight—the sort of thing that garners a "C" on a torts exam or even a retake on the bar exam.

The fact that *Bradshaw, Beach, Baldwin,* and *Rabel* focused blindly upon custodial control special relationships stacked the deck against student injury claims. Each of these cases determined that students were beyond university control for purposes of establishing a special relationship because students

---

51. *See id.* at 316.

were not in the *custodial* control of the university. As odd as it might seem to non-lawyers, these courts analogized universities to non-acting bystanders and students to strangers in peril—and then held that universities lacked sufficient custodial control to protect students from injury. Students became a class of people who needed rescue, but no one was responsible to save them except themselves (or possibly outsiders to the college).

Listen carefully to the way *Beach* crafted the issues presented:

> Here, Beach contends that Cuellar [the field trip professor] and the University breached their affirmative duty to supervise and protect her. Ordinarily, a party does not have an affirmative duty to care for another. Absent unusual circumstances, which justify imposing such an affirmative responsibility, "one has no duty to look after the safety of another who has become voluntarily intoxicated and thus limited his ability to protect himself." *Benally v. Robinson*, 14 Utah 2d 6, 9, 376 P.2d 388, 390 (1962). The law imposes upon one party an affirmative duty to act only when certain special relationships exist between the parties. These relationships generally arise when one assumes responsibility for another's safety or deprives another of his or her normal opportunities for self-protection. Restatement (Second) of Torts § 314(A) (1964). The essence of a special relationship is dependence by one party upon the other or mutual dependence between the parties.

Beach put the question of duty to students in terms of no duty/special duty.

> Beach argues that a special relationship, arising out of the state statute prohibiting alcohol consumption by minors and the University's corollary rule, should be deemed to exist for a number of policy reasons. At bottom, however, Beach simply claims that a large, modern university has a custodial relationship with its adult students and that this relationship imposes upon it the duty to prevent students from violating liquor control laws whenever those students are involved directly or indirectly in a University activity. We cannot agree.
>
> ....
>
> [C]olleges and universities are educational institutions, not custodial.[52]

---

52. *Beach*, 726 P.2d at 415–18, 419.

Beach saw no gray area, no middle ground, no subtlety regarding control—students were either in custodial control or legal strangers on campus. *Bradshaw, Baldwin,* and *Rabel* echoed nearly identical sentiments about custody control and the absence of special relationships among students and colleges. *Bradshaw* sought to protect the college's "interest in the nature of its relationship with its *adult* students, as well as an interest in avoiding responsibilities that it is incapable of performing."[53] Viewing the university as a (helpless) bystander, *Bradshaw* specifically invoked the custodial image.[54] *Bradshaw* said that beer drinking by college students was a way of life (and, implicitly, excessive drinking is a fact of that life), that the university is powerless to stop it, and that there is no legal duty to do anything about it. Under *Bradshaw* a college could regulate drinking but would have no legal responsibility to intervene, even when it knew or should have known of likely danger to students. In a bystander universe, a university might literally look the other way or even facilitate conduct that creates risks of injury without creating any liability. *Bradshaw* believed—and ruled—that the causes of college drinking—and its tacit ratification by government and society—run far too deep for colleges to repair.

---

53. *Bradshaw*, 612 F.2d at 318 (emphasis added).

54. *Id.* at 141, 142. As *Bradshaw* stated:

> Bradshaw has concentrated on the school regulation imposing sanctions on the use of alcohol by students. The regulation states: "Possession or consumption of alcohol or malt beverages on the property of the College or at any College sponsored or related affair off campus will result in disciplinary action. The same rule will apply to every student regardless of age." App. at 726a-727a. We are not impressed that this regulation, in and of itself, is sufficient to place the college in a custodial relationship with its students for purposes of imposing a duty of protection in this case . . . . A college regulation that essentially tracks a state law and prohibits conduct that to students under twenty-one is already prohibited by state law does not, in our view, indicate that the college voluntarily assumed a custodial relationship with its students . . . .
>
> . . . .
>
> The centerpiece of Bradshaw's argument is that beer drinking by underage college students, in itself, creates the special relationship on which to predicate liability and, furthermore, that the college has both the opportunity and the means of exercising control over beer drinking by students at an off campus gathering . . . . [Given the realities of beer drinking by college students], we think it would be placing an impossible burden on the college to impose a duty in this case.

Likewise, *Baldwin* specifically determined that university liability raises questions of "nonfeasance rather than misfeasance."[55] This is a technical legal way of saying that the duty question is one of no duty/special duty varieties. *Baldwin* likewise required a special, custodial relationship as a precondition to legal liability for "nonfeasance." Even in the context of alcohol rules and regulated dormitory living arrangements, *Baldwin* said that there was no special custodial relationship between students and the college.

Rabel followed that logic and concluded:

> [W]e do not believe that the university, by its handbook, regulations, or policies voluntarily assumed or placed itself in a *custodial* relationship with its students, for purposes of imposing a duty to protect its students from the injury occasioned here. The university's responsibility to its students, as an institution of higher education, is to properly educate them. It would be *unrealistic* to impose upon a university the additional role of custodian over its adult students and to charge it with the responsibility for assuring their safety and the safety of others. Imposing such a duty of protection would place the university in the position of an *insurer* of the safety of the students.[56]

Rabel, like the other three prominent bystander cases, believed that it would be unrealistic to ask the now disempowered university to exercise the custodial control necessary to protect student safety. According to *Rabel,* if duty were imposed, the university could never meet the standard of care required of it and would always be in breach despite its best lawful efforts. Hence a university would be like an insurer of student safety, rather than a typical reasonable person who would be liable only when conduct in a given situation fell below the minimum level of care expected under the circumstances.

Bradshaw, Beach, Baldwin, and *Rabel* turned a cultural/political image of a helpless university into legal doctrine. These courts determined in effect that universities were not active participants in student life but were passive bystanders/observers whose only power to intervene—custodial control—was the very power they lacked and modern college students had fought to insure that colleges could not have. To win cases—to establish university responsibility for conditions causing student harm—students would have to show a special relationship arising from custodial control. For these courts, being a student subject to rules and regulations was not special enough. There was even the sug-

55. *Baldwin*, 176 Cal. Rptr. at 812.

56. *Rabel*, 514 N.E.2d at 560–61 (emphasis added).

gestion that being in dormitories and participating in school-sponsored events (dangerous, even irresponsible events and activities) was not special. The only relationships that would be sufficiently "special" would be those based on *custodial* control. But according to these cases, all control—especially *custodial* control—was lost for legal liability purposes when *in loco parentis* died (as if *in loco parentis* had created such a special custodial relationship in higher education, which, however, it did not).

The four central cases were, in the end, driven by public policy. These cases were not as candid in their policy analysis as some later courts have been—choosing to address *some* but not *all* of the unique policy issues raised in college safety litigation. The bystander cases brushed over the fact that certain business relationships colleges have with students are legally special—and potentially can create duty. Those cases overlooked the fact that responsibility could arise programmatically—in some cases the university is no mere stranger to risk but creates the very context in which it occurs. In addition, these cases also breezed past obvious problems associated with *enhancing* risk, which can be a predicate for tort duty. The bystander cases contained within them technical doctrinal flaws, oversimplifications, and problems that began to manifest in other cases even during the heyday of the bystander university (the early 1970s to early/mid-1980s). After all, universities were in many respects becoming more like businesses and could not be bystanders to *everything*. Crosscurrents of responsibility appeared in the case law at about the same time the bystander college was born. Explaining this apparent inconsistency in the law—bystander versus crosscurrent cases—has been a central challenge for courts and scholars since the civil rights era. To move one step closer to resolution of the paradox of the bystander era, let's now turn to these crosscurrent cases and see the clues they hold.

* * * *

At the time the fall of insularity was under way the *business* university began to be born. Courts began to ask: Why should universities be treated unlike other similar businesses? Rescue law and bystander images had kept something like the old era of insularity in play, but the rise of business safety law made colleges seem more like activities on the mainland especially as colleges continued to don the garments of businesses. Simultaneously, as universities became more like businesses in the eyes of tort law—and courts began to *mainstream* higher education under law—business safety responsibility law was undergoing major shifts as well. There was a shift within a shift so to speak.

Critically, the no-duty-to-rescue/special duty approach to university/student relations had to confront at least three specific technical problems in legal doctrine. Overall, business tort safety law is generally not governed by bystander images.

First, it is well settled in American tort law that most businesses are in "special" relationships at most times with their business customers on business premises. This means, *inter alia,* that most businesses have a duty to protect customers from unreasonable risks, even when customers, acting negligently, contribute to their own injury. (There are some cases where people walk into traffic barriers in parking lots or try to climb on boxes to get something off a top shelf in a store and are injured: courts almost unanimously agree that these people must be assisted when injured, and that reasonable steps must be taken to protect against such injury. The law now regards it as too draconian and immoral—in most cases—to "punish" an injured person who needs assistance.[57] Generally, the law has a strong preference for mitigating reasonably avoidable further damage, regardless of fault.) Universities own property and buildings and invite students (and the public in many cases) to do the business of education and in many instances businesses simpliciter—such as when students visit restaurants at a student center or buy books in a bookstore. The business "invitor" has a legally special relationship to the business "invitee." Would the modern, non-insularized, university become like businesses now and therefore owe its students reasonable protection as business invitees of the university?

The second legal problem was closely related to the first. Beginning in the 1960s and 1970s, American law radically redefined the relationship between landlord and tenant. Most of the focus early on was on slumlords and slum tenants. Later, the rules spread to most all residential-style tenancies. The old common law idea was that the tenant was in a *caveat emptor* (let the buyer/tenant beware) situation: if you lease an apartment with rats, lead paint, and broken pipes, bargain for a better place to live in on the free market, or put up with it. That longstanding common law attitude died hard in this period; landlords became legally responsible for the basic habitability of an apartment and

57. Antipathy to college students who drink and are injured was reflected in a case in Illinois where a young college drinker landed injured on a train platform and required assistance. The Illinois court treated the student like a trespasser and held that there was no duty to rescue a trespasser whose injuries were from off-premise conditions or activities. *See Rhodes v. Illinois Cent. Gulf R.R.*, 665 N.E.2d 1260 (Ill. 1996). The rule in that case, although very narrow, is still out of step with what most courts have said. The case is very fact driven. The student had been on a dangerous drinking escapade off campus and then the student did receive some care from trained personnel. Only when the student got to the hospital, did anyone discover the severity of the head injury. By then it was too late. It would have been better to view the case in "no breach" terms.

became responsible to exercise reasonable care for the safety of tenants and even guests of tenants. In fact, American courts began to recognize that dangerous conditions in a slum house could cause injury to innocent third parties *off* premises. They reacted by imposing duties on landlords to protect against some such harm—gunshots from known tenant/drug dealers killing innocent third parties and such. This was an area where no duty shifted into duty because of a new special relationship, brought on by shifting social policy.

This shift was highly significant. One feature of much of modern university life has been the often common university desire to have at least some students live on campus, near campus, or in university housing. American campuses are not just educational places; they are also living arrangements for many students. The university legally became a *landlord* with a very unusual, and often unusually large, client base. Were universities legally responsible to fix broken locks, make premises reasonably safe, keep dangerous people out, and protect the public from dangerous students? Was the non-insularized university a *landlord* for legal purposes now?

Third, to trigger rescue law—the law of affirmative duty—courts require that the claim be for "nonfeasance" rather than "misfeasance." Most tort and negligence cases involve misfeasance, and the issue is so obvious that it is never discussed or argued. In a few cases it is an issue. The basic intuitive idea is simple, but the application (which is which?) is often extremely difficult in the handful of unusual cases that raise the issue. Nonfeasance involves the mere failure to act for someone's benefit; misfeasance involves an action you take causing harm.

Simple? I'm on vacation at a lakefront resort and a stranger's child falls in the lake. I could help at no risk to myself. My human instincts tell me to help this child, but I do nothing. I make the news as the moral monster who did nothing. I get sued. I win. I win because my failure to act is "nonfeasance," and there is generally no duty to others for nonfeasance unless there is a special relationship. Just being fellow humans and my being in a position to save a child at no risk to myself is not legally special. Mere knowledge of harm does not create duty; and deliberate indifference to the suffering of strangers is legally, if not morally acceptable.

The flip side is this: If I drive my car at 80 miles an hour into you "by accident," my action is "misfeasance." I *drove* (an action or activity) into you. Action requires that I exercise at least reasonable care for your safety. I have a duty, whether or not I have a special relationship with you. This duty is owed to everyone (or at least foreseeable anyones).

It is now easy to see why characterizing someone as a mere bystander to a person in need of rescue is so important; it negates that person's legal responsibility for harm. Bystanders are innocent until proven special.

Obviously, it is not always this simple. Suppose I am driving along at the speed limit and merely neglect to apply the brakes. Nonfeasance or misfeasance? The courts always say misfeasance. They postulate that although you omitted to put on the brakes, you did so in the overall context of the driving activity. Drawing the line between action and inaction can be tricky. Such line drawing has been controversial, and legal scholars admit that when a court in a tough case characterizes the behavior of a defendant as either nonfeasance or misfeasance, the characterization is really just a conclusion—based on underlying policy considerations—that sets up either a no-duty or duty result with consequent liability implications. In other words, the distinction begs the question—is a duty owed and why, or why not? Some courts have abandoned outdated misfeasance/nonfeasance analysis entirely and simply address the policy questions involved in tough cases straightforwardly.

The central position of the four prominent bystander cases was that, if the university did anything wrong at all, the wrong was only an omission and only the nonfeasance of a non-business entity—a failure to act, like the failure of a bystander to rescue a stranger's child in distress. However, the modern university now carried on activities—some very business-like—with impact on and off campus. Fundamentally, many student injury cases look more and more like the "no foot on the brake pedal" situation. Universities effectively attract and house large groups of people; sponsor events and field trips; often *require* students to live on campus and participate in off-campus activities; and plan, regulate and administer most aspects of student life. Universities literally co-create an environment for students and control almost all of the major strategic decisions—how and how many to house, where to house, types of housing, what activities to promote or prohibit, etc. College is not Disney World, where litter never hits the ground and the parade always runs, but college is also not an entirely accidental or unplanned experience. Universities lie somewhere between sparse rural exurbia and theme park. Is university life an *activity*—a community, a community with business overtones? Or is it a *condition*—a passive backdrop to the activities of students—an essentially non-commercial activity? Are there times when a university is a bystander but other times when it is not? Is a university community always an activity or condition but never both, or constantly alternating?

The bystander image raised three fundamental legal problems—is the college a business, a landlord, and/or an activity? These internal legal/doctrinal problems manifested in crosscurrent case law imposing legal responsibility in apparent contradiction to bystander case law. Truly, the no-duty rules of the bystander cases were far less insulating than the protections of previous eras in university law.

The legal/doctrinal problems were also associated with a major political/moral issue. American courts may say that a mere bystander has no legal duty to assist a stranger, but it is interesting that many courts say that there is a *moral* duty to help others in distress. Bystander cases finding no liability can be pyrrhic victories for any entity with a public reputation. The courts say: "You win, but we condemn you." It is quite a high wire act to win the legal no-duty-to-rescue issue *and* win the political/moral issue. (It's like the insanity defense. I am not guilty—but I'm insane.) You are struck with either admitting that you *should* (morally) have done more or admitting that you were totally helpless, incompetent, or incapable. A university could argue that in a given case there was nothing reasonable to do or that it was too far away to help, but these are technically breach and causation, not no-duty arguments. When you play the no-duty-to-rescue card, you admit to being wrong and/or you admit, in effect, to *global* helplessness in a situation. *Situational* helplessness, far more defensible morally, is not usually a duty argument.

Of course, a modern university does not want to admit to being a moral monster, nor would it be good for business to put messages of incapacity in college catalogs and promotional material. Universities know that parents and most students usually expect the university community to be at least reasonably safe. There are many today that believe colleges are especially safe or protective places. So how did a university find the high road in the bystander cases? How did bystander cases really fit into an emerging duty era?

The undercurrent of the bystander cases was that college-aged drinking (including underage drinking) was not so "unusual or heinous," as *Baldwin* put it, to cry out for some special response from *colleges*. Ironically, the bystander cases articulated the most powerful rationale for what they were doing, least effectively. Bystander cases were creating alcohol law parallelism.

All four bystander cases were decided in the nadir of alcohol risk responsibility law in America. Prohibition had fallen before World War II. When Americans returned victorious from World War II the "Dean Martin" era was born. Social responsibility for alcohol risk, if it existed at all, was almost always the sole responsibility of the voluntary drinker (which usually meant men, as women were a moderating cultural influence on alcohol risk at that time). Businesses and social hosts were almost never responsible for alcohol risk; vendors of alcohol also usually escaped at least tort responsibility. Drunk in public laws were no longer routinely enforced; dram shop laws were the future. Higher education safety law had the peculiar fortune of being born when American alcohol law blamed drinkers of almost any age for risks of drinking, and was otherwise largely laissez-faire. *Baldwin* hit the nail on the head: why should colleges be treated any differently from every other business in America? Even bars were not responsible for drunk driving accidents, why should a college be? Worker compensation laws of that time also favored businesses that created an enhanced alcohol risk: ask anyone who remembers about the office parties of the 1960s–1980s or watch *Mad Men*.

The fossil record left behind in the bystander cases skews our view of history a bit unless we examine the bones carefully. The bystander cases we see discuss the issue of duty, but there would have been a far larger number of cases of that laissez-faire era that were dismissed for lack of proximate causation. (Courts still routinely dismissed alcohol tort cases for lack of proximate causation at that time, except with respect to the drinker.) But right at that moment in time (when the first college safety cases appeared) courts were beginning to reject the drinker as sole proximate cause of harm rules in favor of duty analysis.[58]

In retrospect, the much weaker argument to justify the bystander cases was the *quid pro quo* argument: universities gave the students the rights to do the very things they now wanted the university to protect them from when they got injured. *Bradshaw, Beach, Baldwin,* and *Rabel* each very explicitly tried to yield the moral high ground to the university. Universities were not disempowered; they had used their power to grant civil rights. *Baldwin,* for example, went so far as to state that California colleges had been "in the forefront of extension of student rights."[59] Somehow, even systems that resisted civil rights were now to be *praised* for foresight and largesse. Courts struggled to find the high road by blaming students and by reinterpreting the history of student protests.

---

58. As a leading treatise on tort law has stated:

> X is served alcoholic drinks by D until X becomes intoxicated. En route home, X, due to intoxication, injures P. P certainly has a tort action against X. Does she have a negligence action against D? Should it matter whether D is in the business of selling liquor or is a social host? At a common law, neither sellers of liquor nor social hosts were liable to those injured by those to whom they served alcohol. Courts viewed the inebriated driver, not the supplier of the liquor, as the sole proximate cause of the harm.
>
> Starting in the late 1970s, courts began to reconsider the common law view. Several imposed liability on commercial suppliers of liquor.

John L. Diamond, Lawrence C. Levine & M. Stuart Madden, *Understanding Torts* 131 (2nd ed., Lexis Pub. 2000) (citations omitted).

59. *Baldwin*, 176 Cal. Rptr. at 813.

Was there an essentially zero sum link between the civil rights won by students and rights to safe campuses? The Beastie Boys sing of "fighting for your right to party," but the civil rights cases were about freedom from summary dismissal, freedom of speech, freedom to protest, racial equality, freedom from discrimination, etc. The civil rights era was not about rights to use drugs and alcohol but involved First Amendment, due process, and equal protection type issues.[60] There was an unspoken assumption in the principal bystander cases that long-haired hippie freaks who wanted rights also invariably wanted to smoke pot and drink with underage girls, engage in drag races, etc.

There was some serious revisionist history in the bystander cases. Universities suddenly were portrayed as the champions of many rights they had actually fought so hard to block. In the civil rights era, abuses of *in loco parentis* authority were so bad that students were forced to litigate or quit their college education.[61] Civil rights were often won over the objections of many colleges. The civil rights era was not a battle for license but for basic fairness and justice. The costs of freedom were plenty high, and did not need to be augmented with a backlash of unsafe campuses.

Finally, *so what* if students won civil rights and diminished the powers of universities (which they did)? Does the university have any less of a responsibility to operate a reasonably safe and protective learning environment? Some colleges went so far as to take the messages of *Bradshaw, et al.* to ridiculous extremes, arguing for example, that they owed no duty to minimize the risk that criminal intruders would attack students in their dorms. No one can seriously contend that increased security—which can prevent criminal intrusion and worse—diminishes the overall academic mission or unduly intrudes upon some rights of a "free" student. To the contrary, it has become more and more obvious that resources devoted to more security and safety improve the overall *educational* mission of a school. Fairness and safety are complimentary. *Quid pro quo* arguments were, and are, weak. The bystander cases are best remembered for applying prevailing alcohol law to colleges.

---

60. Some of the rhetoric and imagery in the bystander cases is insulting to the students who pursued the civil rights era's most famous cases. In *Dixon*, students were involved in efforts to desegregate places of public accommodation and demonstrated to protest institutionalized Southern racism.

61. When I met John Dixon, I was struck by the fact that he had never received a college degree. He is a hero of higher education who was driven out of the very system that thrives from his sacrifice.

Cases imposing business-like duty responsibility were very much contemporaries with the bystander cases, but they did not become the dominant images of that era. Instead of being rectified in a field theory that might explain all the cases, the crosscurrent cases—destined to emerge as evolutionary winners—lost the initial political war of images. For reasons involving the politics of university law, the four bystander cases (and some other similar cases) became perceived as "majority" cases; the other (crosscurrent) cases were viewed as "minority," wrong, and as anomalous cases.

* * * *

A digression on the politics of university case law is in order. How could certain cases become the perceived majority in the face of obvious crosscurrents?

Colleges and universities typically spend most of their energy on fairly predicable and repeating legal questions. They usually have their own lawyers, who work in-house (and out) principally for the university client. University lawyers have national organizations and several journals and publications just for them. They are a practice group with reliable institutional clients. On the other hand, student cases involving physical injury are often handled by personal injury attorneys who may see just one university case in a lifetime. Most students never need a lawyer; the few who do are usually one-time clients. Perhaps there should be an organized group of student-rights-to-physical-safety lawyers, and perhaps there should be institutional clients (like student (labor) unions?) to argue their rights. But for the most part there are not. Students and their lawyers approach the law usually as individuals and with individuated claims. In contrast, universities and their lawyers often approach the law collectively and institutionally. A given lawsuit may have long-term policy implications for a college. How the law is made and then promoted has a great deal to do with this.

A concrete example may be offered using the *Beach* case. At oral argument, legal counsel for the injured student conceded a major point that not all students' lawyers would concede in other cases. The lawyer "conceded that the mere relationship of *student to teacher* was not enough" to establish a "special" relationship for duty.[62] Why would a lawyer concede this? Sometimes lawyers concede arguments at oral argument because they feel that tactically it is in the best interests of that client. If a panel of judges seems unsympathetic to a case, it may be best to abandon certain arguments even if a lawyer thinks the arguments are right. A lawyer is not charged, as such, with making good law

62. *See Beach*, 726 P.2d at 416 (emphasis added).

or making good arguments for good law; lawyers' primary duties are to their clients. A given student's lawyer must make the argument that will win for her client, even if every student afterwards will lose. A lawyer does not represent student group rights by representing a given student. It is a little unfair, then, for a court to make law for other students through concessions of specific lawyers for non-institutional student clients.

On the other side, a university lawyer represents an ongoing institution (with very similar interests to other universities). A given case might be one where today's losing argument is tomorrow's winner, or *vice versa.* The university lawyer takes the long look because she must evaluate *all* of her client's interests and all cases a client will be involved in—not just this one case. A university lawyer should be careful not to concede points that might be important in future or other cases (possibly in front of other judges). The university legal counsel's job often requires a more long-term strategy.

This fact has one very important corollary—the cases which get litigated and reported. University lawyers can look at a number of cases and choose to settle some—or all—of them. Almost invariably, they will settle a bad case with bad facts and any case that can make bad or dangerous precedent. Lawyers representing injured students do not have to settle, but often a settlement offer in hand is better than a jury trial and/or lengthy appeals. The plaintiff's lawyer does not have much incentive in most cases "to make law or precedent." In fact, a plaintiff's lawyer caught using a client and injuring his client's rights in trying to make precedent (perhaps hoping to get other clients) could be disciplined professionally. Again, client interests dominate, and one-time individual clients have different interests than long-term institutional clients.

One might surmise that every appellate decision (and that is principally how we have assessed what the law of student safety is) would be a university winner because of this dynamic. Hand-selected university winners—the cases to fight and win in final appeal—would be the only reported cases. But university lawyers sometimes have incentives to fight cases they ultimately lose in the appellate process. This is often a result of a deliberate test of where the margins are in the courts: How far can I push for rules protecting my client's interest until the courts back off? Other times there is a bit of miscalculation that occurs.

So when you read case law in the university field, you will likely see a highly select group of cases, and most should be university winners. These cases were more likely selected to be the appellate cases for their precedential value by university attorneys rather than by any plaintiff attorneys attempting to change a system of law. (Note that almost exactly the opposite phenomenon occurred in many of the civil rights cases. Many plaintiffs knew their cases were test cases and willingly and heroically sacrificed their own good for the greater good of society.) There are many cases settled that never see much, if any, light of day (some unfavorable appellate decisions are actually erased by terms of settlements, which is an overt manipulation of how the law appears). From the university point of view, a settlement makes the case go away; a lost motion to dismiss can produce judicial rhetoric you will live with for a long time, or have to pay extra to settle.

Once these selective cases are decided, they are then discussed among university lawyers. Their clients can see the cases, but need help with judicial rationales and with "what does this mean to me" questions. Here lies the danger of some inbreeding and insularity. University law has the risk of appearing to be what university lawyers say it is. This is not to suggest that university lawyers purposefully give their clients less than the complete picture of the law. Not at all. But there is a tendency to become so convinced of your client's interests that it can color your perception at the margin. The reported record of case law may also bait some self-deception as well.

There is no judicial review of what the clients hear from their attorneys, except for the next case. And because university lawyers are so good at what they do, losing cases are rare and come along very slowly. The cycle builds and can suffer—like stock market corrections—major and unexpected shocks. We may actually be seeing a bit of this right now. Years of bystanderism are being rejected by regulators who, at least for now, appear to be adopting more demanding standards for higher education.

* * * *

In several crosscurrent cases, decided contemporaneously with the bystander cases, courts held that universities had duties to:

- Protect students (especially resident students) from foreseeable criminal intrusions by dangerous people in the community. Students residing in campus housing were owed the basic rights of tenants to a reasonably secure and safe place to live;
- Treat students and some non-students like business invitees and to use reasonable care in premises construction and maintenance. Universities had duties similar to those businesses owed their customers or business visitors;
- Use reasonable care in planning and executing student activities, like field trips. Reasonable care did not mean all possible care, and students

were expected to use care for their own safety and acknowledge and accept certain risks;

- Protect off-campus non-students who were foreseeably endangered by dangerous activities/dangerous persons on campus. On the rare occasions when campus danger spilled over into the community at large, the university became responsible to use reasonable care for the safety of some foreseeably endangered individuals.

These cases *appeared* to run counter to the no-duty position of the four famous bystander cases. Some commentators saw these cases as a return to *in loco parentis*; which as we have seen is mistaken.[63] However, the crosscurrent and bystander cases had more in common than was perceived. American courts had taken their first steps into the world of *duty* paradigms to describe student/university relations. The bystander era was an era of methodical mainstreaming, backlash to student rights, and concerns over the perceived helplessness of modern universities in the face of student alcohol use. It was also an era in which the university shouldered important new legal safety responsibilities, many for the first time ever. The case law reflected a general flow in one new direction towards duty analysis and away from historical legal doctrines creating insularity from law. The cases were also clearly mainstreaming higher education under prevailing business safety law of the day.

The most famous crosscurrent case of the period that acknowledged the rights of students to safe campus housing was the 1983 decision of the Massachusetts Supreme Court in *Mullins v. Pine Manor College*,[64] although it was not the first case to so hold.[65] In *Mullins*, a female student was attacked on campus by a non-student assailant. The college was located in a highly populated area in greater Boston. *Mullins* determined that a resident student, for purposes of living arrangements, is in a sufficient special relationship

---

63. *See* James J. Szablewicz & Annette Gibbs, *Colleges' Increasing Exposure to Liability: The New In Loco Parentis*, 16 J.L. & Educ. 453 (1987); Perry A. Zirkel & Henry F. Reichner, *Is the "In Loco Parentis" Doctrine Dead?*, 15 J.L. & Educ. 271 (1986); Brian Jackson, *The Lingering Legacy of In Loco Parentis: An Historical Survey and Proposal for Reform*, 44 Vand. L. Rev. 1135 (1991); Theodore C. Stamatakos, *The Doctrine of In Loco Parentis, Tort Liability and the Student-College Relationship*, 65 Ind. L.J. 471, 472 (1990).

64. 449 N.E.2d 331 (Mass. 1983).

65. *See Duarte v. State*, 148 Cal. Rptr. 804 (Cal. Ct. App. 1978) *vacated*, 151 Cal. Rptr. 727 (Cal. Ct. App. 1979) (unofficial published opinion) (1978). *Mullins* has been widely followed. *See* Peter F. Lake, *Private Law Continues to Come to Campus: Rights and Responsibilities Revisited*, 31 J.C. & U.L. 621 (2005).

with the college to create duty under special circumstances. Under *Mullins,* a college must use reasonable care to prevent foreseeable criminal attacks on campus.

Mullins held that a duty to protect the resident students existed because:

- Customarily, the college provides for campus security, especially for resident students;
- Pine Manor College featured a high concentration of young people—especially young women—creating a risk in that this is a favorable target for criminal activity (especially sexual assault);
- A college is in a better position to take steps to minimize these risks to students than the students themselves. Students can only do so much to institute personal security measures in residence halls;
- The college retains the authority to determine most security measures, not students;
- The college undertakes, in return for fees and rent, an array of services. When one provides a service (activity/acting: duty), the service must be performed with reasonable care;
- Students who rely upon the fact that the college provides security are lulled into a sense that security is provided and this may work to their detriment in that they will relax their vigilance.

Mullins made two other points perfectly plain.

First, this responsibility was *not* parental, derived from or otherwise *in loco parentis.* No one says that landlords must act *in loco parentis* for tenants. *Mullins* treated resident students in the same general way as the law treats ordinary tenants. What the college asked for in *Mullins* was a standard of care for tenants' safety that would have been *less* than that owed *by slumlords to slum tenants.* The court gave parity, not parenting.

Second, *Mullins* made it crystal clear that student rights were not won at the expense of student safety. In its own (and famous) words the *Mullins* court said:

> [C]hanges in college life, reflected in the general decline of the theory that a college stands *in loco parentis* to its students, arguably cuts against this view. The fact that a college need not police the morals of its resident students . . . *does not entitle it to abandon any effort to ensure their physical safety.* Parents, students, and the general community still have a *reasonable* expectation, *fostered in part by the colleges*

> *themselves*, that reasonable care will be exercised to protect resident students from foreseeable harm.[66]

The *Mullins* court correctly observed that college responsibility for safety in student housing did not rise or fall with *in loco parentis*. The rise of landlord/tenant responsibility was more directly related to the fall of governmental and charitable immunities. In particular, a college has a duty to protect students—using *reasonable, not all possible* care—from foreseeable criminal and dangerous conduct that might come onto campus from the community. If an attack like the one in *Mullins* was unforeseeable, or could not be prevented with reasonable precautions and security, the university was not liable. There *is* a duty; it just does not extend to unforeseeable problems (risks). Moreover, a duty has not been breached if reasonable care has been used.

In addition to landlord/tenant responsibility, a university would have a duty to students and others who come to campus with legitimate university business or related interests (employees, visitors, etc.). This duty arose from the special relationship considered to exist between these entrants as invitees and the landowner/premises-operator/university. Even *Bradshaw* and *Beach* acknowledged that a business invitee—one who comes to a landowner's premises for some business or commercial purpose—is entitled to reasonable care because a special relationship exists.

Again, the standard of care owed to such persons, including students, is reasonable care—not all possible care. In addition to fixing broken stairs, etc., this includes using reasonable care to protect against assaults and room invasions, *if, and to the extent, reasonably possible*. Many attacks will occur that are unforeseeable or not reasonably preventable. But some simple and reasonable steps can be taken to prevent and protect students. Fixing broken locks, better lighting, and security patrols are common solutions to the problem of preventing criminal intrusion, and the law evolved quickly to encourage such measures.

Even during the heyday of the bystander era, courts were thus willing to say that a duty existed to keep safe premises (other than just residential premises for resident students and guests), and that a university would have to maintain reasonably safe grounds (like walkways) for students and others coming to campus with business to conduct.[67] These duties were duties owed by any *business*

66. *Mullins*, 449 N.E.2d at 335–36 (emphasis added) (footnote omitted).

67. *See Isaacson v. Husson Coll.*, 332 A.2d 757 (Me. 1975); *Shannon v. Wash. Univ.*, 575 S.W.2d 235 (Mo. Ct. App. 1975).

to its customers, etc. Courts were quick to see the analogy between students who pay to attend a college and business invitees in other commercial contexts. As we will see in the next chapter, these cases have multiplied, in spite of some attempts by colleges to avoid business-like responsibility. Mainstreaming has moved forward at a steady and irresistible pace.

During the bystander era, only *Rabel* directly contradicted *Mullins* on the issue of premises safety. Functionally, the other three major cases were *off*-premises injury cases. The attack in *Rabel* occurred on premises against a student. *Rabel* rejected a landlord/tenant duty (today, *Rabel* is a clear minority position on this point) but never addressed the (obvious to lawyers) issue of the status of the student as a business invitee. A later case in Illinois has pointed out this flaw (and it is such an obvious flaw that a person taking the bar exam would be marked off for missing it) in *Rabel*.[68] (Technically, the plaintiff did not argue the point in *Rabel*, but appellate courts are usually free to consider issues not raised by counsel, and in a case of this importance the omission is significant. It is particularly significant given that today most courts *would* consider the issue *and* find a duty, and that many courts of even that period did so. Judicial myopia sometimes indicates an intense focus on something else.) American courts have generally not allowed universities to perpetuate sub-standard living or other business facilities. Courts do not see this parity with business law as akin to parental responsibility. Even today parents do not have such tort duties. Businesses do.

As landlord/tenant and business premises liability began to gain secure footing in higher education law, issues of programmatic liability also arose in the bystander era. To what extent would bystander case law be stretched to programmatic activities?

Both *Beach* and *Bradshaw* were programmatic cases. In each instance the university facilitated the activities and/or its employees enhanced risk to students in the context of university programs. *Beach* was a class field trip planned and supervised by a professor; *Bradshaw* was an off-campus class picnic that

---

68. *See Leonardi v. Bradley Univ.*, 625 N.E.2d 431, 434 (Ill. App. Ct. 1993). The *Leonardi* court found no premises duty because the sexual assault occurred in a non-university premises—a fraternity house. The court intimated strongly that the result would have been different if the attack were in a dormitory or on a walkway owned by the university. The court also pointed out that the weight of out-of-state authority now went in favor of premises duties to students. By 1993, the result reached in *Rabel*—the Illinois bystander case—was no longer defensible. Courts were already in the process of chipping away at alcohol/no responsibility rules and imposing duties on businesses to use reasonable care to manage their premises even with respect to alcohol risk.

was aided by college officials signing checks and permitting use of university facilities. The universities in *Bradshaw* and *Beach* were hardly helpless strangers/bystanders.

But *Beach* and *Bradshaw* overplayed the role of custodial control in creating tort responsibility. This mistake would have a significant impact on future higher education safety litigation because it formed a key predicate for a legal non-sequitor—that university *programmatic* responsibility would only extend to situations in which students were under university *custodial* control. In the wake of the bystander era, university counsel often made this argument in court attempting to turn a set of cases driven by a unique moment in the history of alcohol law into a broad programmatic risk immunity for colleges. That maneuver was destined to fail in the courts and may even have precipitated a backlash against colleges in safety law.[69]

Beach and *Bradshaw* assumed duty requires custody and since there was no custody over college students, there was therefore no duty. Superficially, that makes sense, but if you make that argument on almost any bar exam, you will fail because it is dead wrong, even if subtly so. Duty is *also* owed when someone acts, carries on an action, etc. This is misfeasance. *Nonfeasance* qualifies for no duty but is subject to exceptions, *inter alia*, for exercising custodial control. Misfeasance does not require "control" and certainly not *custodial* control: and only *some* nonfeasance issues raise problems of control and only a subset of nonfeasance cases require *custodial* control. Custodial control creates duty but is not the only way duty is created. (Moreover, if there is no way to execute duty with reasonable care—if there is nothing to do that will work, no way to control if so required—you have a legal duty but you are not legally *liable* because you did not *breach* a duty. Courts require you to exercise only the level of control that you actually have, (if they emphasize control at all); there are legally significant forms of control that count for duty that are far short of custodial control. These types of control are ones that universities often do exercise, such as control over field trips and residence security.)

Were the judges in *Bradshaw* and *Beach* unaware that custodial control is only one necessary predicate for affirmative duty? Were they attempting to immunize programmatic responsibility and recreate much of the era of insularity? Again, probably not. Obviously, these two courts in particular (and *Rabel* for a different reason) felt very strongly that there should be no legal liability as a matter of law. They felt that universities should enjoy a type of *immunity*

69. However, as discussed *infra* in Chapter V, regulators may be accelerating expectations of safety beyond reasonable care.

from lawsuits when injury occurred to a student who had become voluntarily intoxicated or had been harmed because of another student's voluntary intoxication. The key to understanding these cases is to realize that this was precisely in line with prevailing alcohol risk law of the day. The bystander cases were declining to impose alcohol risk liability on colleges in exactly the same way they were declining to do so for other businesses.

Beach and *Bradshaw* may have *seemed* like no-programmatic-duty cases, but they were not. They were cases applying prevailing principles of alcohol risk responsibility. Take alcohol out of the mix, you get different results: move forward in time to more modern attitudes about alcohol risk responsibility, you get different results. *Beach* and *Bradshaw* are the lime green leisure suits of higher education law.

There was no judicial plebiscite in the bystander era to recreate the era of insularity via broad no-duty rules immunizing programmatic responsibility. Other courts began to view university-facilitated student activities/student injury litigation through more accurate (in terms of tort law logic) lenses.

The leading case to see university-facilitated student activities/injury cases through a different lens was *Mintz v. State of New York*,[70] a 1975 New York appellate court decision and one of the earliest crosscurrent cases. That case involved the periphery of university-facilitated activity injury cases as it involved an extra-curricular, overnight canoe trip on (dangerous and unpredictable) Lake George in New York State.

Early one May, a time of very cold lake water and changeable weather, a group of students set out on Lake George, as part of an "overnighter" sponsored by an intercollegiate outing club. A bad storm blew in and students were drowned in the lake. Because the intercollegiate outing club had a university charter, the university became a defendant. Nothing in the *Mintz* decision suggests (or even seems concerned) that the university did more than *encourage*, indirectly, the activity as an extracurricular activity. There was no hint of university custody and only very limited control. There was little to no close university supervision of the particular outing in question. *Mintz* featured far less college involvement than the academic field trip situation in *Beach*.

The *Mintz* court dismissed the case against the university, but for very different reasons than *Bradshaw*, *Beach*, *Baldwin*, and *Rabel*. *Mintz* determined that "all reasonable and necessary precautions were taken to guarantee a safe outing."[71] The court noted that the club had conducted outings for ten years with-

70. 362 N.Y.S.2d 619 (N.Y. App. Div. 1975).

71. *Id.* at 621.

out significant incident and had taken many precautions on this particular occasion. Among other precautions, there was a motorboat escort, and there were veteran canoers on the trip. Canoes were equipped with lights and experienced canoers were given the more responsible posts. The accident occurred in pre-Weather Channel 1966: the weather forecast did not foretell of anything dangerous to come. And *Mintz* emphasized that the students were not babies in need of close supervision. Under these circumstances, *Mintz* ruled that the unforeseen weather—not the university—was the "proximate cause" of the deaths.[72]

Mintz did *not* say there was no duty, or that a duty arose only under special circumstances. Even with the tenuous thread of control over such activities, *Mintz* acknowledged duty, but emphasized facts that showed there was no *breach* of duty that would be the legal cause of harm. Simply put, the university avoided liability because it exercised reasonable care in its involvement in the trip. The university did not avoid liability because it assumed a no-duty posture relative to safety precautions, but because it acted responsibly in attempting to make the trip as safe as possible. *Mintz* is distinctly modern in its analysis and uses accurate tort analysis. The result in *Mintz* is also correct from a policy standpoint and in keeping with the responsibility a good university would shoulder in encouraging field trips/outings by professors and students or student organizations.

In essence *Mintz* said: "Yes, you have a duty to use reasonable care towards students in extracurricular programmatic activities. But you *did what was reasonable here* (and perhaps more) and you could not have foreseen this ferocious and unusual (unpredictable) storm. Sometimes accidents just happen, and this is that case." *Mintz* is a classic example of the fact that duty alone does not create strict liability, nor insurance, nor a responsibility to babysit students. Legal liability is a complex of several variables. Duty is just one variable. Duty is not *in loco parentis.* It is possible to have shared legal responsibility and not be liable legally.

Mintz was a field trip case like *Beach* but used a different rationale to reach a no-liability result. Why?

Beach was an *alcohol* case; again *Mintz* was not. American courts of the high bystander period held that a voluntarily or negligently intoxicated individual was the only legally responsible party. The rule appeared regularly in cases involving liquor served in a bar to persons who drove off and killed or injured others or themselves. The bar, bartender, vendor, business, or social host was

---

72. *Id.* at 620–21.

not the legally responsible party. Courts were not praising over-service, just exonerating it. Those rules would soon change, however.

When looking at the bystander cases in the rearview mirror it is essential to understand their place in the rapidly evolving law of alcohol risk responsibility in America. It is now common to impose liability on bars and bartenders who over-serve adults or who serve minors. Business premises that serve alcohol have a responsibility to provide a reasonably safe environment and it is kapu to entrust a dangerous instrumentality—like a car—to a drunk. Yet, not all liquor injury problems come out of bars. When liquor is purchased outside a bar (say at a convenience store) or consumed privately, the law has been more hesitant to impose liability upon such vendors or "social" servers. For instance, so-called "social hosts"—private cocktail party hosts for example—have traditionally escaped liability and still usually do today.

As the old rule that the drinker was the sole proximate cause of harm fell, the law filled the gap immediately with no-duty rules for social hosts for social policy reasons.[73] Professional and commercial vendors of liquor for on-premises consumption—bars and restaurants—were subject to duty regarding liquor service, but virtually everyone else had no duty (there were some important exceptions, the biggest one of which was giving someone who was visibly drunk a dangerous item like a car). The law had moved from a no-liability-for-liquor-related injury rule (except for the drinker), based on no *proximate cause as matter of law*, to a new paradigm—duty for certain commercial vendors, *proximate cause questions for the jury regarding these vendors* (example: I over-served you at noon, and you killed someone in an accident at 11:00 p.m.), but *no duty*, therefore *no liability*, for most others.

Instinctively, *Beach* reacted to the student's injury in that case as an *alcohol-related* injury in a non-commercial, non-bar/bartender setting. Just 10–20 years earlier, such a case would have been dismissed routinely under proximate cause rules in most jurisdictions because the voluntarily intoxicated student would have been the sole proximate cause of her injury as a matter of law. *Beach* did what most courts of that moment in the law did—transitioned the issue of social drinking into a no-duty rule. Anyone other than commercial vendors for on-premises consumption—bars and bartenders—was not subject to legal liability (no duty) for liquor-related injuries if they served a drunk, knew someone was drinking, or even facilitated or promoted drinking activities. Wine with dinner, a private cocktail party, an office party with beer, a

73. But not all. *See, e.g.*, *Kelly v. Gwinnell*, 476 A.2d 1219 (N.J. 1984).

fraternity party, and even a university-sponsored event with liquor (*Bradshaw*) were treated in the social host category (no duty) as contrasted with the bar/bartender category. The legal result would have been the same decades earlier, but using a different rationale—no duty.

Indeed the point—a critical one for understanding the entire bystander era and its paradoxes—is that *Bradshaw, Beach, Baldwin,* and *Rabel* were *all* liquor-related injury cases where injury did not come from commercial bars and bartenders. To the extent that they reflect no-liability results for non-bars/bartenders, the bystander cases are unremarkable cases of their period as liquor injury cases. These cases simply mainstreamed colleges with other businesses. Yet it is instructive that these courts chose legal doctrinal *rationales* (the end of *in loco parentis,* the birth of student freedom, etc.) that were very *atypical* of social host cases—except to the extent that they shifted the legal issue from proximate cause to duty. Bystander era courts were not willing to *justify* college-aged liquor culture but were willing to exonerate colleges from liability for duty based policy reasons. Seen from a wider lens, *Bradshaw, Beach, Baldwin,* and *Rabel* were prominent in a stage in the development of the basic theme in university law in the 20th and 21st centuries—the application of general tort and liability rules to university culture.[74]

---

74. Some final points about liquor liability and social host no-duty rules. In most cases raising the question(s) of liquor-related injury which occurs as a result of conduct *other than* that involving bars and bartenders, courts have often made two critical observations. First, in many instances liquor liability is imposed on bars/bartenders by *statute.* To the extent that the legislature(s) chose not to extend liquor liability to other parties, a kind of immunity existed by legislation to those parties. Second, social hosts (really most entities other than bars and bartenders) had no duty because of policy reasons and social forces that outweighed the policies in favor of imposing liability. In essence, many courts have deliberately provided an immunity for social hosts.

Immunity is subtly different from no duty in that it connotes that a *protection* is afforded for policy reasons, even though the actor is engaging in otherwise unreasonable conduct. No one praises someone who knowingly serves a drunken friend another beer with full knowledge that he will soon drive home. It is not what a reasonable, prudent person would do. When the law says that the social host has no duty to the innocent mother who is injured in the subsequent car wreck, that is not a court's way of condoning or praising the social host's behavior. It is only saying that private drinking is so pervasive, so hard to regulate, etc., that it would be inappropriate to impose liability on a private person who does not and cannot ordinarily insure for that type of risk. Rightly or wrongly, that is *all* that courts are saying when they protect "social" drinking.

In the "bystander" era, then, when a student activity became "wet" in some way, courts were likely to side with a university, as they would with other businesses or social hosts, if they saw colleges as special social hosts. But when the situation was "dry," the courts began

Danger spilled off campus into the community in other non-alcohol related ways. By far, the leading case to address the unusual problems of dangers that carry off campus was a case involving predatory assault—*Tarasoff v. Board of Regents of the University of California.*[75] The University of California, like other modern multi-service universities, offered psychiatric counseling on premises. In *Tarasoff*, a man in outpatient counseling with a psychotherapist confided his intention to kill a specific, named woman. The threat was deemed highly credible and the psychotherapist alerted campus police. Campus police detained the man, but were told by the psychotherapist's supervisor to let him go on his way. No one called the woman to warn her that a danger was headed her way. The man attacked the woman. Until 1976, that would have been the end of the story legally (at least in terms of civil liability).

We have taken so many steps to protect people from relationship violence, stalkers, and predators, that it is hard to think back three or four decades when terms like "battered woman syndrome," "sexual predator," "stalker," etc., were not in common use. Prior to 1976 (yes, 1976) a patient could walk into a psychiatrist's office, outline a murder plan of a specific person set to happen in an hour, and even if the psychiatrist believed in all good professional judgment that the danger was real and present, the psychiatrist could legally sit by and watch the murder go down. This was considered nonfeasance—and the psychiatrist could be said to be a mere bystander. The lunacy of the then majority (nay, unani-

---

to acknowledge duty and the circumstances under which a university could be liable. While *Bradshaw* and *Beach* (alcohol cases) talked about the loss of custody and control, *Mintz* spoke of duty owed and how it can be satisfied. The paradox of these cases (and all of the cases of the era) was rooted in alcohol tort law and the not so easy task of fleshing out the new legal relationships of student and university. Courts took it a case at a time and instinctively and typically found no duty in alcohol cases and duty in others. University personnel and students were forced to try to make sense of this. Two things were happening simultaneously. First new rules were entering higher education, and second those rules themselves were changing rapidly. It was a lot to digest.

In *Bradshaw* and *Baldwin* the courts reached issues of student alcohol-related injury occurring in vehicular mishaps *off* campus. It would have been fascinating to hear these courts on another troubling issue: who would have won if an innocent non-student were injured in the community by student activities which carried over into the community? Suppose a pregnant mother driving to a supermarket had been struck and seriously injured by the drag racers in *Baldwin*? To what extent would a university have been liable for injury occurring off campus to non-students if the university in some way facilitated danger on campus? Most likely in that era, courts would have deployed social host-type reasoning. Today, however, social mores and the law of alcohol responsibility are shifting.

75. 551 P.2d 334 (Cal. 1976) (en banc).

mous) rule that no duty was owed to anyone other than the psychiatrist's patient was changed forever and rapidly by the decision in *Tarasoff*. *Tarasoff*, in one form or other, since has become a majority rule imposing some responsibility on psychologists (and others) to use some care for certain endangered persons.[76]

At root, *Tarasoff* (and later cases) said[77] that, in some instances, a university psychotherapist would owe a duty to an *off-campus non-student* who became endangered from forces/individuals on campus. To oversimplify a bit, if you know who the victim is and she is not aware of the danger, you must warn her of the danger, if reasonable professional judgment would say that she is at risk. The university fought this duty all the way to the California Supreme Court. That court unanimously ruled against the university.

In the heart of the bystander era, an important seed was planted. If a university facilitates or knows of a manifest danger to an *off-campus non-student*, the university must calculate the possibility that courts will ask them to respond for harm caused or use reasonable care to protect off-campus interests. Modern universities are increasingly integrating their activities into the larger community. New responsibilities have followed. As we shall see in Chapter V, these responsibilities have developed in several new dimensions.

The bystander era is often seen as a time of paradox in a post-insularity and post-*in loco parentis* period. The perception was common that universities were relieved of most if not all duties to protect student safety—even programmatic and residential safety. But the cases defied that simplistic model. Strong no-duty, bystander rhetoric—fueled by social movements on and off campus, the loss of confidence in law enforcement powers, and laissez-faire alcohol risk law—were most prominent in cases involving liquor-related injuries to students or by students. Yet equally powerful crosscurrents were at work. Cases arose in which the university was held responsible to its tenants, to its business "customers" (invitees), for its programmatic activities, and even to the community with respect to certain dangers exported off campus. The bystander era was a stage in the development of duty law: the idea of duty had been suppressed in the *insularity* era, but slowly rose in the bystander era.

This bystander era was a transitional era, however. The no-liability case law was rife with hard rhetoric and strained rationales. There was a vision of newly

76. *See, e.g.*, *Santana v. Rainbow Cleaners, Inc.*, 969 A.2d 653 (R.I. 2009).

77. Precise parameters of *Tarasoff* and its implications for psychotherapeutic practice are complex and there is considerable debate about the margins of responsibility. *See* Peter F. Lake, *Revisiting Tarasoff*, 58 Alb. L. Rev. 97 (1994); *Fraser v. U.S.*, 674 A.2d 811 (Conn. 1996); *Santana v. Rainbow Cleaners, Inc.*, 969 A.2d 653 (R.I. 2009).

emancipated students who were now free to harm each other and be harmed: the vision was cold and left the university in a helpless role. Many cases used legal reasoning with inherent flaws. The pro-duty cases were politically marginalized by the politics of university law. With some exceptions, even these cross-current cases were lacking in overall vision. Although *Mullins* discussed the duties of a university landlord, even that case did little to offer a significant comprehensive post-insularity vision of university/student relationships.

Tarasoff, *Mintz*, and other cases were decided without much attention to the fact that they were *university* cases (*Mintz* is commonly cited in non-university cases; *Tarasoff* applies to psychotherapy generally, and only a small fraction of cases like *Tarasoff* come from university situations). The bystander image—defective and contradicted—was the most significant legal image of its era. The duty era in university law was forming but had no appropriate legal image to support it.

The central question remained even with the brief ascent of the bystander era: "What is the nature of the student/university relationship?" The answers of the bystander era were incomplete, or in some cases, inappropriate. For sure, it was now settled that the student/college relationship was not *in loco parentis*. The bystander era also settled that university/student relations would now be cast in terms of duty or no duty. Beyond alcohol injury cases, it was hard to accept the image of a helpless bystander university. When the issue was fixing broken locks on lobby doors, sweeping sidewalks, getting a weather report before taking students on an icy lake, or turning your back to off-campus danger, the issues seemed, and were, different. The truth is that sometimes the university did just stand by, but at other times it was a co-participant in an association of complex shared responsibilities. Bystander images could not suffice to replace the demise of *in loco parentis* and the fall of insularity. Bystander imagery was in many ways the absence of image. Such an image could not do justice to modern college life. What images could?

V

Millennial Student/University Relationships

The Duty Era in an Age of Accountability

The period since the early 1980s has seen the erosion of no-duty-to-student bystander case law. Courts have been mainstreaming higher education under law. Accountability under law is increasing rapidly; however, that does not necessarily mean *liability* is increasing at the same rate. Courts today increasingly enforce business-like responsibilities and rights while preserving some uniqueness in college affairs. There has been a steady rise in the application of typical negligence rules to university life—this is the duty era. There is less judicial willingness to create or recreate rules of legal insularity in the duty era. Nonetheless, the law largely remains sensitive to the unique roles and circumstances that characterize the American college experience. However, years of resistance to accepting reasonable care as a governing norm for managing a campus environment may be causing a regulatory backlash: colleges may be facing new and accelerated legal safety standards.

Today a university owes duties to students and students owe duties to protect themselves. Courts continue to recognize that the university is a unique, if sometimes business-like, environment where special applications of more general negligence and duty rules sometimes are needed. The dominant judicial image is one of *shared* responsibility, and a balancing of university authority and student freedom. The law of duty is a primary legal vehicle that courts use to make this happen. Colleges still "win" many reported safety law cases, but scrutiny under duty standards has increased levels of accountability.

In this new era of legal duty, courts confront the law of student/university relations on a situational basis—one case at a time—and are demonstrably influenced by two counter-balancing notions. On the one hand, courts in the duty era can see direct analogies between cases involving student injuries and cases involving business responsibility, professional and amateur sports, and, in some instances, municipal liability for certain governmental operations, *inter alia*. On the other hand, courts continue to view the university as a unique environment that deserves at least some protection from rules, which, while appropriate for some entities/activities, are not always strictly appropriate for universities. The university is not a government, nor is it a typical business (e.g., manufacturer). The university has a special social mission. Courts increasingly give careful consideration of the policies and factors that should govern the college experience. Courts are also aware that higher education is not one uniform experience for all students in all contexts. Duty is an organic concept and needs to be carefully fitted: it is ill suited to fast, off-the-rack, solutions.

Ultimately, the value of a given court decision lies in the guidance it gives. However, there are many cases and they are not always consistent—facially or otherwise. Concretely, for instance, an administration must decide through counsel whether *Bradshaw* or some other more recent case rejecting *Bradshaw* applies: what do the apparent (if not real) inconsistencies in the cases mean here, for *this* college in *this* situation? "Trends" in the law are hard to discern and work with (even for lawyers), but this is especially so when there is doctrinal complexity and a genuine lack of easily observable overall vision in the cases. University officials and students are asked to step back from the brush strokes that are the cases and be Monet, even when there is no real assurance that there is a painting at all. The challenge is to construct coherence—as much as possible—and a guiding vision. The law today on the subject of college student safety and security is not simple. While it is possible to construct a coherent vision of how complex rules of negligence apply to colleges, the law lacks a clearly articulated *vision* for the core safety mission of higher education that is a companion to those complex legal rules of student safety. Administrators need both: they need some sense of how the law congeals doctrinally *and* a sense of the spirit of those rules—a vision.

From a legal/doctrinal perspective, say that of a seasoned tort lawyer, university safety law is largely unremarkable. Courts have used, and will continue to use, standard and typical categories of tort responsibility—applicable to a wide array of actors and businesses—and adapt them to institutions of higher learning. There is no body of higher education tort safety law *per se*. The law of student safety in higher education arising in the courts is somewhat tailored prêt á porter, not tailor made.

In developing the law of rights and responsibilities of universities and students with regard to safety and security on campus, the courts have seized upon the complex law of duty to deal with campus safety issues. The basic "strategy" (the courts do not openly collaborate, but training and experience guide them collectively down often predictable paths) is to relate a particular type of claim to general duty rules and to solve problems posed by the "claim" within those parameters.

It is helpful to see *categories* of student safety claims. In many ways the law of duty is a seamless web—none of it makes sense until all of it does. Nonetheless, there are functional categories of safety law like these:

(1) Premises/landlord responsibility with respect to conditions on premises (like broken locks);
(2) Responsibility to control dangerous persons and/or prevent harm caused by them;
(3) Responsibility for sexual assault;
(4) Active shooter prevention;
(5) Responsibility regarding student activities (like chemistry lab, sports, field trips, etc.);
(6) Responsibility for voluntary student alcohol (and other drug) use (and attendant risks) in a non-commercial setting where alcohol is not sold for consumption on premises; and
(7) Responsibility for mental health risk.

As we consider these categories in more depth keep in mind the following:

First, these functional categories are *not exclusive* and they overlap significantly: a court might have to address a matter involving a dangerous male student who attacks a female student—and both are drinking. Always keep in mind that the law of negligence and duty is more seamless and breaking it into parts is somewhat artificial.

Second, the functional *legal* categories are not exactly sorted in the ways that a typical campus administrator might encounter or solve campus problems. Thus, a dangerous student on campus might be a student discipline problem *and* a residence life issue, etc. The law stubbornly organizes and sorts in its own ways, not in ways college officials would. (This is a key reason why an overall vision of college safety law is necessary: college officials have difficultly arranging legal doctrinal icons so as to quick-sort their problems and issues. Think of the law as an iPhone with apps written only by someone who doesn't entirely care about how *you* work.) Very few lawyers, and fewer judges, have ever managed a campus learning environment. There is no inclination to match the law's categories to those of administrators; and little skill or knowledge to do so. (This has sometimes been a problem at a regulatory level as well. Some legislation and regulation is simply not realistic or as efficient as intended in a real world college context.) The law of higher education needs *interdisciplinary* work, a rapidly growing field that, for all practical purposes, did not exist just thirty years ago.

Third, none of the cases in these functional categories reflect any sort of return to an era of insularity or *in loco parentis* by the courts. This is an era of reasonable care, not parental care. The fundamentals of duty law are not *in loco parentis* or insurance. *No modern court* discussing university and student safety duties has ever stated that current rules are parental responsibility-based; indeed, courts sometimes explicitly bend over backwards to state that current rules are *not in loco parentis.* Again, the argument that courts are secretly or unwittingly returning to *in loco parentis* is specious. (As discussed in Chapter II, were we to return to the era of *in loco parentis*—the era of insularity—the results courts reach would not be babysitting or parental liability results, but would rather be results which would tend to insulate the university environment from legal liability by the application of traditional immunities. Moreover, family-based tort immunities—and *in loco parentis*—were historically used to protect the university from lawsuits regarding discipline, regulation, and punishment of students only.) We have seen a profound retreat from the era of insularity in which the doctrine of *in loco parentis* flourished. Colleges still tend to "win" the majority of reported cases, but this is not a return to the era of insularity, or a recreation of it. *Accountability* is clearly on the rise, even if liability is not. This is emblematic of a duty era. Duty means some level of *scrutiny* but the mere existence of legal duty is not sufficient to create liability. The rise of duty has fostered the increased importance of *a standard of care*—usually the reasonable person standard. Unlike Dean Wormer, most administrators are *eminently* reasonable in their decision making most of the time. Duty implies accountability, which implies a standard of care—usually reasonable care. It is a standard that colleges and administrators routinely meet or exceed in practice. Hence, we win a lot of cases.

Fourth, the reality (not especially dramatic) is that university law reflects the process of mainstreaming and tailoring general duty criteria to the specific and unique university context. Somewhat ironically, the seedlings for the current duty era lie in the no-duty bystander era cases themselves. Bystander era cases replaced the immunity rules of the era of insularity with no-duty rules. Those cases made duty prominent in its negation; crosscurrent cases used duty to impose legal accountability. Today, the university community is governed as a duty community, with a complex allocation of rights and responsibilities. This allocation neither immunizes universities generally nor provides students with opportunities to foist their own unreasonable conduct or deliberate risks upon universities. The duty era is a *shared* responsibility era and in that regard does mark a departure from the major periods that preceded it. The prior eras have favored all-or-nothing style approaches in which only a student or a college, or no one, was *the* legally responsible party. The duty era is about a balancing of university control/authority with student freedom/rights and shared responsibility.

Now let's look at the evolution of the law of (legal safety and) duty through these functional categories. As this chapter unfolds, we will look at the law from the other perspectives as well—from the point of view of an administrator looking at administrative tasks and/or meeting safety challenges in a higher learning environment, and to some extent from a more abstract point of view that sees the law of duty as a seamless conceptual system.

1. Premises/Landlord Responsibility

A landowner has a duty to use reasonable care in the operation and maintenance of his premises for the protection of so called "invitees." Such a relationship is legally "special." Universities are landowners, operating classroom, library, and office buildings, walkways, athletic and recreational facilities, parking facilities, cafeterias and bookstores, etc. Some questions are tricky, but in the large, most of the buildings and grounds pictured in college catalogs are university premises. Students are presumptively invitees almost without exception as are employees of the college, and often so are others who come as guests to the college's premises to participate in college functions. The roots of such premises responsibility first dimly appeared in the era of insularity, but college premises responsibility substantially developed in the "bystander" era and then solidified in the current "duty" era.

Landlords, as special premises owners, owe some maintenance responsibilities to their tenants (think of them almost as a sub-class of invitees); students in university-owned residential facilities are treated like tenants. The landlord/tenant relationship is also legally special for many purposes and therefore imposes certain affirmative duties defined by common law (or even statute).

Among university attorneys a most well-known and often-cited university non-tenancy premises case is *Poulin v. Colby College*,[1] which was decided in 1979 in the heyday of the bystander era (as such, another crosscurrent case).

In *Poulin*, a man was injured when he slipped and fell on an icy hill at Colby College. To determine the responsibility owed to the person on college premises, the court had to determine the man's "status" *vis-a-vis* the college. He had come to the college's premises to escort a college-employed maid to the dormitory in which she worked: he was not a student, nor an employee, but just a regular guy helping a college employee in icy New England conditions. Nonetheless, he was considered by the court to be like an invitee. (Note that the college did not actually "invite" him onto the premises. One of the oddities of the law of premises safety is that invitees are rarely actually "invited." Lawyers!) The injured man helped an employee of the college to get to her place of work safely, and he had conferred a benefit on the university. The college therefore owed a duty to make its premises reasonably safe for him.

It might seem odd that a leading university premises liability case is a *non-student* case. *Poulin* involved someone who was, for non-legal purposes, almost a stranger to campus (he was not a prohibited stranger or a vagrant; had he been, the matter would have been differently decided).[2] *Poulins's* significance lies in where the margin is drawn. If the injured *non-student* in *Poulin* were entitled to reasonable care, then a person coming with a more palpable economic benefit to a college campus clearly would be entitled to reasonable care. Commonly, students and their guests (like mom and dad) are either invitees or like invitees, and thus owed reasonable care in premises maintenance and design. Cases solidifying *student* rights to premises safety followed on the heels of *Poulin*. Since *Poulin*, cases involving premises maintenance have held, *inter alia*:

- A university has a duty to use reasonable care to warn students of significant dangers associated with excavation.[3]
- Students as invitees are entitled to reasonable care in premises maintenance.[4]

---

1. 402 A.2d 846 (Me. 1979). *See also Isaacson v. Husson Coll.*, 332 A.2d 757 (Me. 1975) (jury question as to whether a college maintained premises reasonably); *Shannon v. Wash. Univ.*, 575 S.W.2d 235 (Mo. Ct. App. 1975) (jury can decide whether a university negligently maintained a walkway).

2. In cases where homeless people wander onto colleges and get hurt, they are owed a much lower standard of care because in most jurisdictions they are considered "trespassers," especially when efforts are made to keep them from the premises.

3. *See Prairie View A & M Univ. v. Thomas*, 684 S.W.2d 169 (Tex. Ct. App. 1984).

4. *See Baldauf v. Kent State Univ.*, 550 N.E.2d 517 (Ohio Ct. App. 1988).

- A university can be liable for negligently installing a screen door in a student apartment when it leads to injury of the tenant or her child.[5]
- A college has the same duty that any private landowner has regarding removal of dangerous accumulations of snow and ice on its premises.[6]
- A university has a duty to maintain athletic facilities in reasonable condition for the safety of participants and spectators—but not to prevent all student injury from participation in athletics or observation of the athletic events.[7]
- A college must repair broken locks on common exterior entry doors in dormitories or face liability when a student is attacked in her room by an intruder who easily entered because of the broken lock.[8]
- A university has a duty to use reasonable care to maintain a safe parking garage, including fixing dangerous holes.[9]

A few points are critical with regard to these cases. First, no case views routine maintenance responsibility as a form of babysitting, parental responsibility, or strict liability. To the contrary, the cases uniformly require only *reasonable* care, not all possible care. A college does not have to foretell the future. A college does have to fix broken locks, repair windows, and fill in the potholes in garages. These responsibilities are virtually identical to the ones that modern businesses (and in some cases cities) have today. Indeed, the university premises cases are routinely cited and quoted in non-university business and municipal cases and vice-versa. (*Poulin* is an example.) If you were to ask a judge what the law of university premises responsibility is today, the judge would most likely answer, after looking at you a bit cross-eyed, that there are no special rules regarding university maintenance: universities must use reasonable care towards their invitees, just like any other business.

Williams v. Junior College District of Central Southwest Missouri[10] illustrates this point. In that case a high school student enrolled in an auto-mechanics course at the college (there was no special treatment because the student was a high

---

5. *See Bolkhir v. North Carolina State Univ.*, 365 S.E.2d 898 (N.C. 1988).

6. *See Mead v. Nassau Community College*, 483 N.Y.S.2d 953 (N.Y. Sup. Ct. 1985); *Goldman v. New York*, 551 N.Y.S.2d 641 (N.Y. App. Div. 1990).

7. *See Henig v. Hofstra Univ.*, 553 N.Y.S.2d 479 (N.Y. App. Div. 1990); Marcus Misinec, *When the Game Ends, the Pandemonium Begins: University Liability for Field Rushing Injuries*, 12 Sports Law J. 181 (2005).

8. *See Delaney v. Univ. of Houston*, 835 S.W.2d 56 (Tex. 1992).

9. *See Malley v. Youngstown Univ.*, 658 N.E.2d 333 (Ohio Ct. Claims 1995).

10. 906 S.W.2d 400 (Mo. Ct. App. 1995).

school student). He was injured when he slipped and fell on the floor of the shop class. The evidence showed that a petroleum-based substance had been left on the floor between classes. The instructor said that he inspected the floor before the injury occurred, but the jury felt that he did a careless job. In affirming an award of damages based on the jury's determination that a *duty* was *breached*, the appellate court made a point of holding that the duty was one of *reasonable* inspection. Just because something was done did not mean enough was done; just because not enough was done did not mean that everything possible had to be done. The instructor was in the best position to anticipate spills of petroleum matter that might not be obvious to a student or an ordinary and less experienced observer, especially because the instructor repeated the auto-shop class throughout the day. As we shall see later, things would have been dramatically different if a student had actually seen a huge oil spill on the shop floor; if the student knew the floor was slippery and walked on it anyway, his knowledge would have likely reduced or defeated his recovery if he reasonably had been able to avoid the dangerous area. The jury did not ask the instructor to babysit his students but rather just to do his job with reasonable care. Nor was the college *strictly* liable for any injury, no matter how careful it might have been in cleaning its shop floors. Responsibility here was identical to that of a business. Reasonable care.

The second critical point is that when a university fails to properly maintain its premises (including student dormitories), it is no longer entitled to seek protection from the traditional, complete immunities of (1) family, (2) government, or (3) charity. No lawyer today argues a family immunity to protect university misconduct. Charitable immunities have largely been abolished (and were never particularly strong with respect to premises maintenance regarding business properties). Governmental immunities for public universities have not completely disappeared. Indeed, public universities still enjoy substantial immunity from private lawsuits regarding design and planning-level decisions (e.g., what type of dormitory to build; where to place it). However, public universities typically do not enjoy governmental immunity when they operate "proprietary" (business-like) activities such as parking garages, bookstores, etc., nor with respect to routine "ministerial" non-discretionary tasks, like fixing broken door locks or repairing sidewalks. Governmental immunities may pose procedural obstacles for injured students; and states often "cap" responsibility. But the era of the government always wins is over.

In fact, in situations where universities have attempted to push the notion that the public university is immune as a governmental entity too far, the courts have offered stern rebuke. The case which best illustrates this point is *Delaney v. University of Houston.*[11] In *Delaney,* the university apparently received numerous requests from female students in a women's dormitory to fix the lock on a dormitory entry door. The university did not repair the lock. The broken lock became the access point for a criminal intruder. The university seriously contended in court—under cover of alleged governmental immunity—that it had the right to leave the broken lock unrepaired, even after it was a source of danger *and fear* for female students (the university attempted to define the issue as being about the level of campus security it provided to its students, and then argued that police power issues are immune from private tort suit). The university also blamed the intruder as the sole proximate cause of the injury to the student and denied any shared responsibility for the incident.

The Texas Supreme Court—not exactly notorious for strong pro-plaintiff sentiments—rejected both arguments. The *Delaney* court held that the act of fixing a broken lock on the entry door of a student residence hall is not invested with the level of policy making and political judgment that would require courts to defer to the "political" (or discretionary governmental) process, nor was the issue one of campus security as an immunized police power function. Fixing a broken lock is a no-brainer—a simple and routine feature of providing a safe residence hall. *Delaney* basically said that a public university is not entitled to permit unsafe tenant conditions to persist under the false umbrella of sovereign discretion. The university was severely chastised by the court for its attempt to avoid responsibility by seeking immunity from the consequences of its negligence in deferring repair in one of its residence halls.

In addition, *Delaney* took a very modern approach to the proximate cause question. There was a time under landlord-tenant law when the criminal intruder/attacker would have been considered the sole proximate cause of harm and danger and hence the university would have escaped liability. The notion that the deliberate criminal attacker was the determining cause was very much in keeping with a primary belief of police and criminologists at one time—the best and only way to stop crime was to punish criminals. But as recent theorists and practitioners, such as Kelling and Coles, James Q. Wilson, former N.Y.C. Police Commissioner William Bratton, and Felton Earls (and other researchers in

11. 835 S.W.2d 56 (Tex. 1992).

the Chicago study and on the topic of collective efficacy)[12] have now convincingly pointed out, crime strategies focused simply on punishment (and incarceration) are not as effective as other strategies.[13] One reason such myopic crime strategies failed was that they misperceived and disconnected the links between *disorder* and crime. Failing to fix broken windows and locks facilitates major criminality.[14] Preventing crime by restoring order has had substantial success in places like New York's once infamous, but now safer, subway system. Another reason these strategies failed is that they did not account for a crucial factor in deterring crime—collective efficacy. New research strongly indicates that a community that shares responsibility for its own environment enhances the health and well being of its youth—and reduces crime. Science now indicates something intuitive. Degradation of a community is risky and fosters criminality and unwellness.

Moreover, reducing disorder and improving collective efficacy—fixing locks and engaging a community—decreases *fear* of crime. Fearful students (and those forced to waste precious study time repeatedly asking for routine maintenance) are not learning. Fixing locks, as *Delaney* perceived, can stop crime and lead to a (real) sense of safety on campus, thus improving education. *Delaney* correctly intuited that collective efficacy—the opposite of bystanderism—deters crime. In that sense, the university community itself bears some responsibility (proximate) for crime and danger in its midst. Reducing disorder and improving collective efficacy are features of shared responsibility. The students did their part in *Delaney* (unlike some dorms where students deliberately disarm door locks after repeatedly being told not to do so), but the university did not do its part. The rule in *Delaney*—that a public university must defend the reasonableness of its failure to perform maintenance that enhances the opportunity of crime on campus—tends to prevent crime, and fear of crime.

Why would a university have argued such a counter-intuitive position all the way to a state supreme court, rather than admitting fault and agreeing to

---

12. *See* William Bratton with Peter Knobler, *Turnaround – How America's Top Cop Reversed the Crime Epidemic* (Random House 1998); *see also* Felton J. Earls, *Project on Human Development in Chicago Neighborhoods: Longitudinal Cohort Study, 1994–2001* (2002), *available at* http://dvn.iq.harvard.edu/dvn/dv/isq/faces/study/StudyPage.xhtml?studyId=380&tab=catalog.

13. *See* George Kelling & Catherine Coles, *Fixing Broken Windows – Restoring Order and Reducing Crime in Our Communities* (The Free Press 1996, Touchstone 1998).

14. In *Delaney* the university's negligent failure to fix the broken lock provided the opportunity/setting for easy criminal intrusion and attack.

a monetary settlement to compensate a student for her injuries in such a situation? Surprisingly, the answer is that tort rules and procedures, the professional responsibilities of lawyers, insurance, and the corporate management of higher education, often encourage such litigation. Indeed, the very existence of insurance may lull some colleges into a sense that "insurance covers that." The way there is an incentive for a college lawyer to continue to litigate to the margin of responsibility up to the point where "bad" precedent might be made. Moreover, from a management perspective (not talking specifically about *Delaney*) a very real political issue may exist as to how much to spend on very politically unglamorous buildings and grounds maintenance. A legislature may not want to give a school money for maintenance—particularly money without a political tag—and private donors often want to give money to *new* buildings and major renovations or restorations. College leaders in the boom times following World War II chose an interesting path—pour money into larger and more expensive buildings—larger and more expensive buildings often require more maintenance. The corporate strategy of bigger is better in physical footprint has caused a reverse pyramid effect for safety—straining future budgets with high costs of maintenance and administrators with ever more difficult tasks to manage facilities. In retrospect, and from the point of view of the great recession, this long-term corporate strategy amounted to a form of hoarding—with a predictable effect of causing implosion. Many of the modern risks of college are at root corporate errors on a massive scale. However, the law provides virtually no remedy for corporate decisions that cause deferred maintenance, etc. Decisions to build and build at public universities are immune under so called "discretionary function" rules: there are few realistic methods of corporate accountability for most private colleges.[15] Questionable corporate strategic decision making, which led to deferred maintenance, has fostered lawsuits over operational-level administrative choices and compliance with the reasonable care standard. A dollar spent on buildings and grounds maintenance (or on campus law enforcement) is a dollar that donors and university leadership may want to go somewhere else. But in the end it can be the root of safety litigation. Tort law tries to create an incentive by *legally* requiring certain minimum maintenance standards. A dollar not spent on required maintenance is many dollars more in litigation fees and injury awards, not to mention the potential public relations problems that can follow from failure

15. *See* Peter F. Lake, *What's Next for Private Universities? Accountability*, Chron. of Higher Educ. (Dec. 5, 2010), *available at* http://chronicle.com/article/Whats-Next-for-Private/125599/.

to stop reasonably preventable injury. The tort system may not always be enough to incentivize universities, however.

The third critical point is that bystander arguments do not apply to invitees on premises. An invitee is in a "special" relationship with the college even if the problem is one of omission or "nonfeasance."

The final, and perhaps most critical, aspect of the recent premises responsibility cases is that they are a very conscious effort by courts to balance university responsibility with *students'* responsibility for their own safety. Early American common law stated that a person who was injured as the result of another's negligence could not recover *any* civil reparation for the harm done by the other's negligence if the injured person had himself been careless (negligent). That rule persisted into relatively recent times (well into the 1960s). But in the 1970s, the old "all or nothing" rule was abrogated in favor of a rule that apportioned liability for injury—and thus damages—between the parties, according to the extent that their fault (negligence usually) had contributed to the injured party's damages. The concept is called *comparative* negligence. It has been one of the most important changes in American negligence law. The doctrinal shift from the all or nothing approach of contributory negligence to comparative fault was an important legal step to a system of shared and apportioned responsibility. The all or nothing effect of a contributory negligence rule often unfairly barred the partial recovery of damages by an injured person. The old rule caused the legal system—sympathetic to the plight of an injured person who might recover nothing from a negligent defendant—to employ strange rules and tactics to overlook a victim's own carelessness so as to grant her damages for her injury. But, these rules and tactics were then harsh on defendants because some faulty plaintiffs received windfalls. The logical middle ground was to ask the parties to *share* responsibility for the injury and apportion it.

Today, the typical faulty accident victim recovers something for her/his injuries[16] but is asked to bear the relative costs of her own fault. Common sense and experience in a university community suggest that students are often architects of the problems that injure them and are—most importantly—sometimes the ones in the best position to help themselves. Sometimes students clamor for locks and the university fails to provide them; sometimes universities provide reasonably safe premises but confront students who foolishly take risks. Some of the most senseless acts of Bluto Blutarski-style self-inflicted

16. In the period after the adoption of comparative fault, some courts have retained the idea that a party who voluntarily proceeds in the face of a known danger can recover nothing at all. All this is most typical today when an individual expressly so proceeds.

injury inhabit university tort case law with predictable no-liability results.[17] In such cases, it is virtually impossible to imagine that even the highest level of care could prevent such harm from occurring—certainly not reasonable care.

In this context, the messages the courts are sending at one level are very clear. A university has a responsibility to use reasonable care to prevent premises/residence life injury, but not to the extent that the danger presented is "open and obvious" to a student who voluntarily encounters it anyway or is created or enhanced by the student's own action (with reasonable alternatives available of course: the broken locks were painfully obvious in *Delaney*, but what are students to do about that?). A university can diminish or even defeat liability if a student is comparatively at fault, either by failing to use reasonable care for his or her own safety and/or by assuming a risk voluntarily and knowingly (especially an open and obvious danger) in the face of safer alternatives. A university may have a duty to maintain its premises, but it has ways to avoid liability. Courts are not reluctant to send the message to students that they are sometimes solely responsible for their own safety. The courts most often send that message when the students themselves are in the best position to avoid an injury. Newer systems of shared responsibility account for the fact that in some cases no sharing is appropriate.

Students have a responsibility not to be negligent in their conduct and must be willing to share or bear the consequences of their own voluntary, informed choices. Safety on campus depends on shared responsibility. The more reckless students are, the more an activity with known dangers should be guided and facilitated. However, the more risk students assume, the more responsibility they bear. The college student is a *legal adult* insofar as he or she is responsible to

17. *See, e.g.*, *Robertson v. State ex rel. Dept. of Planning and Control*, 747 So.2d 1276 (La. Ct. App. 1999), *writ denied*, 755 So.2d 882 (La. 2000) (intoxicated student recklessly climbs onto roof of natatorium and falls); *Nichols v. Northeast La. Univ.*, 729 So.2d 733 (La. Ct. App. 1999), *writ denied*, 744 So.2d 633 (La. 1999) (intoxicated student chooses to spit over railing of upper floor dormitory and falls); *Bash v. Clark Univ.*, No. 06745A 2006 WL 4114297 (Mass. Super. Ct. Nov. 20, 2006); 2007 WL 1418528 (Mass. Super. Ct. April 5, 2007) (student unforeseeably overdoses on heroin in her dormitory room); *Brody v. Wheaton Coll.*, 904 N.E.2d 493, (Mass. App. Ct. 2009), *review denied*, 908 N.E.2d 307 (Mass. 2009) (Underage adult guest of a resident summer employee drives after drinking and crashes. As the court stated: "Public policy considerations support our conclusion that no duty exists. No one was in a better position to prevent harm to Brody than Brody himself... he was an adult capable of and responsible for avoiding the combination of drinking and driving... Wheaton is not responsible for Brody's decision to put his own life in danger.").

exercise *reasonable care* for her/his own safety and the safety of others, and accept certain risks.

Thus, in many situations, it may be said that the student is responsible for her own injury or the injury of another. Even in those situations where the college is negligent in some respect, such as in the allegedly negligent failure to barricade an excavation site, a student may be comparatively negligent in entering the construction area when the risk of doing so is unreasonable. Negligence law holds the college student to the standard of care that a reasonable person would exercise under the circumstances for their own safety. Damages resulting from a student's injuries should be reduced to the extent of that student's own careless conduct. The law recognizes a significant responsibility residing in students to understand and deal with matters of their safety and the safety of other students and third parties. Where the college acts as a facilitator of student safety by actively educating students in ways of self-protection and civility toward others, the student who ignores the university's efforts can be held legally accountable for his or her own injuries or injury to others. In some cases, where the college has exercised reasonable care in facilitating student life, the burden of shared responsibility will fall heavily upon the shoulders of a student.

For example, in *Banks v. Trustees of the University of Pennsylvania,*[18] a student who fell on university property sued the university and lost. This was no ordinary fall, however. She had encountered a fraternity protest blocking a pedestrian right of way and elected to scale a wall to bypass the protest. She was not as nimble as she supposed and fell. When she sued, the university successfully pointed out that a wall is a known and obvious fixture, which if one were to climb it, poses obvious risks (unlike the petroleum-based substance on the floor in the *Williams* case, *supra,* which would not have been apparent to a typical student). A wall is a wall after all.

The *Banks* court did point out two important things. First, the student had other, more reasonable options to get to where she was going. Second, the *Banks* court specifically noted that even if a danger is open and obvious, a university (or any business) has a responsibility to use care to prevent danger if it is foreseeable that a student (consumer or business visitor) will, due to extenuating circumstances, overlook the otherwise obvious danger and proceed in the face of it.

A very famous case[19] involving a K-Mart store illustrates the latter rule. A K-Mart customer passed some large, post-like barriers as he entered the store

---

18. 666 A.2d 329 (Pa. Super. Ct. 1995).

19. *Ward v. K-Mart Corp.*, 554 N.E.2d 223 (Ill. 1990).

to make a purchase. He was injured by the barriers when he exited while carrying his large, bulky purchase. (The barriers were designed to stop vehicles from getting too close to the entrance and hitting pedestrians walking out of the store.) The man obviously saw the barriers on his way into the store; but after he shopped, he either forgot about them or was distracted when he walked his large purchase out the exit door (which obstructed his view). What is open and obvious at one moment can become foreseeably less so under other circumstances, such as when a customer is distracted, carrying a bundle of goods, or a period of time has elapsed since first encountering the danger:

> [T]he modern majority rule is that a landowner is liable to an invitee on his premises if the landowner (1) knows, or should know of a condition that presents an unreasonable risk to the invitee, and (2) should expect that the invitee will not discover or appreciate the dangerous condition, or will fail to protect himself against it. Thus, the landowner may be liable where he should anticipate that an invitee might be injured by a condition, despite its obviousness. Such situations include those in which the invitee's attention is foreseeably distracted, or where the condition is unexpected or forgotten by the invitee.[20]

The *Banks* court determined that there was nothing to indicate—as in the K-Mart case—that someone would be so distracted. At the moment you climb a wall, you know you are climbing a wall; when you walk through a door, you may forget what is, or may be, on the other side.

What happens if a student does proceed (unlike *Banks)* in the face of a should-be-obvious danger, or proceeds into non-obvious danger when an alert person would hesitate? Again, the current legal answer is not a coddle-the-student answer, but a balancing of rights and responsibilities approach that emphasizes shared responsibility.

There are two excellent examples.

In *Weller v. College of the Senecas*[21] a student suffered serious paralytic injuries when he fell from his bicycle on campus. The injured student had elected to ride on a grassy path between some trees instead of riding on the paved path. However, other students had ridden off the paved path in the area where the plaintiff rode, and the university (through its maintenance contractor) knew of these deviations from the paved path. The fall in this case was caused

---

20. Robert Bickel, *Tort Accident Cases Involving Colleges and Universities: A Review of the 1995 Decisions,* 23 J.C. & U.L. 357, 363 (1997) (footnotes omitted).

21. 635 N.Y.S.2d 990 (N.Y. App. Div. 1995). *See* Bickel, *supra* note 20.

by impact with an exposed, but not obvious, tree root: the plaintiff did not know about the root until it was too late. (Tree roots are not necessarily common hazards on paths, even unpaved ones.) So the danger was not "open and obvious." However, the court held that the student's failure to use care for his own safety could be used by a jury to reduce or eliminate recovery, even assuming some university negligence in the maintenance of the path. The fact that a student made what some jurors would consider a bad choice did not relieve the university of its *responsibility* but instead potentially relieved the university of some (or all) *liability. Weller* reminds us that in accidents sometimes no one is at fault, sometimes only one entity or individual is at fault, and at many other times fault is shared. Responsibility for fault can thus be shared: just because you are at fault does not *ipso facto* mean that I am not. Legal rules in the university context sometimes openly acknowledge that apportioning responsibility is best. This is mainstream comparative negligence law.

Sometimes, apportioning responsibility or fault between the university and the student can be very tricky even for the courts, as is illustrated in the *Pitre v. Louisiana Tech University* litigation.[22] In *Pitre,* a rare, Jim Cantore-type winter storm covered the campus of Louisiana Tech with snow. In good form, the university had anticipated the storm and issued an appropriate bulletin including warnings (because many of these students were unfamiliar or inexperienced with heavy snow or serious winter weather). The bulletin encouraged students to enjoy the snow, build snow people, and sled in proper areas using good judgment. The bulletin also discouraged stupid, "Jackass" style sledding, etc.; "Do not sled into the path of cars, or on certain bad hills, or allow yourself to be dragged behind cars" (popular, if stupidly dangerous, ploys are made worse by movies like Napoleon Dynamite that glorify them—"sweet jumps" are rarely so, and "a tow into town" invites injury). The bulletin was a classic example of how modern student affairs engages student activity: the bulletin was neither babysitting, parental, or custodial. It was also not some draconian control missive: the bulletin of the *Gott-Hunt* era might have read "All students caught sledding will be expelled." Instead, the bulletin provided needed information and admonitions.

When the snow hit, it was a big one. Classes were canceled and several thousand students were trapped on campus. Earl Pitre, a student from Louisiana, decided to take advantage of the unusual conditions and went to an 85-foot hill. Louisiana is not exactly the land of sleds, saucers, or the luge, so students had

22. 673 So. 2d 585 (La. 1996).

to make do. Homemade sleds and cardboard, plastic signs, cafeteria trays (a sport once known at snowy Wellesley College as "traying"), and even a toilet seat became makeshift snow/gravity conveyances. Pitre elected a large plastic garbage can lid. It should have been lots of fun; but sledding on steep slopes can be dangerous, particularly when one is sledding into a parking area with concrete light poles. On his eighth ride, he struck a light pole base and was paralyzed. He had chosen, with some friends, to go downhill backwards (on your back, feet facing uphill), which is exciting but as an author raised in Massachusetts can attest to, is trouble. You cannot see what is coming and you almost always go head over back, or worse. As Pitre headed towards the pole, other students shouted warnings while jumping up and down, but it was too late. Tragically, he struck the fixture and suffered horrible injuries.

At one level, the events of that evening were tragic and confusing. A student was seriously injured. Had the university done enough? Too much? Was the student at fault? Was this just an accident that happens? What is the appropriate balance between student responsibility for their own safety and university responsibility to provide safe conditions for students?

On these issues, the Louisiana court system predictably flip-flopped and finally settled the issue in a split decision (with a vigorous dissent) of the Louisiana Supreme Court that ruled slenderly in favor of the university. At the trial court, Earl Pitre lost when the trial judge granted summary judgment (the judge believed that most of the facts were not in dispute; the real questions were what is the law) on the grounds that the danger associated with striking the concrete base of the light pole was obvious and apparent, and therefore there was no duty to warn Pitre or prevent the danger. On the first appeal, the intermediate lower court reversed the summary judgment and sent the case back for trial (believing that there were fact issues for a jury to consider). The trial was held and things went against Pitre again. On the second appeal, the Louisiana intermediate appellate court reversed (again) and determined that *both* the university and Pitre were negligent and should share responsibility legally under principles of comparative fault. The university appealed the "split-it-up-the-middle" decision to the Louisiana Supreme Court.

The majority of that court sided—albeit narrowly and fact specifically—with the university and reversed the intermediate appellate court. The Louisiana Supreme Court recognized the typical duty owed to invitees/students to make university premises reasonably safe by either warning of danger or correcting it, *except* where a condition was as obvious to the student as it was to the university. If a danger is obvious to a student, the court reasoned, that is an important factor in determining whether the university's handling of the condition was unreasonable. A condition that is obvious to anyone and everyone, the court concluded, was not unreasonably dangerous and there would be no duty. The court clearly weighed a university's responsibility against the responsibility of students to watch out for their own safety.

In that vein—balancing of responsibilities and risks—the *Pitre* court determined that the concrete base and its light pole were "clearly visible" and "observable" to virtually all the sledding students: the parking lot was still lit and Pitre himself apparently had observed students slide past the light poles and also saw students collide with stationary objects.[23] It was, after all, a light pole and a large fixed, hard object. Because the light pole was so obvious and sledding is not unusually or highly dangerous (no more dangerous than hiking or skateboarding, two other popular student activities), the court reasoned that the general risk of injury was slight.[24] On the other hand, light poles prevent other accidents and attacks on students on typical days and nights in Louisiana when there is no snow (and even prevent injury by illuminating an area). Moreover, the court reasoned that it would be burdensome on a university to *eliminate* this risk; for example: the cost of posting police at every possible point of injury during the storm would be too high. As such, the university did what was reasonable under the circumstances (*Pitre* is suspiciously similar to a duty *and* breach decision: recall that courts sometimes use duty in the combined sense of duty and breach).[25]

Pitre tried to argue that there were bases for duty other than a landowner/invitee theory. Unfortunately for him, once the court made its reasonableness/policy factor determination—balancing the risk of harm against the cost of its prevention—these arguments had no chance. If the university did what was reasonable, then it did what was reasonable under other duty theories. The court did not protect the university from accountability for unreasonable conduct: it determined that the university did what was reasonable under the circumstances.

---

23. *See Pitre,* 673 So. 2d at 591–92.

24. *See id.*

25. The university did have a responsibility to patrol areas used by unusually high numbers of students during the highly unusual storm—but the university did make reasonable efforts in this regard, and the presence of student affairs administrators or campus police might not have prevented Pitre's injuries. For an in-depth treatment of how courts use the term "duty" in several senses, *see* Peter F. Lake, *Common Law Duty in Negligence Law: The Recent Consolidation of a Consensus on the Expansion of the Analysis of Duty and the New Conservative Liability Limiting Use of Policy Considerations,* 34 San Diego L. Rev. 1503 (1997). Courts increasingly use multi-factor policy balancing tests to determine close cases of "duty."

Thus, when Pitre argued that his status as a *college student* alone created a duty on the part of the university to protect him from harm it was to no avail. The *Pitre* court recognized that status as a college student was relevant to the duty owed regarding conditions on university premises, but otherwise did not entitle him to care in the form of supervision, etc. The university/student relationship, *Pitre* said, is not sufficient in itself to create a duty.[26] Of course, it *is* the basis for the landowner duty owed. The *Pitre* court stated that a duty premised merely on a student/university relationship would be an *in loco parentis* duty; in this regard, *Pitre* could all too easily be interpreted to fall into the trap created by *Bradshaw*, *Beach*, *Rabel*, and more recently *Freeman v. Burch*, when those cases suggest—in a historically false way —that *in loco parentis* once legally protected college student safety.[27] *Pitre's* determination to say that student status itself does not create duty might seem gratuitous and even hypertechnical. But the point is clear: courts like *Pitre* wish to make certain that the law does not require the university to always follow students on or off campus to protect their safety simply because they are students. The point is often obvious since many on and off-campus actions of students are beyond reasonable efforts of the college to monitor or guide. When courts say that a student/university relationship in itself does not create duty, remember that students are a unique set of invitees on campus who are entitled to reasonable, even affirmative, care. A university does not guarantee safety or provide the type of supervision of student activities that would be required for elementary or high school students. Thus, to the extent that there is a modern *in loco parentis* legal safety rule for K-12 students, it does not apply to college students.[28]

---

26. *See* Peter F. Lake, *The Special Relationship(s) Between a College and a Student: Law and Policy Ramifications for the Post* In Loco Parentis *College*, 37 Idaho L. Rev. 531 (2001).

27. Consider how the power of the false and fallacious reasoning of the key bystander cases persists when courts uncritically follow old precedent. *See, e.g.*, *Freeman v. Busch*, 349 F.3d 582, 587 (8th Cir. 2003). ("In fact, since the late 1970s, the general rule is that no special relationship exists between a college and its own students because a college is not an insurer of the safety of its students," citing *Bradshaw v. Rawlings*, 612 F.2d 135 (3d Cir. 1979), and cases following *Bradshaw.*) *Freeman* commits the "*Bradshaw* fallacy." The statement implies that there were "special" relationships in college based on the college/student relationship prior to 1970—there were not. Even if there were and again, there were not, special relationships create duties of reasonable care, not insurance.

28. In recent K-12 education law, there is a doctrine of *in loco parentis* regarding student safety. These rules developed largely after the fall of *in loco parentis* for colleges and were never applied to college law. This is the root of some of the confusion in higher education law.

Earl Pitre also tried to argue that a duty to warn arose because the university had sent an encouraging bulletin on snow activities to students and the campus police had some general, *ad hoc* powers to use their judgment to intervene in dangerous student behavior. Pitre in essence argued that the university thus assumed a duty to him and facilitated his injury. The court disagreed: other students testified that the bulletin did not motivate them to sled. And the campus police were not legally required to stop sledding, just use good judgment. Critically, the court seemed of the view that the university's actions had not proceeded so far as to work a positive wrong or to show a particular assumption of responsibility to Earl Pitre himself. That ruling is very much in line with modern rules regarding police duties to citizens. When police issue general warnings or police a beat, they do not typically assume special duties *ipso facto*. No doubt the *Pitre* court was influenced by the similarity of the problem to non-university police situations.

Pitre did not specifically relate its holding to the rules in the K-Mart case, but it is roughly consistent with them. Although the university knew of the danger, the court ruled that it could expect students to also observe the danger and protect themselves. It is easy to see where some judges might see it the other way. Excited students, late at night, might be tempted (and pushed by their peers) into overlooking danger, like a very last minute shopper on Christmas Eve might race down an aisle looking for one last gift. And perhaps at a commonly snowbound college with a hill leading to a parking lot, a university might place padding around concrete poles or even promote "traying" at safer locales. These might be inexpensive solutions. Perhaps a judge might view this type of question as more appropriate for a jury not the court. In essence, the dissent in *Pitre* argued that a jury should be given the opportunity to balance the relative responsibilities of university and student. The fact that a majority went the other way gives some indication that deference to university prerogatives—and a concern over opening a flood gate of litigation—still governs in many of the close cases. It is a precarious position of deference, one which universities could easily lose in the imaginations of judges.

In sum, *Pitre* is a tough case with a tough result and a tough message. If students fool around on campus, they risk literally everything. A university is *not* an insurer of student safety even though it does have responsibility for student safety on campus. In some instances, accidents do just happen or are attributable to students' own conduct (misconduct). Courts are aware of the need to place some responsibility for student injury on the heads of the students themselves. Courts are sensitive to the burdens that a university might face otherwise and to the almost infinite ways in which college students can get hurt. The other tough message is that the court was divided—and could easily have gone the other way (as had the intermediate appellate court)—on the shared responsibility of the university and its student(s) in this situation. A university could easily then lose a case like this one in the future if it were to fail to bring less than obvious risks to the attention of students and to take other reasonable steps to minimize the risk of injury.

The message of *Pitre* is complex. Modern administrators can surmise that the existence of "duty" will now only be knowable after the fact—at least in close cases. Modern administrators must often act *as if* duty were owed, even if it turns out otherwise after years of litigation. This is a complex message from the courts to higher education—accountability, but not necessarily liability—and the complexity of the message is no accident but a key feature in a universe of shared responsibility. Courts do not seek to crucify higher education, or impose impossible to discharge responsibilities (hence the rhetoric of many of the bystander cases); but courts also do not want to let colleges just walk away from all responsibility to their students. The right legal messages are often hard to articulate and even harder to understand sometimes.

In recent times the most challenging cases have been those involving more complex relationships among students, injuries, and campus boundaries—particularly "off-campus" injuries. Colleges often retain vestiges of a bygone era—defining themselves by physical plant and physical campus boundaries. However, modern learning is increasingly less and less defined by physical boundaries as students tune into cyberspace and move fluidly from campus operated facilities to externships, study abroad, etc. Risk does not respect physical boundaries and flows indiscriminately into cyberspace and on/off campus. The modern higher education learning environment is larger than its physical boundaries and students live in a fluid "riskscape" not just a (often beautiful) landscape. Lord Voldemort ultimately was not content to vex only Hogwarts.

Several recent cases illustrate the challenges of defining the boundaries of the modern riskscape and fairly allotting respective rights and responsibilities.

Perhaps the most important case arose at the University of Nebraska, Lincoln (which has become a national leader in alcohol prevention efforts, discussed further in this chapter).[29]

---

29. The following discussion of the *Knoll* case is adopted and adapted from Peter F. Lake, *Private Law Continues to Come to Campus: Rights and Responsibilities Revisited*, 31 J.C. & U.L. 621 (2005).

Knoll v. Board of Regents of the University of Nebraska[30] involved an incident at a fraternity.[31] A student at the University of Nebraska was involved in a hazing incident that resulted in a very serious falling injury.[32] During a pledge induction process, members of a fraternity met the plaintiff student at a university building on campus and brought the student to an off-campus, but university regulated, fraternity house.[33] The injured student consumed alcohol over a several hour period.[34] At one point the student was handcuffed to a radiator.[35] The student managed to become free of the handcuffs and attempted an escape out an upstairs window.[36] During the attempted escape, the student suffered serious injuries on the fall.[37]

The critical issue in *Knoll* revolved around the fact that the injuries ultimately took place at premises not owned or operated by the university; nor on the "campus."[38] Although the fraternity house was not on university-owned property, it was subject to the student code of conduct, which created sanctions for certain forms of dangerous conduct.[39] The Nebraska Supreme Court, though, did not focus upon the regulation of the off-campus property because regulation does not create duty in itself. The court focused instead on the fact that the incident began on university property.[40] In deploying the totality of the circumstances test—virtually identical to tests employed by many other courts[41]—the Nebraska Supreme Court relied heavily upon the fact that there had been prior hazing incidents where students had been snatched and removed from buildings or otherwise coerced into high-risk alcohol consumption or other harassing hazing activities.[42] From this the court concluded "the University owes a landowner-invitee duty to students to take reasonable steps to protect against foreseeable acts of hazing, including student abduction on the University's property, and the harm that naturally flows therefrom."[43]

30. 601 N.W.2d 757 (Neb. 1999).
31. *Id.* at 760.
32. *Id.*
33. *Id.*
34. *Id.*
35. *Id.*
36. *Id.*
37. *Id.*
38. *Id.* at 761–62.
39. *Id.* at 764.
40. *Id.*
41. *See, e.g., L.W. v. W. Golf Ass'n*, 712 N.E.2d 983, 983–85 (Ind. 1999).
42. *Knoll*, 601 N.W.2d 764–65.
43. *Id.* at 765.

In so holding, the court made it clear that events on campus leading to an eventual injury off campus do not themselves have to be injurious or even seriously dangerous.[44] Importantly, off-campus injuries to students sometimes occur when students are lured from a university premise to an off-premise location. If the *Knoll* reasoning is correct, there could be a sufficient link—subject to possible proximate cause limitations—between almost any off-campus event that initially commences on campus and the ultimate injury that arises from that event. Therefore, whether a college or university has a duty to a victim may hinge upon where an attacker commences contact with the victim, even if the initial contact itself is neither harmful, nor portends harm. In this sense, duty may lie in the hands of an attacker in some contexts.

Existence of a duty in a given case may turn upon circumstances largely beyond the control of the institution or its administrators. A risk may result from a series of specific events that thus may or may not trigger a legal duty; it is often impossible to predict how harmful events will unfold. After cases like *Knoll*, a college or university must often behave *as if* duty were owed, even if ultimately a court were to determine that the college or university has no duty. Tests like the totality of the circumstances test make it difficult for a student or administrator to predict in advance whether a duty will be owed in a given fact pattern. Colleges and universities should be cautious when relying upon bystander case law to deduce the limits of college responsibility *a priori*. The law of duty in higher education law no longer guards the gates of the courthouse as it once did.[45] Duty law now serves the primary function of being a major factor in limiting or eliminating liability *post hoc*. Duty no longer routinely keeps cases involving physical injury to students occurring within some proximity to campus blocked from the courthouse door. More cases than ever proceed to discovery and to summary judgment.

Knoll also made clear that it was not essential that a specific prior incident occur with respect to a specific fraternity. Using the totality of the circumstances test, the Nebraska Supreme Court was willing to look at prior acts of sneaking and grabbing of students and also prior, but not identical, criminal

44. *Id.* at 762.

45. Courts began using "duty" as a way to reduce access to extended litigation in the early part of the twentieth century. Virtually all lawyers are trained to recognize the case that signaled the start of the duty era. *Palsgraf v. Long Island R.R. Co.*, 162 N.E. 99 (N.Y. 1928). If you are not a lawyer you are almost better off for not knowing about this case: if you are a lawyer, you will be unlearning it in your career.

activity in the fraternity community.[46] Crucially, the court made it clear that "prior acts need not have occurred on the [specific] premises [where the injury occurred]."[47] Sufficiently similar incidents occurring in a nearby community can give rise to an inference that such criminal activity is foreseeable on a nearby landowner's property.[48]

The *Knoll* court did address the fact that the university had asserted some control over fraternity houses by regulating them under the student code.[49] Nonetheless, it appears from the court's reasoning with respect to landowner duties that the mere fact that control was or was not exercised over an off-campus property would not be dispositive.[50] The court included the exercise of university control over students as *one* of the factors in the totality of circumstances test, but the court did not find university control to be the only—or even most important—factor in determining liability.[51] Thus, one critical implication of *Knoll* is that it does *not* hold that regulating off-campus behavior itself imposes duty. *Knoll* is not an "assumed duty" via regulation case ("assumed duty" is discussed later in this chapter). The reverse is also certainly not true: not choosing to regulate off-campus behavior does not insulate an institution from liability. The Nebraska Supreme Court, by reversing the trial court's grant of summary judgment for the University of Nebraska, suggested, to the contrary, that the failure to enforce regulations involving off-campus behavior could be a factor under the totality of the circumstances test. The question ultimately turns on what a reasonable person would do with respect to business invitees considering all the circumstances.[52] *Knoll* may be the first American case to imply that not being proactive is itself a factor in creating duty.[53] A small amount of prevention may be a cure for potential liability.[54]

In retrospect, it seems that the University of Nebraska's strong and proactive concern for student behavior off campus (and certain safety measures that were taken, such as working security phones) may have ultimately resulted in minimal exposure to the university. By way of settlement with the university,

46. *Knoll*, 601 N.W.2d at 764.

47. *Id.*

48. *Id.*

49. *Id.*

50. *Id.*

51. *Id.*

52. *Id.* at 764–65.

53. *Id.* at 761–65.

54. *See id.* at 764 (indicating that the university was aware of hazing and created regulations prohibiting hazing, but that the university did not enforce those regulations off campus).

the injured student received only $25,000.[55] This relatively small sum in the range of tort injury settlements[56] seemed related to the fact that the institution had regulated pledge sneak events and had offered security phones, one of which the injured student had admitted that he had chosen not to use because he wanted to participate in the event.[57] Again, students are principally responsible for their own safety in many situations.

A case that illustrates just how fine the battle lines of premises responsibility may be drawn is *Guest v. Hansen*.[58] *Guest* is another off/on campus injury case, involving alcohol.

In *Guest*, a snowmobile accident fueled by alcohol cost the lives of a student and a guest of the student near the sylvan campus of Paul Smith College in upstate New York. The reported decision in *Guest* focused on the claim relating to the guest's death. Some students at Paul Smith had "occasionally built bonfires and consumed alcohol" on a nearby lake in wintertime on state property adjacent to the campus.[59] As is so common in millennial[60] student risk and injury situations, events unfolded at night culminating in injury in the wee hours of the morning. The guest was a 20-year-old student at Quinnipiac University in Connecticut, who had been invited to campus by a student of Paul Smith College to celebrate his twentieth birthday.[61] Drinking began around 8:00–9:00 p.m. in the student's room on campus in preparation for trips back and forth to a nearby lake.[62] As the court related:

> [The guest] and her friends returned to [the student's] dorm room around 3:30 a.m. . . . . They headed back out to the lake, hoping, in due course, to watch the sunrise. A heavy fog . . . had begun to lift, and [a friend of the student] [drove] his snowmobile around the

---

55. *See* Peter F. Lake, *Tort Litigation in Higher Education*, 27 J.C. & U.L. 255, 274–275 (2000).

56. *Id.* at 275.

57. The $25,000 *Knoll* settlement is relatively small in comparison to known settlements in recent cases. Consider the $6 million settlement paid by the Massachusetts Institute of Technology (MIT) to the family of Scott Krueger, an MIT student, for his death from alcohol poisoning. Higher Educ. Ctr., *MIT Settlement Makes Other Colleges and Universities Take Notice* (Sept. 15, 2000), *available at* http://www.higheredcenter.org/files/thisweek/tw000915.html. By terms of that settlement MIT agreed to make significant changes in preventing alcohol risk on campus.

58. 603 F.3d 15 (2nd Cir. 2010).

59. *Id.* at 17.

60. *See* Chapter VI.

61. *Guest*, 603 F.3d. at 18.

62. *Id.*

> lake . . . [the student] drove out further onto the lake with [the guest]. . . . The two crashed into a promontory at a peninsula called Peter's Rock, a piece of land owned by the College.[63]

Both the student and the guest were killed in the horrific crash; neither was wearing helmets.[64]

Still, the *Guest* case created a bar examination hypothetical—if only it were unreal. Danger and poor decision making were transpired on and off campus, in and out of an area interwoven with campus, but not owned by the college.[65] The injury producing event technically occurred "on" premises but strangely so—the promontory was not itself a hazardous condition on campus, but a natural feature of an Adirondack Lake.[66] (*Guest* is also unusual because of its David v. Goliath procedural posture as the estate of the guest was represented *pro se* by her father.[67])

Guest is another federal court decision under the *Erie* doctrine, which requires a federal court to guess as to how the state court (here New York) would have ruled. The case does illustrate a trend in the federal courts to hold in favor of colleges in injury cases involving the voluntary consumption of alcohol.[68] It

---

63. *Id.*

64. *Id.* at 18–19.

65. *Id.* at 17–19. The lake was immediately adjacent to campus, and it was a promotional draw attracting students.

66. *Id.* at 19.

67. *Id.* at 21.

68. Federal courts—at least lower federal courts—have been deferential to colleges since *Bradshaw* and the bystander era. There is a noticeable division of state law precedent decided by state courts and state law precedent articulated by federal courts making *Erie* guesses. Federal courts are not supposed to create a federal common law of torts independent of state law but in college cases they have come close to doing so. Failing to correct precedent like *Bradshaw* fuels this impression, and motivates litigants to engage in forum shopping in hopes of achieving different results in different systems (federal vs. state court). Moreover, lower federal courts are inundated with criminal cases and may simply be sending the message that student alcohol injury cases should be heard in state courts. This may go a long way in explaining why federal courts have persistently followed *Bradshaw* despite the fact that its state law foundations are no longer secure. The law of Pennsylvania articulated in *Bradshaw* may never have been, but it is surely now dead. The *Erie* doctrine is dead. *Bradshaw* has created a ghost. However, the impact of *Erie* "ghosts" like *Bradshaw* is nefarious, especially when state courts use federal *Erie*-based precedent as persuasive articulations of the state law of sister states. *See, e.g.*, *Pawlowski v. Delta Sigma Phi*, CV-03-0484661S 2009 WL 415667, at *6 (Conn. Super. 2009). This is how ghosts become real.

is hardly clear that New York courts would agree with *Guest* on its no-duty ruling. *Guest* is not a *student* vs. college case, but a *guest* vs. college case and the victim was voluntarily involved in very high-risk behaviors—snowmobiling at night, in the fog, without a helmet and while intoxicated and with a similarly intoxicated driver. Guests of colleges are hardly free game; New York uses a somewhat plaintiff-friendly version of comparative fault. However, the student and guest were clearly more faulty than the college, and it is not unreasonable to surmise that *Guest* is little more than a ruling as a matter of law on comparative/contributory fault and causation—styled as a "no-duty" rule. *Guest* is hardly emblematic of the sweeping language of the high bystander era; and *Guest* is readily distinguishable from other situations because of its unusual facts.

"Gray-space" landowner duty cases—ones that straddle campus boundaries—often struggle to articulate rationales for their rulings. Consider the following. After correctly observing that mere foreseeability of danger alone does not create duty, that the ability to control a situation does not always imply that one has a duty to do so, and that a modern college is not *in loco parentis*,[69] *Guest* held as follows:

> Assuming *arguendo* that the college had the ability to control off-campus social activities, it was under no obligation to do so. Moreover, the fact that [administration] knew students were congregating on the lake did not mean that [the administration] was required to ban their activities on this off-campus site. The same conclusion obtains even if the drinking at issue began on the College's premises because [the guest] and [the student] left school property prior to the accident and the circumstances of their return—in the early morning hours, in dark and foggy conditions, and only for the instant of the accident—did not permit the College to supervise [the guest's] activities or those of [the student] driving the snowmobile on which [the guest] was killed.[70]

In this passage *Guest* suggested that the key rationale was even if there were a duty to supervise, there was no chance to do so. That sounds precariously similar to ruling that there was no breach of duty as a matter of law.

69. *See* 603 F.3d at 21–22.
70. *Id.* at 22.

Guest went on to admit that New York law "has suggested that landowners may be liable for dangerous conditions that they 'created or contributed to.' . . . [but] this theory of liability is quite narrow and does not appear to apply to activities that are dangerous independent of the landowner's actions."[71] *Guest* admitted that this one was at least close to the plate under New York law.

Pairing *Knoll* with *Guest* it should become clearer that duty and liability cases occurring in the "riskscape" are anything but clear—even to experts—and are often only clear in the rear-view mirror. Consider how things might have gone differently in *Guest* if the claim was by a *student*, or the injuries were the result of some other incident back in a dormitory room. The latter is the open question in *Guest* that will perplex student affairs administrators everywhere. Almost any night on a college campus somewhere a student/guest combo stumbles back to residence hall and someone is injured—is the dormitory a foggy promontory of no-duty/liability or not? The answers lie in levels of legal analysis that vex even experts in the field.

However, a "riskscape" is not infinite and not all questions are hard like *Guest*. There are essentially three "zones" of potential responsibility. The first zone is more or less on campus or in university-operated facilities—here duty creates special relationships that are most likely to trigger accountability under reasonable care standards. Living and learning in a riskscape does not make physical boundaries, and control of those boundaries, irrelevant. The second zone is "gray-space"—the straddle zone between on and off campus. This zone is the hottest zone area of recent litigation over student safety; and results in court are predictably mixed, very fact-specific and usually turn on extremely complex legal analysis. However, some cases are neither in the first or second zone—and they are not "gray" at all.

A good example is *Falkner v. Arizona State University*.[72] In *Falkner*, a football player shot and killed a man (non-student) at an off-campus night club. At some point—and clearly so in this case—the only relationship between a college and an injury is the fact that someone is a student. *Falkner* correctly held that there was no duty owed to the victim and no special relationship with the victim (or the student) in these circumstances. There are times on premises when duty is created by virtue of knowledge of a specific individual's dangerous

71. *Id.* at 22, quoting *Galindo v. Town of Clarkstown*, 814 N.E.2d 419 (N.Y. 2004) and citing to *Hayman v. Pettit*, 880 N.E.2d 416 (N.Y. 2007).

72. CV 2006-050660 2006 WL6654499 (Ariz. Sup. Ct.).

propensities.[73] It is critical, however, that the victim enjoys the status of business invitee at some point during the attack.[74] *Falkner* illustrates that there must be a tether to create duty: the mere fact of a student/university relationship is not a tether and *Falkner* is an easy no-duty case.

To summarize, when a student asserts a right to safe premises or residence living, modern courts balance university responsibilities to students/invitees and student/tenants against responsibilities of students for their own safety. The outcomes of the balancing process are not always easy to predict because courts must weigh various policies in fact specific contexts to find appropriate results. University duty to students as invitees or tenants is not parental, babysitting, or insurance—but there is at least the spectre of a duty to exercise reasonable care. That duty is subject to the limitation that students do assume some risks of college life and must shoulder some (and in a few cases all) responsibility for their own safety.

The premises liability/landlord-tenant cases of the current duty era are not heavy on images of what makes the university environment special or unique, although some vestigial deference to university culture can still be detected in the cases. In many ways courts treat universities like other businesses or entities in society, and courts do say what university life is not—it is *not in loco parentis,* nor is it insular. The university, as any other business or landlord, has a duty to manage risks to student safety reasonably, and students are subject to legal requirements that they exercise reasonable care for their own safety.

2. Dangerous Persons on Campus

Arguably the fastest evolving area in university liability law in the modern duty period is the growing responsibility of universities to protect students on campus from dangerous persons who come from off campus or who come from the student ranks themselves. Already a major issue in litigation prior to events at

73. Contrast *Falkner* with *Thompson v. Skate Am., Inc.*, 540 S.E.2d 123 (Va. 2001). Generally landowners owe their business invitees a duty of reasonable care to protect against foreseeable criminal danger (*Mullins*) but this is usually a background responsibility to reduce the risk of criminal attack often discharged by having a security force, fixing broken locks, etc. What if a business space is generally safe but becomes dangerous by virtue of a known dangerous person? That is *Skate America.* A special relationship with a business invitee can create a duty to protect in these circumstances if there is a known dangerous individual present on the premises who presents an imminent risk of serious harm to a business invitee. *See id.* at 129–30.

74. *Id.* at 128–30.

Virginia Tech, that event and subsequent events have brought this issue to the forefront of national attention. (In subsection 4, *infra*, the specific topic of active shooter intervention and "Virginia Tech" responses is developed in more depth.)

The message of the cases in the preceding "bystander" era was radically ambiguous on this issue. In cases like *Rabel*, the message was that there was no duty to protect a student from an attack by another (drunken) student on campus or in a dormitory. Yet without any attempt to make sense of the obvious incongruity, cases following *Mullins* found that a university had a responsibility to protect students from non-student intruders. The cases, when placed side-by-side, seemed almost unaware of each other and sent a paradoxical message to colleges: protect students on campus in dormitories from non-students, but do not protect them from each other. Incredibly, for a time, a student raped in her dorm by a fellow student was less likely to recover than one raped in her dormitory by a non-student intruder. Courts made no effort to explain—let alone justify or even recognize—this facially problematic difference in the protection of student safety.

The bystander era cases were beset by another powerful and ambiguous development—the rule in the famous *Tarasoff* case, which in many ways is the father of all dangerous person cases and the law relating to active shooter prevention. *Tarasoff* imposed a duty to protect some individuals from foreseeable danger arising from university relationships with dangerous persons on campus. If a campus psychotherapist had a duty to protect a non-student off campus from a non-student on campus, what would happen if a known dangerous student attacked another student on campus (or someone else, off campus)? There was nothing in the language of *Tarasoff* to suggest that it was just an "export" case. Indeed, the case resounded with a broadside fired against preventable danger to (particularly) female students by rapists, stalkers, etc. The implications for campus safety were manifest, yet cases like *Rabel* needed to be reconciled with *Tarasoff.*

Today, universities increasingly face responsibility for student injuries that arise from the presence of dangerous persons or groups on campus—whether the bad person is a student or not—whenever there is a foreseeable risk of danger and/or the university has a relationship with the dangerous person from which danger is predictable and imminent to a known or readily identifiable student. While in some cases courts speak of special relationships, it is clear that a relationship does not necessarily have to be custodial to be legally special for these purposes. It is in this area that university attorneys and commentators have perceived the biggest shift in decisional law in the post-bystander era. Again, there are intimations by some commentators that these cases are a return to *in loco parentis*, or the appearance of strict liability. However, these cases neither ask a college to be Nostradamus nor to use every possible means to protect every student from attack. The danger to a student must be known or reasonably foreseeable by a university, and then reasonable care must be able to prevent such a foreseeable, sometimes imminent attack.[75]

There is a substantial overlap in these cases with the landowner/landlord cases as to the legal doctrinal basis for duty. Universities do not encourage students or actors to attack students, so they are often cast in the passive, "nonfeasance" role. As such, the legal question presented is typically a special question of duty—affirmative duty or duty under special circumstances. Again, being a landowner to an invitee, or a landlord to a tenant, is an adequate special relationship to create an affirmative duty of reasonable care toward a student. Courts essentially view the potential or actual presence of dangerous persons on land or in a tenancy as a very special type of *condition*—a condition that makes the campus or residence hall unsafe.

Courts do see dangerous person cases as doctrinally analogous to slippery floor cases, but also treat them differently in analysis, tone, and, ultimately, liability.

In the 1950s and early 1960s a dominant rule of proximate cause would have determined, *per se*, that the dangerous person was the only party legally responsible, and that a landowner or landlord was not responsible to prevent the risk of harm from criminal intrusion. Today, the dangerous person on campus is not necessarily the sole proximate cause, even if the dangerous person is a student or an off-campus intruder. The proximate cause rule has been relaxed, opening the door for cases like *Tarasoff*.

Since *Tarasoff*, tort courts severally have recognized that a relationship to a dangerous person—student or other—*itself* can sometimes be a predicate for responsibility under *some* circumstances.[76] One can have an affirmative duty to protect even a stranger from certain foreseeably dangerous individuals. This

---

75. Modern tort cases illustrate that landowners cannot be oblivious to known dangerous persons on campus and may have the responsibility to anticipate that individuals will escalate into more dangerous actions. *See, e.g.*, *Sharkey v. Bd. of Regents of the Univ. of Neb.*, 615 N.W.2d 889 (Neb. 2000), *abrogated by A.W. v. Lancaster Cnty. Sch. Dist.*, 784 N.W.2d 907 (Neb. 2010). *See also Thompson*, 540 S.E.2d 123.

76. Courts following *Tarasoff* have emphasized a necessary combination of control (often custodial control) plus identifiability of a victim or set of victims, plus foreseeability of dangerousness by the dangerous person. You need all three, typically, and courts vary somewhat in the tests they use. Moreover, *Tarasoff*-like duties are the most likely to be imposed in cases involving medical professionals or in landowner duty cases.

responsibility is *in addition* to any responsibility owed to a student in a landowner or landlord context; because many incidents do occur on campus and/or in residence living, those incidents trigger multiple duty theories.

* * * *

Because *Tarasoff* makes special relationships so prominent in terms of duty and dangerous people, a brief digression on duty, students, and special relationships is in order. Courts will not say that a duty is owed simply because a victim or attacker is a student.[77] As we have seen, being a student does not itself create a special relationship sufficient to impose a duty according to courts of the bystander and current duty eras. Judicial reluctance to treat students as intrinsically special must be viewed in context, however. Students *are* in a special duty-creating relationship on campus (as invitees), in their residence halls (as tenants), in certain circumstances when there is foreseeable endangerment by a dangerous individual (*Tarasoff*), when involved in a program of instruction broadly conceived, and also when working on campus or for the college (employees). Students are also owed a duty of reasonable care when colleges undertake safety precautions but fail to perform them reasonably,[78] increasing risk or inducing students to rely on the college's undertakings or services. Thus, for many purposes students *are* in a presumptive duty relationship with a college because of special relationships or special circumstances. College is not special, except when it is.

So, students are not in a special relationship with the university except when certain things they do or experience as students put them in a special relationship. It's all very Monty Python— "I came here for an argument—no you did not." Needless to say, this state of affairs is very confusing to college ad-

77. Student safety law was once the almost sole province of the courts. Frustrated by the persistence of insularity and bystander positions, legislatures and regulators have increasingly asserted themselves in student safety issues. For example, the Clery Act has grown from its infancy as a very basic campus crime reporting act into ever expanding campus safety legislation. *See* Jeanne Clery Disclosure of Campus Security Policy and Campus Crime Statistics Act (Clery Act), 20 U.S.C. §1092(f) (2006). The U.S. Department of Education can, and does, dispense significant fines for non-compliance. Trench warfare over bystander principles has created a backlash at the regulatory level: consumer expectations of college safety now outpace those established in litigation. Regulators may have a different view of the college/student relationship.

78. According to the *Restatement (Second) of Torts,* a person or entity which undertakes a safety service for another person can be liable if the failure to perform that service increases the risk of harm, makes a person worse off, or induces that person to rely on the undertaking to her detriment. This is technically not a special relationship rule but an independent way to create duty under what we call "special circumstances." *See Restatement (Second) of Torts* §§ 323, 324 (1965).

ministrators attempting to come into compliance in the line of duty. If one were to restate the law today in these areas, it would be easy to say, "you have no duty to students, except when you do." Confusing? Courts have reached this state of affairs very methodically and interstitially by applying and adapting doctrines used in other contexts. To date, the courts have yet to step back and identify the collection of patches as a college responsibility quilt. College law remains in transition and the current post-bystander duty era will continue to evolve perhaps for several decades to come. The case law is close to critical mass in terms of identifying the legal *vision* of modern college and university relations, apart from simply offering a seemingly *ad hoc* collection of complex duty and special relationship rules.

* * * *

Now, the case that most university persons regard as the signal of the beginning of the end of college bystander rules, specifically regarding dangerous persons/activities on campus, is *Furek v. The University of Delaware*,[79] decided in 1991. For many, *Furek* brought tethers of tort responsibility together.[80]

---

79. 594 A.2d 506 (Del. 1991).

80. There are still courts (particularly federal courts) that prevaricate about the impact of *Furek* and cases that follow. Consider how *Freeman v. Busch* (again, a federal case under *Erie*), 349 F.3d 582, minimizes *Furek*. In an overbroad statement of the law, *Freeman* stated: "Since the late 1970s, the general rule is that no special relationship exists between a college and its *own* students because a college is not an insurer of the safety of its students." 349 F.3d at 587 (citing *Bradshaw*, *inter alia*). Taken at face value, the statement is demonstrably false: colleges and students enjoy special relationships in many circumstances, notably when students are business invitees on campus and for certain purposes in a tenancy in residence hall facilities. Duty is also not insurance. Stepping far beyond an *Erie* rule of deciding a matter under the specific state law at issue in the case, *Freeman* attempted some form of trans-jurisdictional generalization about college tort law in America—and muffed it. The case is argumentative, and this is visible in the way that the court related clearly contrary precedent like *Furek* via *footnote*. As *Freeman* stated:

> However, the rule is not absolute, and in very limited circumstances, courts have found such a [special] relationship. See Kleinknecht v. Gettysburg College, 989F.2d 1360, 1368 (3d Cir. 1993) (holding that there is a distinction between the relationship of a college and its students and the relationship of a college and its student-athletes); Schieszler v. Ferrum College, 236 F.Supp.2d 602, 609 (E.D.Va.2002) (finding in general that no university/student relationship exists, but in this specific case in which a college had repeated warnings that a student had emotional problems, had made threats of suicide, and had required the student to sign a statement that "he would no longer hurt himself," a special relationship did exist); see also Furek v. Univ. of Delaware, 594 A.2d 506, 521–22 (Del. 1991) (finding a duty in the context of fraternity hazing); McClure v. Fairfield Univ., 35 Conn.

In or around 1977 (yes, 1977—university cases can take over a decade to resolve in the courts), the University of Delaware began to take note of students who were injured in fraternity pledging activities. The director of health services at the university specifically reported two injuries to the vice president for student affairs and labeled them "hazing" incidents. The university then responded in writing by promptly admonishing fraternities about hazing. The dean of students issued a formal statement that hazing would not be permitted *on* or *off* campus. Later, an assistant dean gathered the presidents of the fraternities and discussed matters involving disruptive behavior and hazing. Ultimately, another top administrator spoke to the campus about hazing deaths occurring around the country and the dean made it clear that the university was willing to revoke the charter of any Animal House.

Yet, hazing went on at the university. A breakdown occurred in policy implementation.[81] The campus police were not properly instructed or empowered concerning the university's position on hazing. There were formal policy statements and announcements regarding fraternity-related disorder and danger, but there was an insufficient plan of implementation. Sometimes "making it wrong" can actually play into the hands of perpetrators whose intentions are to engage in secret, prohibited conduct as a way to bond and gain control over others. A public statement by administration can actually sometimes *worsen* a problem like this, especially if it is not supported by other environmental interventions.

In one sense, it certainly did worsen the situation. The campus police appeared hamstrung. Campus police officers (and other campus personnel) observed obvious indicia of fraternity hazing such as the marching of pledges with paddles, pledge "line-ups," and pranks. On a night just before "Hell

---

L. Rept. 169, available at 2003 WL 21524786, at *4 (Conn.Super.2003) (holding that the rule of Bradshaw and Beach is not absolute and that a university had a duty to its students under Restatement § 322). [Sic. McClure did not find a duty under § 322 but instead relied on §323]

349 F.3d at 588 n. 6 (emphasis added). It is hyperbole to suggest that special relationships—particularly those created by landowner/landlord relationships—are "very limited." It is also significant that *Freeman* never once mentions the case—widely followed—that contradicts the above analysis in *Freeman*, *Mullins v. Pine Manor*. I discuss *Freeman* in greater depth later in this chapter. *Freeman* is a prime example of how federal courts have (mis)used *Erie* to create a form of federal common law tort law, but there is even more going on in the case. Stay tuned.

81. At least that is the inference to be gained from the appellate court's opinion.

Night," (consider the mixed message of tolerating a "hell night" and condemning hazing) suspicious looking students were actually stopped by campus police, but no action was taken because there appeared to be no clear rules regarding such disorder for the police to enforce nor any effective instruction on how to use police discretion in these matters. Had an individual campus law enforcement officer decided to use her discretion and seize a paddle or disperse a group, she perhaps would have risked a great deal—reprimand, lack of support from above, lawsuits, etc. Case law like *Rabel* would not have indicated the need to intervene; to the contrary, it would have counseled standing by.

Yet the link between disorder, lack of community efficacy and the dangers of efficacy to combat bad behavior of hazing is clear: seize a paddle or a paddler and you may prevent a beating. You may also obtain more information to prevent other dangerous episodes and may set the tone that high-risk behavior is not permitted. Fix broken windows, as Kelling says, and the drug dealers move out: when Bratton arrested fare beaters in the Subway he caught criminals with guns and other dangerous items. Communities where citizens take ownership of their environment and intervene to stop criminal behavior have lower rates of crime. (One potential implication of the community efficacy work is that overreliance on police as a tool of environmental enforcement may actually *increase* crime. It may be that citizens are lured into deflecting their responsibility to create a safe environment onto others—the police.)

In the fall term of 1980, Furek pledged a fraternity. He entered "Hell Night"—a long hazing ritual featuring paddling, eating from a toilet, and being covered with food and other organics. This pointless ritual was exactly what the university had sought to prohibit. Here is why: one foolish fraternity member poured *oven cleaner* over Furek while he was blindfolded during a "ritual." Furek was chemically burned and scarred severely and permanently. Hazing has a way of getting way out of hand.

The *Furek* case squarely presented the question of how to deal with dangerous students and dangerous group activities on campus. The answer in *Rabel* and other bystander cases had been that to have responsibility, a university must be in a special relationship with students premised on *custodial* control. *Furek* saw the question differently and sensed that more subtle forms of relationships between students and universities exist in a modern era. As *Furek* said: "The university-student relationship is certainly unique. While its primary function is to foster intellectual development through an academic curriculum, the institution is involved in all aspects of student life [a clear rejection of *Bradshaw* and *Beach*]."[82] Many aspects of university life are "university guided,"[83] including housing, food service, security, extracurricular activities, and student life. Students are not *solely* responsible for their own safety simply because they are adults. (*Furek* saw no empirical or other support—as suggested in other cases of the bystander era—that university supervision was inversely related to the maturation of college students or that supervision of dangerous student activities would make for an inhospitable or educationally dysfunctional college experience.) The fact that students may be adults does not make university efforts to reduce high-risk alcohol use inappropriate (*Furek* noted that in both *Beach* and *Bradshaw* the students *were not* adults under drinking law). The university is in a unique relationship with students because of the "concentration of young people on a college campus and the ability of the university to protect its students."[84]

Furek saw a very different vision of university/student relations than that of the bystander era. Students are in the process of full maturation, whether calendrically adults or not. The university was not powerless. It could act without placing students in custody. It could facilitate and guide students into many of the circumstances that increase or decrease risk. *Furek* did not see the university as a helpless bystander but as guide and co-creator of campus life and student activities for individuals in an important transitional stage.

The legal principles that *Furek* used to reach its ultimate conclusion that the university had a duty to the student reflected a shift away from the affirmative duty/special relationship/custody concepts of *Bradshaw, Baldwin, Beach,* and *Rabel.* The duty of care in *Furek* arose not from special relationships, *per se,* but from ideas of "reliance" and assumption of responsibility/creation of risky conditions. Indeed, *Furek* was about starting something and finishing it properly when people (mainly students) have come to rely on what you have started.[85]

---

82. *Furek,* 594 A.2d at 516 (emphasis added).

83. *See id.*

84. *Id.* at 519.

85. *Furek* is sometimes minimalized as an "assumed duty" case by courts and commentators. *Furek* is, however, like *Mullins,* a case about *creating* risk as well as *assuming* responsibility. The very creation of a college environment engenders risk that would not exist but for that environment. Courts in another era had difficulty comprehending enterprise risk creation; many modern courts do not. Indeed, risk management efforts have increasingly focused on enterprise risk management strategies. This is not to say that there is always duty: but some risks, like the risk of hazing, are engendered by aggregating individuals in certain ways. Often, as happened after *Furek,* once such unique enterprise risks are identified, swift judicial and legislative solutions follow. For instance, statutory prohibitions against "hazing" are now ubiquitous.

Furek is about duty existing under unique or special circumstances: a college is not merely a passive educational repository for students, like parentheses in an equation, but is one of the most important variables and part of the functions. Colleges, according to *Furek*, often guide the creation of a community in which the college remains a major player in what actions or activities are promoted or discouraged. The college itself guides the level of safety that occurs on campus in the way a director determines how a play will be performed. Once the college "play" is in motion, there is an illusion that there is no director. If you see the director —or if you see too much of the director's hand in the play—the play is not working because the director must facilitate the vision of the playwright and the talents of the actors while keeping the expectations of the audience in mind.

In this vein, *Furek* held that the university had been committed to providing security on the campus in *general* and in *particular* had formulated general policies regarding hazing. In both these regards the university had undertaken to provide a level of security to students on campus and endeavored to eliminate hazing by fraternities. To the extent the university did not see its undertaking through, it could be legally responsible. Duty—to use *reasonable, not all possible care*—thus arose under the unique and special circumstances of the university's affirmative commitment to student safety in the context of long-term and well-known hazing problems. Such a duty can be breached by a university when the campus police are given an ineffective implementation plan regarding an acknowledged danger, thereby permitting students to flagrantly disregard anti-hazing policies. This is not a campus policing failure but a university administrative policy failure. It would be as if the director refused to direct the final act of the play, and then blamed the actors for the play's failure.

There are some important points to recognize about the implications of *Furek* for the modern college. These points fit under three headings—reasonable care, not strict liability; student responsibility; and assumption of duty.

Furek—Reasonable Care, Not Strict Liability

The *Furek* decision does not impose strict liability nor does it require babysitting or seeing students in a custodial relationship with the university. The duty owed is *only* that of *reasonable* care. This means that, despite reasonable efforts, some students will be severely injured in hazing or other incidents. However, *Furek* sends an unmistakable message that a university cannot make rules and policies against hazing, etc., and then do nothing to enforce them beyond verbal threats and admonition or fail to give campus police the authority and guidelines to enforce them through intervention. Moreover, non-draconian actions can prevent harm reasonably and discourage unwanted behavior. Had the campus police seized a paddle and taken some names—a visit with an associate dean to follow—a life might not have been damaged. Instead, campus policies unwittingly facilitated negative behavior. Bad students learned quickly that the rules would not be enforced and drew good students (and wannabes) into their dangerous activities; the fact that the conduct was "wrong" only enhanced the motivations of students whose attitudes about hazing were precisely to act out secret, prohibited, or unacceptable behavior. The fact that the campus police appeared to students to be disempowered only accelerated the sense that students were in charge and there were no real rules. As any parent or businessperson knows, making rules and not enforcing them leads to trouble.[86]

High-risk alcohol use is very dangerous for college students; as developed further in Chapter VI, high-risk college alcohol use is a major social problem and a major source of risk on campus. *Furek*'s intuition was, and is, correct. However, there are some reasonable steps that universities can take to reduce risks from alcohol-related activities. Unlike *Furek*, some courts still throw up their hands—no doubt recalling the futility of prohibition—at college drinking and its risks.[87] The issue, however, is not prohibition but *prevention* and reduction of risk. Many of the social causes of drinking on campus (and off) may be beyond the control of a university but the consequential danger engendered by campus drinking is not.

Courts cannot say—as a matter of law—and categorically—that there are no reasonable solutions to alcohol and/or *Furek*-type incidents. Decisions like *Bradshaw, Beach,* and *Rabel* seemingly protect university defendants, but they actually institute a stridently negative vision of students on campus and a negative view of attempts to restore reasonable safety and order on campus. These cases have done more damage than courts may have realized. In retrospect *Bradshaw, Beach,* and *Rabel* aspired to do little more than parallel alcohol risk

---

86. Active prevention, rather than post-injury discipline, is often a more effective risk management strategy. All universities have inherent, contractual, or governmental (constitutional) authority to restrict conduct that poses unreasonable risks to student safety. There is no need to return to *in loco parentis* to intervene and protect student safety.

87. The *Bradshaw* and *Beach* courts could well be criticized for essentially advising universities to give up attempts to reduce drinking by college students. Many colleges and universities bought into these decisions for years, creating problems from which many are still recovering. Much of the delay in the response by the colleges to the problem of alcohol-related student injury was counseled by embracing *Bradshaw's* and *Beach's* no-duty/bystander rules—and a failure to believe in high-risk alcohol use prevention science.

law of their day. They are dated legal leisure suits. They do not fit the law, the science, or the times.

"Protecting" universities from liability in improper ways can actually *facilitate* extreme student libertarianism and needless danger and disorder that threaten student safety. To promote the growth of student personal accountability, universities must facilitate the conditions of order and safety that make higher education possible under conditions of acceptable risk. It did not take totalitarians to clean up the subways of New York; it will not take a Mussolini to clean up American colleges. The vision of *Furek* is the faith restored in the possibility of reasonable solutions. Chapter VI sketches ways in which this faith can be made concrete on campus and in the courts.

Furek—Student Shared Responsibility

Furek did not see the university as the solely responsible party in matters of student safety. To the contrary, *Furek* is very much a *shared* responsibility case. In *Furek* both the student who poured the oven cleaner and the fraternity were responsible parties. In this sense *Furek* is at odds with cases like *Beach,* which assume that responsibility is a zero-sum game; shared responsibility does not diminish but can actually enhance student personal accountability. College student personal accountability is more likely to thrive in an environment that models responsibility and believes in civic efficacy.

Today, it is very common for courts to hold individuals *and* associations like fraternities liable for injuries negligently caused. For example, in one Mississippi case, a fraternity was liable both for gross negligence and punitive damages after a female student was forcibly grabbed against her will and thrown off a high railing into a shallow pool.[88] The court criticized the fraternity for failing to properly supervise the party, for maintaining the dangerous pool, and for failing to comply with university alcohol and party rules. Holding individuals, associations, and distributors of alcohol liable was also a feature of the bystander era.

Moreover, a student victim is not always entirely blameless. As we have seen, a student who deliberately goes along with known unauthorized activities and fails to use care to protect himself faces hard questions— potentially for a jury to decide in each case—regarding what, if any, offset any defendants are entitled to. Cases that have relied upon no-duty rules may thus be overreacting to

88. *See Beta Beta Chapter of Beta Theta Pi Fraternity v. May*, 611 So. 2d 889 (Miss. 1993).

plaintiff misconduct (e.g., *Baldwin,* where the students were clearly at fault). Recall that at one time a negligent plaintiff was entitled to nothing—a rule that is a great deal similar to no duty, at least in result. *Furek* does not disable affirmative defenses, but merely states that a university can properly be considered as *one* of the responsible parties in an accident. There will be situations where student misconduct is so egregious that courts should bar claims as a matter of law. They should, however, make it clear that they are not saying that a college has *no duty*. Courts no longer automatically need to say no duty in contexts like *Baldwin,* and doing so disserves the college community in a number of instances.[89]

Furek—Assuming Duties and Ostrichism

One unfortunate consequence of *Furek* is the perception that if you become involved you become liable, so, the logic goes, it is better to be uninvolved or push the students and their dangerous activities off campus. This perception is part of a larger legal and social milieu in which the belief is that you are better off not to get involved. Popular culture seems obsessed with this theme and we construct heroes like Kick-Ass to assuage our fears of ostrichism.[90] The question is white-hot in university affairs today.

"Assumption of duty" is a particularly scary phrase for university administrators (and university attorneys for that matter). It connotes, in legal effect, that when an actor (here the college or university) voluntarily assumes a duty not imposed by law, it is bound to carry out the duty with reasonable care and is liable for its negligence if it does not. Now, if an administrator believes that the general rule for college law is a no-duty bystander rule (because *in loco parentis* is dead, etc.), there is fear that to affirmatively intervene in student activities, programs, conduct, etc. (even in ways that establish parameters which clearly

89. That is not to say that no-duty rulings are *never* appropriate—indeed sometimes they are.

90. *See Kick-Ass* (Lionsgate 2010). For example, the final episode of the popular *Seinfeld* television series placed questions of deliberate indifference squarely on the table. In what might have been a truly pointless "Sein-off," the writers of the hit show chose to put a premise of the show on trial. The principle characters were arrested and convicted for being bystanders who deliberately mocked a man being robbed. They suffered a form of extreme disconnection—a world of farce and fantasy—and at their trial it was shown that their lives were generally characterized by a lack of caring much at all about others or even each other. (Although Kramer once noted to Jerry that if he—Jerry—killed someone, he (Kramer) would "turn him in without hesitation.")

reduce risk of injury), will lead to liability in the event of failure. The seductive option will be the temptation to not engage at all: be careful not to "assume" a duty that you would not otherwise have.

Major problems exist with this approach. First, as is evident even in *Furek*, most college and university administrators are not about to ignore student conduct or activities that invite danger (indifference is both counterintuitive and unlikely given their professional education training and articulated standards and competencies). Following strategies of deliberate indifference is professionally distasteful and disempowering. It makes a career in student affairs like life in a Dilbert cartoon. Indifference is also hard to pull off: the active involvement of student affairs professionals, campus law enforcement officers, and other university administrators in student activities is an inherent feature of the modern college or university. Indeed, engagement is increasingly being mandated by regulators and legislators. Moreover, deliberate indifference increases the chances that student injury will occur and thus enhances the likelihood of a finding of negligence. The best way to defeat a lawsuit is to avoid the injury in the first place. Finally, the strategy is now legally doomed to backfire because the law is much less likely to see a college as a true passive bystander and increasingly sees students and colleges in legally special relationships. Even as some courts cling to bystander ideals, regulators have begun to engineer a vision completely opposite to bystanderism. Bystander positions are not politically viable for a generation of parents and politicians who may expect colleges to use *more* than reasonable care.

As to this latter point, only a small number of college and university programs are so disengaged from student life and activities that they could credibly be seen as having taken no affirmative steps to facilitate the environment in which risk occurs. Certainly, a college that features substantial on-campus housing, student life, and provides a panoply of student services including campus police, medical services, sports and recreation programs, and other co-curricular and extracurricular experiences and events has engaged itself in student life to a point where withdrawal or disengagement from student life and safety issues would be impracticable and unprofessional. It is not the creation of regulations alone that legally engages a college; it is the creation of a guided, facilitated environment that suffuses student/university relationships with a responsibility of reasonable care to guide student growth and development. Indeed, student affairs professionals see their role as student *development*, and thus have an inherent problem with legal rules that encourage disconnection or passivity in student/administrator relationships.

Another example is illustrative. As Arthur Levine and Jeanette Cureton pointed out in 1998 in *When Hope and Fear Collide—A Portrait of Today's Col-*

lege Student,[91] college students like to "party" off campus. In some instances, as in *Baldwin* (the drag race case) or *Guest* (the snowmobile case), activities begin on campus but carry on off campus. Colleges struggle with whether it is preferable to encourage students to stay on campus or to push danger off campus (or *de facto* encourage that state of affairs). *Furek* logic might seem to encourage an administrator to establish *de facto* policies that put college drinking problems in the lap of the greater community. The problem again—at the root of all bystander-style legal solutions—is that the best way to avoid legal liability is not to avoid involvement with others but *to avoid the accidents, however caused, which might give rise to lawsuits.* Community efficacy, not ostrichism, is the winning hand. The best way to proceed with student affairs/campus security is the way that will result in reasonable and tolerable levels of danger. Deliberate indifference results in the worst-case scenario for a college: (1) students are injured, (2) the university may pay damages in a lawsuit, and (3) the university could face potentially humiliating public relations problems. For the modern college, looking the other way regarding off-campus drinking is a dangerous and incongruous option. There may be no simplistic solutions to how to manage college-aged drinking—but this does not mean that there are no reasonable measures to be taken. Deliberate indifference is not a reasonable solution. Ironically, it is by behaving as if duty were owed that a college is best situated to win no-duty arguments in court.

Courts, regulators, and especially parents, are increasingly less likely to view modern universities as true bystanders. The law is more likely to view colleges as co-creators of a campus, and even off-campus, dynamic. The cases that saw the university as a bystander were partially a throwback to the idea of insularity and/or belief in the futility of university control over student behavior, particularly drinking. But modern courts are often less influenced by the "rather myopic view" that "to control" someone always requires custodial control or constraint.[92] As the Ohio Supreme Court stated in a non-university, *Tarasoff*-type case, "the duty to control the conduct of a ... person is commensurate with such ability to control as the defendant actually has at that time.... In other words ... there will be diverse levels of control which give rise to corresponding degrees of responsibility."[93] There is a growing sentiment that universities *have* done

---

91. *See also* Arthur Levine, *When Dreams and Heroes Died* (Jossey-Bass 1980).

92. *See Estates of Morgan v. Fairfield Family Counseling, Ctr.*, 673 N.E.2d 1311, 1323 (Ohio 1997). *Estates of Morgan* was eventually superseded by a statute in Ohio. *See* Ohio Rev. Code Ann. §2305.51 (2008).

93. *Id.* (citations omitted).

things, *can* do things, and *should* do things to prevent unreasonable student injury. Ostrichism is bad policy and increasingly legally suspect. It invites a backlash. Reasonable solutions are not always obvious or easy, but the law in the duty era—an era of accountability—will expect colleges to look for them.

For example, a typical first response to alcohol problems is a campus alcohol ban (whole or partial). This "solution" can cause some students to react with confrontation—riots—and/or avoidance behaviors, including moving off campus.

There are effective, reasonable alternative solutions, however. Student affairs administrators and campus police can confront a small and *recidivist* group of dangerous students who seem to delight in risky rituals and bullying others into problem behavior. A discreet group of very high-risk students takes its toll on administration and the campus itself; they become the source of a disproportionate number of lawsuits, injuries, etc. The larger student population makes its share of mistakes, but not as intensely and not with a focus to draw others down with them. These hard-core students resist prevention strategies. For example, when Greek life is exorcized and campus drinking is curtailed, some individuals will use their "martyrdom" to cajole drinking off campus. They often form quasi-criminal partnerships with less reputable off-campus drinking establishments (who comply with the law less and are notorious places of disorder) and try to set up their own alternative student organizations. They sometimes do this with impunity, and in a strange way the college has unintentionally facilitated them. An important strategy to impact high-risk college drinking is to identify these individuals, disempower them, and separate them from the college environment if necessary. Targeted enforcement and prevention efforts are more subtle ways to control high-risk college drinking. Such efforts would be more effective than, for example, total campus alcohol bans, or lowering the drinking age, especially when used in a scientifically-based environmental management strategy.

This does not mean, of course, that all universities are responsible to operate exactly the same way. Each environment is unique. Courts will look to the unique situation of each college to assess *its* relations with *its* students. Thus, a pure commuter college—offering classes in one building and few student life activities to speak of—will not be similarly situated to a residential college with substantial Greek life. Isolated rural colleges will be different from urban colleges, etc. The ramifications of duty assumed—and the amount of care necessary so as not to be in breach of duty—will necessarily vary from college to college. But, *Furek* and *Mullins* clearly signaled the end of blind judicial acceptance of the notion that there is no legal duty to students to provide a safe learning environment. As students were injured in preventable ways, universities began to lose insularity.

3. Sexual Assault, Duty and Accountability

The spirit of *Furek* has been manifest in cases dealing with a most serious issue on modern campuses—college sexual assault. Reported cases tend to follow the *Mullins/Furek* approach, but courts are clearly vexed by acquaintance rape cases. Regulators, however, recently have been accelerating accountability for sexual assault, potentially going past *Furek* and *Mullins*, and even the standard of reasonable care itself. The recent cases have abandoned almost entirely the notion that someone must be in a custodial relationship with the university as a precondition to university responsibility to prevent this type of harm.

There are five illustrative cases demonstrating how modern courts respond to dangerous persons on campus who sexually assault students—*Johnson v. State of Washington,*[94] *Nero v. Kansas State University,*[95] *Stanton v. University of Maine System,*[96] *L.W. v. Western Golf Association,*[97] *Delta Tau Delta v. Johnson,*[98] and *Freeman v. Busch,*[99] from Washington state, Kansas, Maine, Indiana, and a federal court, respectively.

In *Johnson,* a first-year student was abducted and raped near her dormitory on the campus of Washington State University. The university argued that as a public governmental entity, it was entitled to a form of governmental immunity. Usually, governments are immune from suit by private citizens over the negligent failure to provide *general* police protection.[100] This is known as the "public duty" doctrine, which means that a duty to provide police protection is owed to the public at large, but not to specific members of the public—a misleading position

94. 894 P.2d 1366 (Wash. Ct. App. 1995), *review denied*, 904 P.2d 299 (Wash. 1995).
95. 861 P.2d 768 (Kan. 1993).
96. 773 A.2d 1045 (Me. 2001).
97. 712 N.E.2d 983 (Ind. 1999).
98. 712 N.E.2d 968 (Ind. 1999).
99. 349 F.3d 582 (8th Cir. 2003).
100. Lawyers often associate this rule with *Riss v. City of N.Y.*, 240 N.E.2d 860 (N.Y. 1968), which as such is a majority rule. The *Riss* rule is subject to powerful exceptions, however. Among other exceptions, a duty does attach to a private citizen if the police assume a duty to a particular person or class of persons (as in sending a crossing guard to an elementary school).

because there really is no duty at all (as no citizen can enforce the duty in a court). In essence, the university argued that it had no legal duty whatsoever to protect young women from abduction and rape—a throwback argument harkening to the era of insularity. A trial judge agreed, and dismissed the case.

The Washington appellate court rejected this argument. The *Johnson* court agreed that duty did not arise from notions of *in loco parentis*, or even from the fact that the victim was a student; however, duty *did* arise from the fact that the student was an invitee/tenant of the university. As such, a duty was owed to her, irrespective of the public duty doctrine. The public university could not hide under the cloak of being a government agency or functionary to avoid using reasonable steps to prevent sexual attacks on students. The duty owed to the student was thus similar to that owed at a private school to a student or to any invitee/tenant. If the location of the premises or prior criminal events makes criminal danger foreseeable, the university has a duty to provide reasonable—not all possible—security. *Johnson* adopted the modern rule that a criminal attack or intrusion is not the sole proximate cause of harm. A university landlord can be a (concurring) proximate cause if criminal attack is foreseeable.[101]

Johnson did not say that the university was strictly liable. A jury would have to decide whether unreasonable acts or omissions of the university landlord significantly contributed to or created the opportunity for the assault and whether or not a criminal attack was reasonably foreseeable. The university

---

101. This rule was carefully explained by the New York Court of Appeals (the highest court in New York) in *Nallan v. Helmsley-Spear, Inc.*, 407 N.E.2d 451 (1980), a case arising when a union member was shot in the lobby of the defendant's office building while there to attend a meeting. Citing the *Restatement (Second) of Torts*, § 344, the court observed: "A possessor of land who holds it open to the public . . . is subject to liability . . . for physical harm [to a business visitor] caused by . . . the intentionally harmful acts of third persons [e.g., a criminal] . . . and by the failure of the [landowner] to exercise reasonable care to (a) discover that such acts are being done or [protect them against it]." The court emphasized that the landowner is not liable merely because of the presence of criminal activity. Rather, the victim of an attack must show that crimes on the premises were sufficiently related to the conduct that caused plaintiff's injury to encourage a reasonable landowner to take precautions against future attacks. If the landowner knew or had reason to know of such prior crimes in the building and further found that the landowner should have anticipated a risk of harm from criminal activity in the lobby, it properly could have gone on to conclude that the defendant failed to make the premises safe for the visiting public. The fact that the "instrumentality" of harm was the criminal conduct of a third person does not preclude liability where the criminal activity was itself foreseeable and reasonably preventable. Where that plaintiff can show that the presence of a lobby attendant or security guard would have likely reduced the risk of an attack, the landowner may be held accountable.

certainly could not prevent all attacks and would not be responsible if there were no reasons—apart from general background criminal activity—to suspect and foresee danger to its students.

Johnson represents the application of general business/landlord rules to a university. It is *Mullins* and follows *Kline v. 1500 Massachusetts Ave. Apartment Corporation,*[102] the seminal non-university, *landlord/tenant* duty case. This is no "return" to *in loco parentis*; *Johnson* and other cases are charting a mainstream business tort law path for colleges, rightly or wrongly.

Nero is *Johnson* and *Mullins* with a twist. *Nero* deals with the more legally controversial problem of dangerous sexual predators *who are students* and who attack other students. The problems of dangerous *students* are always at least binary: how to protect other students and how to deal with the problem students themselves. *Nero's* facts presaged recent concerns over the rise of sexual predation on campus.[103] Violence in *general* continues to plague modern higher education. Sadly even violent gangs[104] are already present on some campuses as outsiders and as students and active shooter issues have gained prominence after Virginia Tech. Moreover, some of today's high school students bring drugs, guns, violence, fear, and disorder with them when they come to college as students.

In *Nero,* Kansas State University assigned a male student to a dormitory. One month later that student was accused of raping a resident student. The male student was reassigned by the university to an all-male dormitory and instructed to stay away from certain areas. The academic year came to a close and summer session began. The problem—only one residence hall was available and it was a male/female dormitory. Despite the fact that he had been removed and boundaried and was awaiting criminal trial for sexual battery, the student was given a spot in the summer dormitory, perhaps because of the university's fear of depriving *him* of *his* rights.

Shana Nero, a transfer student from Oklahoma, was also assigned to the summer session dormitory. She was unaware of the presence of a charged felon in the dormitory, and she was not aware of the male student's prior history or status. She was sexually attacked by this male student in the basement televi-

---

102. 439 F.2d 477 (D.C. Cir. 1970). *Kline* ended one aspect of a nasty slumlord era; *Mullins* brought pro-tenant rules to campus.

103. *See, e.g.*, Sara Lipka, *Colleges Face Conflicting Pressures in Dealing with Cases of Sexual Assault*, Chron. Higher Educ. (March 20, 2011), *available at* http://chronicle.com/article/Colleges-Face-Conflicting/126818/.

104. *See Gragg v. Wichita State Univ.*, 934 P.2d 121 (Kan. 1997).

sion room where the two were watching television. It is the type of situation that makes parents sick.

Once again, a trial court—no doubt reading *Bradshaw et al.*—held that no duty was owed to the student by the university. The Kansas Supreme Court could not stomach that result. The *Nero* court reviewed the bystander era cases—including *Bradshaw* and *Baldwin*—and noted that those cases were different. In those cases, *Nero* said, the injured students asked the courts to impose a general obligation on colleges to prohibit underage drinking on and off campus. Like a city police department, there was no general obligation of a college to enforce regulations, although *Nero* did question those cases in light of countervailing authority.

Nero instead looked to *Mullins* and *Furek* for duties regarding student safety. Universities actively manage student housing. Reasonable care is owed to tenants, including, as in *Johnson*, reasonable protection against foreseeable attacks. The duty is not based on *in loco parentis*; students pay for housing just like residential tenants, and do so in a market in which colleges compete against private landlords. The fact that a decision to house a student is "discretionary" does not mean that there are no consequences for a college once assignment is made. The college may have the power to place an alleged rapist in a dormitory, but once they do, they must use reasonable care to protect other students (and that student).

Nero held that the placing of the students in the coed dormitory presented issues of fact for a jury to decide. The jury could consider what the victim knew and whether she was lulled into a false sense of security. The court realized, as *Estates of Morgan* did, that one way to control dangerous students on campus is to give appropriate warnings or information to potential victims so that they can protect themselves.[105] Again, the questions were ones of reasonableness and foreseeability.

---

105. When concern for student peril is evident, common law privacy rules, as well as federal and most state statutes and regulations regarding student records, permit the sharing of information about dangerous behavior between or among institutional officials in the "need to know" chain and/or to protect the health and safety of students and others. Federal privacy law was recently changed to increase the flow of necessary safety information. Family Educational Rights and Privacy Act (FERPA), 20 U.S.C. § 1232g; Peter F. Lake, *Student-Privacy Rules Show A Renewed Trust in Colleges*, Chron. Higher Educ. (Feb. 6, 2009), *available at* http://chronicle.com/article/Student-Privacy-Rules-Show-a/20332. The sharing of information certainly compromises privacy. However, information sharing may be critical to the safety of a student, and is a vital aspect of university responsibility when consistent with case law and legislative protections of privacy.

Two points about *Nero* are worth noting, as it raises important issues about assignments to dorms and even classes and co-curricular activities. These two points revolve around the fact that the attacker was an "alleged" rapist at the time of dormitory assignment and that there was but one summer residence.

First, a potentially dangerous student on campus does have rights, but we must be careful not to overstate these rights. For one thing, removing the male student from housing was not the only option in *Nero,* although it was the best option. Students could have been warned of the presence of a potentially dangerous male student, for example. More importantly, however, denying or terminating student housing is not a matter of high constitutional scrutiny (in contrast to, say, racial classifications) but a matter of ordinary discretion. Certainly, a student is entitled to *some* appropriate process regarding cancellation of his dormitory lease or contract—but there is nothing in the idea of due process that requires *undue* or *too much* process. A student being removed from a dormitory is not being *convicted* of a crime; instead a decision is being made on policy grounds to resolve a lease issue. Such a decision does not require anything like criminal trial in full battle dress. To the contrary, it would be absurd to give that much process. Indeed, to do so pragmatically denies other students *the process they deserve* to protect their safety interests in safe dormitory housing. Too much deference to process "rights" can be as bad as too little—*Nero* is the flip side of cases like *Dixon.*

Second, a college has a legal responsibility to provide a reasonably safe learning environment, and cannot defer all responsibility to others—including the criminal justice system—to deal with violence and sexual assault. In particular, a campus must make its own decision about whether someone belongs in a learning environment irrespective of how they fare in criminal court. Some individuals, like quarterback Ben Roethlisberger, will not be criminally prosecuted for sexual assault; but may have made grave errors transgressing the rules and values of a college and/or may present risk and danger to others in a college setting. Or, a person may be found guilty of a crime—even crimes against children—and present little to no danger to others on campuses. For instance, colleges will see individuals accused of "sexting" minors, perhaps when they were in K–12 themselves. These individuals may well have committed several serious crimes including the distribution and possession of child pornography. Some of these individuals may have made bad decisions with terrible consequences, but not all are predators or pedophiles. In short, the mistake in *Nero* was too much deference to the criminal law system to protect a campus. After *Nero*, it is not reasonable to categorically turn the problems created by crime over to the criminal justice system alone.

The *Stanton* case raises a different, and modern set of issues. Our campuses are flowing with guests, sleepover visitors, summer residents, and even K–12 aged individuals. Sexual predators may actually seek out those who come to campus under special circumstances, and the law recognizes the special need for reasonable care in these circumstances. *Stanton* is that case.[106]

In *Stanton v. University of Maine System*, the plaintiff was taking classes at the university prior to receiving a high school diploma.[107] Stanton attended a pre-season soccer program and stayed in dorms on the campus. She was sexually assaulted in her dorm room after being walked back to her dorm by a young man, her future assailant, whom she met at a party.[108] *Stanton* is an example of all too frequent predatory acquaintance rape on modern college campuses.

Although there had been few rapes reported at that institution, Maine's university system had engaged in significant safety planning for full-time students regarding dorm room security.[109] Importantly however, the plaintiff—a special student—had not received instruction on the rules and regulations regarding safety in the dormitory facilities and there were no signs indicating who should be permitted in and out of the dorms.[110] *Stanton* pointed out that the university, as a premise owner, owed a duty to students as business invitees.[111] There was "a duty to exercise reasonable care in taking such measures as were reasonably necessary for [the plaintiff's] safety in light of all then existing circumstances."[112] The court recognized that under previous decisions a landowner is under no duty to anticipate attacks utterly without warning.[113] Following *Mullins v. Pine Manor College*,[114] however, *Stanton* stated that sexual assault was foreseeable at the university since the university environment

---

106. The discussion of *Stanton* that follows is drawn heavily from Peter F. Lake, *Private Law Continues to Come to Campus*, *supra* note 29.

107. 773 A.2d 1045, 1047–48 (Me. 2001).

108. *Id.*

109. *Id.* at 1048.

110. *Id.*

111. *Id.* at 1049 (citing *Schultz v. Gould Acad.*, 322 A.2d 368, 370 (Me. 1975)).

112. *Id.*

113. *Id.* at 1049 (citing *Brewer v. Roosevelt Motor Lodge*, 295 A.2d 647 (Me. 1972)).

114. The Maine Supreme Judicial Court is a Court whose jurisdiction is intimately connected to the Massachusetts Supreme Judicial Court, which decided *Mullins*. At one time, the Supreme Judicial Court of Massachusetts actually had jurisdiction over much of what is now Maine. The two courts consider each other as sister courts and precedent from one court is often closely followed in the other.

is favorable for crime because of the high concentration of young people, and that the university took notice of this fact by implementing some preventative procedures.[115] On this basis, the plaintiff and the type of injury that occurred, sexual assault, were foreseeable.[116]

Stanton is a unique adaptation of *Mullins* in that it relates to special students who come to campus for particular programs.[117] After *Stanton*, students coming to campus for alternative programs are entitled to the same level of safety training that full-time residential students receive if those students will be exposed to the same types of risks as full-time residential students.[118] Colleges and universities typically provide orientation and safety training to full-time traditional students, but may let certain groups of individuals who come to campus for special programs or overnight stays slip through the cracks. Dangers to atypical students or visitors may be equal to, or even greater than, risks to typical students, since the former are often new to an area and not familiar with specific risks or the best means to protect themselves.

Stanton also illustrates a tragic pattern of sexual predation on modern campuses. The plaintiff/victim was "partying" with an "acquaintance"/future assailant, who lured her away from others, identified her as vulnerable and used a position of trust to invade her room and sexually assault her. Reasonable care in a high-risk sexual culture means that universities must be vigilant to close the gaps in safety prevention efforts that predators might seize upon.

Twin decisions from the Indiana Supreme Court, *L.W. v. Western Golf Association* and *Delta Tau Delta v. Johnson*, are also helpful in understanding responsibility to prevent sexual assault in the duty era.[119] In *L.W.*, a student at Purdue University was raped after returning home from a bar.[120] A fellow tenant of the victim's residence hall raped the victim. The victim was required to live in this building pursuant to a scholarship program. The victim became intoxicated at a bar and was helped back to her room by several individuals. The victim passed out from intoxication. One of the individuals who had helped the victim back from the bar raped the victim while she was unconscious.[121] The facts are strikingly similar to *Stanton*—another tragic acquaintance rape. There

---

115. *Id.* at 1050.

116. *Id.*

117. *Id.* at 1047–48.

118. *Id.* at 1047–51.

119. The following discussion of *L.W.* and *Delta Tau Delta* is drawn heavily from Peter F. Lake, *Private Law Continues to Come to Campus*, *supra* note 29.

120. 712 N.E.2d at 984.

121. *Id.*

had been previous safety issues at the university housing where the victim lived, even an attempted act of violence directed at another female in the same housing unit.[122] *L.W.* however, distinguished the general prior incidents that had occurred from the incident that specifically occurred.[123] Crucially, the student was living in an environment where there had been no rape or serious sexual assault.[124] *L.W.* used the totality of the circumstances test to determine foreseeability for purposes of determining duty.[125] Although the totality of the circumstances test does not require an identical or similar incident to the tort in question for finding foreseeability, *L.W.* found that while the housing situation was "childish" and "deplorable at times," there was insufficient evidence of prior dangerous activity for the rape to be foreseeable.[126]

In *Delta Tau Delta*, however, the Indiana Supreme Court recognized that there *were* sufficiently similar prior incidents of sexual misconduct to support foreseeability as an aspect of legal duty owed to a student.[127] In *Delta Tau Delta*, the victim brought suit against local and national offices of a fraternity arising out of a sexual assault at a fraternity house. The victim attended a party at a fraternity house where she met up with an alum of the fraternity. Near the conclusion of the party, the victim sought a ride home, and the alum offered the victim a ride after he "sobered up." The two went to a separate room within the fraternity house to wait for the alumnus to regain his sobriety, and during this time, the alumnus locked the victim into the room and sexually assaulted her. Applying a totality of the circumstances test, the court found that the victim's assault was foreseeable because of prior instances of sexual assault within the defendant fraternity's house.[128] These two cases show that there are sometimes insufficient predicate facts to create a legal duty to a tenant or business invitee. And, duty does not necessarily mean liability. Universities do not insure student safety and duty may turn on sufficient indicia of prior criminality.

Several points are worth noting. First, duty and hence a responsibility to use reasonable care, are often building or area-specific questions in courts of law. The law of negligence focuses on *locations*, not campuses, *per se*. The implicit message is that responsibility follows risk; many portions of campus may

122. *Id.* at 985.
123. *Id.*
124. *Id.*
125. *Id.* at 984–85.
126. *Id.* at 985.
127. 712 N.E.2d at 973–74.
128. *Id.* at 970–73.

require little to no care, but some areas may need heavy and constant attention. Second, predatory violence—involving sexual violence—looks for soft targets and tests safety systems (including those students devise for themselves) for weaknesses. Third, alcohol is a critical factor in sexual assault, and sexual predators use high-risk alcohol culture as a weapon against victims (and sometimes use other drugs as well). Fourth, the case law vividly illustrates the challenges of sexual predation and acquaintance rape on campus brought forth in Professor David Lisak's pioneering work in the field.[129] Modern sexual predators are numerous and often use subtle tactics (instead of hiding in bushes waiting to ambush strangers). Sadly, many predators methodically target victims. There truly are vampires on campus—and they are not like the Cullens in *Twilight*.[130] Finally, even if a college bears some responsibility for a sexual assault, the victim clearly bears the brunt of the event. Indeed, many victims simply leave higher education—their lives shattered. The need for violence prevention efforts[131] and victim efficacy are paramount: we need to stop the sexual predation epidemic in its tracks. We cannot focus all of our efforts on allocating responsibility after the fact. The facilitator university described in the next chapter is deeply motivated by the gravitas of college sexual predation and searches for ways to help potential victims and prevent victimization. Duty, prevention, and risk management are kindred spirits and no discussion by a facilitator of one can ignore the others.[132]

One of the most interesting cases is also one of the most difficult to understand—*Freeman v. Busch*.[133]

---

129. Lisak has authored and gathered numerous articles and pieces. *See, e.g.*, David Lisak & Paul M. Miller, *Repeat Rape and Multiple Offending Among Undetected Rapists*, 17 Violence and Victims 73 (2002).

130. *See Twilight* (Summit Entertainment 2008).

131. For an excellent environmental/public health manual *see, e.g.*, Linda Langford, *Preventing Violence and Promoting Safety in Higher Education Settings: Overview of a Comprehensive Approach*, http://searchpubs.higheredcenter.org/files/product/violence.pdf (last visited June 16, 2011).

132. There are no rights in tort law to good prevention efforts or risk management, *per se*. However, what is reasonable under the circumstance often is good prevention or risk management. Good prevention and risk management efforts can reduce the injuries that generate lawsuits. Facilitator universities, however, are cautious about using prevention/risk management simply for the sake of litigation risk reduction. That can be fool's gold.

133. The following discussion of *Freeman* is adapted heavily from Peter F. Lake, *Private Law Continues to Come to Campus*, *supra* note 29.

In *Freeman*, a sexual assault arose once again out of a college party.[134] The victim was invited to a party at the dorm room of her attacker, became drunk, blacked out, and while unconscious was sexually assaulted.[135]

The victim sued under an unusual theory that the college was responsible under the doctrine of *respondeat superior*[136] for the negligent failure of the resident assistant to prevent the assault.[137] Most of the represented cases against colleges are direct actions against colleges for negligent security, etc. *Freeman* is somewhat unusual in that it is a pin-the-tail on a resident assistant case.

The evidence linking the resident assistant to the incident was relatively thin. Sometime after the victim had passed out from alcohol intoxication, the attacker went downstairs and informed the resident assistant that the attacker had a visitor (the victim) who had consumed alcohol, thrown up, and passed out.[138] The resident assistant informed the attacker to monitor the victim's condition and to report back if things took a turn for the worse.[139] The victim and attacker then had sex.[140] They later disagreed as to whether the sex was consensual.[141] The victim asserted that no consent had been, nor could have been, given due to her unconscious state, while the attacker alleged that the sex had been consensual.[142] After the disputed sexual encounter, two other students returned from a fraternity party and both of them were permitted by the attacker to engage in impermissible touching of the victim.[143]

Freeman declined to hold that there was a special relationship between the resident assistant and the plaintiff-student.[144] *Freeman* correctly stated that there was no special relationship between the resident assistant and the victim (a student) arising simply out of the college-student relationship,[145] *Freeman* reasoned that since there was no special relationship between Freeman and the resident assistant the general rule of section 314A of the *Restatement (Second)*

134. 349 F.3d at 585.

135. *Id.*

136. Under which negligent acts of employees are imputed to employers.

137. *Id.* at 586–87.

138. *Id.* at 585.

139. *Id.*

140. *Id.*

141. *Id.*

142. *Id.*

143. *Id.*

144. *Id.* at 589.

145. *See also Garofalo v. Lambda Chi Alpha Fraternity*, 616 N.W.2d 647, 655–56 (Iowa 2000) (holding that fraternity membership does not create a special relationship).

of Torts applies: generally the mere fact that a party is aware of danger to others does not create a duty to assist.[146] (However, while the resident assistant was not the landlord, the resident assistant was an *agent* of the landlord—the institution.[147] A landlord-tenant relationship creates a special relationship,[148] and this should have been sufficient to create a relationship, or at least with the college, in this case. *Freeman* passed over the landowner and landlord-tenant special relationship issues in the case, summarily dismissing this issue in a conclusory footnote. It would have helped immensely to have heard more from the court on these issues as future readers of *Freeman* may too easily attribute the no-special-relationship reasoning in the case and read past the footnote.)

The *Freeman* court also considered whether the resident assistant had assumed a legal duty to come to the victim's aid under section 324 of the *Restatement (Second) of Torts*.[149] The court held that "a finding that [the residential assistant] 'took charge of' [the victim] requires that he took specific action to exercise control or custody over her."[150] The resident assistant was informed that "[Freeman] had consumed a substantial quantity of alcohol; and that after consuming it, she had thrown up and passed out."[151] The court was not willing to interpret the resident assistant's decision to ask another to monitor and report as a form of taking charge or control of the victim.[152] *Freeman* did not feel that there was enough evidence to find that the resident assistant had "exercise[d] control or custody over Freeman."[153]

It may be that *Freeman* is nothing more than a no-breach-of-duty case lurking as a "no-duty" case. The result in *Freeman* is defensible even if some of the analysis is doctrinally suspect; merely notifying a resident assistant that someone is drunk does not itself alert the resident assistant that a rape is legally foreseeable. On these facts, many juries would likely agree that the resident assistant's con-

---

146. *Restatement (Second) of Torts* § 314A (1965).

147. *Freeman*, 349 F.3d at 586–87.

148. *See Restatement (Second) of Torts* § 314a (1965) (imposing a duty upon the one who voluntarily takes custody of another such that it deprives the individual in custody the opportunity to defend himself). It is unclear from the reported decision whether the landlord/tenant issue was properly raised fully or resolved in any proceeding. *See Freeman*, 349 F.3d 582.

149. *Id.* at 588.

150. *Id.* (citing *Restatement (Second) of Torts* § 324 (1965)).

151. *Id.* at 589.

152. *Id.*

153. *Id.* at 588–89.

duct was not unreasonable. This situation is tragically typical. Students who are drunk but do not need medical transport are often remanded to the care of friends, fellow students, and resident assistants. There are few drunk tanks on college campuses. Resident assistants are the first lieutenants in the college alcohol/sexual predation wars and have become the preferred solution to the problem of what to do with thousands of significantly intoxicated students who are easy targets of abuse and a danger to themselves and others. Resident assistants are often overworked, under-trained and under-equipped. *Freeman* may have recognized (rightly or wrongly) that coping with high-risk alcohol culture triage requires a lower amount of care owed, at least from the point of view of a resident assistant.

It may also be that *Freeman* is yet another example of how federal courts do not want to exercise federal court jurisdiction over student injury cases arising from voluntary student alcohol consumption. There is evidence of this in *Freeman's* heavy reliance on *Bradshaw*, and its minimization of more modern and contrary cases. *Freeman* may also be nothing more than a slender doctrinal reed: its "holding" is technically limited to the very narrow question of whether a resident assistant—who is not the landowner, landlord, or the college itself—has a special relationship with students (although the court seemed to confuse/conflate the issues at times). As such, the case is potentially distinguishable from *Mullins*, *Stanton* et al. because in those cases the college is the direct defendant and a landowner/landlord (not by virtue of employment law rules). It may also be that the court simply confounded itself in hyper-technical reasoning about special relationships. At times *Freeman* seems confused about whether it was analyzing the resident assistant/student special relationship issue *or* whether it was considering the related question of the special relationships between *colleges* and students. (It is an easy thing to mix up in a *respondeat superior* case—trust me, I grade papers on this all the time and it is conceptually very tricky.) It may also be that *Freeman* recognized that in the criminal justice system acquaintance rape cases are almost never prosecuted. *Freeman* may have felt is an unreasonable burden to ask colleges to sort out acquaintance rape cases when the criminal justice system fails to do so effectively.

Freeman is a tough case—a close case—in the duty era. *Freeman* is made that much more interesting by the fact that regulators have staked out a different set of standards for colleges in these instances. *Freeman* may or may not be an ideal explication of tort law. But that may be moot. Administrators may have no freedom to follow the guidance of cases like *Freeman* in light of recent federal regulatory changes.

College safety law traditionally has been almost sole province of the courts—particularly state courts deciding cases under state law. In the last decade or so this has changed, particularly with respect to sexual assault and post-Virginia Tech active shooter prevention and safety law.

In April 2011, Vice President Joseph Biden and Education Secretary Arne Duncan announced a new set of "guidelines" relating to federal sex discrimination law (Title IX) and sexual assault. The Department of Education's Office for Civil Rights issued a "Dear Colleague Letter" on April 4, 2011,[154] and Vice President Biden made the following landmark statement in connection with the rollout of the new Title IX guidelines set forth in that letter: "Students across the country deserve the safest possible environment in which to learn. That's why we're taking new steps to . . . end the cycle of sexual violence on campus."[155] This may well be the first time that public officials have stated a specific aspiration to create and enforce a standard of care higher than reasonable care. Compliance with the new Title IX guidelines will be demanding. Even if *Freeman* remains valid negligence law, a campus would not be allowed to be a "bystander" to acquaintance rape in its residence halls in situations like *Freeman* under Title IX. Colleges must now have significant procedures in place to punish such sexual assault or face serious fines and even the loss of federal funding—in other words institutional death. State tort law no longer dominates legal compliance relating to sexual assault.

In the April 4, 2011, "Dear Colleague Letter," Assistant Secretary for Civil Rights, Russlyn Ali stated the following:

> Education has long been recognized as the great equalizer in America. The U.S. Department of Education and its Office for Civil Rights (OCR) believe that providing all students with an educational environment free from discrimination is extremely important. The sexual harassment of students, including sexual violence, interferes with students' right to receive an education free from discrimination and, in the case of sexual violence, is a crime.
>
> Title IX of the Education Amendments of 1972 (Title IX), 20 U.S.C. §§ 1681 *et seq.*, and its implementing regulations, 34 C.F.R. Part 106, prohibit discrimination on the basis of sex in education programs or activities operated by recipients of Federal financial assistance. Sexual harassment of students, which includes acts of sexual violence, is a

154. Office for Civil Rights, *Dear Colleague Letter* (Apr. 4, 2011), *available at* http://www2.ed.gov/about/offices/list/ocr/letters/colleague-201104.pdf.

155. *See* Lauren Sieben, *Education Dept. Issues New Guidelines for Sexual Assault Investigations*, Chron. Higher Educ. (Apr. 4, 2011), *available at* http://chronicle.com/article/EducationDept-Issues-New/127004/ (emphasis added).

form of sex discrimination prohibited by Title IX. In order to assist recipients, which include school districts, colleges, and universities (hereinafter "schools" or "recipients") in meeting these obligations, this letter explains that the requirements of Title IX pertaining to sexual harassment also cover sexual violence, and lays out the specific Title IX requirements applicable to sexual violence. Sexual violence, as that term is used in this letter, refers to physical sexual acts perpetrated against a person's will or where a person is incapable of giving consent due to the victim's use of drugs or alcohol. An individual also may be unable to give consent due to an intellectual or other disability. A number of different acts fall into the category of sexual violence, including rape, sexual assault, sexual battery, and sexual coercion. All such acts of sexual violence are forms of sexual harassment covered under Title IX.

The statistics on sexual violence are both deeply troubling and a call to action for the nation. A report prepared for National Institute of Justice found that about 1 in 5 women are victims of completed or attempted sexual assault while in college. The report also found that approximately 6.1 percent of males were victims of completed or attempted sexual assault during college. According to data collected under the Jeanne Clery Disclosure of Campus Security and Campus Crime Statistics Act (Clery Act), 20 U.S.C. § 1092(f), in 2009, college campuses reported nearly 3,300 forcible sex offenses as defined by the Clery Act. This problem is not limited to college. During the 2007–2008 school year, there were 800 reported incidents of rape and attempted rape and 3,800 reported incidents of other sexual batteries at public high schools. Additionally, the likelihood that a woman with intellectual disabilities will be sexually assaulted is estimated to be significantly higher than the general population. The Department is deeply concerned about this problem and is *committed to ensuring that all students feel safe* in their school, so that they have the opportunity to benefit fully from the school's programs and activities.

. . . .

Sexual harassment is unwelcome conduct of a sexual nature. It includes unwelcome sexual advances, requests for sexual favors, and other verbal, nonverbal, or physical conduct of a sexual nature. Sexual violence is a form of sexual harassment prohibited by Title IX.[156]

---

156. *Dear Colleague Letter, supra* note 154, at 1–3 (footnotes omitted) (emphasis added).

Note that this letter states an aspiration to make students "feel safe"—a standard not typically connected to the negligence-based reasonable care standard. Presumably, colleges might need to do many things to create a greater sense of safety.

Compliance under a tort-based negligence standard is likely *less* demanding (and certainly not as specific) than under the new guidelines. The April 4 guidance letter states a number of broad compliance directives including the following:

> [I]f a school determines that sexual harassment that creates a hostile environment has occurred, it must take immediate action to eliminate the hostile environment, prevent its recurrence, and address its effects. In addition to counseling or taking disciplinary action against the harasser, effective corrective action may require remedies for the complainant, as well as changes to the school's overall services or policies. Examples of these actions are discussed in greater detail below.
>
> Title IX requires a school to take steps to protect the complainant as necessary, including taking interim steps before the final outcome of the investigation. The school should undertake these steps promptly once it has notice of a sexual harassment or violence allegation. The school should notify the complainant of his or her options to avoid contact with the alleged perpetrator and allow students to change academic or living situations as appropriate. For instance, the school may prohibit the alleged perpetrator from having any contact with the complainant pending the results of the school's investigation. When taking steps to separate the complainant and alleged perpetrator, a school should minimize the burden on the complainant, and thus should not, as a matter of course, remove complainants from classes or housing while allowing alleged perpetrators to remain. In addition, schools should ensure that complainants are aware of their Title IX rights and any available resources, such as counseling, health, and mental health services, and their right to file a complaint with local law enforcement.
>
> Schools should be aware that complaints of sexual harassment or violence might be followed by retaliation by the alleged perpetrator or his or her associates. For instance, friends of the alleged perpetrator may subject the complainant to name-calling and taunting. As part of their Title IX obligations, schools must have policies and procedures in place to protect against retaliatory harassment. At a mini-

> mum, schools must ensure that complainants and their parents, if appropriate, know how to report any subsequent problems, and should follow-up with complainants to determine whether any retaliation or new incidents of harassment have occurred.
>
> When OCR finds that a school has not taken prompt and effective steps to respond to sexual harassment or violence, OCR will seek appropriate remedies for both the complainant and the broader student population. When conducting Title IX enforcement activities, OCR seeks to obtain voluntary compliance from recipients. When a recipient does not come into compliance voluntarily, OCR may initiate proceedings to withdraw Federal funding by the Department or refer the case to the U.S. Department of Justice for litigation.[157]

The April 4 guidance letter sets forth these broad mandates and then goes on to provide a lengthy list of specific potential remedies—a non-exhaustive list—that colleges should consider: these are in addition to procedural safeguards outlined in the letter.[158] Colleges have been frustrated with the non-

---

157. *Id.* at 15–16.

158. *Id.* at 16–19. As the April 4 letter states:

> Schools should proactively consider the following remedies when determining how to respond to sexual harassment or violence. These are the same types of remedies that OCR would seek in its cases.
>
> Depending on the specific nature of the problem, remedies for the complainant might include, but are not limited to:
>
> - providing an escort to ensure that the complainant can move safely between classes and activities;
> - ensuring that the complainant and alleged perpetrator do not attend the same classes;
> - moving the complainant or alleged perpetrator to a different residence hall or, in the case of an elementary or secondary school student, to another school within the district;
> - providing counseling services;
> - providing medical services;
> - providing academic support services, such as tutoring;
> - arranging for the complainant to re-take a course or withdraw from a class without penalty, including ensuring that any changes do not adversely affect the complainant's academic record; and
> - reviewing any disciplinary actions taken against the complainant to see if there is a causal connection between the harassment and the misconduct that may have resulted in the complainant being disciplined.

Remedies for the broader student population might include, but are not limited

specific compliance mandates of state courts demanding "reasonable care." In some ways the new regulatory guidance is exactly the opposite—it sets out what in many situations would be more than what reasonable care would demand in court and does so with a massive list of specific compliance requirements.

A few final observations are in order. First, the Department of Education showed it means business. The Department of Education has investigated schools

---

to:

Counseling and Training

- offering counseling, health, mental health, or other holistic and comprehensive victim services to all students affected by sexual harassment or sexual violence, and notifying students of campus and community counseling, health, mental health, and other student services;
- designating an individual from the school's counseling center to be "on call" to assist victims of sexual harassment or violence whenever needed;
- training the Title IX coordinator and any other employees who are involved in processing, investigating, or resolving complaints of sexual harassment or sexual violence, including providing training on:
    - the school's Title IX responsibilities to address allegations of sexual harassment or violence
    - how to conduct Title IX investigations
    - information on the link between alcohol and drug abuse and sexual harassment or violence and best practices to address that link;
- training all school law enforcement unit personnel on the school's Title IX responsibilities and handling of sexual harassment or violence complaints;
- training all employees who interact with students regularly on recognizing and appropriately addressing allegations of sexual harassment or violence under Title IX; and
- informing students of their options to notify proper law enforcement authorities, including school and local police, and the option to be assisted by school employees in notifying those authorities.

Development of Materials and Implementation of Policies and Procedures

- developing materials on sexual harassment and violence, which should be distributed to students during orientation and upon receipt of complaints, as well as widely posted throughout school buildings and residence halls, and which should include:
    - what constitutes sexual harassment or violence
    - what to do if a student has been the victim of sexual harassment or violence
    - contact information for counseling and victim services on and off school grounds
    - how to file a complaint with the school

  - how to contact the school's Title IX coordinator
  - what the school will do to respond to allegations of sexual harassment or violence, including the interim measures that can be taken
- requiring the Title IX coordinator to communicate regularly with the school's law enforcement unit investigating cases and to provide information to law enforcement unit personnel regarding Title IX requirements;
- requiring the Title IX coordinator to review all evidence in a sexual harassment or sexual violence case brought before the school's disciplinary committee to determine whether the complainant is entitled to a remedy under Title IX that was not available through the disciplinary committee;
- requiring the school to create a committee of students and school officials to identify strategies for ensuring that students:
  - know the school's prohibition against sex discrimination, including sexual harassment and violence
  - recognize sex discrimination, sexual harassment, and sexual violence when they occur
  - understand how and to whom to report any incidents
  - know the connection between alcohol and drug abuse and sexual harassment or violence
  - feel comfortable that school officials will respond promptly and equitably to reports of sexual harassment or violence;
- issuing new policy statements or other steps that clearly communicate that the school does not tolerate sexual harassment and violence and will respond to any incidents and to any student who reports such incidents; and
- revising grievance procedures used to handle sexual harassment and violence complaints to ensure that they are prompt and equitable, as required by Title IX.

School Investigations and Reports to OCR

- conducting periodic assessments of student activities to ensure that the practices and behavior of students do not violate the school's policies against sexual harassment and violence;
- investigating whether any other students also may have been subjected to sexual harassment or violence;
- investigating whether school employees with knowledge of allegations of sexual harassment or violence failed to carry out their duties in responding to those allegations;
- conducting, in conjunction with student leaders, a school or campus "climate check" to assess the effectiveness of efforts to ensure that the school is free from sexual harassment and violence, and using the resulting information to inform future proactive steps that will be taken by the school; and
- submitting to OCR copies of all grievances filed by students alleging sexual harassment or violence and providing OCR with documentation related to the investigation of each complaint, such as witness interviews, investigator notes, evidence submitted by the parties, investigative reports and summaries, any final disposition letters, disciplinary records, and documentation regarding any appeals. *Id.*

for Title IX violations recently.[159] Second, the April 4 guidelines are not set in stone—they may exceed the Department of Education's statutory authority; and the Supreme Court, which has charted a different path for Title IX *private* lawsuits, may not agree with the Department of Education's view of Title IX. Future political and legal battles loom—over due process rights of accused students; contract rights; and freedom of speech, privacy, and association. Third, many years of litigating over "bystander" principles may have cost higher education in the political arena, and with regulators. At least insofar as sexual assault regulation (and active shooter risk to be discussed shortly) is concerned, "bystander" principles are dead, and cases like *Rabel* and *Freeman* are not congruent with public or regulatory expectations of providing a safe environment. A long history of resisting the standards of reasonable care may have released an enormous wave of accountability—focused potential energy. Higher education now faces a battleground that would have been unthinkable in the 1970s—the very real possibility of heavy regulations under compliance standards far more demanding than reasonable care. The facts of *Tarasoff*, *Nero*, *Stanton*, and *Mullins*, if reported today would almost certainly draw the ire of the Department of Education. It's not hard to speculate that each of these cases, if presented today, would provoke major disapprobation from the Department of Education.

159. *See, e.g.*, Elyse Ashburn, *Education Dept. Tells 2 Colleges to Revamp Sexual-Harassment Policies*, Chron. of Higher Educ. (Dec. 10, 2010), *available at* http://chronicle.com/article/Education-Dept-Tells-2/125704/. A great deal of attention was focused on the Dept. of Education investigation of Yale University. *See, e.g.*, Jordi Gasso, *Yale Not Alone in Title IX Probe*, Yale Daily News (Apr. 15, 2011), *available at* http://www.yaledailynews.com/news/2011/apr/15/yale-not-alone-in-title-ix-probe/; Caroline Tan, *UP CLOSE: Title IX, One Year Later*, Yale Daily News (Apr. 9, 2012), *available at* http://www.yaledailynews.com/news/2012/apr/09/up-close-title-ix-one-year-later/. Just as this book was heading to publication, the Dept. of Education announced its favorable resolution of its investigation of Yale University. *See* Gavan Gideon & Caroline Tan, *Department of Education Ends Title IX Investigation*, Yale Daily News (June 15, 2012), *available at* http://www.yaledailynews.com/news/2012/jun/15/department-education-ends-title-ix-investigation/; U.S. Department of Education Office for Civil Rights, Region 1, *Resolution Letter to Yale University* (June 15, 2012), *available at* http://www2.ed.gov/documents/press-releases/yale-letter.pdf; and *Voluntary Resolution Agreement for Yale University* (signed June 11, 2012), *available at* http://www2.ed.gov/documents/press-releases/yale-agreement.pdf. The resolution letter and voluntary agreement will likely serve as a template for a compliance blueprint for other institutions of higher education in the future.

4. Active Shooter Prevention/Virginia Tech

Until April 2007, most lawyers, campus police, and administrators did not think of mass violence on a college campus as a separate issue from dangerous person issues as such events are exceedingly rare. The vast majority of highly violent criminality experienced on campus is either relational (think *Tarasoff*), spontaneous (violent altercations), targeted hate crimes and/or related to other crime (think robbery, arson, drug crimes, rape).[160]

Efforts to respond to mass violence events like those at Virginia Tech in April 2007 have not been directed significantly by negligence-based case law addressing the specific issue of mass violence. As we have seen, guiding case law can take years (even decades) to develop sufficiently to give meaningful guidance.[161] Although general principles of negligence law are helpful in formulating compliance responses, the incident at Virginia Tech illustrated a critical weakness when relying upon the courts alone to allocate safety rights and responsibilities—timeliness and comprehensiveness of necessary legal guidance may be lacking.[162] The limits of the duty era have begun to appear in the new millennium. Risk is evolving faster than the court system can manage on its own.

The aftermath of the events at Virginia Tech have highlighted several major points for the modern university.

First, state and federal regulatory systems largely had been content once to defer the development of college safety law to the courts. Virginia Tech awakened sleeping safety law giants—legislators and regulators. The Clery Act,[163] which

---

160. *See* Gene Deisinger, Marisa Randazzo, Daniel O'Neill & Jenna Savage, *The Handbook for Campus Threat Assessment & Management Teams* 9–10 (Applied Risk Management 2008).

161. For instance, at the time of the publication of this book, some matters involving Virginia Tech were still outstanding although some cases had been settled. *See Judge Overturns Findings and Fines Against Virginia Tech Under Clery Act*, Chron. of Higher Educ. (Mar. 30, 2012), http://chronicle.com/blogs/ticker/education-department-judge-overturns-findings-and-fines-against-virginia-tech-under-clery-act/41849; *Secretary Duncan Will Have Final Word on Virginia Tech*, Chron. Higher Educ. (May 6, 2012), http://chronicle.com/blogs/ticker/secretary-duncan-will-have-final-word-on-virginia-tech/43080; *Judge Upholds Negligence Verdict from Va. Tech Shootings but Reduces Damages*, Chron. of Higher Educ. (June 20, 2012), http://chronicle.com/blogs/ticker/judge-upholds-negligence-verdict-from-va-tech-shootings-but-reduces-damages/44651. Outstanding litigation from the 2007 shootings at Virginia Tech might take years to resolve.

162. The same issue arose in the civil rights era. Courts could only do so much so fast without sweeping civil rights and regulatory legislation enforcement.

163. Jeanne Clery Disclosure of Campus Security Policy and Campus Crime Statistics Act (Clery Act) 20 U.S.C. § 1092(f).

began as a campus crime reporting act, has been evolving steadily to become an omnibus campus crime/safety bill. After Virginia Tech the Clery Act was amended to include timely notification requirements relating to active shooter events, *inter alia*.[164] The Department of Education has even enforced these new rules—controversially—against Virginia Tech in relation to the events on April 16, 2007.[165] These rules, and related enforcement efforts may well signal that higher education has responsibilities in excess of reasonable care: certainly the articulated standards are not equivalent to the reasonable care standard.[166] The reasonable care standard is a different kind of legal compliance mandate. Some states like Virginia have mandated some threat intervention practices[167] and there have been state legislative initiatives including those related to gun possession on campus.[168] A new age of debate about campus safety has emerged and moved well beyond the courtroom. This is a trend that promises to continue. For now, state negligence law continues to dominate the college safety landscape. Will it continue to do so into the future?

Second, the "law" of student safety has been influenced (more than any time since Kent State) by state and federal investigative reports.[169] Such reports do not have the force of law like a statute, regulation, or court decision. They are the "softer side of Sears" so to speak, in the law. However, the impact of investigative reports is significant, and provides guidance—even if controversial—to campuses. Investigative reports sometimes become the basis for "harder" forms of law. There is a noticeable lack of "bystander" rhetoric in recent investigative reports; the message is one of engagement and responsibility (perhaps even beyond what is reasonable, or even realistic) not disengagement. Bystander imagery is fading in the courts, but clearly has not been an animating force in recent campus safety regulation or in investigative reports. Of course, political winds can change, but these are rea-

---

164. *See id.*

165. *See* Terry W. Hartle, *A Federal Outrage Against Virginia Tech*, Chron. Higher Educ. (April 10, 2011), *available at* http://chronicle.com/article/A-Federal-Outrage-Against/127055/.

166. See *id.*

167. *See* J.J. Hermes, *Virginia's Governor Signs Laws Responding to Shootings at Virginia Tech*, Chron. Higher Educ. (April 10, 2008), *available at* http://chronicle.com/article/New-Virginia-Laws-Respond-to/675.

168. *See* Sara Lipka, *Allowing More Guns on Campuses is a Bad Idea, Administrators Argue*, Chron. Higher Educ. (Feb. 19, 2008), *available at* http://chronicle.com/article/More-Guns-Wont-Make-Campuses/519.

169. *See* Deisinger et al., *supra* note 160, at 162–64.

sons to believe (explained in the next chapter) that the current vectors away from bystandardism—and even the reasonable care standard—may accelerate.

Third, events at Virginia Tech spurred a remarkable surge in college self-regulation in advance of clear legal mandates. Since 2007 campuses around the country have formed campus threat assessment and case management teams (with different names, missions, composition, authority, etc.),[170] for instance. In most states there is no specific legal mandate requiring such efforts—although these efforts may be compliance efforts in accord with the reasonable care negligence standard. (As we have seen, however, the reasonable care standard is not a specific mandate and does not specifically mandate compliance maneuvers such as "have a threat assessment team.") Colleges have shown an increasing willingness to engage in proactive efforts in advance of legal mandates—even if nudged by softer forms of law and political pressure to do so.

Fourth, "timely" warning and emergency response/warning systems have become imperative. Primary *legal* focus on timely warnings and emergency notification systems have been dominated in recent times by Clery Act compliance issues.[171] Compliance with federal law in particular is complicated and colleges face serious consequences for non-compliance. Fines leveled against Virginia Tech and others in 2011 demonstrate an ever more aggressive approach to enforcement by federal regulators. Clery Act compliance is not the only issue raised however. Colleges continue to have negligence law responsibilities to warn and respond to crime as well.

Fifth, events at Virginia Tech in April 2007 and the reports that followed drew national attention to issues of information collection, collation and synthesis, and the disturbing issue of information "silo-ing" in colleges. Higher education institutions historically were not designed for rapid information management—especially safety information—and several features of college

170. *See, e.g.*, Deisinger et al., *supra* note 160; Alyssa Keehan, *Threat Assessment Teams for Troubled Students—Putting the Pieces Together* (Risk Management Counsel, United Educators 2009); Higher Education Mental Health Alliance (HEMHA) and The Jed Foundation, *Balancing Safety and Support on Campus: A Guide for Campus Teams* (2012), *available at* http://www.jedfoundation.org/campus_teams_guide.pdf.

171. For helpful resources on Clery Act compliance, *see* Security on Campus at http://www.securityoncampus.org, and The International Association of Campus Law Enforcement Administrators (IACLEA) at http://www.IACLEA.org.

safety law actually slowed the development of safety information management. First, adherence to "bystander" concepts encouraged poor information collection and synthesis, and discouraged proactive interventions to prevent risk. The fear of "assuming duties" and gathering information that would be a predicate for "foreseeability" (and hence duty) stymied campus administrators in efforts to parent and manage risk. The bystander era contributed to a regulatory backlash—as the public has become more concerned with issues of mass violence and sexual assault on campus. Ostrichism—an artifact of the bystander era in part—is a legal dinosaur and contributes to silo-ing of information. Second, the law relating to information "intake" into higher education has been developmentally delayed by several forces. For one, higher education has not been placed under typical employment/business rules like negligent hiring vis-a-vis admission (an analogy to hiring). On the other hand, pressures on access to higher education—and a strong "second chance" mentality—has fueled an "Etch-A-Sketch" culture in admissions in which colleges seek to break the information links between high school and college. Individuals who have serious issues in their K-12 records have found homes in higher education—often taking advantage of "open enrollment" institutions or "second chance" programs. Moreover, consider the difficult problems associated with identifying those students who are "dangerous," particularly in light of prior or alleged criminality. A sizeable number of students have vehicular tickets, DUIs, petty theft, drug possession, vandalism, etc. (Serious crimes of violence are much less common.) Colleges have *some* criminal history information about students but certainly not all. There is a tremendous amount of potentially helpful information in many students' K-12 records. However, admissions committees do not ask for or receive all of this information, and even if they did, there are relatively few administrators who would know how to read and translate the information.

How are colleges to comply with the law of negligence, apart from state and federal regulations? The prime reasonable care directive, if there is one in negligence law, is to look for *similar* criminal behavior that would alert a reasonable person to further danger of *that* kind. This means that students who have been caught speeding or shoplifting prior to college may pose little threat of violence on campus. Students with multiple alcohol, drug, and especially violence conviction charges, however, are potentially greater problems. Reasonable colleges look for trends and patterns, and vectoring of risk.

Colleges should be most concerned about serious physical violence on campus (a shoplifter might steal a ring from the bookstore; a speeder might hit a student's car in a parking lot) and respond to that. The reality is that very few students will present foreseeable risks of great physical violence. And, for reasons discussed below, the few who are at serious risk of being violent may not be detected in criminal background checks, especially if they are of traditional college age (as college populations continue to shift to older learners and individuals who have served in the military this will change somewhat).

Nonetheless, courts have not made the seemingly obvious leap from negligent *hiring* cases in employment law to negligent *admissions* in higher education. (Nor have they rushed to create negligent supervision, retention, or training claims either—except when a student is an employee and someone is injured in relation to that employment.) Why?

First, education is not employment. Second, courts have hesitated to interfere with academic prerogatives and freedom, especially "whom to teach." Third, courts historically have not viewed problems of "negligent admission" as significant safety issues—unlike in employment (keep in mind that many negligent hiring cases are not about prior criminality but the ability to perform the job—at physical risks to others). The widespread perception that college students are at risk from criminals *within* college is a post-*Mullins* phenomenon, and has accelerated after Virginia Tech. Fourth, courts are also confined by open/special admission legislative mandates—that would countervail the common law. A court cannot tell a college that it was negligent to admit a student that lawmakers have determined a college must admit.

A leading case from a previous generation (1987), *Eiseman v. State of New York*,[172] is illustrative of this latter fourth point. In that case a former convict (of serious crimes of violence and drugs) was enrolled at a special New York college program for the disadvantaged, where he raped and murdered a fellow student. The university was not held liable. The New York Court of Appeals held that the state's interest in reintegrating a former convict into society—allowing him to enroll and reside in the university community—could outweigh the state's general interest in student safety. *Eiseman* is emblematic of a period in criminal rehabilitation theory, during which society was more likely to accept dangerous offenders into higher education. Transition to college was thought of as a fresh start. Times have changed. It seems less and less likely the law will chart on an *Eiseman* path.

---

172. 511 N.E.2d 1128 (N.Y. 1987).

One area of recent discussion with respect to the reasonable care standard is criminal background checks.[173] Criminal background checks can be useful in identifying *some* past criminality that is relevant, but there are drawbacks. First, traditional-aged college students often will only have juvenile records—which can be difficult to access. Second, many students are *international* students and international records can be exceedingly difficult to obtain; and can vary widely from jurisdiction to jurisdiction. Third, it takes a trained eye—and judgment—to know what some criminal background information means. Many domestic abusers are never convicted; some individuals, including some (but not all) "sexters" are convicted of heinous crimes but may present little risk of future danger. Fourth, only a very small number of individuals will have significant criminal records. Criminal background checks require volume to get results. Fifth, information gathered could be misread and eliminate students from applicant pools unfairly.

A focus on criminal background checks shows a lack of imagination. K–12 records will often be a far more valuable resource. "Gifted" students—many of whom end up in college—are often given extensive psychological testing. K–12 files have significant information as well as aptitudes, behavioral issues, and disabilities. It is nothing short of a national tragedy that the flow of information is blocked from K–12 to higher education. A focus on criminal background checks directs higher education away from creative and necessary legal reform. The law must shift to improve the sharing and use of information from K-12 to higher education. (Moreover, even inter-institutional sharing of information is still in its infancy in higher education—and dangerous people move from state to private institutions and across state (and international) lines as well.)

Partly in response to events at Virginia Tech and the subsequent investigative reports, and partly motivated by the reasonable care standard, many colleges that had not already done so moved quickly to create a variety of response and action teams. Collection and synthesis of information have been greatly facilitated by the rise of various teams—threat, behavioral assessment, case management, etc. The growth of teams is a positive step in reducing ostrichism, silo-ing and bystanderism.

However, these teams face challenges.

---

173. *See* Sara Lipka, *U. of Virginia President Meets with Governor to Push for Access to Law-Enforcement Records*, Chron. Higher Educ. (May 12, 2010), *available at* http://chronicle.com/article/A-Call-for-Access-to-Students/65482/.

First, most teams operate without any clear and specific legal mandates (unlike in Virginia, which has a mandate). In time, for instance, Congress may require such teams, or a body of duty/negligence law may arise that will give a clearer sense of how teams must operate in light of the reasonable care standard. In a complete flip from the bystander era —in which courts actively discouraged proactivity —the law now finds itself playing catch-up to an industry that is no longer willing or able to wait for comprehensive legal mandates to manage its affairs. Dramatic incidents, public opinion, professional judgment, and investigative reports can be greater motivators than tort law.

Second, there is no agreed upon consensus or "best practices" with respect to teams and campuses face a variety of choices in how best to structure their team efforts. There are good and promising practices, but lawyers and student affairs practitioners must devote some effort to determine the practices that are good and promising, and how to implement and evaluate those practices on campus.

Third, teams run the risk of administrative burnout. Teams are often composed of already taxed administrative personnel. Teams must be careful not to drive too late into the night; operational error increases with fatigue and burnout. In the future, there will be teams that "care" for "care" teams.

Fourth, current teams are heavily oriented to being *response oriented*. Teams are often triggered by events or behavioral concerns. It is necessary to use prevention/early intervention strategies to reduce violence and danger on campus. Many teams lack the time, mission, or resources to engage in significant prevention.

Fifth, teams run the risk of "dumping" decisions on certain personnel—campus police/security and psychotherapists in particular—on the teams. Teams must self-assess to ensure that key decisions are made in light of multiple campus perspectives. Small campuses, or campuses with small or outsourced personnel, will find this particularly challenging.

Sixth, teams may find themselves becoming permanently encamped quasi-self-study teams. Interdisciplinary teams will be asked to deal with all sorts of issues/challenges in the higher education learning environment. There will be constant pressure to turn non-safety issues into issues for the team. For example, a teacher dealing with bad millennial student classroom behavior may refer a student to a team: the real issue however may be pedagogy, not a dangerous student.

In sum, regulatory standards have accelerated changes in law and risk management that started in the duty era. Regulators and consumers of higher education may well be pushing compliance standards past the standard of reasonable care. The courts are developing the reasonable care standard, but the question colleges may ultimately face is whether or not reasonable care-based negligence law will be the determining standard for compliance. Will doing what is reasonable to protect students merely become a defense in tort litigation as colleges scramble to achieve higher levels of safety under regulatory law (or in compliance with investigative reports)?[174] That is not the law today, as a great deal of college safety law is still primarily governed only under duty/reasonable care standards. But for how long?

---

174. Courts applying the reasonable care standard and ordinary rules of duty/negligence understand that there will be many times when violence cannot be stopped. Reasonable care cannot prevent all danger. Consider the following:

(1) At Carroll College in Montana, a college employee (it could just as easily have been a student) was shot by a homeless man. A homeless man went to the college chapel. He was drinking, had a gun in his pants, and hollered and banged on a pew during the priest's preparation for Mass. The priest escorted the man from the chapel but did not have him removed from campus or notify the police. The man went to the college cafeteria and shot an innocent employee. The case went to the jury (hence the duty issue was alive), which brought back a verdict for the college. The Supreme Court of Montana affirmed, holding that the college had been the super-safe sanctuary many imagine colleges to be up to this point: there had never been a serious problem caused by a homeless person and the college had been free of rapes, murders, assaults, and armed robberies. *See Peschke v. Carroll College*, 929 P.2d 874 (Mont. 1996). Today the same facts might warrant a Clery Act fine.

(2) In *Gragg v. Wichita State University*, 934 P.2d 121 (Kan. 1997), a woman was shot and killed while attending a 4th of July fireworks display on campus. The Kansas Supreme Court—which had just decided *Nero*—affirmed a summary judgment for the University. There had been no shooting or violent assault resulting in death on the campus for a quarter century, and the assailant was unknown to the university. There was evidence of gang-related activity in the area, but the university had developed a security protocol and had deployed more than 80 police offices for the event of approximately 20,000 persons. The university had done what was reasonable. Under the same facts today, a campus would have to consider what its obligations are under the Clery Act to warn students of known gang activity prior to an event.

(3) Compare *Tanja H. v. Regents of the University of California*, 278 Cal. Rptr. 918 (Cal. Ct. App. 1991) with *Crow v. State of California*, 271 Cal. Rptr. 349 (Cal. Ct. App. 1990), two cases where athletic team members attacked other students on campus. In both cases, the universities escaped liability for the peer attacks.

In *Tanja H.*, a young woman was sexually attacked by members of the university football team. The attack was the result of alcohol suffused activities on campus. The *Tanja H.* court determined that although drinking was prohibited by university rules, the university was considered to be limited in its power to enforce drinking rules given the privacy rights students enjoyed in their rooms. More importantly, the attack was a spontaneous assault, not specifically or readily foreseeable. *Tanja H.* effectively conceded that while attacks may be generally foreseeable, the culture of student privacy rights would not allow reasonable efforts to prevent this sort of assault. In finding no duty to the student the case turned, as other cases, on foreseeability, and the reasonableness of what would be necessary to stop such atrocious acts.

5. Liability for Student Activities (Curricular, Co-Curricular, etc.): The Scope of the University's Duty with Respect to Programmatic Responsibilities

The cases in the duty era firmly support the idea that a duty to use reasonable care exists to manage and supervise curricular and co-curricular activities,

---

(The *Tanja H.* court also had to grapple with the fact that there was a broken light bulb in the stairway and agreed that a duty to repair defects that facilitate crime exists. However, the court believed that the broken light did not have a meaningful nexus to the particular attack. In this vein, *Tanja H.* correctly established that not all maintenance problems are in fact or proximate causes of injury. Otherwise, a clever plaintiff's lawyer could point to any number of unrelated defects as a way to force a time consuming jury trial. Courts will be reluctant to permit a victim to put the entire university on trial in this way. This is a major purpose of causation requirements in negligence law.)

Tanja H. represents a disturbing concession, however, to unlawfully prohibited underage drinking in dorm rooms and the predictable problems of date rape (and worse) that it can facilitate. *Tanja H.* is similar to *Freeman* and may have much the same fate in the law in the future. The court is empowered to draw its own conclusions, but there is no doubt about the foreseeable connections between drinking and more serious crimes, particularly against young women. Hedging on the issue of the university's responsibility in situations of known alcohol abuse in residence halls, *Tanja H.* emphasized the fact that the victim was herself engaged in unlawful consumption of alcohol (thus the court believed she was not blameless). In this regard, *Tanja H.* represents the bystander era judicial antipathy to student plaintiffs who are themselves participants in alcohol consumption. Victim blaming, especially in rape cases, is a dangerous legal position. However for modern colleges, in light of recent regulatory changes, victim blaming is especially disfavored. There are strong hints of historical no proximate cause, assumption of risk, and comparative negligence theories at work in the court's opinion.

Tanja H. is of questionable future efficacy. To the extent that *Tanja H.* represents the idea that date rape/gang rape on the heels of campus drinking is unforeseeable and/or is unstoppable, the case states a social vision inconsistent with current regulatory enforcement.

Tanja H's sister case is *Crow v. California,* which is more in line with modern trends. The victim was an adult male student drinking beer in a dormitory. He ended up being punched-out by a college athlete. *Crow* noted that there was no claim that the university knew or had reason to know of the particular risks in this dormitory. Reasonable care could not have prevented this attack. As *Crow* indicated, if the athlete/aggressor had been a known danger to others, the matter would have been different. The difference between *Crow* and *Tanja H.* is subtle but important. Reasonable steps do exist to prevent *Tanja H.* occurrences; dormitory fights are a fact of life and when they simply spontaneously erupt, it would be usually too much to ask any university to prevent them. Reasonable efforts cannot prevent all violent human encounters.

including internships, externships, field trips, and study abroad.[175] Again, the applicable standard is reasonable care not insurance, and colleges have significant ways to avoid and limit potential liability—assumed risk and comparative negligence factor heavily.

With the decline of charitable and governmental immunity, duties to provide reasonably safe classroom instruction became more easily enforceable. Universities have been held liable for injuries in chemistry labs and physical education classes, for table saw injuries in a scenery class and injuries in aeronautics courses, for example.[176] Community colleges have similar responsibilities even for classes taught off campus on other premises.[177]

The leading higher education case is *Nova Southeastern University v. Gross.*[178] The victim, a graduate student, was attacked in the parking lot at the site of an assigned off-campus practicum.[179] The university argued that it had no duty to protect the student from the attack because she was off the school premises and was an "adult."[180] The Supreme Court of Florida—in a unanimous decision—held that the university owed the student a duty of reasonable care.[181]

Gross is not an instance of a special relationship arising from a landowner's duties of care *vis-a-vis* the university defendant.[182] *Gross* stated a simple premise: because Nova "had control over the students' conduct by requiring them to do the practicum and by assigning them to a specific location, it also assumed the Hohfeldian correlative duty of acting reasonably in making those assignments."[183] When a university creates an academic program—on or off

175. *See* Kathleen M. Burch, *Going Global: Managing Liability in International Externship Programs—A Case Study*, 36 J.C. & U.L. 455 (2010); Kathleen C. Butler, *Shared Responsibility: The Duty to Legal Externs*, 106 W. Va. L. Rev. 51 (2003).

176. *See* Bickel, *supra* note 20, at 374 n.128.

177. *Delbridge v. Maricopa County Community College Dist.*, 893 P.2d 55 (Ariz. Ct. App. 1994).

178. 758 So. 2d 86 (Fla. 2000). The following discussion is adapted and adopted from Peter F. Lake, *The Special Relationship(s) between a College and a Student: Law and Policy Ramifications for the Post in Loco Parentis College*, 37 Idaho L. Rev. 531 (2001). *Gross* also pointed out that colleges should be held to the same standards as open businesses.

179. 758 So. 2d 86, 90 (Fla. 2000).

180. *Id.*

181. *See id.*

182. *See id.* at 89.

183. *Id.* (citation omitted). Referencing the famous Hohfeldian correlative duty theory, *see, e.g.*, Wesley Newcomb Hohfeld, *Some Fundamental Legal Conceptions as Applied in Judicial Reasoning*, 23 Yale L.J. 16 (1913).

campus—it has a duty to act reasonably to prevent foreseeable danger in the context of that program.[184] *Gross* did not ask the university to babysit the student or place her in custodial care.[185] Instead, the court required only *reasonable care*, which is potentially dischargeable by a warning.[186]

Programmatic duty is *not in loco parentis* and is *not* based on any argument that a student/instructor relationship is custodial. Any actor—business or college—has a duty to use reasonable care in its actions and activities. There is no need for a special relationship analysis in such circumstances (although one may exist on premises when students are business invitees, for instance), any more than the driver of a car would need a special relationship with other motorists and pedestrians before that driver would be required to use reasonable care while motoring. However, students assume the ordinary/inherent risks of the classes they take, and a student's failure to use reasonable care can diminish or defeat recovery.

Curricular activities that are inherently physical, such as certain physical education classes, athletics,[187] and field trips—now numerous and diverse—are governed by basically the same rules whether it is a weightlifting course or a school-sponsored rock climbing class. Students assume the ordinary and obvious risks of such activities. There is no duty to protect against inherent, obvious, or primary risks of such activities. But students do not assume the risk (1) of reckless or deliberate and intentional behavior compromising safety, (2) of hidden (or non-obvious) or non-ordinary dangers, (3) that an institution will take a student to a level of risk that the student is not capable of handling without proper instruction, equipment, and guidance.[188]

---

184. 758 So. 2d at 90.

185. *See id.*

186. *See id.*

187. I do not directly address issues in intercollegiate athletics here. There are special rules, principles and standards at play.

188. (3) was the problem in *Davidson v. Univ. of N.C. at Chapel Hill*, 543 S.E.2d 920, 924–25 (N.C. Ct. App. 2001). That case involved a serious cheerleading accident. The court pointed out the following in determining a duty was owed:

> In sum, the evidence showed that the varsity squad members, who were older, more skilled, and more experienced, were provided with a supervisor, were provided with safety instruction through the UCA camps, were informed of the known risks involved in performing pyramids, and were admonished to create and abide by specific safety guidelines. However, the JV squad members, who were younger, less skilled, and less experienced, did not have a supervisor, received no safety training, received no information regarding risks involved in performing pyramids, and were left on their own to make decisions regarding safety procedures. *Id.*

Perhaps the best expression and explanation of the shared responsibility in a student activity remains *Regents of the University of California v. Roettgen.*[189] In *Roettgen,* a student was killed in a rock climbing class. The court determined that rock climbing is a dangerous sport with some very obvious dangers. Rock anchors can fail and cause falls, which cause injury or death. These are the apparent or ordinary risks of an extra-ordinary activity. The instructor(s) had a responsibility to place the anchors carefully (which they did—but the anchors still failed) and to keep the students within their range of capabilities (which they did). *Roettgen* was very particular in its reasoning process. The responsibility of the student for his/her own safety and the responsibility of a college for non-ordinary risks were considered in light of the nature of the activity, its risks, and the relative experience of a student. As *Roettgen* explained:

> Plaintiff relies on cases involving student/instructor relationships and those involving commercial recreational operations in urging that defendant owed Mr. Roettgen a duty of care simply because he was enrolled as a student in defendant's commercial venture. *The determination of duty in the student/instructor or commercial recreational operation cases turns not on labels given to the sporting participants, but instead on the facts surrounding their levels of experience and/or their relationships to one another in the activity resulting in the plaintiff's injury.*[190]

Roettgen represents the belief that sporting or recreational activities, even when academic in nature, should be governed by flexible rules that focus on the activity rather than on a "label." If you take students on a kayak excursion as a part of a geology course, be prepared to respond at the level of responsibility reasonable for that activity. The rule explained in *Roettgen* is appropriate for field trips, study abroad programs, and, in fact, most instructional activity that mixes inherent risk with aberrant or unusual risk. The basic idea is that students do assume certain risks, but the university has responsibility too.

It is important to keep the other points in mind as well. First, immunity law, especially recreational use immunities, may protect universities in some activities litigation.[191] Second, universities can employ releases/waivers/exculpatory agreements to manage risk: where these agreements do not violate public policy and provide specific and useful risk information to students, courts

---

189. 48 Cal. Rptr. 2d 922 (Cal. Ct. App. 1996).

190. *Id.* at 925 (emphasis added).

191. *See, e.g., Ochoa v. Cal. State Univ., Sacramento,* 85 Cal. Rptr. 2d 768, 768–72 (Cal. Ct. App. 1999).

often enforce them. Third, cases imposing programmatic responsibility do not require *custodial* control before a duty attaches.

6. Responsibility for Student Alcohol Use

The major bystander cases were all alcohol-related injury cases. Cases like *Mullins* and *Gross*, which do not involve alcohol, have been more likely to impose a reasonable care duty. It might be tempting to separate "the alcohol cases" from all the others. There are reasons to do that; and reasons not to. It is also tempting to craft generalization about "the alcohol cases." For instance, the leading casebook in the field written by Dean Judith Areen states: "Although many courts in recent years have been willing to hold colleges and universities liable for some student injuries, *Bradshaw* illustrates the [dominant] judicial view that they are not liable for most alcohol related injuries and deaths."[192] Areen goes on to assert that assuming duties can create legal exposure in alcohol cases.[193] Although this is a widely held view, it overly simplifies the progress of the law of responsibility for student alcohol use. It is actually very difficult to create one rule that captures all the cases that involve alcohol. One must conceptualize this area to grasp its complexity—and its vector heading. It is also dangerous— from a safety and litigation perspective—to oversimplify the law here, as the compliance message colleges could perceive would be "you will keep winning alcohol cases as long as you are careful about proactive intervention." Bystanderism/ostrichism are risky choices in a business where alcohol is a core risk factor in almost every negative outcome on campus.

Consider the following.

First, almost all of "the alcohol cases" involve issues other than alcohol—like *Freeman* and sexual assault. There are only a few reported "pure" intoxication cases where alcohol poisoning causes death. Moreover, even doctrinally the cases are usually "mixed drinks"—for example, is *Beach* a programmatic responsibility case or a "rescue" case? Whenever you read an "alcohol case," ask yourself—is this a pure alcohol case? What other factors are in play? There certainly are a large number of reported cases where alcohol caused injury or significantly enhanced injury. There also are some cases where alcohol was present but did not cause

192. Judith Areen, *Higher Education and the Law: Cases and Materials* 817 (Foundation Press 2009) (citations omitted).

193. *See id.*

harm or enhance risk. Which cases do you have to emphasize or de-emphasize to state a general rule about "the alcohol cases?"

Second, quite apart from college law there is continued adherence in society at large to legal rules that treat liquor liability within narrow boundaries. Critically, social hosts have historically not been subject to lawsuits, and most courts and legislatures still adhere to this rule. Essentially, so do federal regulators.

Third, there has been a sense of futility about alcohol prevention: high-risk drinking, like subway graffiti, seems to many an inevitable feature of college life. Charles Homer Haskins, writing in the 1920s on the rise of universities, did not overlook the featured role of alcohol in the earliest accounts of student life.[194] It is as if college and liquor go together. There is that picture of John Belushi as Bluto Blutarski from *Animal House*: Bluto stands wearing his "College" sweater and has a dazed, confused, post/pre-alcohol visage and a vacant "Why?" and "Where is the next beer?" look in his eyes. This type of vision has become an archetype of modern post-secondary education and is remarkably multigenerational. Ernest Boyer reported in the 1980s that alcohol is the drug of choice.[195] In two books, Arthur Levine described the power of alcohol on campus in the 1990s and very recent studies relating to millennial students show their preference for alcohol use. The law has taken notice of this archetype. Courts are loathe to make rules that will fail; fighting campus alcohol culture is like prohibition, which failed miserably. The limits of the law as a tool for social reform seem stronger in cases involving alcohol. The archetype may be false, as we shall see, but it is no less perceived.

Fourth, many plaintiffs/victims have not been sympathetic victims to courts. In cases like *Beach*, the drinking student sought refuge in tort liability. Courts see assumed risk and contributory negligence as appropriate to bar recovery in many college injury situations. In most states today, even where liquor liability flows more freely, rarely can the *drinker* sue for his or her injuries. The state of Florida, for instance, has actually adopted a specific rule for drinking plaintiffs that bars recovery in many cases. Tort liquor liability rules do not generally operate to protect drinkers from drinking. Old proximate cause ideas have never really left—they have just mutated.

Fifth, many no-duty cases are more like no *breach* of duty as a matter of law cases. In some instances, like *Bash* (technically that case involved *heroin*),

---

194. Charles Homer Haskins, *The Rise of Universities* (Cornell University Press 1957) (1923).

195. Ernest Boyer, *College: The Undergraduate Experience in America* 201 (Harper & Row 1987).

there is little to nothing reasonable, or even realistic that an institution could do to prevent a specific injury.[196] Since *Palsgraf* courts have used "no-duty" rulings to screen cases out: this generation of judges was taught in law school—almost universally—how to use no-duty rulings as a weeding out tool. (The next generation will have been taught more complex rules for duty analysis.)

Sixth, some states have powerful governmental immunities that limit negligence cases against public institutions. This can significantly impact the viability of alcohol-based claims in a state. Governmental immunity has receded significantly on a national basis, but some states have significant barriers to tort litigation in place—all tort litigation, including alcohol.

Seventh, there is a noticeable difference in federal court—even the language/analysis of such cases is often noticeably more strident against student claims (e.g., *Bradshaw*, *Freeman*). There is little doubt federal courts are fearful that they will be flooded with "diversity jurisdiction" cases from college if they are not careful. College cases can end up in federal court: college students often travel across state lines for college creating a necessary predicate to trigger federal court jurisdiction. Federal court judges are already swamped with criminal jurisdiction and are not looking to attract new business. The federal court bias in favor of "no duty" has little to do with protecting colleges. It is far more influenced by the fact that since the drug wars of the late 1970s and 1980s began in earnest federal courts have been overwhelmed with criminal cases. Federal judges are underpaid and their courts are understaffed to meet the demands of the new federal criminal jurisdiction. The college alcohol cases in federal court are jurisdictional triage. This helps to explain why federal courts so confidentially and emphatically "guess" at state law under *Erie*. *Bradshaw* is indefensible under modern Pennsylvania tort and regulatory law; *Freeman* is inconsistent with current Title IX sexual assault enforcement. Yet it is doubtful that this will stop federal courts from relying on those cases anytime soon. (However shame on *state* courts that follow federal court precedent blindly; and fair warning to lawyers who argue cases in court without apprising judges of any knowable *Erie* (or other) defects in cases they argue.)

Eighth, alcohol responsibility law, prevention science, and student development theory have been changing significantly since the laissez-faire 1960s and 1970s. Alcohol responsibility law has a vector heading, and it is discernably towards more, not less, accountability. Changes have been incremental; social host immunity remains the most resistant to change but there have been

196. *See* Lake, *supra* note 55, at 261–64.

noticeable inroads even into that one legal concept that remains most protective of modern colleges in alcohol litigation. Many courts persist in framing alcohol issues on campus by analogy to social/personal drinking—and resist viewing college alcohol use as similar to alcohol risk in employment or business. This will undoubtedly change as alcohol prevention science makes broader connections to high-risk alcohol use and core mission challenges—elongated completion rates, poor attainment rates, poor classroom performance and attendance, sexual violence, etc. Alcohol risk is still not universally appreciated for what it is—the core enterprise risk in modern higher education. High-risk alcohol use is a personal choice (usually), it is a social phenomenon *and* it is a central challenge in delivering quality higher education in the United States. It is *all* of these things.

Ninth, generalization about "the alcohol cases" should be sensitive to another "bystander era" reality. Reported cases are the tip of an iceberg—a tip that is more the creation of university lawyers than any other single force. You may notice that a number of intermediate state appellate court decisions state no-duty rules. Intermediate state appellate courts are much less likely to carve new paths in common law (unlike the high court of that state) and university counsel can and do settle cases to preserve "good" precedent (as discussed earlier). The visible "history" is skewed towards what the business of higher education would like it to look like. Here is a prime example: in the last ten years or so there has been a significant uptick in alcohol-related college litigation. Much of it settles, sometimes confidentially. A few cases become well known, however. Consider the record-breaking settlement in the alcohol overdose death of Scott Krueger at MIT, as just one example.[197] Sometimes parents insist on public settlements if there is to be a settlement, but there is no legal requirement to do so (and there can be powerful incentives not to do so). However, the "evidence" must be understood in the context of how the litigation system operates. Sometimes the litigation system hides evidence of its operation. (This will become even more pronounced if higher education cases move into arbitration. To date, arbitration is not a major form of dispute resolution in student injury cases—but that could change.)

Tenth, quite apart from social host issues, students can assume risks and can be contributorily negligent. It is common in the United States to bar a plaintiff from the courthouse if that plaintiff cannot show that the defen-

197. Leo Reisberg, *MIT Pays $6-Million to Settle Lawsuit over a Student's Death*, Chron. Higher Educ. (Sept. 29, 2000), *available at* http://chronicle.com/article/MIT-Pays-6-Million-to-Sett/32171/.

dant(s) were *more* at fault for the accident causing injury.[198] Recklessness is a good way to walk your way out of court as a plaintiff, and in many situations, voluntary intoxication and voluntary high-risk behavior *is* reckless. Many alcohol injury plaintiffs are not well postured for recovery in the tort system because of their own fault—assumed risk or contributory fault (watch for discussion of the *Knoll* case, *infra*).[199] Drinking and getting on trampolines, drag racing, riding motorcycles, navigating rocky trails, climbing on the roof of a natatorium, etc., undermines a plaintiff's case, to say the least. It is very easy to conflate no *liability* with no *duty*. For courts the "alcohol cases" are often not alcohol cases. They are cases involving substantial plaintiff fault. Almost anything that will get you cast for *Jackass* (or *The Real World*) will get you kicked out of court.

---

198. *See* John L. Diamond, Lawrence C. Levine & M. Stuart Madden, *Understanding Torts* 263–71 (Lexis 2000).

199. The following cases are prime examples of this (there are others):

- The Colorado Supreme Court found that a university was not liable for injuries suffered by an intoxicated student as a result of his use of a trampoline at a campus fraternity (*Univ. of Denver v. Whitlock*, 744 P.2d 54 (Colo. 1987));
- In *Booker v. Lehigh University*, 800 F. Supp. 234 (E.D. Pa. 1992), a female student admitted she voluntarily consumed significant amounts of alcohol before she chose to navigate a rocky trail and fell as she went home to her sorority. She asserted that the university had a general duty to control student consumption of alcohol on campus and that the breach of this duty caused her fall. She lost. (The court did note however, that if the university, not a fraternity, had served liquor or otherwise planned or purchased and supplied liquor, the result would have been different—an interesting observation, given the facts *of Bradshaw*);
- A student was killed riding a motorcycle on a public street after drinking at a fraternity party. The university was not liable (*Millard v. Osborne*, 611 A.2d 715 (Pa. Super. Ct. 1992));
- In a very unusual case, a college freshman "got wasted" and belligerent off campus and after taking some sort of a beating (that he may well have instigated) stumbled into a commuter rail platform and collapsed, in need of a rescue. As a drunken trespasser, he was not entitled to immediate assistance by the railroad (*Rhodes v. Illinois Cent. Gulf R.R.*, 665 N.E.2d 1260 (Ill. 1996).
- No liability when a student is injured in a "Fast and Furious" style drag race while intoxicated (*Baldwin v. Zoradi*, 176 Cal. Rptr. 809 (Cal. App. 1981)).
- No liability in a fall at a football stadium; an intoxicated student vaulted a wall. The case went to a jury; the university was not a proximate cause (*Allen v. Rutgers*, 523 A.2d 262 (N.J. Super. App. Div. 1987)).
- No liability when a student jumped into an elevator shaft intoxicated (*Houck v. Univ. of Washington*, 803 P.2d 47 (1991)).

The "alcohol cases" are therefore the result of a complex play of forces. To add to the complexity, some of these forces have been changing—vectoring—over time. Alcohol-related case law refuses to sit still. There has been a demonstrable shift in prevention science, social attitudes, and the law since the 1970s and 1980s. The widespread acquiescence in college alcohol risk is destined to change, and it has been changing:

> Perhaps the first signal of changing judicial attitudes occurred in the 1980s when courts began imposing liability upon fraternities—usually the local chapter—for alcohol risk. These cases constituted a shift away from notions of exclusive student personal responsibility for high-risk drinking injuries. Courts were beginning to reimagine responsibility for alcohol risks in terms of shared responsibility.[200]

However, high-risk alcohol use is a college problem, not simply a Greek life issue.

Recognizing this, cases in the new millennium have charted a different path from the bystander case law and expanded responsibility for risks in a high-risk alcohol culture—recognizing duty, shared responsibility, and the need to manage a modern higher educational riskscape. These cases have been augmented by aggressive changes in anti-hazing laws—laws that can implicate students, Greek groups, administrative personnel, and even institutions.[201]

---

200. *See* Peter F. Lake & Joel C. Epstein, *Modern Liability Rules and Policies Regarding College Student Alcohol Injuries: Reducing High-Risk Alcohol Use Through Norms of Shared Responsibility and Environmental Management*, 53 Okla. L. Rev. 611, 616–17 (2000) (footnote omitted).

201. *See* Areen, *supra* note 192, at 776–77 n. 1. As Areen succinctly summarizes:

> Hazing is common at many universities, both in Greek organizations and in sports. One survey found that eighty percent of college athletes had been subjected to some form of hazing. Joshua A. Sussberg, Note, Shattered Dreams: Hazing in College Athletics, 24 Cardozo L. Rev. 1421, 1427 (2003). Anti-hazing laws have been passed in almost every state and some students have been formally charged in hazing incidents. Massachusetts, for example, has made hazing punishable by a fine of up to three thousand dollars and/or one year in prison. Mass. Gen. Laws ch. 269 § 17 (2002). The statute defines hazing as "any conduct or method of initiation into any student organization . . . which willfully or recklessly endangers the physical or mental health of any student or other person" and removes consent as a defense to prosecution. Id. Massachusetts also has made failure to report hazing punishable. Mass. Gen. Laws ch. 269, §18 (2002). See also Cal. Penal Code § 245.6 (West 2007); N.Y. Penal Law § 120.16 (McKinney 2004).
>
> Florida has enacted one of the toughest anti-hazing laws, making hazing resulting in serious physical injury a felony punishable by up to five years in prison. Fla. Stat. § 1006.63(2) (2004). In a recent case, two members of Kappa Alpha Psi

In *Knoll v. Board of Regents of the University of Nebraska*,[202] a student sued the university in negligence regarding a hazing incident that caused him very serious injury.[203] The case went to the Supreme Court of Nebraska after a trial court granted summary judgment to the university on the grounds that no duty was owed.[204] The Supreme Court of Nebraska reversed the no duty ruling and determined that the University of Nebraska did indeed owe a duty to Knoll as a landowner, with respect to the hazing injuries.[205] During a "pledge sneak" process, several members of a fraternity met Knoll in a university building on campus.[206] They walked to an off-campus, but related, fraternity house. Knoll drank hard liquor and beer provided by members over a period of approximately two and one-half hours. Knoll became severely intoxicated and ill.[207] He was taken upstairs to a restroom in the fraternity house and then handcuffed to a pipe.[208] Somehow, Knoll managed to break loose from the manacles while left unattended: he attempted an escape out of the third floor window,

---

at Florida A & M University were sentenced to two years in prison for felony hazing. Elia Powers, *Testing an Anti-Hazing Law*, Inside Higher Ed., Jan. 31, 2007, *available at* http://insidehighered.com/layout/set/print/news/2007/01/31/hazing. The fraternity members beat a pledge with a wooden paddle and boxing gloves, causing the pledge to suffer a ruptured eardrum and injury to his buttocks. *Id.* While not speaking on behalf of the university, some university officials, including the former president, a former Board of Trustees chairman, and the current assistant director for recreation, pleaded for leniency in the sentencing. Susan Lipkins, a psychologist specializing in campus conflict, criticized the university officials for sending "mixed messages." *Id. See also* Lisa W. Foderaro, *3 Plead Guilty in Inquiry into Fatal College Hazing*, N.Y. Times, Oct. 11, 2003 at B5; Joseph A. Slobodzian, *Penn Students Guilty in '05 hazing Inciden*t, Philly.com, Nov. 21, 2006, *available at* http://www.insidehazing.com/ headline.php?id=344.

Virtually every state abolishes the defense of assumption of the risk—a prime impediment to alcohol cases for plaintiffs, and hazing situations essentially trump social host immunities as well. (Some hazing does not involve alcohol of course.) Only Alabama is out of step with this development. See Ex Parte Barran, 730 So.2d 203 (Ala. 1998) (retaining assumption of the risk defense).

202. 601 N.W.2d 757 (Neb. 1999). The following discussion of *Knoll* is adopted and adapted from Peter F. Lake, *Tort Litigation in Higher Education*, 27 J.C. & U.L. 255 (2000).

203. 601 N.W.2d at 760.

204. *See id.*

205. *See id.*

206. *See id.*

207. *See id.*

208. *See id.*

fell and suffered severe injuries.[209] The injured student was 19 years old (under the legal drinking age) at the time of the incident.[210] The fraternity house sat on non-university owned property, but was considered to be a student housing unit under the code of conduct.[211] The student conduct code included violations for possession of alcohol, hazing, and for unreasonably dangerous conduct, inter alia.[212]At the University of Nebraska, pledge sneak events were planned events, and a fraternity was required to file a form with the university in advance of a pledge sneak event.[213] The university had not received a form from this particular fraternity.[214]

In *Knoll* the incident incepted on university premises, but the consumption of alcohol and the subsequent injuries occurred off campus at a regulated property that was not owned by the university. *Knoll* is a "grayscape" landowner duty case, an alcohol case, and a hazing crime. In applying landowner duty analysis, the Nebraska Supreme Court pointed out that "prior criminal history need not involve the same suspect to make the further criminal acts reasonably foreseeable," and, "prior acts need not have occurred on the premises."[215] In determining foreseeability, the court turned to the commonly used "totality of the circumstances test" to determine whether or not prior incidents created foreseeability of danger.[216] Under the "totality of the circumstances" test, the number or location of prior incidents alone is not dispositive when determining foreseeability.[217] In

---

209. *See id.* Using the totality of the circumstances test, the court characterized the stipulated facts as follows:

> [T]he University was aware of prior hazing instances where students had grabbed and physically removed other students from buildings, had coerced other students into drinking alcohol, and had engaged in other harassing activities. The record reflects that the University had noticed that pledge sneaks could lead to illegal hazing. Thus, the University could have foreseen various forms of student hazing on its property, even though FIJI failed to disclose the pledge sneak event . . . As such, we conclude that the University owes a landowner-invitee duty to students to take reasonable steps to protect against foreseeable acts of hazing, including student abduction on the University's property, and the harm that naturally flows therefrom.

Id. at 764–65.

210. *See id.*

211. *See id.* at 761.

212. *See id.*

213. *See id.*

214. *See id.*

215. *See id.* at 764.

216. *See id.*

217. *Id.*

analyzing this issue, the *Knoll* court pointed out that there were two incidents of fraternity hazing that had occurred previously that did not involve the specific fraternity in question and that the university was aware of several incidents involving the particular fraternity. These incidents included a fraternity member resisting arrest, several members being found in possession of alcohol at the fraternity house, violations of rules regarding the presence of females at the fraternity house after the expiration of visitation hours, a conviction of sexual assault on a female high school student by a member of the fraternity at the fraternity house, the discovery of a fraternity member who was intoxicated and unconscious in a third floor restroom of the fraternity house, and an altercation that had occurred between fraternity members and another fraternity, which had caused the necessity for campus police to intervene.[218] In addition, there had been an attempted break-in of a sorority house.[219] Importantly, *Knoll* made the following observation: "It is true there is no evidence that any of this activity occurred on the University's property. However, there is evidence that the FIJI house is located near the University's property."[220] Moreover, the court pointed out that the university had "exercised control over the FIJI house by considering it to be a 'student housing unit' subject to the code."[221]

It is common for students to live off campus in regulated and/or unregulated housing: risks transport on and off campus in a variety of ways. *Knoll* signals the breakdown of the image that landowner duties are inexorably tied to incidents where the injury producing events occur. However, again duty does not mean liability. In *Knoll* the university was able to limit its responsibility by settling with Knoll for a mere $25,000.[222]

How was the University of Nebraska able to limit its liability? It drew attention to certain facts that were not portrayed in the appellate opinion in *Knoll*. For example, there were indications that Knoll had passed by telephones that would have connected with the university police and that could have been used to avert the tragedy that lay ahead. Shared responsibility is not the end of personal accountability.

Knoll is a reminder that even in an age of increasing college accountability, students must use reasonable care to protect themselves. Students are usually

218. *See id.*

219. *See id.*

220. *Id.*

221. *Id.*

222. *See* Robynn Tysver, *Ex-Student Settles with UNL in Fall from Fraternity House*, Omaha World Herald, Aug. 9, 2000, at 15.

in the best position to protect their own safety. This is often the case in alcohol-related injuries.

A couple of final points are in order. *Knoll* is not a true hazing case as such—it is a landowner duty case (although the facts would demonstrate unlawful hazing in many states). Second, *Knoll* is not an assumed duty case. *Knoll*, when juxtaposed with *Gross*, instead illustrates a shift away from strict *geophysical* responsibility to a more *conceptual* form of responsibility based on where programs take place and how danger actually interacts with a campus. Finally, *Knoll* is more like *Furek* than *Bradshaw*: it is not a bystander case. (Neither was the University of Nebraska at Lincoln—as discussed *infra*, the campus is and has been a national award winning campus in adopting successful prevention strategies based on environmental management.)

Another important case is *Coghlan v. Beta Theta Pi Fraternity*.[223] In *Coghlan*, an 18-year-old student at the University of Idaho had recently been admitted into the Alpha Phi sorority. She was involved in an ongoing rush week, an event sponsored and sanctioned by the university in conjunction with its Greek activities. Coghlan attended fraternity parties in connection with rush week.[224] There was significant party management in effect during rush week. For example, there were policies prohibiting underage drinking and requiring sororities to assign a "guardian angel" to any underage student that sought induction into a sorority.

The "guardian angel" was to shadow the student during rush week, particularly during evening activities.[225] Advisors from the Greek system and the university jointly monitored the evening events, which were a series of alcohol parties.[226] The injured student managed to obtain alcohol at two parties entitled "Jack Daniels' Birthday" and "Fifty-Ways to Lose Your Liver"—and became so intoxicated that she later fell and suffered injuries.[227] Another sorority sister—not her assigned "guardian angel"—had escorted her from a party and put her into bed in a sorority house, but this did not prevent her from sustaining permanent injuries by later falling thirty feet from the sorority's fire escape.[228]

223. 987 P.2d 300 (Idaho 1999). The discussion of *Coghlan* is adopted and adapted heavily from Peter F. Lake, *Tort Litigation in Higher Education*, *supra* note 55; and Peter F. Lake & Joel C. Epstein, *Modern Liability Rules*, *supra* note 200.

224. Lake, *supra* note 55, at 305.

225. *Id.*

226. *Id.*

227. *Id.*

228. *Id.*

Idaho's Dram Shop Act was highly protective of servers: it protects a server from being sued by a person who voluntarily consumes alcohol from that server, even though the individual who consumes the alcohol is underage.[229] As a result of this loophole in the Idaho Dram Shop Law, the lawsuit against the fraternity defendants was dismissed as they were deemed servers.[230] The university, however, was not a server and, therefore, did not quality for Idaho Dram Shop immunity.[231]

Coghlan correctly noted that the student/university relationship is not itself a special relationship imposing an affirmative duty.[232] Finding it unnecessary to discuss issues related to landowner duties, the court determined that the injured party's pleadings were sufficient to create an issue regarding an assumption of duty toward Coghlan.[233] *Coghlan* pointed out that there were university employees at parties who were charged with supervisory responsibilities, and that there were allegations that the employees either knew or should have known that Coghlan was drunk and required reasonable care to protect her from injury.[234] The matter was remanded for further determinations with respect to the issue of voluntary assumption of duty.[235]

Does *Coghlan* mean that the best course of action for college and university officials is to decline to participate in supervision of student events? The answer is almost certainly no. For one thing, substantial interaction with student life and Greek affairs is well entrenched in modern student affairs.

Such a strategy would also be legally unsound. As in *Knoll*, danger has a nasty habit of transporting on and off premises: the failure to attend to a risk that occurs near campus or at a student off-campus event is as likely to create college or university liability as a failure to attend to a risk on campus.[236] Landowner duty analysis in *Coghlan* might have created a foundation for that court's conclusion that the university shared responsibility for the injuries to the plaintiff.[237] Crucially, many factual situations might create triable issues of fact on whether a duty has been assumed. The modern college or university is

---

229. *Id.*

230. *Id.*

231. *Id.* at 311–12.

232. *Id.*

233. *Id.* at 312.

234. *Id.*

235. *Id.* at 314.

236. *See Knoll*, 601 N.W.2d at 764.

237. The *Coghlan* court did not engage in landowner duty analysis because it found that the defendant university assumed a duty to the plaintiff. *Coghlan*, 987 P.2d at 312.

so interactive in student life—and offers many interlocking business activities concentrated in time and space[238]—that any time a student is injured on or near campus, a college or university employee may be involved to an extent that a fact issue on assumed duty may exist. Again, this is something that may be knowable only *ex post facto*. A university may not have assumed a duty but will discover this after summary judgment, trial or appeal and years after an event.

Knoll, *Gross*, and *Coghlan*, all descendants of *Furek*, send very similar messages. Duty and accountability are environmental and conceptual issues. Duty and accountability can extend where programs go, where foreseeable danger goes, and where students involve themselves in a broadly contoured living-learning environment. After litigation, lawyers may well be able to limit, even eliminate liability, but in many, many instances the epistemology of college risk is not one with *a priori* knowledge—even for experts in the field. From an operational standpoint bystanderism, ostrichism and no-duty positions are exceedingly risky; especially when a university can use reasonable care to manage its environment. (Consider as well that cases like *Freeman* and *Tanja H.* have held that "no duty" is owed in acquaintance sexual assault matters: can a college truly operationalize this in light of the Department of Education's recent Title IX guidance and enforcement efforts?)

Knoll and *Coghlan* also connect with a major shift in alcohol and other drug prevention science. The bystander era was built on core beliefs about alcohol use and college students that modern science-based prevention dispels.

Indeed, recent alcohol cases have begun to toe into a world of science/scientific research—and shift focus away from a singular focus on personal accountability to shared responsibility. The law and alcohol prevention science have often paralleled each other. There was a time in the bystander era when both focused on individual choices:

> For various historical policy reasons, colleges and universities traditionally put emphasis on the education of individual students, and on intervention with respect to individual students, in trying to fight high-risk alcohol use. Until relatively recently, high-risk drinking—including alcoholism—was commonly considered an individual problem that arose out of personal choices and weak character. To a certain extent, individuals were considered to be unfortunate in their life experiences or to have inherited genetic propensities for high-risk

238. *See, e.g.*, *Coghlan*, 987 P.2d 300; *Knoll*, 601 N.W.2d at 761.

> alcohol use. A consistent theme in traditional efforts to prevent high-risk drinking has been a focus on individuals and their ability to determine the course of their own lives.[239]

Consistent with this notion that alcohol problems are primarily issues of personal choice, the focus in prevention efforts was on *education* (and recall that *Bradshaw* cast the mission of colleges as primarily "educational"—note the parallel):

> Campuses have developed, for example, alcohol awareness programs, awareness weeks, peer education programs, special events associated with preventing high-risk alcohol use, and other education and informational programs. In keeping with traditional norms, even faculty have begun, in recent times, to bring messages of prevention and education into their assigned courses; this process is widely known as "curriculum infusion." Again, it has traditionally been thought that if people are made aware of various legal rules and various dangers regarding high-risk alcohol use, they are more likely to exercise self-determination and resist high-risk drinking.[240]

Today, a singular focus on individual drinker responsibility and education—in law and prevention—has given way to broader environmental management strategies. Modern prevention science recognizes that alcohol risk is the result of a complex interplay of individual choices and the environments in which the choices are made. Largely based on pioneering and foundational words by Professor William DeJong, former director of the U.S. Department of Education Higher Education Center, public health-based alcohol and drug prevention models made the transition into *environmental management strategies.*[241] Major national reports have supported environmental management strategies.[242] Environmental management strategies have shown great promise when imple-

---

239. Lake & Epstein, *supra* note 200, at 618 (footnotes omitted).

240. *Id.* (footnote omitted).

241. *See* William DeJong et al., Higher Educ. Ctr. for Alcohol and Other Drug Prevention, *Environmental Management: A Comprehensive Strategy for Reducing Alcohol and Other Drug Use on College Campuses* 31–32 (1998), *available at* http://www.higheredcenter.org/services/publications/environmental-management-comprehensive-strategy-reducing-alcohol-and-other-dru. DeJong's work has also been foundational in violence prevention strategies as well.

242. *See, e.g.*, National Institute on Alcohol Abuse and Alcoholism (NIAAA), *A Call to Action: Changing the Culture of Drinking at U.S. Colleges* (2002), *available at* http://www.collegedrinkingprevention.gov/niaaacollegematerials/taskforce/taskforce_toc.aspx.

mented on a college campus.[243] The U.S. Department of Education provided a number of resources to the field via the now-defunct Higher Education Center (HEC), which helped colleges implement a variety of coordinating environmental strategies. The core idea of environmental management is as follows:

> A comprehensive environmental approach does not limit itself to educational harm reduction programs and also does not limit itself to one level of impact. Instead, the perspective of a comprehensive environmental approach is to focus not upon the individual in isolation, but upon bringing about fundamental changes in the array of institutional, community, and public policy forces that may have, inadvertently, facilitated high-risk alcohol use. The environmental management approach draws its force from the well-accepted notion in public health policy that individual choices regarding alcohol use will (at least in part) revolve around various factors in the environment in which individuals reside. The environment includes a number of factors including social factors, economic factors, background legal rules, the physical environment in which students reside and the datascape in which they are immersed. The college student's environment is not a constant or static feature of his or her existence. In fact, deliberate efforts by higher education administrators, individuals involved with the law and people trained in areas

---

243. As a prime example, the University of Nebraska-Lincoln has had great success in reducing binge drinking rates through their "NU Directions" program. UNL was one of ten universities to receive an "A Matter of Degree" (AMOD) grant from the Robert Wood Johnson Foundation in the late 1990s, which required the formation of a comprehensive environmental management plan to address high-risk alcohol use among college students. *See* Linda Major & Thomas Workman, *Organizing a Community Coalition: Lessons Learned from Lincoln, Nebraska*, http://bcm.academia.edu/ThomasWorkman/Papers/125408/Organizing_a_Campus_Community_Coalition (last visited Sept. 22, 2011). The NU Directions project reduced binge drinking rates among 16,000 undergraduates from 62.5% in 1997 to 47% in 2003—a remarkable drop. They reported similar reductions in both self-reported primary and secondary harms related to alcohol consumption. *See* Ian M. Newman et al., *Use of Policy, Education, and Enforcement to Reduce Binge Drinking Among University Students: The NU Directions Project*, 17 Int'l J. of Drug Policy 339–49 (2006). In 2006, UNL's binge drinking rate dropped to 43%, yet another remarkable feat as UNL has succeeded in lowering drinking rates *below* national averages. *See* UNL College Drinking Data at http://www.nudirections.org/drinkingData.php (last visited Sept. 22, 2011). Linda Major and Tom Workman, both of whom worked with the NU Directions project, received the Facilitator Award in 2009 at the 30th Annual National Conference on Law and Higher Education held by Stetson University College of Law. The UNL experience is proof that a college *can* combat high-risk alcohol use successfully.

> of prevention can have a dramatic effect on the overall environmental factors that foster or diminish high-risk alcohol use.[244]

Environmental management is a "combined-arms" approach to combatting high-risk drinking, and eschews "magic bullet" approaches.

One arrow in the environmental management quiver that is particularly notable is the "social norming approach."[245] Social norming aims to alter perceptions in an environment:

> The principal idea has been to provide sufficient and accurate information about the real patterns of high-risk alcohol use on campus. Research has indicated that students tend to believe that their peers drink more heavily than they actually do. However, the belief—or misbelief—that students drink more heavily than they actually do, can be a powerful force in determining campus culture. Thus, where expectations regarding other students' alcohol use are out of sync with the reality of alcohol use, peer pressure to drink in a high-risk way may be greater. This presents an important opportunity to correct misbeliefs in order to potentially reduce the rates of high-risk drinking. Changing the overall social environment of college students through social norming has shown great potential as a prevention strategy when coupled with other prevention strategies and traditional educational approaches.[246]

Social norming can be very effective when used in combination with other environmental management strategies.

---

244. Lake & Epstein, *supra* note 200, at 620 (footnotes omitted).

245. *Id.* at nn. 50–53. *See* Higher Education Center for Alcohol and Other Drug Prevention, U.S. Department of Education, http://www.higheredcenter.org (last visited Sept. 22, 2011); Robert Zimmerman, *U.S. Dep't of Educ., Social Marketing Strategies for Campus Prevention of Alcohol and Other Drug Problems* (1997), *available at* http://www.higheredcenter.org/services/publications/social-marketing-strategies-campus-prevention-alcohol-and-other-drug-problems; H. Wesley Perkins & Henry Wechsler, *Variation in Perceived College Drinking Norms and Its Impact on Alcohol Abuse: A Nationwide Study*, 26 J. Drug Issues 961–74 (1996); Michael P. Haines & Sherilyn F. Spear, *Changing the Perception of the Norm: A Strategy to Decrease Binge Drinking Among College Students*, 45 J. Am. C. Health 134 (1996); Michael P. Haines, *U.S. Dep't of Educ., A Social Norms Approach to Preventing Binge Drinking at Colleges and Universities* (1996), *available at* http://www.higheredcenter.org/files/product/socnorms.pdf; *see also Correcting Misperceptions of Norms on Seven Campuses*, Catalyst (Higher Educ. Ctr. for Alcohol & Other Drug Prevention, Newton, Mass.), Summer/Fall 1998, at 6 (vol. 4, no.1), *available at* http://www.higheredcenter.org/files/product/catalyst11.pdf.

246. Lake & Epstein, *supra* note 200, at 619 (footnotes omitted).

Environmental management strategies are reflected in several recent alcohol cases. Much of the recent case law has:

- Focused on a riskscape—the environment.
- Promoted shared responsibility, where appropriate (this is not the death of personal accountability but the expansion of it).
- Paid attention to environmental messages, e.g., social norming. (Who comes to a "Kill Your Liver Party," anyhow?)
- Sought data-driven, science-based approaches to prevention.
- Been suspicious of simplistic, magic bullet approaches. The magic bullet, if there is one, is an enfilade of coordinated strategies and requires persistence and assessment.

The science has also contradicted *Bradshaw* and core bystander era beliefs. *Bradshaw* took judicial notice of the following beliefs in the left column, but here is what modern prevention science now shows in the right column:

1. Students are adults.	1. Today many students are not full adults. Most traditional-age college students' brains are still developing, even past college years. The development is slowed/harmed by high-risk alcohol use. The part of the brain that is developing involves judgment and decision-making, inter alia.
2. College alcohol use is uncontrollable; only "custodial" control could change that.	2. High-risk alcohol use can be lowered using science-based strategies, most of which involve very limited "control." We can manage and facilitate environmental change.
3. College is where students learn to drink, and socialize into drinking.	3. Few college students "learn to drink" in college. Most bring high-risk behaviors from K–12. Sadly, some evidence shows that drinking patterns persist—even become worse for some—in college and carry into graduate school.
4. Courts should take judicial notice of pre-scientific prevention "facts."	4. Science gives increasingly better insight into realities of college drinking.
5. The core mission of college is education.	5. High-risk alcohol use degrades that core mission.

The law may sometimes continue to be resistant to science and scientific prevention strategies. Nonetheless, it is more common than ever for colleges and plaintiff's lawyers to "arm up" with prevention science and scientific experts. Evidence of science-based litigation is now reflected even in the reported case law as a new era of data, assessment and law emerges.

Consider twin cases from Connecticut, *McClure* and *Pawlowski*.[247] In *McClure v. Fairfield University*,[248] a Connecticut superior court considered a situation involving a vehicular accident stemming from an off-campus outing at a beach involving alcohol use, for which the university offered a safe ride program.[249] The complaint alleged various forms of negligence against the university including failing to adequately supervise and monitor off-campus and underage drinking.[250] In considering whether a duty was owed from the university to the injured students, the court specifically considered the bystander trilogy of *Beach*, *Bradshaw*, and *Rabel*.[251] The court, however, sided with *Furek* in rejecting the reasoning of that line of cases.[252] While the court's reasoning seemed to turn upon an assumption of duty argument—based upon the fact that the university had provided a safe ride program between the beach and campus[253]—its comments about *Beach* and *Bradshaw*, the change in the minimum drinking age, and alcohol issues are instructive:

> Both *Furek* and *Mullins* are distinguishable from the present case in that the events in those cases occurred on campus. However, while the events in the present case occurred off campus, the university's providing information about the beach area housing in the student binder was an imprimatur. It was well known that students would attend parties at the beach residences where they would consume alcohol. When *Bradshaw* and *Beach* were decided, the legal drinking age in a majority of jurisdictions was 18 years of age. In Connecticut, the legal drinking age is presently 21 years of age, as it was at the time of the accident. A large percentage of university students are there-

---

247. The following discussion of *McClure* is adopted and adapted heavily from Peter F. Lake, *Private Law Continues to Come to Campus*, *supra* note 29.

248. No. CV000159028, 2003 WL 21524786 (Conn. Super. Ct. June 19, 2003).

249. *Id.* at *1.

250. *Id.* at *1 n.1.

251. *Id.* at *3–4.

252. *Id.* at *5.

253. *Id.* A safe ride program enlists volunteers to safely drive individuals who have been consuming alcohol to and from locations. *Id.* at *4.

> fore below the age of majority with respect to the usage of alcohol. Student alcohol use has become an increasingly serious problem in recent years. The university has acknowledged this in that it has an anti-alcohol policy that applies to all underage students. While the university had knowledge that underage drinking frequently occurred at the beach area, it did nothing to enforce the policy there, which indirectly encouraged students to go to the beach area in order to drink alcohol.[254]

The interesting question after *McClure*—in addition to whether it will ultimately remain the law of Connecticut—is whether the case would have turned out differently if there had been no safe ride programs in place. Safe rides are promising prevention practices with some scientific support. Is *McClure* an assumed duty case? Would institutions in Connecticut be better off legally to adopt science-based prevention strategies? Technically, the case is "unpublished"; however, it has been cited and referred to.[255] The *McClure* matter went to arbitration, and in a subsequent decision the same Connecticut court decided that the arbitration award barred further recovery by the plaintiff against the university defendant in the matter.[256]

The fraternal twin Connecticut case is *Pawlowski v. Delta Sigma Phi*[257] (also "unpublished"). In *Pawlowski* Judge Linda Lager (You can't make this stuff up!) determined that Quinnipiac University did not assume a duty to an underage student who left a private party at an off-campus residence—significantly intoxicated—and was struck and killed while crossing the street in the middle of the block.[258] The private party was at a house—not a chapter house—that was populated by current and former members of a fraternity that had trouble in the past. *Pawlowski* is a modern grayspace case; both in terms of duty but also with terms of registered student organization (RSO) management—events at living arrangements like this occur throughout the country.

There were campus rules against what happened at the "party." However, *Pawlowski* correctly observed that having rules—even negligently not enforc-

254. *Id.* at *7.

255. *Freeman v. Busch*, 349 F.3d 582, 588 n.6 (8th Cir. 2003); *see also* Areen, *supra* note 192.

256. *McClure v. Fairfield Univ.*, No. CV000159028S, 2004 WL 203001, at *1 (Conn. Super. Ct. Jan. 14, 2004).

257. No. CV-03-0484661S 2009 WL 415667 (Conn. Super. Ct. Jan. 23, 2009).

258. *Id.* at *1.

ing rules—does not create a duty.[259] Colleges can, and should, have rules and the existence of rules *in itself is not* "assuming a duty" or a "special relationship." Moreover, *Pawlowski* pointed out that while it was "literally foreseeable" that students might go to an off-campus party, mere foreseeability is not enough to create a duty.[260] The court also pointed out that past enforcement did not *enhance* risks (indeed the science would suggest that having rules and enforcing them *reduces* risks).[261]

Recognizing the limits of law, and even legal duty, to create a safe campus *Pawlowski* stated:

> Since the plaintiffs seek to extend the university's affirmative control of student behavior to students living privately off-campus, there is the potential for restrictions that could be far more extensive than those in effect when the doctrine of *in loco parentis* governed the university-student relationship. Under the *in loco parentis* doctrine, a university had a custodial relationship over its students. It exercised stringent control over student conduct but, in exchange, was required to provide certain protections to the students. [Note the *Bradshaw* error here. Ed.] See, e.g., *Bradshaw v. Rawlings*, 612 F.2d 135, 139–40 (3rd Cir. 1979). "The demise of *in loco parentis* . . . has been a direct result of changes that have occurred in society's perception of the most beneficial allocation of rights and responsibilities in the university-student relationship." *University of Denver v. Whitlock*, 744 P.2d 54, 60 (Colo. 1987). "The transfer of prerogatives and rights from college administrators to students is salubrious when seen in the context of a proper goal of postsecondary education the maturation of the students. Only by giving them responsibilities can students grow into responsible adulthood." *Baldwin v. Zoradi, supra,* at 123 Cal.App.3d 291, 176 Cal.Rptr. 818.
>
> Additionally, a conclusion that a duty arises based on policies contained in a student handbook and past practices of the university in enforcing those polices could potentially discourage institutions of higher education from having policies and implementing enforcement practices that govern such things as students' alcohol consumption and students' unlawful behavior, if the absence of a policy means the

---

259. *Id* at *3.

260. *See id.* at *5.

261. *Id.* at *5. Indeed the court went on to intimate that there would have been no breach of duty in the case. *Id.* at *6, n. 5.

> absence of any duty, a rational institution could opt for laxity over enforcement to the detriment of its student population.
>
> Thus, recognizing a § 323 duty under the circumstances presented by this case poses a risk of a university engaging in either over enforcement, i.e., excessive control, or under enforcement, i.e., no control, of its students' private off-campus recreational activities. Neither of these are desirable outcomes. As desirable as it may be to address the serious problem of students' underage drinking and its adverse consequences, courts recognize [Note the judicial "notice" of the perceived state of prevention science. Ed.] that it is "difficult to so police a modern university campus as to eradicate alcohol ingestion." *Baldwin v. Zoradi, supra,* at 123 Cal.App.3d 290. As a practical matter, it may be impossible for a university to police students' off-campus alcohol consumption. [Same. Ed.] The practical limitations on the proactive measures a university may be able to undertake, combined with the attendant costs of such measures [*Pawlowski* relates no information on the costs of prevention. In fact, good prevention is not extremely costly. Ed.], further militates against finding any duty on the part of the university.[262]

Pawlowski may have committed the *Bradshaw* error with *in loco parentis* and assumed too much about prevention science, but much is forgiven in the candor the court shows in its analysis. Too much enforcement in colleges will not *teach* but *police* students—destroying the educational mission we are trying to protect. Finding a duty based on policy creation and enforcement could encourage colleges to be bystanders. *Pawlowski* is perhaps the first clear case of using duty analysis to at once encourage colleges to have policies and enforce them, create a facilitative educational environment, and keep colleges accountable without holding them liable. *Pawlowski* is as brilliant as the ending of Harry Potter—subtle, profound, modern, timeless. Would you dare pursue ostrichism after reading the case? Would you cancel your safe ride program? I suspect not: the no-duty ruling is a direct result of active, reasonable engagement. The paradox of duty analysis—especially in "alcohol cases" may lie in the fact that it is most powerful when courts do *not* find liability. Anyone who still believes that legal compliance merely means avoiding "assuming duties" has missed the point, and does so at their peril in and out of court. Welcome to the age of duty, balancing rights and responsibilities, and accountability. At least in the

---

262. *Id.* at *6 (footnotes omitted; editorial comment inserted).

courts. It may well be the case that doing what is reasonable provides the greatest chance of winning "no-duty" arguments in court.

Keep in mind however, that this may be a fleeting moment if regulators continue down a path of heightened expectations for colleges and student safety. The great post-World War II alcohol party could end at any time. Colleges have been protected by social host immunities and rules of comparative fault. However regulators might step up enforcement under the Safe and Drug-Free Schools and Communities Act.[263] Current Title IX enforcement efforts will also impact college alcohol responsibility cases: cases like *Freeman* and *Tanja H.* are particularly vulnerable. Will regulators make the leap and recognize that alcohol is the central risk factor in virtually all college risks including academic achievement, attainment, and safety? If they do, this will be the final bell for bystanderism.

Nonetheless, courts have rejected college liability for student alcohol-related injuries in the following circumstances, *inter alia*:

- The Colorado Supreme Court found that a university was not liable for injuries suffered by an intoxicated student as a result of his use of a trampoline at a campus fraternity. The court insisted—similar to *Bradshaw*—hat a special relationship be shown *(Univ. of Denver v. Whitlock,* 744 P.2d 54 (Colo. 1987));
- In *Hartman v. Bethany College*, 778 F. Supp. 286 (N.D.W. Va. 1991) a college freshman claimed that because she was a minor, the college had a duty to prevent her off-campus drinking. She lost;
- A student was killed riding a motorcycle on a public street after drinking at a fraternity party. The university was not liable *(Millard v. Osborne,* 611 A.2d 715 (Pa. Super. Ct. 1992));
- In an unusual case, a college freshman "got wasted" off campus and after taking some sort of a beating, stumbled into a commuter rail platform and collapsed, in need of rescue. As a drunken trespasser, he was not entitled to immediate assistance by the railroad *(Rhodes v. Illinois Cent. Gulf R.R.,* 665 N.E.2d 1260 (Ill. 1996).

The alcohol cases may seem to split but there are some fairly consistent themes. The mere fact that a university regulates alcohol use does not create a specific duty to particular individuals. While alcohol dangers are *generally foreseeable,* specific foreseeable danger will be necessary to attach liability for a particular student/victim. In the courts, bad plaintiffs deserve comparative fault: even un-

263. 20 U.S.C. § 7101 (2006).

derage drinkers are rarely afforded the benefit of the doubt. Some parties, like the liquor vendor and local Greek chapters, may be legally responsible for harm. Gray space cases vex courts and generate intensely intricate legal analysis.

Finally, while the alcohol litigation wars continue in court, and as regulators may be poised to intervene, college alcohol policy is generating major debate in social policy circles.

First, beyond the confines of college life, there has been a steady increase in responsibility for liquor injuries. Importantly, the law increasingly holds employers and businesses liable for liquor injuries arising from company events. Also, some courts are relaxing the notions of what it means to "furnish" liquor to a minor. Some states have rejected wholesale social host immunities. In sum, social mores about drinking and liability are shifting, and the law is shifting too.

Second, there is a sense of urgency about liquor problems on campus. It is not realistic (or desirable) to seek prohibition on campuses. However, there are effective techniques to affect some of the most dangerous aspects of disorder that are connected with alcohol use. The university is not a bystander, and it is not helpless—there are reasonable solutions.

Third, attitudes are shifting towards college drinkers. As cases have made the press, there is an increasing sentiment from the public and parents that *general* risks of alcohol culture are foreseeable and that students are not solely responsible for alcohol-related injuries. Parents and the media see that students are being injured, attacked, raped, and killed as a result of an alcohol culture and may not continue to accept the argument that dangerous behavior and risk of injury—including sexual assault—that results from high-risk alcohol use on campus is beyond the college's power to manage.

The duty era is an era of transition. It is a period that features a powerful judicial alignment around rules of "duty"—particularly familiar business and liquor liability rules. The messages of the cases *seem* mixed at first: e.g., *Tanja H.* plaintiff loses, *Furek* plaintiff wins. However, from a wider perspective there are several themes at work—the strongest is the steady mainstreaming of higher education under widely used alcohol law principles.

7. Mental Health and Suicide

In 2002, Nancy Tribbensee and I published the first major piece on the emerging mental health challenges for college campuses.[264] At that time, a wave

264. *The Emerging Crisis of College Student Suicide: Law and Policy Responses to Serious Forms of Self-Inflicted Injury*, 32 Stetson L. Rev. 125 (2002).

of mental health issues was evident in K–12, which broke in higher education (and is now spilling into graduate programs).[265]

Researchers have pointed out the disturbing statistics of suicidality in college-aged populations and noted the surge in those who seek access to mental health services:

> Suicide is the third leading cause of death for youths between the ages of 15 and 24 years, following accidental injury and homicide, and is believed to be the second leading cause of death for college students because of the low rate of homicide in this population (Centers for Disease Control and Prevention, 2007; Suicide Prevention Resource Center, 2004). Although the rate of completed suicides for college students is estimated at between 6.5 and 7.5 per 100,000, or approximately half that of the nonstudent matched cohort, nearly all of this reduction in suicide completions may be attributable to the reduced access to firearms on college campuses (Schwartz, 2006a; Silverman, Meyer, Sloane, Raffel, & Pratt, 1997). Additionally, the apparent decline in college suicide rates that has been noted over the past 3 decades (Schwartz, 2006b) correlates almost perfectly with the decreasing proportion of men in college, as the suicide completion rate for male students is over twice that of female students (Silverman et al., 1997). One might therefore conclude that campus prevention efforts are either non-existent or ineffective, especially because nearly 80% of those students who die by suicide never participate in counseling services (Gallagher, 2004; Kisch, Leino, & Silverman, 2005). However, for those students who do receive help from their college counseling centers, these services are effective. An analysis of the prevalence and effect of known risk factors among counseling center clients suggests that these students would complete suicide at a rate 18 times greater than the general student suicide rate, when in fact the actual rate of suicide among counseling center clients is only 3 times greater than in the nonclient student population (Schwartz, 2006a).

265. *See, e.g.*, Trip Gabriel, *Mental Health Needs Seen Growing at Colleges*, N.Y. Times, Dec. 19, 2010; Richard D. Kadison & Theresa Foy DiGeronimo, *College of the Overwhelmed: The Campus Mental Health Crisis and What to Do About It* (Jossey-Bass 2004); David J. Drum, Chris Brownson, Adryon Burton Denmark & Shanna E. Smith, *New Data of the Nature of Suicidal Crises in College Students: Shifting the Paradigm*, 40 Professional Psychology: Research and Practice 3, 213 (2009) [Drum Study].

> Although the benefits of seeking counseling may be due, in part, to the self-selection of those who seek help, efforts to raise awareness about the mental health services available on campus remain important. This is particularly important considering that only 26% of college students are aware of their campus's mental health resources (Westefeld et al., 2005). Yet, even if it were possible to increase the sensitivity and accuracy of existing referral systems so that the majority of students at risk of committing suicide were seen at their college counseling centers, meeting the needs of these students would be extremely costly and could require up to a 75% increase in counseling staff (Schwartz, 2006a). An effective approach to suicide prevention cannot continue to rely entirely on individual-focused counseling services. Further reductions in suicide ideation, attempts, and completions must derive from a thorough understanding of all aspects of the suicidal spectrum and from use of that information to plan more robust programs of prevention and intervention.[266]

These observations are especially disturbing in light of the push in some states for weapons on campus—will we see greater suicide completion rates on campus if the efforts succeed? Moreover, statistics also hide another safety reality—some suicidal individuals complete or attempt suicide off campus, after graduation, or after dropping out—representing as "non-college" student suicides. College suicidal problems may be greater than we imagine given our still relatively primitive data gathering systems. Moreover, suicide has been averred to be the leading cause of death among GLBT students; and some suicides are caused/impacted by bullying behavior.[267]

Suicide is the tip of an iceberg in an ongoing wellness challenge on campus including self-injury/cutting, eating disorders, learning disabilities, personality disorders, social phobias, and the list goes on. It may be that in time wellness issues will overtake alcohol risk as the greatest challenge to modern college students. The law has been painfully slow to develop in this area.[268] Safety law developed primarily around situations where an individual harms another; for

266. *See* Drum Study, *supra* note 265, at 214.

267. *See* Richard Fossey, Suzanne Eckes & Todd A. DeMitchell, *Anti-Gay T-Shirt Litigation in the Seventh and Ninth Circuits: Conflicts of Outcomes, But Changing Values*, 256 Ed. Law Rep. 1, 1 n. 5 (2010).

268. *See* Peter F. Lake, *Still Waiting: The Slow Evolution of the Law in Light of the Ongoing Student Suicide Crisis*, 34 J.C. & U.L. 253 (2008).

many mental health risks the victim is the one who has wellness challenges. Lawsuits are much more likely to arise in the context of disability accommodations, or in breach of contract, than negligence. Moreover, the law of liability for suicide has generally been unfavorable to negligence claims and there has been little to no indication that courts will impose broad-based duties of suicide prevention upon colleges.

In 2002, Nancy Tribbensee and I surveyed the law of suicide "duty" as follows:

> For many years the American legal system categorically refused to find civil liability arising out of a failure to prevent suicide. Suicide was considered an illegal, deliberate, and intentional act, that was an intervening proximate cause that precluded liability. As the Supreme Court of New Hampshire correctly has observed
>
>> [I]n recent years, however, tort actions seeking damages for the suicide of another have been recognized under two exceptions to the general rule, namely, where the defendant is found to have actually *caused* the suicide, or where the defendant is found to have had a *duty to prevent* the suicide from occurring.
>
> An individual or entity may fall within the first exception—that of causing the suicide—in a number of limited circumstances. For example, when an individual causes severe physical injury to another, leading that individual to a state of mental incapacity that results in suicide, the individual causing the physical injury may be held responsible for the resulting suicide. Additionally, if a defendant causes severe mental injury through serious physical abuse, torture, abuse of process, or improper confinement, and that mental injury leads to suicide, that defendant may be held responsible for causing an uncontrollable impulse to commit suicide that prevented the individual from realizing the wrongful and serious nature of the suicidal act. As the *McLaughlin* court correctly observed, an exception based on causing the suicide
>
>> involves cases where a tortious act is found to have caused a mental condition in the decedent that proximately resulted in an uncontrollable impulse to commit suicide, or prevented the decedent from realizing the nature of his act.... Such cases typically involve the infliction of severe physical injury, or, in rare cases, the intentional infliction of severe mental or emotional injury through wrongful accusation, false arrest or torture.

Indeed, it is common for courts to regard this exception in a "very narrow" way.

Courts also have considered that an individual who or entity that provides illegal substances or liquor in an illegal or improper way also can be liable for resulting suicide. This type of liability can be statutory in nature and encompasses "a duty to refrain from knowingly making available the means of an individual's self-destruction."

• • • •

A second well-recognized exception to the no-duty-to-prevent-suicide rule arises when the defendant has a legally recognized special relationship with a suicidal individual sufficient to create a duty to prevent suicide. Generally American tort law does not hold individuals responsible for preventing harm by others merely from the knowledge of danger. The duty to prevent suicide (when it is not an issue of whether the defendant caused the suicide) is a creature of the law of affirmative duty.

Most typically, courts look for a special relationship between the parties to impose an affirmative duty on an individual for the benefit of another party. In discussing the duty to prevent suicide, courts typically speak of special relationships in the context of custodial care. Some courts appear to impose a custodial requirement that goes even beyond mere custody and control to the level of the responsibility of a suicide watch—a highly controlled custodial care environment. Courts have been most likely to impose duties arising from such a special relationship on a jail, hospital, or reform school, and on others having actual physical custody and control over individuals. Mental hospitals, psychiatrists, and other trained professionals in the mental-health field are also often deemed to have the type of training and experience to permit them to be aware of behavior patterns that may increase the potential for suicide. It appears that courts sometimes equate special knowledge and experience in this field with a type of control sufficient to impose a duty to prevent suicide.

• • • •

In each of the two exceptional scenarios in which a defendant may be liable for a suicide (the case in which the defendant's acts are deemed to have caused the person to commit suicide or the case in which the defendant has a special relationship that creates a duty to protect), the traditional, no-proximate-causation rule is no longer accepted. Instead, with respect to these two exceptions, courts typically say that a

> suicide is foreseeable. Suicide is no longer an intervening act that cuts off the chain of liability. Therefore, a defendant who falls within either of these two exceptions may be subject to liability for the resulting suicide. Historically suicide rules focused very heavily upon the idea of proximate causation, as opposed to duty. Yet, strict rules of proximate causation have waned in modern times.[269]

There have been exceptionally few cases of *any* kind applying these two exceptions in tort law, and precious few in higher education. Colleges or administrators rarely "cause" a suicide,[270] and again in rare instances colleges do put students in something like the necessary *custodial* care. Perhaps there is some relaxation of old rules in college litigation;[271] recent bullying-related suicides may prompt legislative and regulatory change that will force colleges to face higher levels of accountability for student suicide (or if a suicide is precipitated by a sexual

---

269. Lake & Tribbensee, *supra* note 264, at 129–34 (footnotes omitted) (quoting *McLaughlin v. Sullivan*, 461 A.2d 123, 123–124 (N.H. 1983).

270. It does happen, however. *See, e.g.*, *Wallace v. Broyles*, 961 S.W.2d 712 (Ark. 1998) (duty can arise from allowing access to drugs that can cause suicidal ideation).

271. Consider *Schieszler v. Ferrum Coll.*, 233 F. Supp. 2d 796 (W.D. Va. 2002):

> In a recent case involving Ferrum College, the court upheld a claim involving an alleged duty to prevent suicide. Michael Frentzel was a freshman at the time of his self-inflicted death. He experienced some "disciplinary issues" during his first semester, and the College required that he fulfill certain conditions such as anger management counseling prior to the start of the second semester. Early in that semester, Frentzel had an argument with his girlfriend. Campus police and the resident assistant at Frentzel's dormitory responded to the incident and were aware that Frentzel sent a note to his girlfriend stating that he would hang himself with this belt. During the next few days, Frentzel wrote several other notes of a suicidal nature and was found in his dormitory room with self-inflicted bruises to his head. The College responded by requiring Frentzel to sign a statement promising not to harm himself and by refusing to allow his girlfriend to return to his dormitory room. Frentzel hanged himself by his belt in his dormitory room three days after the argument with his girlfriend.
>
> Representatives of his estate sued the College, alleging that it owed a duty to Frentzel to prevent his suicide. The College moved to dismiss the complaint, arguing that no such duty was owed. However, the court refused to dismiss the action, holding that Frentzel's suicide was arguably foreseeable because there was an "imminent probability" of harm and the college had "notice of this specific harm." The court noted that there is usually no affirmative duty to aid others "absent unusual circumstances." One such circumstance is the existence of a special relationship sufficient to impose a duty to aid. The court acknowledged that the relationship be-

assault).[272] Nonetheless, there has been no avalanche of reported suicide case law, or regulation, or statutes, and it appears that many jurisdictions may be content to wait this one out.

A third potential form of responsibility has evolved. However, it is also without much firm footing. Some litigants argue that colleges may have a duty to warn or notify someone—usually parents—of a student's suicidal ideation. This idea *might* have taken root at the time of *Tarasoff* (1970s)—it did not. In *Nally v. Grace Church*, the California Supreme Court rejected the idea of broadening *Tarasoff* duties in a suicide context.[273] Other courts agreed. Decades later college plaintiffs have tried their hand at essentially the same theory in a string of cases that are inconsistent and inconclusive.[274] The "notification" theory has a fatal flaw in most suicide situations—suicidal ideation is rarely a "sudden" event and parents/family are often aware for years of a student's suicidal ideation. It is not unusual to see families place suicidal family members into higher education to take advantage of the protective factors present in a college environment. It is not unusual that the college is the entity that is the last to know about a student's suicidal ideation—and may also know the least. Even counseling staff may be in the dark; suicidal students sometimes hide their suicidal ideations or attempts.

Mental health and wellness issues push the limits of what the law can do to facilitate safer and more responsible campuses. While some research sug-

---

> tween college and student is not necessarily special; however, a special relationship can "exist between particular plaintiffs and defendants . . . because of the particular factual circumstances in a given case." Therefore, the special relationship at issue arose from the College's knowledge of the imminent danger to Frentzel. The court did not suggest that the holding relied on the "assumed duty" theory because the duty owed by the College did not arise from its voluntary attempt to work with Frentzel after his first semester difficulties. The existence of the special relationship also did not stem from custodial control as the court acknowledged that, unlike a high school student, no *in loco parentis* relationship existed. Instead, the College's duty arose from a special relationship based upon the particular facts of the case.

Lake & Tribbensee, supra note 264, at 135–36 (footnotes omitted).

272. *See* Will Creeley, *Why the Tyler Clementi Act Threatens Free Speech on Campuses*, Chron. Higher Educ. (Apr. 10, 2011), *available at* http://chronicle.com/article/Why-the-Tyler-Clementi-Act/127062/; *Some Student Bullying May Violate Federal Law, Education Department Says*, Chron. Higher Educ. (Oct. 25, 2010), *available at* http://chronicle.com/blogs/ticker/some-student-bullying-may-violate-federal-law-education-department-says/27906 (referencing the Department of Education's Oct. 10, 2010 "Dear Colleague" letter).

273. *Nally v. Grace Cmty. Church*, 763 P.2d 948 (Cal. 1988).

274. *See* Lake & Tribbensee, *supra* note 264, at 137–51 and cases discussed there.

gests the power of legalisms to deter suicide, the simple fact is that colleges and students will not achieve wellness through tort litigation. The duty era encounters its own limits in the face of such a crisis. Law and legalisms have shaped the modern university, but it is ironic that as the era of duty and accountability advances, the limits of law as a tool to reshape college have become more apparent. Wellness and mental health challenges cry out for *educational* and *public health* interventions. That being said, courts can help higher education by clearly articulating the boundaries of what they will, and will not, require and when they will, or will not, intervene. The spectre of intervention, under a thin cloud of conflicting case law, can be paralyzing to good student affairs practice. We wait for the law to acknowledge our challenges and to speak.

Three other points are important by way of conclusion. Federal privacy law has changed in a way that facilitates the free flow of safety-related information. The law has encouraged and facilitated educational and proactive public health interventions. This is law beyond "duty" or "liability": it is a form of legal intervention that empowers, instead of judges. There is a glimpse here of the future of higher education law; the possibility of creating a collaborative, facilitative structure of higher education law and legal principles that transcends a culture of responsibility avoidance, blame litigation, and denial. There is indeed a place beyond the dialectic of balancing rights and responsibilities: the law of "duty" in higher education (even the concept of legal accountability) is a creature of that dialectic, its mediating concept. This is an evolutionary leap that seems far in the future from this vantage point.

Second, some suicidal individuals are homicidal or could easily cause unintended injuries to others. When a suicidal person foreseeably endangers others, the analysis shifts to duty principles discussed earlier. Moreover, suicide never just affects the suicidal person; sometimes suicide endangers others.

Third, any "duty"/"accountability" discussion of wellness and suicide risks overlooks the obvious. Without good intervention strategies—like those proposed by the JED Foundation[275]—the core mission of higher education will be at risk. Higher education as a business has little choice but to confront these challenges proactively. Bystanding is not a real business option.

---

275. *See* JED Foundation, *Student Mental Health and the Law: A Resource for Institutions of Higher Education* (2008), *available at* https://www.jedfoundation.org/assets/Programs/Program_downloads/StudentMentalHealth_Law_2008.pdf.

Conclusion

The modern university has faced the steady application of business law safety principles and rules. The Florida Supreme Court may have said it best:

> It is clearly established that one who undertakes to act, even when under no obligation to do so, there by becomes obligated to act with reasonable care . . . We find this fundamental principle of tort law is equally applicable in this case. There is no reason why a university may act without regard to the consequences of its actions while every other legal entity is charged with acting as a reasonable person would in like or similar circumstances.[276]

Higher education has been mainstreamed steadily under tort and safety law, and the complex concept of legal duty has been the primary organizing principle.

A "duty" can arise in a number of ways:

- From a business landowner to its customers (special relationship)
- From a landlord/tenant relationship (special relationship)
- Programmatically
- When a college causes, created, or significantly enhances a risk
- When duty is "assumed"
- From statutory/regulatory mandates
- Occasionally from a contract (rarely though)
- From custodial control

Courts and commentators often talk of "special" relationships, or assumed duty, as a necessary predicate for duty. Indeed, a special relationship/assumed duty can create legal duty, but these are not the only way legal entities become charged with a duty to act reasonably (or more). Over reliance on special relationships/assumed duty analysis in higher education law is a direct result of bystander era conceptualization of college safety law as a rescue/affirmative duty problem. Moreover, exercising custodial control can create duty but custodial control—indeed control of any kind—is not always a necessary predicate for duty. (Unless one is a "control freak" and imagines that the power to act reasonably is a form of "control." Courts do not think like that.)

The existence of duty, *vel non*, is a complex conceptual question and does not reduce easily to simple rules. In fact, duty is as much a function of rules

276. *Nova Southeastern Univ.*, 758 So. 2d at 90.

as other determinants of human behavior, like principles and policies. Moreover, the duty calculus is always shifting, in motion. Duty is a living, evolving concept. To truly understand duty you must get in touch with its organic qualities.

The application of bystander principles is, from a wider perspective, the application of *some* features of the law of duty to higher education. The leading bystander cases like *Bradshaw* and *Freeman* are creatures of time and place, and the specific safety issues they addressed. No-duty/no-liability rules for "social" drinking were extant broadly at the time of *Bradshaw*, and persist in many states even today. Federal courts have had no interest in baiting college safety litigation via diversity jurisdiction and, not surprisingly, have rejected social alcohol consumption and acquaintance sexual assault cases. As to sexual assault, state and federal courts recognize that the criminal justice system does not routinely address acquaintance sexual assault cases, especially where the victim has been drinking and socializing in an alcohol culture with the attacker. Cases like *Freeman* create a parallel: colleges are not required under a reasonable care standard to do what criminal prosecutors have not done.

From the myopic perspective of higher education law it is tempting to elevate the bystander era to mean things it does not. Crosscurrent cases of the same timeframe—like *Mullins*—illustrate this.

It is also crucial to realize that while the duty era inclines towards shared responsibility, proactive interventions, and responsibility in a conceptual educational riskscape, duty is *not* liability. As in the tort system generally, it is difficult for plaintiffs to win. Courts routinely block claims for lack of proof of causation for instance. Importantly, negligence law generally disfavors highly faulty plaintiffs from making claims. Johnny Knoxville is not a good plaintiff. In many instances affirmative defenses bar claims, or reduce them to small amounts (think *Knoll*). Governmental immunity is also a significant issue in a large range of safety cases against public colleges and administrators. Most importantly legal duty can be discharged through the exercise of reasonable care (think *Gragg v. Wichita State*). Indeed, in the paradox of college litigation, colleges may actually win on duty issues in court because courts perceive that they have been acting reasonably or that no reasonable care could have prevented an incident.

The rise of duty is not the rise of liability, simpliciter, although an increase in legal exposure is part of the mix. The rise of duty is evidence of increasing accountability under law, in a complex conceptual/doctrinal system. In an age of accountability colleges will face increasing costs related to compliance efforts and will likely see settlements, not judgments. Finally, if there is one enduring truth in higher education safety law in the modern period it is this: students typically bear the lion's share of responsibility for risk.

The great challenge for colleges in the duty era is to try to reduce the complex messages of the law to operational principles. From an administrative standpoint, the search for compliance is paramount. A core compliance message from the courts is clear, even if it is not specific and stated in single, cookie-cutter compliance steps. Operate in good faith and with reasonable care and you will never lose under a reasonable care standard. Trying to "game" duty law has real legal risk—look at how institutions/administrators tried to avoid litigation only to find it in cases like *Nero*. It is always theoretically possible that a college might, in a highly unusual case, have created a duty where none existed. However, a college will have no way to know this *a priori*: it is quite a gamble to choose a path inconsistent with professional practice and with what is reasonable in the hopes that either no one will get hurt, or if someone does get hurt, there will be a no-duty ruling years after the event.

Persistence with "bystander" era beliefs and rhetoric is increasingly dangerous business as well. Administrators and lawyers retreat to facile positions like "students are adults," or "to impose duty would be to insure students," or "alcohol risk is uncontrollable," or "suicide risk is exaggerated," or "these cases are a return to *in loco parentis*," in large measure because of sheer frustration with compliance directives that are both conceptually complex and deliberately do not provide *specific* guidance.[277] The next chapter explores ways to work within such a system of compliance and accountability—this is the path of a facilitator university. You may be surprised to learn that higher education is a culture of Dorothys—the way home is closer than we may be tempted to think when the fear of the wicked witch of law looms.

In some ways, the path ahead for the modern university will be as easy, or as hard as we make it. Ours is a culture of responsibility and accountability and was so long before law arrived. When we resist our prime directives via ostrichism, bystanding, undue victim blaming, etc., we risk a backlash. Legislators and regulators have shown increasing frustration with higher education. The days of dialogue alone regarding hazing (*Furek*) are done: most states have enacted severe criminal and civil penalties for hazing and insist that campuses enforce the law. Courts may have been sympathetic to the challenges of acquaintance sexual assault in a high-risk alcohol culture; regulators are not so

277. *See, e.g.*, *Nova Southeastern Univ.*, 758 So.2d at 90 ("We do not make any specific findings as to what duty Nova owed Gross, other than to hold a jury should determine whether Nova acted reasonably . . .").

sympathetic. Higher education should also be careful in what it is asking for. Complaints and hyperbole about the non-specific mandates of the reasonable care standard may mutate into strict regulatory compliance directives—setting standards in excess of reasonable care. Fear of reasonable care baits the emergence of the compliance university. Will the duty era be replaced by a new, fifth era, the era of legislative/regulatory intervention? Will the expectation be that colleges should be as safe as possible as Vice President Biden articulated? Will our days be packed with filling out forms and reports, "processing" everything but teaching less?

As we look to the next chapter, and the horizons, it is not inconceivable that there will be legal evolution beyond the duty era into a new age of college accountability under law. This has been the pathogenesis of much safety law in other areas—from legal insularity, to duty, to regulation. We should be particularly mindful of potential changes in alcohol law. Will social host immunities persist in colleges as regulators push for higher levels of accountability in core mission delivery—safety, graduation and attainment rates, debt to outcome ratios—if the science shows the connections between high-risk college alcohol culture and sexual assault, dropout rates, impaired learning and debt? Will *Bradshaw* and the other icons of the bystander era die in Congress or the Department of Education? These questions will loom in the decades ahead as the duty era consolidates and sows seeds for the next era.

VI

The Rise of the Facilitator University

The law of student safety has evolved in four discernable periods, with a potential fifth era on the horizon. First, the university was insularized from the application of legal norms, although the law did protect the power and prerogatives of higher education.[1] In the second era, emphasizing civil rights on campus, university insularity eroded when students won civil rights on campus. In the third phase—the bystander era—governmental, parental, and charitable immunities fell and no-duty rules emerged. Legally, a college could

1. Nancy L. Thomas describes the development of law and lawyers on campus:

> In 1960, nine attorneys representing 15 campuses held a retreat in Ann Arbor, Michigan. Their theme was "The Function of House Counsel at State Universities." At the time, no body of "college law" existed, and members of this small group saw a need to examine legal problems and solutions common to their universities. When they met again in 1966 to consider in loco parentis and student rights, they distributed one handout fewer than 15 pages long.
>
> Today, this group (called the National Association of College and University Attorneys, or NACUA) has grown to more than 2,700 attorneys who represent nearly 1,400 campuses. NACUA, which averages 40 new members a year, provides continuing legal education for university attorneys by producing publications and sponsoring frequent seminars. Its annual conference lasts five days and offers sessions on more than 50 subjects. . . .
>
> [T]he field of higher education law has evolved from an informal "interest" to a complex and sophisticated legal specialty. West Publishing Company, the primary publisher of judicial opinions, publishes the *Education Law Reporter,* which includes a comprehensive descriptive-word directory of college and university topics. Once considered "immune charities," colleges and universities are now living the curse, "May your life be full of lawyers."

stand back from many student safety concerns, particularly alcohol risk. The 1960s and 1970s were unusual times: universities began to distance themselves from students and bifurcated academic and student affairs. The fourth era, the duty era, has rooted firmly today in modern university law (although it was certainly immanent in the bystander era). The duty era is doctrinally complex—as we saw in Chapter V—and seemingly paints ambiguous images of the modern university and its relationship to its students. This chapter describes the way that the duty era has reshaped student/university relationships. Even as the duty era has consolidated, a new period—the compliance era—is burgeoning. More than ever, it is important to stake out an operational vision for the relationship between students and their institutions.

There have been a variety of images of the modern college and its students discussed by courts and commentators. This plethora of images is emblematic of a time of transition in both higher education law and tort law. Table 1 sets out, in brief form, the most commonly stated university/student relationships with some brief parenthetical information on the relationships that this chapter discusses further.

Table 1

The university is . . .	The student is . . .
"Business"/"Producer of Educational Product" (A dominant view.)	"Consumer" *(Id.)*
"Parent"/"Babysitter" (*In loco parentis.*) (Almost universally rejected.) (Sometimes used instead of a positive description—"college is *not* a babysitter.")	"Child"/"Minor" *(Id.)* *(Id.)*

> The presence of attorneys on campus has been met with mixed reactions. To some academics, attorneys are trusted advisors and key members of an administrative team. To others, they are naysayers or "Monday morning quarterbacks," are unnecessarily confrontational, or wield too much power. To most, they cost too much.
>
> Sometimes the negative reaction to attorneys is simply a response to their too frequent role as messenger, warning of problematic situations and legal hazards. Other times, an institution has, regrettably, selected an attorney who is unnecessarily cautious, confrontational, or domineering, or who is a mismatch with the institution's culture and needs.

Nancy L. Thomas, *The Attorney's Role on Campus—Options for Colleges and Universities,* 30 Change: The Magazine of Higher Learning 34, 35 (May/June 1998).

Table 1 (Continued)

The university is . . .	**The student is . . .**
"Bystander"/"Stranger" (The dominant idea of *Bradshaw* et al.)	"Uncontrollable"/"Stranger" *(Id.)*
"Insurer of Student Safety" (Overwhelmingly rejected with "parent," etc., and sometimes considered as an alternative to being a "bystander." Duty era cases distinguish this "strict liability" from duty.)	"Protected"/"Insured" (Confusion over the differences between strict liability, duty, and insurance. Subtle mistakes about "moral hazard."[2])
"Landlord" (Prior to 1960, almost unheard of as such; major development/recognition in recent cases.) (similar ⟶ *landowner)*	"Tenant"/"Resident Student" (There are many creative ways to describe a dormitory or residential student tenant, but courts treat them basically the same.) (similar ⟶ *invitee)*
"Custodian" (Used in K-12 case law, but rejected for law in bystander era, except when college actually brings children into programs. Suggestions that this was the role of the parental, *in loco parentis* university, although there is no case law support for this idea.)	"Persons in Custody" (Never used.)
"Education"/"In a Purely Educational Role" (Limited role/no educational malpractice.)	"Pure Student"[3] (The student comes to college *only* to be educated in class.)

2. The term "moral hazard" is an insurance term of art with a common sense idea tucked inside. Insurance law is concerned that the existence of insurance will facilitate and encourage increasingly risky, deliberate misconduct, or deliberate indifference. For example, the existence of life insurance could create some perverse incentives to kill someone. Liability insurance includes some level of moral hazard for institutions of higher education. In student safety litigation a college's insurance pays many attorney costs—often greater than exposure to liability—and verdicts and settlements are typically well within the covered limits of insurance. Although colleges must absorb premium increases and self-insured retentions, the real financial risks of student litigation over safety are often quite modest in relation to other budget items. As a result, college leadership tends to discount the cost of safety litigation. Insurers themselves have been pushing for greater risk management efforts on campus, with mixed results.

3. This view, a reaction to the abatement of *in loco parentis,* that the student/university relationship is purely educational (as an alternative to custodial) was an attempt to recreate insularity of university conduct from legal scrutiny, since claims of educational malpractice were and still are for the most part summarily rejected by courts.

Table 1 (Continued)

The university is . . .	The student is . . .
"Supervisor" (Sometimes used negatively as similar to custodian; in recent times used, as in *Mintz*, in regard to field trips, etc.)	"Supervised" *(Id.)*
"Employer" (In some cases, a student is actually employed by the college.)	"Employee" (Student enjoys legal status of appropriate category of worker; can include workers' compensation.)
"Manager"/"Organizer of Student Life Activities" (An idea, associated with *Furek*, that a college co-creates the environment on campus.)	"Participant" (Not a consumer, or employee; one whose conduct is channeled, guided or directed but not dictated.)
"Fiduciary" (Sometimes referred to in certain financial/educational/confidential relations situations.)	"One to Whom Fiduciary Duties Are Owed" (Hints of relationships like banking and trusteeship where one relies on the ability and authority of the other; sometimes confidential.)
"In a 'Special' Relationship" (By virtue of being a landlord, a premises owner, or having some relationship to dangerous or endangered persons: because of misinterpretation of *Bradshaw* et al., often used inter-changeably with duty, as if duty *only* exists when a special relationship exists, which is false. Technically, special relationships are only necessary when a university is being entirely unconnected and passive, which law in the duty era is increasingly less likely to see. Reluctance to see university relationship to student as *per se* special, but most aspects of student life are special or infused with duty.)	"Person Entitled to 'Duty' Because of Special Relationship, or Not, for Lack Thereof" *(Id.)*
"Charity" (A feature of the *in loco parentis* era.)	"Beneficiary" *(Id.)*
"In a Unique or Delicate Situation" (Seen by university attorneys, and administrators, as synonymous with *in loco parentis.*)	"In a Unique or Delicate Situation" (A throwback idea to the era of insularity; a view that student relations are too sensitive for a heavy-handed legal system; perceives law as bad, or dangerous.) (Alternatively, a sense that business paradigms are not adequate or appropriate.)

Table 1 (Continued)

The university is . . .	**The student is . . .**
"In a Contract Relationship"/"Promisor" (Many courts say that the student/university relationship is based in "contract," although most of these cases deal with financial, procedural, civil, and intangible rights.)	"In a Contract Relationship"/"Promisee" *(Id.)* (Student is typically contracting party, not parent.)
"A Public Governmental Entity" (Once a source of near total immunity, now a source of limited immunity, but includes constitutional responsibilities of a government to provide "due process," "equal protection," etc.)	"A Citizen"/"Student" (Student falls back to "consumer" image, if activities causing injury are similar to what businesses do, yet still retains substantive constitutional and procedural rights, etc.)
"In Transition from Industrial Age to Technological Age" (Levine & Cureton's thesis.)	"Caught in Transition Where Hope and Fear Collide" *(Id.)*(Unsure, unsteady, fractal community.)
"Facilitator" (Drawn as a synthesis of the various modern images.)	"Responsible"/"Student as Visitor"[4] (A balance between the *in loco parentis* student and the completely "free" student. University and student legally share *responsibility* for student safety; university is neither strictly responsible for student safety, nor insulated or immune from legal accountability for its operational negligence.)

University administrators face a perplexing—sometimes conflicting, other times overlapping—array of images to describe how they interface with students. A decision to treat a student as a "customer" can conflict with treating students like learners. Complex legal rules add to the challenges: the variety of competing images animating duty rules makes it nearly impossible for a conscientious college administrator to do the job without fear of walking into a crossfire of intentionality. The facilitator university model is primarily designed to

4. The concept of the student as "visitor" is devised in a companion work, Peter F. Lake, *Beyond Discipline—Managing the Modern Higher Education Environment* (Hierophant Enterprises, Inc. 2009).

offer a *comprehensive, adaptable, legal and practical model* for university/student safety affairs.[5]

The facilitator model is both the sum of the valuable parts of the images and is also greater. It is principally aimed at establishing balance in college and university law and responsibilities. It is particularly valuable to first examine the various images and place them on a continuum from most "university authority" to most "student freedom" oriented. The views sort into a distinct pattern.

Table 2 graphically depicts what can be gleaned from the images themselves. One thing that is clear is that many conceptions fall rather narrowly to one extreme (leaving a hole in the middle) or span a very wide range in encompassing the center. Thus, the images either provide too much university authority (or too little), too much student freedom (or too little), or encompass wide extremes of both, sending impossible-to-manage messages regarding who is responsible for what. Most images are either too extreme or too wide.[6] Balancing the rights and responsibilities of universities and students is a process of both eliminating extremes and defining an appropriately wide center. The facilitator model is fundamentally a vision of *shared* responsibility—too wide a grant

---

5. In the best student-authored article on higher education law I have ever read, Jane Dall discussed the facilitator model as "an ideal" and argued that the "model does not provide a perfect paradigm for higher education tort liability . . . [T]hat image provides little guidance to a judge considering a college defendant's motion for summary judgment on its motion to dismiss." *See* Jane A. Dall, *Determining Duty in Collegiate Tort Litigation: Shifting Paradigms of the College-Student Relationship*, 29 J.C. & U.L. 485, 518 (2003). Dall also argued that the facilitator "paradigm fails to provide sufficient *legal* guidance. It leaves undefined those policy considerations most relevant to a court's duty determination." *Id.* Indeed the facilitator model is an ideal, but it is also designed to guide decision-making at an intuitive, sometimes abstract level. It is deliberately designed to be practical in a different way from, say "best practices," or as specific guidance on operational compliance. I delve into this further, *infra*. Moreover, in its first iteration the facilitator model was directed first to student affairs administrators, next to college attorneys and was not designed specifically to be a *ratio decendi* in court, *per se*. Upon reflection, the facilitator model can be adapted to duty and liability analysis in higher education litigation. A court could use the facilitator concept to apply rules of shared responsibility in a "grayspace" case for example. Dall's point about policy factor analysis is particularly prescient. In the first iteration of the facilitator university model, I was of the mindset that the policy factors to be balanced in a college case would be those courts normally use in duty analysis. However, there is value in articulating *special* policy considerations applicable in higher education cases and Dall was correct to push this point. Courts are in fact articulating special policy factors for higher education. *See, e.g.*, *Pawlowski v. Delta Sigma Phi*, No. CV-03-0484661S 2009 WL 415667 at *6 (Conn. Super. Ct. Jan. 23, 2009).

6. Charlie Brown once observed to Linus that although winter days are shorter, they are wider.

Table 2

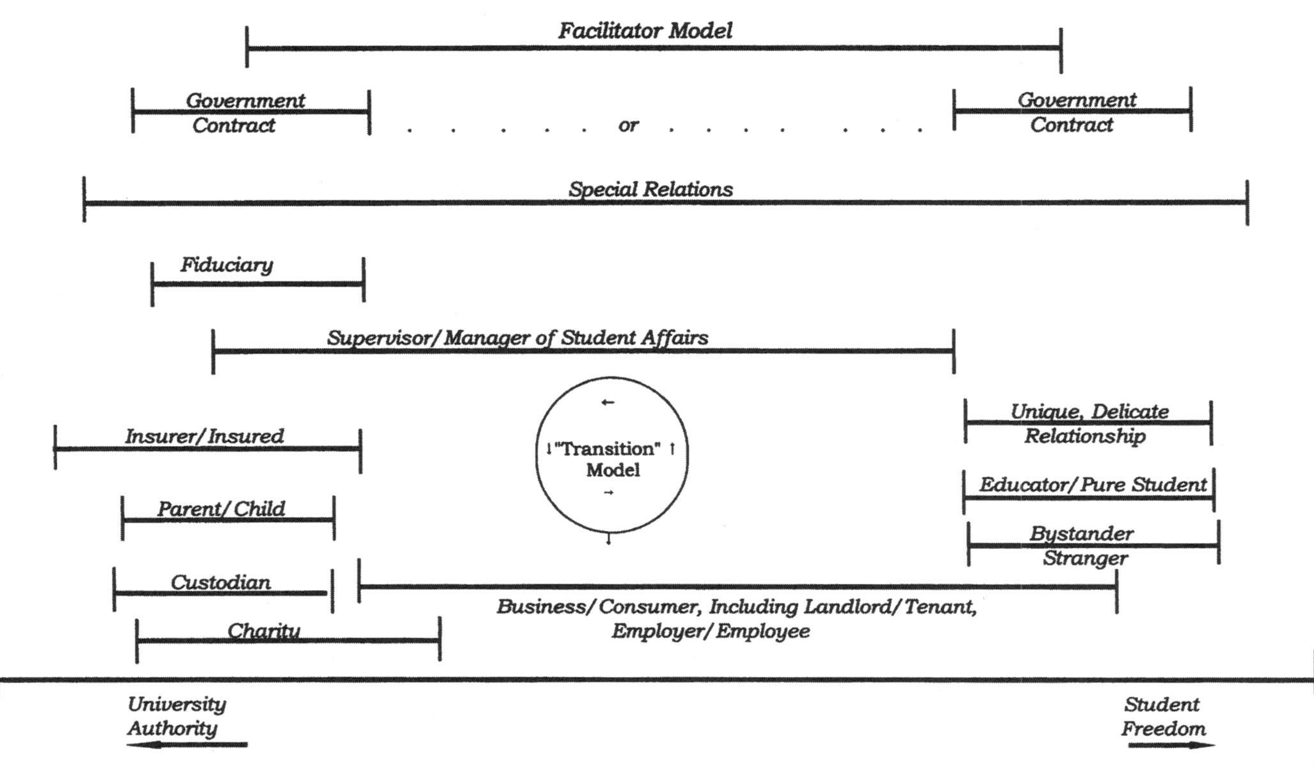

Facilitator Model
Government Contract
or
Government Contract
Special Relations
Fiduciary
Supervisor/Manager of Student Affairs
"Transition" Model
Insurer/Insured
Unique, Delicate Relationship
Educator/Pure Student
Parent/Child
Bystander Stranger
Custodian
Business/Consumer, Including Landlord/Tenant, Employer/Employee
Charity
University Authority
Student Freedom

of freedom or too heavy a dose of authority may disempower the college or the student.

There has been some rather significant image shifts in university law and policy in the last half-century. In the 1960s/1970s there was a *dramatic* swing from extreme university control to radical student freedom-oriented images. Images of the relationships between students and universities are sometimes overlapping. For example, special relationships images are intimately connected to "business/consumer" images. Courts and commentators often use one set of images without reference to competing images in play in other cases/situations. The explosion in college/student images reflects some profound questions about the nature of college education and the appropriate rules for student safety and the security of the learning environment. The facilitator model attempts to organize and distill the competing images in a coherent vision that best approximates the goals of law and good student affairs practice.

I. Looking at the Images of the Legal Relationships Between Student and University

Each of the images of student/university legal relationships has its inherent strengths and weaknesses. The perspective of the facilitator college builds upon the various images and discards weaknesses inherent in them. It is helpful, in this regard, to sort the analysis of each image and its strengths and weaknesses roughly in sequence from models of the insularity/power and prerogative, civil rights, bystander, and duty eras, respectively. However, some of the images span epochs or do not necessarily associate with one period, so this approach is only an approximation.

A. Insularity, Power and Prerogative Era Images

*(1.) Parent/Babysitter/*In Loco Parentis*/Child*

These were some of the dominant images of the era of insularity, and they have since been rejected.[7] The belief of courts since the bystander era onwards has been that modern college students would not accept parental control nor would such a level of control be appropriate for the modern university. Stu-

7. *See* Lake, *supra* note 4, at 27–61.

dents today are seen as "adults" (or better yet "non-children") even though some students come to campus below the age of majority, many are below the legal drinking age, and brain science now demonstrates that many students remain in a transitional maturation stage into their mid-to-late 20s. A major weakness of the "parent"[8] view was based in common law doctrine of the insularity era—that the college as "surrogate parent" had nearly limitless power over students. The image was oriented to strong control (but no correlative responsibility, at least in law) paradigms. When universities exercised extreme and unreasonable (unconstitutional) disciplinary power in the 1960s, the courts reacted and rejected parental imagery.

The parent/child model had little sense of nuance. Under an *in loco parentis* legal paradigm, a six-year-old, a twelve-year-old, and an eighteen-year-old were all seen as children. The image was not adaptable to age, experience, maturity, context, intelligence, etc. From parents' and educators' points of view, it is important and necessary to make such distinctions. For example, a barely eighteen-year-old college freshman who spent high school years in a highly structured and protected home environment may have a difficult time with pressures in the freshman year.

The demographics of college students are changing. There are those students right out of high school *and* returning adults (second career, military, part-time college students for example). Colleges with large numbers of "traditional" students (almost always the places with the most alcohol-based risks) must cope with developmental realities. Many of these students (but not all) are not fully mature and responsible adults. Some of them are away from home (at least physically) for the first time. Many have only limited experience on their own, and are at risk of challenges arising from poor mentoring, poor planning, poorly formed intentions/purposes for pursuing a college education.[9] The loss of a highly structured K–12 environment is often a devastating blow to a student. Students need structure, mentoring and guidance, and many greatly need to learn to grow more independent from parental/familial influence.

The parental legal model has demonstrated that there is a need to revise strictly linear, sharply divided categories of development. There is rarely one magic moment when a person stops childhood and enters adulthood as such

8. Although the parent/child view is dead, there are persistent concerns expressed that it will return. *See* Christopher Jayson Swartz, *The Revivification of In Loco Parentis Behavioral Regulation in Public Institutions of Higher Education to Combat the Obesity Epidemic*, 45 New Eng. L. Rev. 101 (2010).

9. *See* Lake, *supra* note 4.

(June 6, 1944 and similar dates excepted). This guidance that modern students need differs from strict control and discipline, where an authority figure or a parent makes all or most of the life choices. Modern students need structure, guidance, support, mentors, and services, with an eye towards facilitating self-leadership skills. It is critical that students learn to choose and plan for themselves and to take responsibility for their decisions. However, for many modern students these choices need to be guided and mentored.

Our social system, historically, once had significant mechanisms in place to transform adolescents into mature adults. In the industrial age, the primary mechanisms were army, new family (e.g., the 1950s marriage), workplace, or college. A trend began in the 1960s: more young people started the transition to true adulthood *through* college. College in the 1950s *mimicked* the highly disciplinary climate of army, family, and workplace (example: professors were armed with threats of lost deferments). But the college lost its quasi-military/workplace/family authority in the 1960s and *then* was asked to shoulder an ever-increasing burden of more college students of all ages, and at diverse points in the maturation process. College has also become an *elongated* experience: four years in college is now six to seven years in college.

As a society, we must fashion law to address these crucial years in a person's development. There is an in-between stage that social institutions must address—or else. Families play a major role for many students. The parent, grandparent, uncle/aunt, or older sibling, etc., represent the critical guidance of elders. *However a legal paradigm that prevents the educator/administrator from performing the role of mentor for fear of being sued, or which encourages a "look the other way" attitude in situations where guidance or intervention is necessary to the students' wellbeing, is seriously flawed.*[10]

Facilitation, unlike babysitting, is Socratic. Consider *Star Wars* when Luke "enrolls" in "Dagobah Force Academy." Yoda chides Luke not to encounter Darth Vader—"you're not ready." Luke is warned. If Luke were a child, Yoda would ground him; if Luke were an adult stranger, Yoda might not be involved (Luke's friend Biggs never sees Yoda but could have used his guidance). Yoda charts the middle path—inform, guide, teach, chide, and observe. Indeed, Yoda provides the near perfect college experience for Luke—moral, physical, and intellectual training—even experiential learning (recall the cave where

10. The law of another generation advanced "adulthood" by fiat and deliberately distanced parents from the higher education process. *See, e.g.*, FERPA, Family Educational Rights and Privacy Act, 20 U.S.C. §1232(g) (2006) and supporting regulations. This has become very problematic in modern times. FERPA's privacy provisions have anachronistic features.

Luke "imagines" an encounter with Darth Vader). In one sense, it turns out that Luke was not ready to face Vader the first time: he lost his hand in their first duel. Yet it was precisely that loss that helps him to learn the "lesson of the cave"—the real power of the force is not force at all. Luke later defeats Darth Vader *and* resurrects his father by learning these lessons in his own time and at exactly the right moment—compassion and responsibility—that Yoda could not teach by dictating to Luke. Some lessons must be experienced to be learned, and learned at the learner's pace at the right moment. "Do or do not," said Yoda. Luke had to learn this for himself through his own experience.

Yoda *also* learns that in a very important sense Luke *was* ready—the timing of Luke's epiphany was perfect. In a facilitator relationship "teacher" and "learner" both grow. Had Yoda just met Luke, taught him nothing, and let him face Darth Vader, Luke would be dead and Yoda would be a bad bystander. If Yoda fully trained Luke to be a Jedi Knight robot-killer, Darth Vader would be dead *and so would Luke's father.* Little gained, nothing learned, especially if Luke takes another step in an endless cycle of violence. Yoda needs to find the *middle* path for Luke, Darth Vader, and himself. Now that Luke has mastered his tests, *Luke* now stands next in line as the next master facilitator. Higher learners, like Luke Skywalker, need magnificent guidance—not control, condemnation, or apathy—to succeed in life. The task of facilitating is at once difficult and essential, and requires trust and finesse.

Consider the lessons of the Star Wars prequels. We get to observe the same teachers—Obi Wan and Yoda (with the help of other Jedi)—blow a chance at facilitation with Anakin Skywalker. They often treat him like a child, chastise him constantly, hold him back and tell him he is full of the dark side (go figure, he is a young man). They even insist on calling him "padawan." According to Wookieepedia, a padawan "is subject to the demands of the master."[11] It is no wonder Anakin is susceptible to evil de-facilitation. The Jedi had more to learn from him, than he did from them.

(2.) Insurer/Insured

This image actually first appeared in the bystander era and was used to describe a perceived consequence of potentially "returning" *in loco parentis.* The idea is that a university agrees to guarantee a safe environment or pay if injury

11. *See* Wookieepedia, *Padawan*, http://starwars.wikia.com/wiki/Padawan (last visited Oct. 4, 2011) (footnotes omitted).

occurs. *Such a system has never existed* in higher education, but like Camelot, it is a powerful rhetorical icon.

The main weakness of this view is that it places no responsibility on students for their own safety or, at least, seriously diminishes it. By knowing they are "insured," students would be encouraged to displace the costs of aberrant behavior on the university. The burden on the finances of a university would then be catastrophic, or the university would have to reinstitute draconian control, or both. The allocation of risk and rights/responsibility would be drastically skewed.

Of course, insurance does not function quite the way courts have described it in university law regarding student safety. Nonetheless, there is a kernel of truth to the way courts see it. Students generally lack adequate insurance to protect themselves from other dangerous persons, and they do not always have adequate health and medical benefits in the event of *Furek*-type injuries.

Now, an insurance mentality is often a loss-avoidance, *risk management*, pro-active mentality. In this regard, universities could use more of an "insurance mentality." Workers' compensation insurers have been very successful in reducing claims *and* injuries with pro-active, risk management, loss reduction programs.[12] By analogy, better education of faculty, staff, and students regarding the scope of their shared responsibility for safety (in typical scenarios) and more resources devoted to safety implications of activities (facilities maintenance, campus law enforcement, safety technology, etc.) could avoid student injury and litigation. Sometimes the simplest strategy—being proactive—is most effective. This is the mind-set of an insurer, a risk manager, and a facilitator.[13]

---

12. Modern higher education insurers have promoted the use of risk management techniques. Some colleges have stepped into the world of risk management boldly, but the field of higher education remains relatively primitive compared to other industries. Change has come slowly in part because some institutions cling to bystander imagery. *See* Eric Kelderman, *Most Colleges Avoid Risk Management, Report Says*, Chron. Higher Educ. (June 25, 2009), *available at* http://chronicle.com/article/Most-Colleges-Avoid-Risk/47806; Association of Governing Boards & United Educators, *State of Enterprise Risk Management at Colleges and Universities Today* (2009), *available at* http://agb.org/sites/agb.org/files/u3/AGBUE_FINAL.pdf.

13. The first edition of this book impacted the rise of risk management in colleges by connecting tort liability, risk management and a proactive vision of student affairs. As I wrote for the Journal of College and University Law in 2005:

> Recently, there have been many attempts to create risk management programs in higher education. Insurers of college student risk have engaged in programs of risk management information dissemination and training. Many institutions have undertaken their own independent risk management programs, including several that have been influenced specifically by facilitator concepts. . . . Texas A&M University and DePauw University have been overt in their adoption of key pre-

Bystander and parental universities are legally *re-active*. In the bystander model, the incentive is to avoid liability by non-involvement. This is a counterproductive strategy and legally risky. The duty era increasingly fosters *pro-active* college administration, although there is still a distinct tendency for a campus to man-

---

cepts of the facilitator model. In addition, facilitator concepts are so closely aligned with environmental management strategies outlined by the U.S. Department of Education's Higher Education Center that risk management approaches taken on campus could easily be identified with either or both philosophical approaches.

Virtually all risk management programs feature some of the same basic principles. For example, risk management programs are based on principles of proactive intervention designed to reduce the possibility of future harm. This approach also has the incidental effect of potentially reducing litigation—however, litigation reduction is not a first goal of proactive intervention. Risk management programs are not litigation avoidance programs per se. Nonetheless, risk management programs are sensitive to the fact that litigation is often spawned when an injured party or his or her family feels aggrieved by an institution for a perceived mishandling of an incident. Conversely, institutions often avoid liability when an incident has been handled carefully and compassionately. Risk management must be based upon a genuine concern for student safety; only then does it seem to have the required effect.

Risk management is concerned with environmental factors. Few risk management programs are executed in isolation from comprehensive planning. Risk management today is based on principles of student empowerment. Integral to successful risk management is the use of students as agents of safety and the training of students to assist other students. Risk management principles acknowledge that some activities carry with them inherent dangers, along with ordinary background risks. Injury or even death may occur in a program at any time despite best efforts. Risk management principles are not designed to eliminate all possible risks from every possible activity. Instead, consistent with legal principles, risk management typically focuses upon the reduction of risks that are not inherent or reasonable in an activity or sport while maintaining the principles of the activity or sport in question.

Risk management recognizes that some activities are simply too unreasonably dangerous to continue. Texas A&M's unusual saga involving its bonfire tradition illustrates that even after careful review certain activities are simply too dangerous to justify their continued existence. In this sense, risk management often conflicts with local tradition. These local traditions and customs in colleges and universities often do not develop along safety boundaries. In fact, local traditions and customs often create unusual risks that seem odd or out of place at other colleges and universities. A risk management approach attempts to respect local traditions and customs to the extent that those traditions and customs are consistent with a reasonably safe environment. Many traditions and customs can easily be re-made to work within reasonable risk management guidelines.

In due course, a full body of scholarship and research regarding risk manage risks only *after* a tragedy or other events. (Note how even duty law still encourages this in some cases with its foreseeability requirement.) So while bystander courts attacked the idea of an "insurer" university—rightly so for some purposes—there are *aspects* of the insurance image that can help to balance risk and responsibility and thus reduce risk.

(3.) Custodian

Like the insurance image, this strong image is very much a product of looking back on the *in loco parentis* era. K-12 students are considered to be in this type of relationship.[14] However, the cases do not, nor have they ever, applied the notion of "custody" to college students to create duty or liability based merely upon the status of being a student. Some "bystander" courts have stated that custody would be necessary for duty, but that custody did not exist. In that sense, the idea of a custodial relationship with college students is a legal straw man. Control can create duty, but it is not the only predicate for duty: not all forms of control are custodial. The rhetorical effect of the bystander decisions was to suggest that, both practically and legally, the only forms of *control* that would work to create duty would be *the most draconian forms of control.* The phrase "custodial control" usually refers to patients in sanitariums, prisoners, and others held in a confined space and/or heavily guarded. The college was never like a sanitarium or a prison, so the analogy has had a *reductio ad absurdum* feel to it.

However, by engaging in such hyperbole—that the only possible control is the control of a prison guard—bystander courts set the stage for other courts to see the need for a more nuanced approach to control. "Control"—sometimes thought of as necessary for "special relationships"—and hence "duty," can be exerted in other ways. For example, one way to control behavior is to eliminate options or offer alternatives to undesirable conduct. Importantly, the law has evolved to ask individuals (and thus increasingly colleges and universities)

> agement will develop. This development may be one of the most important in the history of higher education safety. *Rights and Responsibilities* cannot claim to be the theoretical foundation for the current risk management culture. It is clear, however, that themes in *Rights and Responsibilities*, particularly with regard to the facilitator university concept, are consistent with and form the theoretical foundation for many risk management programs.

Peter F. Lake, *Private Law Continues to Come to Campus: Rights and Responsibilities Revisited*, 31 J.C. & U.L. 621, 656–58 (2005) (footnotes omitted).

14. The doctrine therefore has *some* applicability on the college campus—e.g., during youth camps—insofar as it has imposed a duty on schools to supervise elementary and secondary level students who come to campus. *See Rupp v. Bryant*, 417 So. 2d 658 (Fla. 1982).

to exercise *only that degree of control they actually possess.*[15] To exercise crowd "control," for example, police do not take all of the crowd into custody. A "lock down" of a campus does not mean that everyone is literally locked behind bars.[16] And control does not connote a guarantee of success over that which is controlled; we often ask who was "in control" at the time of an accident, and not oxymoronically. In a university setting for example, a student can be "controlled" without expulsion, incarceration, or institutionalization. One way to control a dangerous student attacker—as in *Nero,* for example—would be to remove him from a dormitory and thus eliminate numerous options for attacks. Just like criminal intrusion, you can control it, but sometimes you cannot stop it. Another way to "control" behavior is to create incentive systems that promote favorable behaviors.

The custodial image requires an extreme degree of university authority as a predicate for involvement. "Custody" is inconsistent with the college environment today and, for the most part, with college even in the era of insularity. It is worth remembering that when Kent State called in the National Guard in 1970, this attempt at control failed and backfired.[17]

(4.) Charity

In the era of insularity, the idea that a private college was a charitable organization was a powerful way to avoid duty-based liability for injuries to students.[18] Calling a college "charitable" augmented university power and authority and left students legally powerless. It also disempowered students politically: like challenging the Girl Scouts, there was an air of ingratitude to biting the hand of little girls with mint cookies.

The charity model crashed for universities: almost all charitable organizations lost blanket immunities. Courts today rarely recognize significant chari-

---

15. *See Estates of Morgan v. Fairfield Family Counseling Ctr.*, 673 N.E.2d 1311 (Ohio 1997).

16. "A lockdown is a pre-set and rehearsed crisis response plan . . ." Crisis Reality Training, *Lockdown Development and Implementation*, https://www.crisisrealitytraining.com/conference_list.php?sid=14 (last visited October 5, 2011).

17. *See* Lake, *supra* note 4, at 122–36 (discussing Kent State and the use of force to manage a campus).

18. For those who would argue that *custodial* duty relations existed in the era of *in loco parentis,* it is worth noting that truly custodial duties, when exercised by a charity (a sanitarium, for example), were generally actionable and not subject to the immunity of more ordinary charitable activities. Had students truly been in custody, the law would have recognized special duty-based safety rights. A minor point, but worth noting for those who would engage in revisionist history.

table immunities in safety litigation. Thus, today, virtually no one argues that a college is a charitable institution when the issue is student safety. The defunct charity image, however, contained a kernel of wisdom. By viewing the (usually private) university in this way, the university took on the look of an institution with grand aims, public goals, and transpersonal missions. In short, as a charity the university was aspirational, more public, and not simply some private agreement or limited voluntary association. Colleges served their own communities *and* a greater public interest.[19]

What endures today is a sense of the special mission of higher education in society. The Supreme Court for example has regularly referred to the unique role of education in American society.[20] The Supreme Court often defers to the judgment of academics in the academy, and recently broadened the vision of the academic mission in the *Christian Legal Society* case to include student activities.[21] In stark contrast to *Bradshaw* the Supreme Court now views student affairs work as *central* to core mission delivery—the Supreme Court has expanded the sense of the educational mission and rejected *Bradshaw*'s narrow vision of classroom instruction as the primary modality of "education."

(5.) Governmental Entity

In the era of insularity, the public university was protected from student lawsuits over safety issues by governmental immunities. It was an arm of the state and was making important policy decisions on a macro and micro level. University decisions on most matters were insulated from judicial intervention on behalf of private citizens. The extreme deference to governmental authority declined appreciably (although many states retain very powerful governmental immunities) after World War II, and in the civil rights era the governmental aspects of university life shifted from emphasis on the power and prerogative of a college to its responsibility to treat its citizen/students within constitutional and lawful boundaries.

The decline of governmental immunity (or its transmutation) set the stage for stronger "private rights" notions. In fact, the success of due process and civil rights litigation in the 1960s spurred on an equally powerful idea that the

---

19. *See* Lake, *supra* note 4, at 27–61(discussing the role of charitable corporations in early higher education).

20. *See, e.g.*, *Christian Legal Soc'y. Chapter of Univ. of Cal., Hastings Coll. of the Law v. Martinez*, 130 S. Ct. 2971, 2997–98 (2010) [hereafter *Christian Legal Society*] (Stevens, J. concurring) (discussing the "distinctive role" of public colleges).

21. *See id.*

private university was *contractually* responsible for rights owed publicly. The fall of governmental power facilitated the rise of student consumerism and the image of the college as a business—public and private.

Although many powerful governmental immunities remain, public institutions often find that political/softer legal scrutiny more than makes up for any protection from civil litigation. Governmental immunity may trump legal duty, but may not screen public institutions from heightened accountability. Consider the fate of Virginia Tech in the wake of events in April 2007. As discussed previously in Chapter V, although at the date of the publication of this book Virginia Tech has settled many personal injury claims (within a structure of statutory caps on liability), Virginia Tech was chastised by state officials and fined by the federal government. The court of public regulation, so to speak, may be setting standards well in excess of reasonable care.[22] (It is particularly noteworthy that a true hero, Professor Liviu Librescu, a holocaust survivor and professor at Virginia Tech, sacrificed his life to save students that day. There are few "businesses" where employees willingly put the "customer's" lives ahead of their own.)[23]

(6.) Contract

For over a century, courts have said that the essence of the student/university relationship lies in contract law. The image pops up even today, although most of the tort/safety cases no longer even mention contract law in their doctrinal analysis. Contract is one of the most elusive and enduring images in university law. Contract imagery smacks of freedom and voluntary associations, and also limitations on authority.

In the era of insularity, contract notions at times served important college authority functions. Authority sometimes arose from *contract* with parent and/or in delegation of authority from the state and from the social contract. In much the way that governments prior to John Locke would trace the divine rights of kings, courts would establish the authority to insularize university affairs through contract and/or delegation. Contract was related to ideas of sovereignty—sovereignty of government, family, and voluntary associations. Historically, courts

---

22. *See* Terry W. Hartle, *A Federal Outrage Against Virginia Tech*, Chron. Higher Educ. (Apr. 10, 2011), *available at* http://chronicle.com/article/A-Federal-Outrage-Against/127055/ (sharply criticizing the president of Virginia Tech for failing to give "timely warnings" under the Clery Act).

23. In issuing fines, the Department of Education made no reference to this. If this is not legally relevant, then shame on the law!

rarely saw the contract image as a way to empower students or to protect their rights. Students were the subjects of "contracts," not its architects.

Eventually, however, contract images, like governmental images, transmuted into student rights-conferring images in two ways.

First, contract thinking was used from the 1960s on to review and restrain private college authority. The contract was now between *student* and university, and was a unique contract deserving of special rules of construction that sometimes favored student rights. These rights were (and are) invariably economic and intangible rights—rights to associate, rights of fair process, etc. Contract images, like government rights, shifted from university authority to student rights and freedom images.

Second, the contract image began to view the student in a business/consumer relation, an image that first rooted in the bystander era and has dominated in the duty era ever since. Still, somewhat paradoxically, some courts have imagined a contract relationship but also talked about the limits of the contract imagery.[24] The facilitator model helps to make sense of this apparent contradiction.

The strengths of the contract images are related to their weaknesses. Courts like to view colleges as a special form of voluntary association, and the pull of contract in this sense is obvious. Yet contract law has required special adaptation to work. Students are given essentially take-it-or-leave-it deals on the universities' terms and are often not well informed of all the ramifications of their agreement.[25] Is college *simply* a consumer/transactional experience between college and students? Has college lost its "noblesse oblige" and become a bargain? Contract imagery has baited students and their families to see themselves as empowered *consumers*.

B. Civil Rights Era Images

The dominant images of the civil rights era cases were the government/contract images. The significance (as in (1), (5), and (6) above) was in the *shift*. Suddenly, the student became a citizen with constitutional rights and/or a contracting party with basic entitlements to fair treatment. These images were

---

24. *See, e.g.*, *Kashmiri v. Regents of Univ. of Cal.*, 67 Cal. Rptr. 3d 635, 646 (Cal. Dist. Ct. App. 2007) ("contract law should not be strictly applied").

25. In a potentially disturbing trend, some colleges have foisted arbitration clauses on students. *See* Molly Redden, *Supreme Court Decision on Arbitration May Have Eroded For-Profit Students' Right to Sue*, Chron. Higher Educ. (June 21, 2011), *available at* http://chronicle.com/article/Supreme-Court-Decision-May/127964/.

used to empower students and promote student freedom paradigms, but were generally restricted to the concern for fundamental constitutional/civil rights and, to some extent, commercial fairness. The focus was on intangible and economic rights, not safety rights.

C. Bystander Era Images

A great deal of bystander imagery was negative, reactive, and passive. Courts were anxious to say what universities were *not* and what they could *not do.* Images of eras past—whether real or straw men—dominated. As we have seen, many courts rejected parent/babysitter/*in loco parentis* images, refused "insurer" (strict liability) ideas, and decried "custodial" images (that were in use by them in elementary and secondary education). Some courts simply ignored the expanding safety responsibilities of charitable organizations and/or governmental agencies for operational negligence that caused injuries. The university was *not* the Girl Scouts, and not big brother; the university would not hold hands, nor indemnify, nor control, nor accept the mantle of some benign greater public purpose. The university had a limited role to fill—it was a classroom *educator.* Otherwise it was—legally—a bystander to student "strangers." Insularity gave way to two-dimensionality and bifurcation of core mission into academic and student affairs missions.

(1.) Educator

One of the most powerful legal ideas to emerge in the bystander era case law was that the college had a limited mission—to educate. The purely educational role was narrowly conceived as classroom instruction, etc., but not as education in any larger sense (as in socialization). This image saw the college as only marginally involved in non-classroom affairs. Fraternities, extra-curricular activities, almost all off-campus events (whether curricular or not) were not "purely educational." The responsibility was, then, to provide reasonably safe classroom instruction, etc. Of course, since there was (and still is virtually) no legal remedy for educational malpractice in college—the purely educational vision of college was in the nature of immunity *not* duty thinking.

The purely educational college model was a radical affirmation of student freedom and a very narrow vision of university power. The university could decide with impunity who got "A's"; otherwise students could do almost anything without the college being legally accountable. Moreover, the courts would say that the college had the *right* to enforce regulations regarding student conduct but did not have legal *responsibility* to do so. As in *Rabel,* the university could have rules regarding drinking and fraternities but did not have to enforce them. This was a subtle message to colleges, but it became very clear in its implication. The college had the legal right to construct a paper utopia but no duty to manifest it; the college had no duty to enforce the rules, and actually had legal incentives *not* to do so. *Courts told colleges, "You cannot control these students," and college attorneys translated this to mean that if you try too hard (and "assume a duty") you just might be liable if, despite your efforts, students are injured. The idea that a college is purely educational became a judicial invitation, with the active encouragement of some legal counsel,*[26] *to be a bystander.* It also became an invitation to market campus safety to the public in unrealistic ways.

A legal model that sees the university as having no legal relationship with its students outside the classroom—one which sees the student/college relationship as purely educational in a narrow sense—fails in at least four major respects. First, it enlarges student rights by allowing students to exercise so-called student freedoms to the point of the unreasonable endangerment of other students. Second, such a legal model fails to impose any sense of shared responsibility in matters of student/university relations because it precludes a balancing of university conduct and student conduct in matters of student safety and well being. An "all-or-nothing" model simply fails to recognize that the college or university and the student *both* have some control over the safety and security of the learning environment. Third, the limited classroom/educational model ignores the reality of modern higher education—that in many institutions learning occurs in and out of the classroom on equal footing. This is the message of the recent Supreme Court decision in *Christian Legal Society*—arousing empowerment of "student affairs" as equal partners in an educational mission. Fourth, bystander imagery of "education" timed out almost exactly with the bifurcation of higher education into academic and student affairs functions. What was once whole cloth was rent, causing dangerous consequences like the information "silos" noted after Virginia Tech.

---

26. Many college and university attorneys, in fact, supported the desires of student affairs administrators to assume responsibility in matters of student safety but were constrained by their understanding of the major cases of the era (about affirmative and negative duty—misfeasance and nonfeasance). In doing their jobs, university attorneys were aware that if the university were to have "no duty" regarding student injury, judicial rules of procedure permitted student personal injury lawsuits to be dismissed as a matter of law. The bystander courts baited lawyers to seek this line of defense as it held the promise of marginal legal scrutiny of university affairs. The false promises of the bystander era may have actually created a backlash in the form of recent heightened regulatory scrutiny. Sometimes victory in court is a precursor to losing in the court of public policy.

An all-or-nothing, education-only legal paradigm discourages active university efforts to create a sense of civility in student affairs beyond the mere enforcement of rules and regulations. A legal model that makes student affairs administrators fear that their intervention will produce a bad legal consequence for the university is a model under which efforts to teach students civility are doomed to failure.

Courts in the duty era typically have not challenged the idea that the college is purely educational on its face. Instead, they decide cases that place more than narrowly drawn "educational" duties on the college. The image of a "pure" educational college has lost vitality in the duty era.[27] Courts accept that colleges do have an educational role but see it in the wider context of the college living/learning experience. Ultimately, education is only possible under conditions of reasonable safety.

(2.) Strangers/Uncontrollable Students

Bystander ideas are to student freedom what *in loco parentis* was to university authority. The bystander university gave students freedom from university "control." The freedom was really the freedom of a college from lawsuits regarding student safety. The freedom was also a chimera: bystander case law empowered radical libertarian "Animal House" behavior at the expense of other students' liberties. On balance, true freedom and the value of freedom declined. It was also a strange type of freedom considering the fact that courts routinely upheld college discipline power over student behavior.

As the bystander era emerged, it centered around no-duty rules and a perceived lack of special relationships. With the fall of charitable, governmental, and familial immunities, the courts embraced an odd analogy—college safety law evolved as *rescue* law. There was a sense that college had gone bad. It seemed that hordes of young revolutionaries, demanding to be grown-ups, had descended on colleges and overwhelmed their support systems. The students did not want guidance and control and would not accept either. The college was placed in a state of siege and triage; where people were injured, they then sued to be "rescued."

That image, like all of the images, had a kernel of truth. The baby-boom generation was (or is) a demographic force of historic proportions. Families of the 1940s and 1950s likely did not foresee that they were creating the largest class ever of teenagers and college students for future decades. When the baby

27. *See Christian Legal Soc'y.*, 130 S. Ct. 2971.

boomers went to college in record numbers and hit political critical mass, traditional colleges were strained and overwhelmed. As an *intermediate* response to a *temporary* transitional phrase caused by bizarre demographics, the bystander era in part reflected the way that American courts typically treat nascent enterprises or enterprises in a developmental stage—substantial legal latitude is allowed. At first. Examples of similar legal protection for new enterprises: railroads, automobiles, consumer products, and polluting industries. Even the computer industry had this protection in its fledgling phases.

There was very clear concern—expressed in *Bradshaw* et al.—that liability for student safety would deal crushing financial and management blows to modern colleges. New quasi-immunities defined in terms of "no-duty-to-rescue" were appropriate, or so the courts thought, and not just because of alcohol rules. The bystander image was faulty, however, because it promoted the university's abdication of *its* responsibility to exercise reasonable care. In recent times, the notion that a college could turn away from student life issues has also become politically unacceptable.

The bystander image was loaded towards the idea that duty exists only if there is a "special" relationship. In other words, the rescue image was especially associated with some of the most peculiar tort rules that exist, and pushed people to view the college as a passive receptacle, non-acting and almost invisible apart from classroom instruction. "The college" became little more than an educational container outside the classroom. Inside the classroom students were actors, active not passive, and were seen as the primary vehicles of dangerous or endangering behavior.

Bystander imagery became immensely powerful for a time. Levine and Cureton and Boyer described how increasingly distant college administration became from student life. The college system and community efficacy eroded under the bystander rules. The very idea that a college *is* a community faded, although many lamented its passing. Bystander imagery was promoting the breakdown of the very features of a college community that make it safer, and a more effective learning environment.

Yet, as we have seen, college safety law of the 1970s, 1980s, and early 1990s painted a schizophrenic, paranoid picture. On the one hand there was *Bradshaw*, et al. and on the other was *Mullins*. If you assume duties, you then may have them; but you may already have had them. Bystander imagery fractured the soul of higher education into competing personalities—academic and non-academic. *The facilitator university, however, is not routinely passive and does not accept the idea that because some student injury is inevitable all reasonable and positive avenues of protecting student safety are shut off.* The facilitator university is also suspicious of the bifurcation of the core mission. Professors and administrators share one common goal, which is to create a safe, sound, and responsible learning environment. Both bystander and facilitator models believe in "duty" but just draw different conclusions about the role of the college and its true power.

(3.) Landlord/Tenant/Landowner/Invitee

The evolution of university law has downplayed the dual-personality college of the bystander era. The bystander era (in retrospect, the first evolutionary step of the duty era) birthed cases like *Mullins* as well as *Bradshaw*. The bystander era—dominated by the "university as stranger" image—was also a time when the university began to be perceived by many courts as a landlord and premises owner. Truly, the concept that a college is a "business" rooted in the bystander era. Prior to that time, the college was like a charity, a government, or a family to courts—strict analogies to business and business law were generally not used yet. The idea that the college was a business or landlord was seemingly inconsistent with the bystander image. Courts in many cases, made no attempt to reconcile the dissonance between cases like *Bradshaw* and *Mullins*. Even today some courts imagine the law of college safety as a "split of authority."[28] A few courts here and there treat *Bradshaw* simplistically and overlook countervailing precedent that establishes duty based on business/land relationships with students.[29]

---

28. *See, e.g.*, Judith C. Areen, *Higher Education and the Law: Cases and Materials* 817, n. 1 (Foundation Press 2009).

29. Consider the poorly reasoned 1997 decision of the 10th Federal Circuit Court of Appeals (includes Utah) in *Orr v. Brigham Young Univ.*,108 F.3d 1388 (10th Cir. 1997). In fairness, the decision is an unpublished decision and is not binding precedent by rule of the court. This is good, because the case is wrong. In *Orr*, a student athlete complained that the BYU football staff injured him. As the court related:

> Orr's complaint alleged that BYU football coaching staff and athletic trainers failed to provide adequate medical care for a series of back injury episodes he suffered while playing college football for BYU. He claimed that BYU's coaching staff placed enormous pressure on him to continue playing while he was hurt, which further exacerbated his injuries. Orr advanced several theories for holding BYU liable for his back injuries. He theorized that BYU owed a duty of care to him based on the special relationship created by this status as a student athlete at BYU; that BYU's conduct created a situation in which playing him would cause him harm, thus imposing on BYU an affirmative duty to protect him from injury; that BYU allowed its trainers to practice medicine without a license; and that BYU breached its duty of care to him in its diagnosis and treatment of his medical injuries.

In one sense, business/land images are positive for students and invitees. Colleges cannot offer slum-tenant conditions or fail to perform routine premises maintenance (and do not forget that some colleges tried to establish the legal right to offer substandard housing). Students were still responsible for ordinary and obvious risks. However, as these rules have evolved to become more powerful vehicles for student safety litigation, there is the chance that student/college relations will become similar to those of customers to shops in a shopping

---

Id. at 1388.

At the trial court level, summary judgment was granted on the claim (one claim was voluntarily dismissed). The trial court's decision was affirmed by the Court of Appeals on the issue of duty (there were obvious questions of breach, causation, and plaintiff's assumption of risk, etc.). Thus the only question raised was whether there was a *duty* to the student. Because the law controlling was Utah law, the *Beach* case controlled. The court rejected the plaintiff's claims generally, based on *Beach:*

> The rule Orr contends for would result in a broad, nearly unprecedented expansion of duty . . . for Utah's colleges and universities. At present, the boundaries of Utah law are defined by the Beach case, which rejected the claim that colleges and universities owe a special duty to their adult students, even when the students are participating in university-sponsored activities. As a federal court, we are reticent to expand state law in the absence of clear guidance from Utah's highest court, or at least a strong and well-reasoned trend among other courts which Utah might find persuasive, in favor of such expansion. See Taylor v. Phelan, 9F.3d 882, 887 (10th Cir. 1993) (declining to expand concept of special relationships between police and citizens beyond bounds created by Kansas courts); see also Great Central Ins. Co. v. Insurance Services Office, Inc., 74F.3d 778, 786, (7th Cir. 1996) (innovations in the law are better sought in state court than in federal court). We find no indication, either in the Utah courts or in a trend developing elsewhere, that the Utah courts would impose a duty on BYU based on a special relationship, under these circumstances. The district court properly granted summary judgment on Orr's claim that BYU breached a duty created by a special relationship between himself and BYU.

Id.

The case was clearly a simplistic reaction to *Beach.* A federal court can safely hide behind a state supreme court decision. However, the *Orr* court missed the game entirely. For one thing, the *Orr* allegations were different. In *Orr*, the plaintiff contended that he was pushed into service—that the university took affirmative steps that placed him in a position of danger. This would have been the equivalent of an allegation that a professor encouraged a student who had been drinking to walk near a dangerous cliff. Orr's claims contained obvious allegations of *misfeasance* that *do not require* (even in Utah courts) *a special relationship.* Moreover, the court acknowledged only one case on point, but overlooked the holdings of cases like *Mintz, Nero,* and *Roettgen.*

In 2005 in *Webb v. University of Utah*, 125 P.3d 906 (Utah 2005), the Utah Supreme Court completely refashioned *Beach*, making *Orr* untenable under Utah law. The Federal Court "guessed" incorrectly.

mall. Will college safety responsibility be nothing other than the collection of various business responsibilities?

D. Duty Era Images

(1.) Business/Consumer (Special Relationships and Duty)

By far, this is the dominant current conception of modern university relations, if one aggregates the cases. Although dominant, business images do not convey a complete or completely adequate picture, however. In re-imagining the student/college relationship through business law doctrines, modern courts only rarely see the college as just a bystander. The no-liability logic of some modern cases is much more oriented towards lack of foreseeability of risk by the university or accountability of students for their decisions—not college passivity or lack of power. Courts are quick to pick up on business analogies to campus problems and to apply the law of torts to those subjects. Colleges have been mainstreamed under many business categories and some courts openly refer to colleges as businesses.

(a.) Specific Relations

Colleges play various business roles to students—landlord, landowner (premises maintenance), employer, and administrator or supervisor of student activities actively managed or facilitated by the college. A prominent feature of business relations in other environments is that they impose significant tort/accident responsibility. Not only does a business have a general duty to avoid actions and activities which foreseeably cause unreasonable danger, but invitees, tenants, consumers, and others are also owed *affirmative duties* because they are in special relationships with the business. Applying business rules to the student/university relationship forces the college as a business to use due care to minimize the risk of student injury, within the scope of the business relationship. Traditional tort law also emphasizes that whenever the university *acts* it is responsible to use care. For example, when the university in the *Nero* case affirmatively assigned students to a summer residence hall, it was legally responsible to use reasonable care to avoid placing students in positions of unreasonable risk. Therefore, when the university knows that a student is awaiting a criminal trial for rape, it is fair to ask whether a reasonable person would assign that student to a residence hall and thereby facilitate access to residents in common areas of the dormitory like hallways, laundry rooms, and lounges.

Because many business law cases do arise in situations of *affirmative* duty only, there is a strong connection between business law and the law of special relationships. Some courts and commentators confuse this a bit and assume that because special relationships are a feature of some business/college law, duty is owed only under special circumstances.[30] To make this perfectly clear: *Universities can owe duties to their students on and off campus irrespective of whether there is a special relationship of any kind. Legal special relationships potentially enhance responsibility, and include affirmative duties to proactively prevent harm caused by third parties, non-negligent forces, and/or students themselves. Special relations are not prerequisites to duty, per se, but only prerequisites to certain kinds of duty to take affirmative action. Custodial relations are only a subset of special relationships.* This is basic tort law.

Confusion on these points has led on occasion to bad court decisions and misguided secondary commentary. It is a seductive and easy mistake to follow the logic of *Bradshaw* too far. Of course, courts are free to fashion law anyway they please, but if courts are making distinct tort rules for colleges they should say so in plain terms. And if federal courts are erecting barriers to student safety litigation, they should say so as well, and not manhandle the *Erie* doctrine in the process.

A facilitator model permits courts inclined to protect universities as a matter of law to do so with more correct rules of decision. A facilitator university does not try to manipulate the law of duty, or rules of federal court jurisdiction, or reduce the law's complexity to misleading "truisms." *Bradshaw* is more rhetorical than doctrinal. There is a better, more straightforward and candid way to do what some courts wish to do when they use special relationships analysis to protect colleges. A decision that is correct for the wrong reason hurts university/student relations. *Bradshaw* has not protected colleges; it has scared them away from doing the right things.

A business law/consumer mentality has some additional advantages and disadvantages. For example, colleges as businesses increasingly use risk management techniques. To some extent, this is an excellent development, except

30. There is an intuitive reason to conflate special relations with duty in the business context as well. Particularly in the residence life context and in many instances of premises responsibility, courts use special relationship analysis as a proxy for the idea that being a landlord or a business premises owner is much like carrying on an ongoing activity in which omissions are like misfeasance (active misconduct); the failure to fix a broken lock in a dormitory is like a driver who fails to apply the brakes, not like a stranger who refuses to jump in a lake to save a drowning swimmer.

that the campus is not exactly like a corporate workplace. Risk management strategies designed for the workplace must be tailored to student life situations. For example, certain alcohol problems on college campuses are more difficult to manage and are more dangerous than analogous problems at many businesses and residential tenancies. A business strategy may fail because college problems have unique difficulties and require special solutions. Risk management consultants, risk underwriters, and campus administrators are acutely aware of the special nature of student life risk and use appropriate approaches to risk management.[31]

(b.) Shared Responsibility—Strengths and Weaknesses of Business Law

The business/consumer model is very appealing to courts for some obvious reasons. For one thing, business law is familiar territory to courts. Universities can be treated like other businesses, without special legal rules. For another, that model supplies an array of rules that often balance university responsibility with student responsibilities. An experienced set-design student who disregards a professor's clear instructions and admonitions not to use a power saw that is obviously broken and who is then injured while cutting a piece of scenery for a theater class on his own time will have no valid claim for damages from the university. On the other hand, when a first-year undergraduate student who has never before experimented with certain chemicals is burned while conducting an experiment without proper supervision by the instructor, that student may have a valid claim that the university shares some responsibility for her injuries.

Courts have a penchant for balancing approaches and thus have come to prefer business law solutions for colleges to many other approaches. The essence of business law images and rules is a search for the reasonable center. Nonetheless, business/consumer images have still suffered from "width" problems. Business law-type court decisions are not particularly sensitive to the balance between college and student responsibility *as such*. The balance of authority and freedom struck for colleges under an unqualified business paradigm would mimic the approaches that courts use for malls, furniture delivery businesses, restaurants, etc. And so, business law strictly applied to universities goes too far in both directions. The facilitator model adapts business law to the unique university community and to each college uniquely (a two-year college may

31. *See, e.g.*, *Managing Liability*, United Educators (2008), http://www.unh.edu/cie/pdf/risk-ue-understanding-risks.pdf (last visited May 17, 2012).

have different responsibilities than a traditional four-year college with more underage students).

The key to the reconciliation of business law approaches in higher education law lies in the resolution of problems with the analogy to business/consumer paradigms. Students are not ordinary consumers buying a sandwich or shirt. Students buy into immersive living/learning environments at many colleges. Housing, roommates, meals, sports, activities, education, etc., often are all "purchased" in one transaction, which is most like building a complex set of option contracts (except different). In addition, the college deal is "offered" on a take-it-or-leave-it basis. Ms. Nero was in no position to bargain for more safety; students in *Delaney* begged for an entry door lock to be fixed to no avail. The student/university relationship is an unusual consumer relationship at best. Once a student has purchased an education, the power over the deal shifts radically in favor of a college. (For what it is worth, this problem animates the arguments for a fiduciary model—the responsibility to deal with students in good faith and from a position of trust. That model has not caught on widely in student safety cases, but the core idea is an aspect of a facilitator model.)

A business paradigm suggests that students are consumers. For some time now, higher education commentators like Arthur Levine, Jeanette Cureton, Gary Pavela, and Jean Twenge have noted that students view themselves as consumers.

Gary Pavela wrote:

> The momentum for greater student rights was accelerated in the late 1970s and 1980s by the consumer protection movement. Students began to see themselves as "customers" seeking services—a view reinforced by federal and state legislation protecting student privacy, and requiring that 'consumer information' about financial aid, campus security, and other services be made available to applicants for admission.[32]

Students have increasingly looked upon education in terms of commodification.

Arthur Levine and Jeanette Cureton eloquently described the same phenomena. In *When Hope and Fear Collide*, Levine and Cureton devoted an entire section to what they call "A Consumer Mentality,"[33] and the theme permeated

32. 7 Synthesis: Law and Policy in Higher Education 530–31 (1992).

33. *See* Arthur Levine and Jeanette S. Cureton, *When Hope and Fear Collide: A Portrait of Today's College Student* 50 (Jossey-Bass 1998).

the book. They described the causes and consequences of consumerism. First, Levine and Cureton pointed out that consumerism did not first appear on college campuses in the 1990s;[34] it was evident in the late 1970s (the bystander era). The "new consumerism" they described, is specifically targeted at colleges and universities, and modern students bring to campus a true consumer mentality: "[t]heir focus is on convenience, quality, service and cost."[35] Prescient comments, written years before the great recession of 2008–2010.

This consumerism has been fueled by the changing demographics of the college. Most students are now "non-traditional." College is also not typically a central life focus of a specific time and age as it once was for so many of us—it is just one activity, and often work and families are far more important.[36]

According to Levine and Cureton, the new consumerism is deeply related to the rise of "me" values.[37] Recent research on "millennial" students supports this

---

34. *Id.* at 51.

35. Id. at 50.

36. As Levine and Cureton said:

> [Older], part-time, and working students, especially those with children, often say they want a different type of relationship with their colleges from the one undergraduates have historically had. They prefer a relationship like those they already enjoy with their bank, the telephone company, and the supermarket.
>
> Think about what you want from your bank. We (the authors) know what we want: an ATM on every corner. We want to know that, when we get to the ATM, there will be no line. We would like a parking spot right in front of the ATM. We want our checks deposited the moment they arrive at the bank, or perhaps the day before. And we want no mistake in processing—unless they are in our favor. We also know what we do not want from our banks. We do not want them to provide us with softball leagues, religious counseling, or health services. We can arrange all of these things for ourselves and don't wish to pay extra fees for the bank to offer them.
>
> Students are asking roughly the same thing from their colleges. They want their colleges nearby and operating at the hours most useful to them, preferably around the clock. They want convenience: easy, accessible parking (in the classroom would not be at all bad); no lines; and polite, helpful, and efficient staff service. They also want high-quality education but are eager for low costs. For the most part, they are very willing to comparison shop, placing a premium on time and money. They do not want to pay for activities and programs they do not use. In short, students are increasingly bringing to higher education exactly the same consumer expectations they have for every other commercial enterprise with which they deal.

See id. at 49–50.

37. *See id.* at 53.

consumerist thesis.[38] Jean Twenge has described the "me" generation and contends that a broad group of Americans are "generation me"; we may have even created a large group of narcissists.[39]

Educators, however, tend to cling to notions of community in favor of marketplace.[40] The rise of student "consumerism" is related to a growing divide between what faculty and staff perceive and desire and what students and their families perceive and desire.

There are deep problems with the consumer image and strict business law applications. While these images are better in terms of shared responsibility and safety than predecessor images, they need tailoring to function well in the unique college community. If students are consumers, then they should be entitled to get what they want and pay for. Students and families often want demonstrable success and the opportunity for good jobs after graduation. Many "consumers" of higher education resist academic challenge and being held responsible. Moreover, consumers might really want "fun" over other outcomes, and may expect to be treated like consumers in a modern customer service world. Moreover, if consumers are not sophisticated they may desire that which harms them, or not know what they *should* bargain for. As a consumer group, consumers of higher education have actually placed a very low premium on college safety—preferring prestige and degree attainment, for instance.[41]

As a *legal* liability approach, business law applications are ambiguous. At times, business law does not think in terms of shared responsibility. In many business settings it is the consumers' job to look out for themselves only, other times the business shoulders the responsibly for all shared risk. For instance, it

---

38. *See, e.g.*, Neil Howe & William Strauss, *Millennials Rising: The Next Great Generation* 265 (Vintage Books 2000) ("millennials are a consumer behemoth . . ."). There is some debate about when the millennial generation incepted, and even whether such "stereotyping" should be used at all. *See* Eric Hoover, *The Millennial Muddle: How Stereotyping Students Became a Thriving Industry and a Bundle of Contradictions*, Chron. Higher Educ. (Oct. 11, 2009), *available at* http://chronicle.com/article/The-Millennial-Muddle-How/48772/.

39. *See* Jean M. Twenge, *Generation Me: Why Today's Young Americans are More Confident, Assertive, Entitled—and More Miserable Than Ever Before* (Free Press 2006); Jean M. Twenge & W. Keith Campbell, *The Narcissism Epidemic: Living in the Age of Entitlement* (Free Press 2009).

40. Twenge & Campbell, *supra* note 39 at 52.

41. The Department of Education has been moving towards ensuring greater core mission accountability. *See* Kelly Field & Goldie Blumenstyk, *What the 'Gainful Employment' Rule Means for Colleges*, Chron. Higher Educ. (June 2, 2011), *available at* http://chronicle.com/article/Audio-What-the-Gainful/127750/.

would be odd to ask one-time visitors to a theme park to do much more than the obvious to protect their own safety. Obeying the safety rules works well there. However, a dormitory or college campus is a familiar place to students; asking for shared responsibility, such as asking all students to keep the landing door locked, is appropriate. Colleges need *community* efficacy to be safe. The texture of shared responsibility for a business depends on the business and its customers.

Ambiguity in safety responsibility has serious consequences. The phenomenon bears a strikingly similar parallel to the divide between police and citizens described by Kelling, Coles, Wilson, Bratton, and researchers in the Chicago Project. Modern work on criminality has stimulated a major rethinking of traditional police strategies in cities. Police might assume *too* much responsibility for what citizens should do as a community for themselves. On campuses (and in cities) disorder, danger, and fear have been products of the gulf created by *legal paradigms that de-emphasized shared responsibility or failed to give clear senses of the lines of responsibility.* Business rules, like bystander rules, can emphasize "freedom" and "me" instead of *community*, *community efficacy*, and *shared responsibility* on campus. Business law categories often divide responsibility as well—"college is responsible for this, students for that"—with less emphasis on *shared* responsibility. So, while business law has served student interests in many ways by introducing some notions of shared responsibility, a purely business campus does not meet all the basic safety needs of many college students. More *shared* responsibility is necessary and appropriate. More clarity on what "sharing" models look like is needed as well.

Restoring community values, sharing responsibilities, and improving community efficacy on campus can make campuses safer and less violent places. Business rules work well to promote safety at K-Mart, but students do not *live or learn* at K-Mart, or even spend significant amounts of their lives there. Business rules might work well for *some* pure commuter colleges (although even here community efficacy is essential), but not major residential campuses, which require more than the division of rights and responsibilities in a shopping mall. A consumer has little investment in making a store safer for others; every student depends on other students for safety on campus.

A *business* community campus is not the safest campus. It is a safer campus than a bystander campus but still facilitates some unreasonable risk because it emphasizes too much consumeristic thinking and not enough shared, community thinking.

(2.) Fiduciary

Perhaps sensing that courts tend to see universities as businesses with business duties, some commentators have suggested that college is a different kind of business imbued with "trust." A fiduciary model would reimagine the college in a "trusting" relationship in which the college would act for the benefit of the student across several areas of concern.

Many years ago Fowler and Goldman[42] advocated such an approach. Goldman described his view:

> All of the elements of a fiduciary relation are present in the student-university relationship. It is no small trust—no small display of confidence to place oneself under the educational mentorship of a particular university. The value of an educational experience is directly affected by the school's conscientious, faithful performance of its duties—duties which are directed toward the student's benefit.... In addition to often making confidential disclosures about his background, his health and his financial situation in applications for admission and [financial] assistance, the student is expected to confide in course and career counselors who are appointed by the university.... In making these disclosures, the student reposes confidence in the school's skill and objectivity....[43]

It is an image of confidence, counseling disclosures, and the gaining of trust.

Courts have not embraced the view vis-à-vis student safety. The power in such a view lies in the fact that it treats college/student relationships as unique and as more intimate and dependent than ordinary business relations. It is, however, a view that relies upon greater university control/authority and significantly less student freedom and responsibility. A fiduciary

---

42. *See* Gerard A. Fowler, *The Legal Relationship Between the American College Student and the College: An Historical Perspective and the Renewal of a Proposal,* 13 J.L. & Educ. 401 (1984); Alvin L. Goldman, *The University and the Liberty of Its Students—A Fiduciary Theory,* 54 Ky. L.J. 643 (1966); *see also* Kent Weeks & Rich Haglund, *Fiduciary Duties of College and University Faculty and Administrators,* 29 J.C. & U.L. 153 (2002). It may have been Warren Seavey who started this idea in the 1950s. *See* Warren A. Seavey, *Dismissal of Students: "Due Process,"* 70 Harv. L. Rev. 1406, 1407 (1957).

43. Goldman, *supra* note 42, at 671–72.

view is not a shared responsibility view as much as it is a shift in one direction on the continuum. Several commentators have made these points. As Stamatakos stated:

> The fiduciary model recognizes the trust a student places in the institution she attends. In response to this trust, a legally stringent standard of conduct is imposed upon the university.
>
> However, the fiduciary model is not practical. Whenever the student-college relationship is implicated, an institution must justify all actions affecting the relationship with fully-defensible explanations. Further, placing a fiduciary responsibility on institutions reduces students' responsibilities. This state of affairs compromises the institution's ability to foster responsible student decision-making and mature behavior. More damaging to the fiduciary model, however, is judicial resistance towards its adoption. To date, no court has characterized an educational institution as owing a fiduciary duty to its students. Thus, even if the fiduciary model were theoretically tailored to sound dimensions, the model has failed to be viable in practice.[44]

In a similar vein, Munch argued even in the 1960s that such a model would reduce student accountability.[45]

From an image point of view, the law of fiduciary relations was a natural place to look when the parental image died. Its judicial unpopularity as a general image lies in, among other things, its allocation of responsibilities and the fact that fiduciary duties most often arise in transactional contexts where the issue is money, not safety. It is not a centrist, shared responsibility view. It also is primarily a view that courts use in economic, not safety, relationships. On the plus side, its core value lies in its recognition that many students require something special from college life to mature safely and productively. The fiduciary model recognizes that if college is a transaction, it is not always among equally situated parties.

---

44. Theodore C. Stamatakos, *The Doctrine of In Loco Parentis, Tort Liability and the Student-College Relationship,* 65 Ind. L.J. 471, 478–79 (1990) (footnotes omitted).

45. *See* Christopher H. Munch, *Comment,* 45 Den. L.J. 533, 535 (1968).

E. Images of Transition, the Facilitator University, and Generations

The facilitator image helps to organize a vision of higher education's regulation under law (especially complex duty rules), provides a vision for student affairs administration in a world of legal accountability, and supplies a model for the appropriate relationship between modern universities, students, and their families.

Modern college student populations are constantly evolving. "Millennial" students now dominate as traditional students, but more and more higher education also includes second career and late life learners, part-time students, former military personnel, etc. Our relationships with students are also changing; as is the very practice of student affairs administration. The law has been moving from one set of guiding legal rules and principles to another. The duty era is still evolving in the courts and will continue to do so. We may even be on the cusp of a new *regulatory* phase in which the *compliance* university will emerge. Public attitudes towards campus safety have recently shifted to significantly less tolerance for alcohol and drug abuse, dangers of travel abroad, sexual assault, hazing, etc. There is either a growing concern that campuses have become more dangerous or simply less acceptance of college risk coupled with greater awareness of risk.

This is a time of transition in higher education populations. As Levine and Cureton described in *When Hope and Fear Collide*:

> There are rare times in the history of a society in which rapid and profound change occurs. The change is so broad and so deep that the routine and ordinary cycles of readjustment cease. There is a sharp break between the old and the new. It is a time of *discontinuity.*[46]

Levine and Cureton saw two such break points—the industrial revolution, which transformed America from an agricultural nation to an industrialized nation, and now. As they pointed out, "We name periods of profound change only in retrospect."[47] Levine and Cureton underscored that we are experiencing tremendous demographic, economic, global, and technological change, and there is a sense that major social institutions of the industrial age are failing—politics and government, public education, manufacturing and service industries, the health care system, family, church, many professional sports,

46. Levine & Cureton, *supra* note 33, at 151 (emphasis added).
47. *Id.* at 153.

and law and lawyers (including tort law *and* tort lawyers).[48] Everything once sacred, and "solid" (to paraphrase the character Juno in the movie *Juno*[49]), has come under fire (or is scandalized) it seems.

Levine and Cureton thought that the "emerging order is unknowable and unrecognizable"[50] and that there are profound tides of loss and frustration in American culture. They argued it is "fantasy" to describe our society as it will be seen in the future.[51] Colleges and students are caught in this period of "unceasing, unknowable change."[52] College life is straddling two worlds, one of which was once familiar, and one which is emerging but is still unfamiliar. There is literally global revolution in the air, as *billions* of people emerge from dictatorship and forced ignorance into a world of greater freedom and educational opportunity. It is no surprise that the law itself reflects this profound shifting. As the world awakes to a potential second period of enlightenment, American courts have the challenge of articulating a vision of education for the planet, not just the United States.

It is not just a time of transition in law, higher education, and global culture—it is a time when college students are experiencing those changes personally, generationally, politically, and legally. Levine and Cureton described students who were frightened because of change, concerned about their security (especially financial), sexually active but isolated, heavy drinkers, overworked, lonely and tired, typically weak in basic skills but able to learn from their instructors in ways that the instructors often do not make use of, distant from college administrators and instructors, pragmatic, careerist, idealistic, altruistic, and surprisingly optimistic; politically students are more diverse than ever and also more divided and separated, consumer-oriented, disenchanted with American politics and most major social institutions, oriented away from centrist political attitudes, liberal in social mores, focused on local issues more than global, and socially conscious and active.[53] In their summary, Levine and Cureton saw students as "[d]esperately committed to preserving the American dream"[54] but often unsure of what this would mean for them and whether they would be able to manifest it.

48. *See id.* at 152–53.

49. *Juno* (Fox Searchlight Pictures 2007).

50. Levine & Cureton, *supra* note 33, at 153.

51. *Id.* at 154.

52. *Id.* Levine and Cureton's descriptions dovetail substantially with many later descriptions of "millennial students." *See, e.g.*, Strauss & Howe, *supra* note 38.

53. *See* Levine & Cureton, *supra* note 33, at 156–57.

54. *Id.* at 157.

Levine and Cureton's work anticipated an onslaught of the so-called "millennial" generation of college students—and their families.[55] Much of the research focuses on "traditional" students—those who more or less go straight to college from high school. However, the "traditional" student is an evaporating concept: students are more diverse and older than ever; attainment is different (and usually longer than in the past, six to seven years is common); students have access to more distance education; campuses are increasingly more global; etc. A facilitator university is highly interested in populations and demographics and the profound shifts in student populations are critically important.

In the last decade, there has been an explosion of interest in so-called "millennial" students.[56] Who are the millennials? What are their core characteristics? These questions are hotly debated. According to many researchers this is a generation of students born in the early 1980s to the early 2000s.[57] Strauss and Howe identified seven core traits of millennials in *Millennials Go to College*:

- Special
- Sheltered
- Confident
- Team-oriented

---

55. *See* Hoover, *supra* note 38. Hoover, a long time writer of higher education topics for the Chronicle of Higher Education, is a rare combination of journalist/scholar. This Humean piece is the definitive attack on "generationalism" in higher education, and a must read for anyone interested in the study of millennials. *Inter alia*, the piece does a fine job of discussing leading theorists and their (sometimes conflicting) ideas. It is also something of a mirror: it is an excellent glimpse into how "millennials" view being grouped or categorized.

56. I draw heavily here upon the words of Strauss & Howe, *supra* note 38, and Twenge, *supra* note 39. Much of what I have learned about students and millennials is from my colleague Jim Hundrieser.

57. *See* Hoover, *supra* note 38. It is wise to keep in mind that a key point I learned from Eric Hoover and Jim Hundrieser—identifying "millennials" says as much about *us* as it does about them. In many ways we have created millennials in the way *we* approach student populations, whether we are "millennials" ourselves or not. A facilitator university is keenly aware of the pitfalls of stereotyping. The spectre of Dean Wormer, the evil king of "isms," is a constant reminder about our past. Nevertheless, in the era of insularity students came to higher education to assume their place in ordinal society. The civil rights and bystander era—baby boom and generation X students—sought independence from many social institutions (especially family) and desired political power and personal freedom. Shifting demographics was a singular feature of the end of the era of insularity—a lesson facilitators never forget. Generationism, for better or worse, is somewhat embedded in facilitators, who seek a model that both fits many generations but adapts as well. It will not be long before children of the great recession come to college.

- Conventional
- Pressured
- Achieving

There is much to say about these traits (and perhaps others as well) from the perspective of law, student life management, and a facilitator university. Moreover, a facilitator university views students as *visitors*, with important generational, and trans-generational implications. The concept of students as visitors is developed in the book *Beyond Discipline*.[58]

Millennial students, as visitors in a facilitative environment, may tend to discount risks. As "special" individuals, bad things happen to others, not them. Confidence can be a weakness if it is too extreme and does not alert a student to danger. An "I've got this" attitude is sometimes visible in situations when students clearly do not. Teamwork can be a detriment as well, if students pick the wrong team. For instance, in *Garofalo v. Lambda Chi Alpha*,[59] the Iowa Supreme Court addressed multiple liability issues arising out of the alcohol death of a fraternity member. In that case, instead of calling for help, fraternity brothers confidently chose to follow their own mentoring. They were wrong. Several individual fraternity members faced serious legal ramifications.[60] An "It won't happen here" mentality, coupled with over-confidence in the wrong team's decision-making, contributed to a student's death.

Society may also have lured millennial students into false safety consciousness. For one, this is the first generation for whom child safety has become a top priority. It is possible that no human society has ever placed such strong emphasis on child safety. As a baby boomer, I ate rare hamburgers, lived on peanuts, a "hand wash" was a garden hose, I thought only people in France wore helmets on bicycles, and our family car had seat belts but they quickly slipped under the seats and were never used. This has translated into heightened expectation of safety—some expectations bordering on the absurd. Some recent legal cases bear this out; courts have responded by insisting on plaintiff accountability in such cases. New attitudes towards safety have also become apparent in recent regulatory initiatives that push for colleges to provide care levels beyond reasonable care.

A facilitator university plays an important role in teaching and fostering self-responsibility. It is almost inconceivable to imagine what an "as safe as

58. Lake, *supra* note 4, at 329–38.

59. 616 N.W.2d 647 (Iowa 2000).

60. *See* Peter F. Lake, *Private Law Continues to Come to Campus: Rights and Responsibilities Revisited*, *supra* note 13,at 635–36.

possible" university looks like. The simple fact is that higher education *is* risky business—it always has been and must be to succeed. A facilitator university accepts *reasonable* risk as part of the core mission. A facilitator university believes deeply in student autonomy: knowing and voluntary choices are the prerogative of higher learners.

It is troubling for colleges that emphasis in the K–12 experience has been so skewed towards risk avoidance. That is a topic for another book. However, we must face the reality that late-stage transition to adulthood is a time of great risk on a variety of fronts for our visitors. Generations of higher learners have been called to face evil—on the beaches of the Pacific and Europe; in brutal civil rights confrontations in the south; in disaster-stricken Haiti, etc. Luke Skywalker lost a hand and his friend Biggs was killed; Anakin Skywalker suffered horribly. Even *Animal House* had a violent riot. *Every* college student is "at risk:" sometimes taking reasonable risks is essential to learning and growing. This is the salvageable message of the bystander cases: do not destroy higher education by trying to save or protect it. Overconfidence and sheltering can be enemies of a facilitator university if taken too far. Students can *learn* in risky situations, from encountering risks, from failure, and from accepting responsibility. There is peril—even educational peril—in setting too high expectations for risk avoidance.

Millennial populations also have been raised with near constant supervision and in a safety world where others have carefully crafted a world of heightened safety—a world like that in the movie *The Truman Show*[61]—that looks safer from the inside than out. Consider the MTV reality show *The Real World*, which from a safety point of view is anything but reality. A recent cast visited New Orleans, and included a young woman who had frequent blackouts from high-risk alcohol use.[62] What you do not see on camera is a production team constantly monitoring her. In reality, a young woman like her is highly likely to be sexually assaulted: most college students do not have guardian angel production teams. Many millennials have been lulled into risk complacency—even marketed into it—assuming falsely that things are as safe as they appear to be and have been in the past. A facilitator university is keenly aware of the fact that our populations may be particularly at risk because of past experiences. Students themselves are usually the best first agents of safety. Colleges can do their part; so must students. A lifetime of protectivism can backfire into new forms of risk. A facilitator university seeks the right balance of intervention and hold-

61. *The Truman Show* (Paramount Pictures 1998).

62. *The Real World: New Orleans* (MTV television broadcast 2010).

ing students accountable for their own decisions. A facilitator university also appreciates the need to teach risk management, and to some extent, retrain certain populations. This is especially challenging when many administrators and teachers are themselves part of the generation of parents who raised millennials.

Risk management and facilitation fail when colleges seek to avoid the responsibility of using judgment when balancing tough safety questions and focusing instead on black and white compliance steps. Facilitation and risk management have irreducible cores of human care and concern, instinct, and judgment. No grid, or matrix, or form could ever fully capture that. Facilitation can be intuitive and lives in the *spirit* of risk management, not the letter. Facilitation is pragmatic—it exists in the doing—not just in the saying, or the ticking off of "steps" or forms. Students as visitors are not going to a movie of their educational experience—they are starring in the movie and it is real.

Cases of the duty era have impliedly accepted these ideas. Duty is constantly striving to promote responsibility and accountability, and is keenly aware of the balancing that good safety decisions require. In extreme cases—like *Bash* (heroin overdose) or *Robertson* (natatorium roof fall)—courts cannot ignore shared responsibility—there is little to nothing that reasonable care could do to prevent some forms of essentially self-inflicted harm. Indeed, the kind of care that would prevent such injures might well destroy the very educational environment that we seek to preserve. Clear doors in residence halls? A three-foot high, rubberized campus like a child's play area? Awful ideas. Indeed, the only reasonable solutions to situations like *Bash* and *Robertson* lie beyond the potential of the duty era—even law—to regulate.[63]

Many colleges could deploy reasonable and scientifically promising prevention strategies. In the aggregate, such efforts would tend to reduce incidents like *Bash* and *Robertson*. However, the law of duty was not designed to incentivize such reasonable efforts, causing further pressure on regulators to intervene.

Let's explore the limits of duty. First, duty law is typically very point-of-injury specific in application. A plaintiff must prove *causation*, usually with a

63. The duty era has become keenly aware of its own limits—and the limits of a tort system alone to create safe and responsible campuses under law. The duty era implies a future era that includes a partnership with other forms of law. The emergence of a compliance university is a first, perhaps fumbling, step towards a wider relationship with law. A push for accountability invariably matures into an opportunity for facilitation. Someday, law will facilitate us.

"preponderance of the evidence." It would be virtually impossible to show that a given injury—as in *Bash* or *Robertson*—was *caused*, in that sense, by the failure to deploy reasonable prevention efforts directed towards modifying aggregate behaviors. There are still plenty of alcohol/duty-related injuries at campuses that deploy the best, state-of-the-art alcohol prevention strategies. Indeed, many campuses *are* using reasonable prevention strategies; and some individual students are not using reasonable care for their own safety.

Second, and related, many duty cases—again, as in *Bash* and *Robertson*—essentially ask a college to *anticipate* the need for a rescue, not simply rescue someone in known danger. There is a big difference between seeing a drowning child and walking by, and waking up as a hero in a comic book and thinking, "Who needs a rescue today!" The duty paradigm was not designed to create legal responsibility for anticipated rescue, except in situations where a business has actual or constructive knowledge of an unreasonable hazard (like oil spilled on the floor), and imminent/foreseeable danger arising from that hazard. In *some* ways the law of duty has evolved to provide incentives for proactive, aggregate interventions—the most obvious is the duty to protect business invitees/tenants from foreseeable criminal attacks. Even in those cases, however, a plaintiff might still show that a failure to procure reasonable security caused/facilitated a foreseeable or imminent specific attack.[64]

---

64. *See, e.g., Saelzler v. Advanced 400 Grp.*, 23 P.3d 1143 (Cal. 2001). *Saelzler* is a very difficult causation case but the following illustrates the point well:

> *Saelzler* . . . involved an attack on a woman who was making a delivery at a low-income housing project. In a sharply divided, four-to-three decision, the *Saelzler* court determined that the plaintiff failed to show causation-in-fact, resulting in the dismissal of Saelzler's claim.
>
> The case involved Marianne Saelzler, a delivery employee who attempted a delivery at a three hundred-unit multi-building apartment complex. As Saelzler attempted to leave the premises, several men attacked her and attempted to sexually assault her. Saelzler staged a valiant defense and prevented the men from raping her, but she was seriously injured in defending herself. The complex was rife with crime and the police frequented the premises. Security patrols were deployed during the evening, but not during the daytime, presumably as a cost-saving measure. There was a security gate, but at the time of the attack it was propped open. The majority painted a very dark and terrifying picture of the apartment complex and its state of security and repair. Unsurprisingly, Saelzler was unable to identify her attacker. Crucially to her case, neither she nor anyone else was able to identify whether the assailants were living in the complex or had entered the premises either through the gate or by some other means.

More or less, plaintiffs in cases like *Bash* or *Robertson* could never mount a better argument than that a college deprived a victim of a statistical *chance* of improved safety (and by no means am I suggesting that was the situation in those cases). The idea of recovery in a duty system for a loss of chance of recovery—or you might think of this as "anticipatory rescue"—is extremely limited in American tort law. The prime examples of loss of chance of recovery claims arise in medical malpractice cases: example, a doctor commits malpractice when treating a very sick patient who was highly likely to die without treatment. However, in those cases the existence of a duty is usually quite easy to establish. A doctor has performed surgery, and has a doctor/patient rela-

---

> *Saelzler* had a tortured path toward its four-to-three decision in the California Supreme Court.
>
> ....
>
> The issues of duty and breach were not contested. In language reminiscent of cases on duty, rather than causation, the court engaged in policy analysis and acknowledged that the case presented a particularly difficult dilemma of attempting to determine whether to place financial burdens of increased security on low-income business defendants or to provide greater safety for victims in those complexes. The majority opinion reads as if the opinion had originally been written to state that no duty was owed, but in order to flip a judge to the majority, the opinion was edited to become a causation case.
>
> The majority's reasoning was fairly straightforward. Since the gate was designed to deal with intruders, Saelzler's failure to identify the assailants as either insiders or intruders was fatal to her claim because she would never be able to show by a preponderance of the evidence that it was the negligence of the complex that caused the assault. It is equally likely that the attack came from the inside and, if so, poor security and the broken gate would not have been the cause. Security patrols theoretically could have impacted crime within the complex. Nonetheless, the majority stated effectively as a matter of judicial notice that increased security cannot be shown to prevent the causation of crime, either specifically or in general. Thus, Saelzler's failure to identify her assailants and whether they were from inside or outside the complex was fatal to her case because without that evidence she would be unable to establish causation between the defendant's breach of duty and her injury.
>
> Following *Saelzler*, many claims will fail where there is a defect in proof of causation. Although it is usually clear whether an assailant came, for example, from inside or outside a dormitory, there will be situations where it may be hard for an injured student to prove the identity of an assailant. *Saelzler* suggests that issues will shift from questions of duty and breach to questions of causation. Causation law in higher education portends significant development in the next several decades.

Lake, *supra* note 13, at 654–56 (footnotes omitted).

tionship with the victim. This is all very technical tort stuff, but can you see how the duty paradigm was not designed to manage much of the risk of modern alcohol culture on campus?

Third, we now live in a society with extraordinary rescue and triage systems. Emergency rescue and triage services in America are routinely given tort immunities that protect them from liability except in situations of gross negligence, recklessness, or willful or malicious injury. As society developed a professional rescue/triage system, tort law evolved immunities for such systems. The reason is simple: in an emergency what is reasonable is different. It is much easier to make mistakes without full knowledge and the opportunity for measured, careful decision-making. Modern colleges have populations that require emergency services and triage on a regular basis; but except for public colleges with background governmental immunity, colleges as entities routinely face rescue/triage litigation without much legal protection in the form of rescue immunities. Courts implicitly recognize the differential application of rescue protection—magnified because many college "rescue" cases are really more than mere rescue cases, they are anticipatory rescue cases. There is a gap in the law of safety—a crack—that colleges neatly fall into: there is something unfair about treating colleges less favorably *and* asking them to do more than simply rescue by anticipating the need for rescue.[65] Truly, for parity's sake colleges should at least receive the same Good Samaritan protection that other actors in society have. However, most Good Samaritan laws are written for emergency rooms, emergency/triage personnel, and motorists on highways (because our highways are an enormous source of risk). Now look back at the alcohol cases for a minute. Can you see how courts emphasizing personal student accountability in some of the cases were simply mirroring the good faith immunities available to other "rescue" entities in society? If *Gross* is right, that colleges should be treated like other entities in society, then it should be a two way street. However, courts that once created broad immunities saw legislatures tear them down. In modern times, courts have been reluctant to craft immunities as such, deferring to legislatures. New tort "immunities" lurk like the peas mom hid in the mashed potatoes.

The law of duty sometimes reaches its analytic, historical, and practical limits in college cases. Yet duty law applies to populations that have grown up

65. This is the essence of the concern over the Virginia Tech fines levied under a timely warning standard. The application of that standard to Virginia Tech—assuming for the moment that warnings were not "timely" or "reasonable"—is the application of a standard that is not consistent with the law applied to most emergency/triage personnel in analyzing real time decision-making.

with assurances of safety and the existence of superb triage/emergency intervention services. This sets the stage for a clash of expectations and reality—and even the core mission of a college. The modern college faces the daunting task at times of playing the role of a bucket of cold water or Clint Eastwood: life and higher learning are often very dangerous, and if a student expects to be safe that student had better recognize that, in many instances, safety begins with that individual student. Previous generations were more likely to assume responsibility for their own safety: many millennials and their families have been lulled into false expectations about the reality of college life. A facilitator university accepts generational challenges and wants to create ever more favorable conditions under which students will internalize risk management concepts and accept the spirit of living and learning in a reasonably safe way—as compared to ticking off compliance steps or avoiding responsibility. One way to do this is to build on the strengths of other populations—older students, for instance.

Millennial students also create safety challenges because they are often adroit *avoiders*. Self-efficacy and confidence generate a common theme on college campuses today. Individuals "judging" or applying rules to a millennial student are "haters" and are to be avoided. Modern students often smile and nod and then find ways to dodge risk management rules and safety systems they do not like. College populations are so adroit at avoidance that risk management under rule systems is next to impossible for some: as soon as a campus has a new set of rules, students find a way to circumvent these rules. A facilitator university recognizes that safety management under rules alone has limitations, particularly with certain populations.

Closely related, many millennial students were raised primarily in bribe and reward cultures, not rule and punishment cultures. Self-esteem building emphasized becoming a better "me." Awards and trophies were common, even for modest achievements. The evolution of McDonald's and the "Happy Meal" tells all. When I was a child just going to McDonald's was the happy meal, then they invented a "Happy Meal," and then the toys in the meal became much cooler. Millennials are not even truly "rule" people. Rules have been embedded in their experiences and they did not always have to learn rules to participate (compare video games with Monopoly); millennials are much more accustomed to motivation via praise or reward, not rules and punishment. Many modern students were simply not taught to be as rule-oriented as past generations.

A facilitator university understands the need for helping students to learn to live better, safer, rule-governed lives: internalizing the spirit of rules becomes a primary goal.[66] A facilitator university is also keenly aware that rule avoidance behavior, and lack of rule comprehension, can be very risky for some populations.

The "sheltered" and "conventional" generation is also highly connected to parents/key family members. Boomers and Gen X'ers often sought emancipation from parents: millennials view parents as friends and mentors. Indeed, in a very real sense many parents are going to college simultaneously with their children and are as much new students as parents. A facilitator university is keenly aware of how students make safety choices, and with what information, and with whom.

Higher education is recovering from a long period of deliberately distancing parents as a feature of a student development philosophy. In fact, parents are an under-utilized safety and educational resource. However, a facilitator university recognizes that parents may not *always* be the best informal mentors, that their motivation may conflict with certain necessary safety and educational goals, and that students will need to learn to take mastery of their own destinies and not defer the responsibility to mentors, teachers, or Jedi-masters.

Strauss and Howe refer to today's parents as "helicopter" parents—primarily because they "hover."[67] This is a very baby-boom image—Huey helicopters hovering over Vietnam. However, that image misses the mark. Parents do not hover; they participate. Critically, they have often set achievement goals for the children and are determined to see those goals through to conclusion. Parents are much more like builders/construction site managers. They have been building a dream child since before birth, and have meticulously sub-contracted work for years. College represents the last stages of the project; and parents will challenge any intervention that interferes with their goals.

Facilitator universities frequently encounter parent/family opposition to solid risk management plans and systems of accountability. Parents, as a resource, can de-facilitate students unintentionally if not used and trained properly. We can presume that most parents generally do what they think is best for their children. The facilitator university faces and embraces the generational challenge of re-integrating parents into the higher education process.

Emerging brain science also suggests some interesting features of the millennial generation. We now are more keenly aware of brain development in college. Many students are at risk of delaying their maturation and learning. High-risk alcohol use is a great barrier to achievement and safety, and may

---

66. *See generally* Lake, *supra* note 4.
67. *See generally* Straus & Howe, *supra* note 38.

cause long-term effects. Millennial populations are in an in-between state developmentally—to call students simply "adults" misses the mark. A facilitator university embraces the opportunity for pro-active intervention in late-stage learning development and maturation. It may be that educated humans in a technology-based society mature into full, independent adulthood in the late 20s or early 30s, not at 18 or 21.

Finally, millennials are the most culturally diverse group of students higher education has ever seen. This creates challenges for generalization about millennials, and pushes a facilitator university to consider students as individuals first.[68] Environmental management begins with the environment of one—each individual student. A facilitator university recognizes the *tendencies* of its populations but ultimately seeks to empower students—and hold them accountable—on an individual as well as aggregate basis. A facilitator university is micro and macroscopic.

The larger message is that a facilitator university—exactly unlike Faber College in *Animal House*—is population sensitive. We must balance the need to know our students—and their propensities—with the need to prepare them for the society they will enter. Thus when brain science tells us that millennials are not at peak intellectual performance in the early morning hours, we can better structure our curriculum for safety and learning outcomes. However, we do our students no service at all if we lead them to think that the world will always accommodate their preferences or maximize their opportunities or their terms. The era of insularity weeded out those deemed unsuitable for roles in an established hierarchy. The civil rights era opened the door to human potential in higher education. The facilitator university recognizes that the relationship with its visitors is liminal, transitional, and Socratic. There is a deliberate balance to be struck. We must bend to our students, and they to us.

A facilitator university is always looking ahead in time (as well as in the rearview mirror). Our great hope lies in the ever-renewing energy of what our new learners—visitors—bring to our institutions to teach us.

II. Imagining a Facilitator University

The model that can synthesize the best aspects of the competing images and reconcile existing case law is a facilitator model. A facilitator model can help

68. This is a central theme of *Beyond Discipline*, *supra* note 4, and in the law for that matter.

courts and lawyers better identify and describe trends in the law and use familiar rules of decision that are adapted for the unique context of higher education. The facilitator model can also guide student affairs practice. The model is descriptive, predictive, practical, and theoretical. It is also liminal and interdisciplinary in that it can be used to describe university and legal reality, and as a tool of communication between the two worlds.

A facilitator college balances rights and responsibilities—it is neither extremely authoritarian nor overly solicitous of student freedom. Importantly, a facilitator college seeks *shared* responsibility rather than allocating it unilaterally (or not at all). Facilitation implies that there is an appropriate and reasonable degree of risk in higher education—some students will be hurt by the inherent risks of an activity or even their own unreasonable actions. However, there is no reason for a woman to be sexually assaulted in a dormitory by a criminal intruder whose opportunity for entry was the university's failure to repair a door lock that it knew was broken.

The facilitator model best describes case law in the duty era. The facilitator model is in the nature of regression analysis. Some cases are hard to reconcile with centrist positions like the facilitator model. However, most cases (especially recent duty era cases) are easily reconciled using the facilitator model, and several legal paradoxes/problems are resolved as well.

When thinking of a facilitator, think of a guide or mentor who provides as much support, information, interaction, and control as is reasonably necessary and appropriate in the situation. A facilitator stands somewhere between a dominating parent or authority figure and a pure stranger or bystander. The facilitator is not a parent, but does pick up on the idea that some students need more nurturing than others. For many students, familial roles may be appropriate, particularly when it is the first time away from home at age seventeen or eighteen, and the student is thrust into an environment that is unfamiliar. The many facets of college life can be overwhelming without structure and guidance. A facilitator adapts to the student *body* and to students as individuals; however *not all students* need special guidance, except perhaps in very particular ways (financial aid, course selection, etc.). Many older, non-traditional students at two-year institutions want and need much less mentoring than younger students at traditional four-year colleges. But that is hardly a universal truth.

Unlike parents with children, facilitators do not *choose for* students. Students must choose *for themselves* and shoulder significant responsibility for outcomes of their choice. The facilitator university manages the parameters under which choices are made. Information, training, instruction and supervision, discussion, options, and, in some cases, withdrawal of options are all appropriate for facilitators. A facilitator (instructor or student affairs professional) is keenly aware of aberrant risks and risks known only to the more experienced. A facilitator is also very aware of the diversity in a particular university community. Limited involvement may be just fine for second career students who want "just classroom education." Greater involvement is warranted for less mature or inexperienced students, particularly traditional-age students in full-time, on-campus living arrangements. In other words, a facilitator *adapts* and varies the level and nature of involvement.

The facilitator university is different from a fiduciary in all but very unusual circumstances. A fiduciary is usually just involved in financial/economic affairs; a facilitator engages the full range of relevant experience.[69] A fiduciary enjoys a position of trust; often a facilitator will do so too, but it is not always necessary or appropriate to require a facilitator to have such a relationship. For example, an honor code system facilitates the fairness of the academic setting but does not act as a fiduciary. There are times when students need or want adversaries, not fiduciaries. Moreover, a fiduciary typically can exercise too much control and take on too much responsibility. A facilitator plays a role but is not a legal guardian or trust officer. Trust officers often make choices for their charges; a facilitator honors the choices of the student. A fiduciary often directs decisions.

A modern facilitator university offers services uniquely to each community: many are traditional business services. The university can pose as dormitory landlord, education-mall superintendent, activities director, security force, or health services coordinator. Indeed, many universities provide a range of services that individuals would otherwise avail themselves of in the private business sector by interacting with many different business entities. The range of services a facilitator university provides is more like a package or bundle.

Yet in the context of college life, these services have a special feel to them. Nothing is exactly the same as in the private sector (just walk into any student union). Intercollegiate athletics or field trips are not like the pay-per-use gym; dormitories are not always configured or managed like apartment complexes for working twenty-somethings. A campus rarely looks like a shopping mall. College is meaningfully different. The college bundle of services often serves to offer a lifestyle and a training ground for future patterns in life.

Students are not children to facilitators nor are they typical consumers—they are *visitors*.[70] Part of facilitation is teaching how to "consume" university life safely and consistently with overall educational goals. Noise and alcohol re-

69. *See* Lake, *supra* note 4.

70. *See id.* at 329–38.

strictions facilitate studying. College-sponsored activities and athletics can teach students cooperation and offer skills that can lead to a lifetime of fun, health, and safe recreation. The facilitator is not like the rude waiter in the snobbish French restaurant who refuses to assist you in reading the French-only menu. The facilitator will help you read the menu, but the choice is yours. The facilitator will remind you that escargot is snails, but will serve them to you if you choose to order them. Consumers often enter a world of *caveat emptor,* a very poor social world for college life. Facilitators help students make intelligent, fair, and reasonable choices; a facilitator university does not seek to make money at the expense of consumers subject only to minimal legal constraints of fairness. College is not an arms-length bargaining process. Most students "bargain" in a place in-between pure consumers and those under fiduciary care.

To be sure, it is important that a college "do business" with its students. But this business should be done in light of the unique objectives of the college. Education (in the broader sense, not just classroom instruction) is the primary focus of the college, and each of its operations can either facilitate education, or not. A facilitator college in its business role does not simply give consumers what they want; left without guidance, students may desire grade inflation (which arises in complex ways) and a party-til-you-drop campus. In sum, the facilitator college must consider inter-generational and long-term equities and interests. Education is a "product" for a lifetime. As Dean Wormer observed in *Animal House,* drunk and stupid is no way to go through life, and although it may seem appealing in the short run, it is cheating the consumer student to sell this product. (Don't forget that students often say later on "that teacher was hard, and I liked that.")

A facilitator *is sometimes* a bystander—but a bystander who chooses to be in that role as a way to facilitate student education and student development. Control-dominated management is ultimately inconsistent with the objective of helping to facilitate choices of young adults. Thus, much like relatives, friends, and others who must watch with dismay as a student chooses a course of action, the facilitator too must be willing to stand down at times. However, this does not mean abdication of authority or needless victim blaming. In this sense, the college that accepts responsibility for instruction, counseling, residence life, student activities, etc., cannot simply stand by like a stranger. Deliberate non-intervention is very different from indifference.

If students and/or faculty wish to canoe on sometimes very dangerous Lake George in New York, then the college can choose to facilitate reasonably safe excursions or field trips through appropriate warnings and precautions. As the students set out, the college must then hold its breath and allow the students to choose—upon full knowledge and in reasonable safety—to take the *inherent* risks that for many make life worth living. College students were on the Gulf Coast after Katrina; in Haiti after the earthquake, went south in the 1960s to fight for civil rights: wherever there is crisis, college students are certain to be there helping, learning, and taking risks. A proper line of facilitation draws at what is reasonable, but recognizes that the choice to encounter risk lies with students. A facilitator cannot and does not eliminate all risks, but neither does it ask students to assume those unreasonable risks that would arise from lack of proper university planning, guidance, warning, instruction, etc. A facilitator university would allow students to assume the inherent risks of rock climbing but would not allow an instructor to abandon the responsibility to see that inexperienced students did not exceed the scope of their ability. A facilitator university would acknowledge that a faculty member has a responsibility not to actively participate in alcohol consumption with students in a way that openly violates university policy and endangers students. A facilitator university would allow a student to visit a family services center off campus on her own as part of a class, but it would not assign her there as an intern without making some determination that it was a reasonably safe place for her to be and that she would receive proper orientation, etc., at the facility.

And, a facilitator does not accept the idea that students are "uncontrollable." For one thing, this view misses the point of the college/student relationship. Learning is not a control drama, but a delicate act of facilitation. Under all but the most extreme situations, why would a facilitator want to "control" a student in a strong sense? A facilitator desires to be a guide and a source of positive influence but also trusts in the inherent wisdom of students. This is exactly where Yoda and Obi Wan failed with Anakin Skywalker and succeeded with his son, Luke. If a college is concerned about the risks of certain student activities, it can offer alternatives to the less desirable activities, thus minimizing risk. The facilitator is creative and practical, not stifling and reactive. Only the most extreme forms of student misconduct need control in a strong sense.

There is an important analogy to law and jurisprudence. In legal theory, the so-called command theory of law (often attributed to jurisprudential writer John Austin) has been very influential. The Austinian idea is that law exists only when there is a command—a threat backed by sanctions—issued from a supreme commander. Dean Wormer is this "commander" but fails precisely because he knows only the more extreme forms of control and power. Modern legal theorists (like H. L. A. Hart) believe that law is not just a series of explicit and hidden commands but often consists of powers and opportunities conferred. The legal power to associate and create a corporation is not a command in any ordinary sense, if at all. Modern law *commands* less and facilitates more. Over-emphasis on control is a reactionary model of what law is and can be. A modern transitional and transitory world requires *pro-action*. For every problem that might or might not be solved by control, the facilitator believes—until proven wrong—that there exists an opportunity to fix that problem by facilitating positive actions. A facilitator is not a zero sum game theorist. Sometimes Captain Kirk is a facilitator: the facilitator is an optimist at heart.

On the other hand, a facilitator is not averse to controlling disorder on campus, especially activity of any nature that compromises student safety and security. Indeed, by leaving locks unrepaired or looking the other way while students parade to fraternity hazing events, a college facilitates bad behavior, disrespect for rules, and the unreasonable physical danger that follows. A facilitator college can embrace fixing broken windows and community efficacy ideas. There are even moments when students must be dealt with severely. A facilitator accepts that a few students do not seek generally what they say they seek. There are sexual predators and drug dealers in our communities. There is no "facilitating" that—they need to go. There must be some willingness to work with the reasonable constraint of our communities. A facilitator is not a chump or a doormat.

Unlike any other paradigm, the facilitator model *works* to provide proper legal guidance in cases of alcohol-related student injury or death. The facilitator model is *simpatico* with modern environmental management alcohol prevention models. Facilitation is to law and student safety as environmental management is to alcohol prevention. Both concepts stress shared responsibility, collective efficacy, the need for individualized intervention, science, reasonableness and a focus on an environment or riskscape. In addition, both concepts are realistic and optimistic. Environmental management is not prohibition any more than a facilitator university aims to end all risk. Both concepts stress reasonable risk reduction. Both concepts acknowledge a role for law and rule enforcement as well.

A university as a facilitator is *not* an "insurer" of student safety. First, there is a risk that insurance facilitates unreasonable behavior by creating a "moral hazard." Students cannot learn responsibility without consequences. Moreover, it is unfair to ask a college to shoulder all responsibility for all risks. When courts say that a college is not an insurer, they mean this. For example, comparative negligence is critical. A student whose own unreasonable conduct has significantly contributed to her/his own injury should not profit from that conduct or escape responsibility for it. A student's recovery should be diminished or barred—upon proper jury findings—according to principles of comparative negligence applicable in the college's jurisdiction.

Yet, the university can learn a great deal from modern risk management—and insurance strategies in loss avoidance and loss spreading. Looking for innovative ways to stop injury stops legal liability *before it ever starts.* And, a facilitator is conscious that a catastrophic case disproportionately allocates loss to some (a few) students when many others engage in similar risky behavior with more fortunate consequences. The college is in a unique position, along with its insurers, to assess types of risk and find creative and fair ways to reallocate risk. The facilitator model recognizes that students and parents may systematically discount low probability events, yet statistically a certain number of injuries inevitably occur.

A facilitator is an educator but not just in a pure "classroom" sense. Delivery of higher education has rapidly expanded from this narrow sense of pure classroom instruction. Since the 1960s and 1970s, externships, internships, travel abroad, and a vast array of student life experiences augment classroom instruction. Notably, student affairs administrators now co-create a living/learning environment for students. *Bradshaw's* limited vision of the core mission of higher education has no place in highly digital, fluid living/learning environments.

A facilitator university stresses and supports community efficacy. We are not a "community" of bystanders; if we are, we all suffer. Campus and community coalitions, for instance, have had demonstrable safety impacts on college communities. Safety is not a background feature of an education. Participating in a community of efficacy is an integral feature of being a visitorial student in a facilitator university.

A facilitator model embraces appropriate opportunities to manage and supervise student activities and affairs and interact with students. By following no-duty, bystander paradigms and intervening only after injury occurred, universities distanced themselves from students in the day-to-day ways that prevent danger—in much the ways that police once left the neighborhood beat for police cars and rapid response 911 calls. Police strategies once focused upon responding to crime rather than preventing it: so too did the college bystander. As such, the college became out of touch. We must now foster strong community involvement with students in ways that can prevent harm. Consider *Beach:* someone should have made sure the student got back to her tent in one piece so that she would not wander off alone; or, if she had a known, serious drinking problem, she should not have been included in a potentially dangerous field excursion at all. Fears of "assumed duties" have led colleges to be reticent in situations that demand proper college-student/facilitation. Fear *is* dangerous.

A facilitator model also reacts to notions of charity, contract, and government. Colleges are special mission organizations and are invested with public interest. College dangers are increasingly being exported to the community at large and vice versa. A facilitator formulates the greater public interest into the educational equation. As campus risks move off campus and as students integrate more with the community, the connections to the greater community good will be more and more apparent.

The facilitator model also reflects the fact that colleges have a strong flavor, as Gary Pavela has written, of being voluntary associations. A college feels something like John Locke's social contract, and the large university often provides all the basic services of any municipality. To some, college can be like city/state Athens filled with versions of Socrates, Plato, and Aristotle. It is a free and socio-contractual political society unto itself. As such, the facilitator model respects the power of the collective community to define itself. Student involvement teaches participatory values and citizenship—key components of a secure learning environment. Legal models that encourage the mutual disempowerment of students and administration permit, and perhaps foster, disorderly and even dangerous circumstances. Students do not aspire to run a college, but they are not "inmates" in a prison or asylum, or purchasers of services who are to be left on their own in their community affairs.

The facilitator model accepts the idea that college/student relationships are unique and, in a sense "special." But the term "special relationship" is so loaded with legal imagery in the university law context that to make this point it is necessary to put the law, as such, aside for just a minute. In general, a relationship to any higher education institution, whether two-year community college or four-year residential college, is a unique and unparalleled experience in a person's life. Teaching is special. Learning in an organized program is special. Experiencing teaching and learning among similarly situated peers is special. It is no surprise that graduates often look back at college years as the most fortunate and challenging periods in life. Courts can say legally that there is nothing "special" about the relationship of student and university and infuse the law with business rules, but there will always be something different about college. It is a mixture of many things: a dash of family, personal freedom, a variety of quasi-commercial services, a voluntary association (often with genuine governmental responsibilities), the public good and public interest, fellowships and friendships, and, of course, unique educational opportunities. One can form oneself for the future in a place like this and set the tone for a lifetime of vocations, avocations, associations, friendships, and activities (including further learning). The Supreme Court of Delaware was correct when it said that student life is university *guided.*

Moreover, the university is also special in that it is not a singular concept. Higher education is served up in a variety of formats with different expectations and different responsibilities. There is no way to avoid looking at the particular circumstances of a given college in balancing risk and responsibility. A snow "traying" problem should be handled differently in Louisiana than in Massachusetts. A small college in Montana does not face the complexity of security issues that are relevant to a large, urban university like the University of Washington. And colleges themselves are constantly in transition as every few years a new generation of students enters with regenerated needs and expectations and new sets of dangers associated with their generation.

The non-legal special sense of college life is only heightened during times of social transition or upheaval of the kind Levine and Cureton described. All of society will benefit—or not—according to how higher education responds during stress periods. There are few legal/cultural/social issues of more long-term significance. College is special in this sense. This is very evident in the core mission accountability debate going on in the United States right now. From the wider perspective of a facilitator something is very noticeable. A very large number of extremely well-educated individuals are bottled up geographically. A world of billions cries out for law, fairness, education, science, and the college educated. Soon the educational big bang will occur. What seems like an education/economic crisis in the United States is actually the predicate for an unparalleled expansion in human higher education. A facilitator university is increasingly a global enterprise. Today we talk of study abroad; tomorrow, study in a global community. The United States has been so used to being a place that people immigrate to, that it is hard to grasp the diaspora to come.

Fundamentally, a facilitator university continues to search for the right balance between student responsibility and university responsibility—and the appropriate amount of *shared* responsibility. There will always be situations where student or college is more (or totally) responsible, but there are significant areas of shared responsibility. The facilitator model is not polar and prefers centrist and balanced approaches. In essence, the failure of bystander and *in loco parentis* paradigms lay in their extreme allocation of rights and responsibilities. In one system, students were forced to fight in the streets for basic rights; in the other they were encouraged to disconnect, drink, and turn their energies to fights over consumer-style rights. Ultimately, even *in loco parentis* and bystander images facilitated a reality on campus, but it was the wrong reality. Universities should not be either police states or Gomorrah. As we recognize that actual physical danger to students and the security of their learning/living environment is connected to the images and legal rules we use, the facilitator vision can help to find the proper balance of responsibilities and tolerable levels of risks.

III. The Facilitator University and Legal Doctrine

The current duty era case law is complex, ambiguous, and even paradoxical at times. Yet the duty era is readily adaptable to constructing legal rules that facilitate college life through a shared university/student responsibility for the security of the campus environment. Some courts, like *Furek*, *Knoll*, and *Gross*, virtually adopt the facilitator model as such. Duty (and special relationship) rules can balance university authority with student freedom and can adapt to changing circumstances and different college and university environments. As one court stated:

> Duty is not sacrosanct in itself, but is only an expression of the sum total of those considerations of policy which lead the law to say that the plaintiff is entitled to protection.... Accordingly, there is no more magic inherent in the conclusory term "special relation" than there is in the term "duty." Both are part and parcel of the same inquiry into whether and how the law should regulate the activities and dealings that people have with each other. As society changes, as our sciences develop and our activities become more interdependent, so our relations to one another change, and the law must adjust accordingly.... [r]elations perhaps regarded as tenuous in a bygone era may now be of such importance in our modern complicated society as to require certain assurances that risks associated therewith be contained.[71]

Duty in the broad sense of "legal responsibility" and in the narrow *prima facie* case sense is an organic and elastic legal concept, yet is capable of generating very concrete legal results. Duty, special relationships, and legal liability are often used interchangeably to denote the same ultimate conclusion—whether under a given set of circumstances legal responsibility for harm should or should not attach to whom, and why.

The decision to impose liability or not is a function of a variety of factors, policies, and considerations. The following factors are basically the ones that modern courts have used in decisions from *Bradshaw* and *Beach* to *Furek* and *Nero.* In short, whether holding a college liable for physical danger to students or not, courts largely agree on the relevant factors to consider regarding duty and liability [for ease of reference, "the *Tarasoff* Seven Factors"]:

71. *Estates of Morgan*, 673 N.E.2d at 1322.

(1) foreseeability of harm;
(2) nature of the risk;
(3) closeness of the connection between the college's act or omission, and student injury;
(4) moral blame and responsibility;
(5) the social policy of preventing future harm (whether finding duty will tend to prevent future harm);
(6) the burden on the university and the larger community if duty is recognized;
(7) the availability of insurance.

These factors essentially draw their roots from the *Tarasoff*[72] case and have been frequently cited, with little variation, in many of the major university cases of the last twenty years. This may be the only point of near consensus among all the disparate cases of the last few decades. In the heat of litigation, it is easy to miss the convergence of so many courts on such a fundamental level.

In applying these factors to the university context, courts have also come to some agreement on how they work out in given scenarios.

For example, in basic dormitory and premises maintenance cases, duty era courts have been sympathetic to student's injury claims and are intolerant of unreasonably unsafe campus premises. Basically safe conditions in a dormitory and other campus buildings and grounds are essential to successful education—a tenancy unreasonably vulnerable to foreseeable criminal intrusion is not a place to learn.

Courts especially consider foreseeability of harm as the key (but not only) factor. A facilitator college prevents foreseeable risks with reasonable care but asks students to share responsibility via an open and obvious danger rule. If a premises defect/danger is as obvious to a student as it is to the university and the student can avoid it, the calculus may well shift in favor of less, to no, university liability. Courts will consider the *nature of the risk* and how *preventable* it is. For example, an unstable banister on a stairwell that looks safe is different from stone walls around a campus courtyard. The former presents some unusual (latent) risks, and rules imposing responsibility on a college would tend to deter unreasonable delays in maintenance. Courts have seen these rules work for shopping malls and supermarkets. However, a stone wall presents no unusual

---

72. Ultimately, these factors draw their roots to Professor William Prosser, the father of modern tort law. *See* Peter F. Lake, *Common Law Duty in Negligence Law: The Recent Consolidation of a Consensus on the Expansion of the Analysis of Duty and the New Conservative Liability Limiting Use of Policy Considerations*, 34 San Diego L. Rev. 1503 (1997).

risks *per se* and imposing duty on the university as to a student who voluntarily scales the wall (knowing the risk) and falls would not likely prevent much future harm (What would change?).

And while students will be responsible to *use* their door locks, courts will not accept *morally reprehensible* arguments that there is no legal responsibility to fix broken door locks in residence halls after reasonable notice is given to a college that a danger exists. The student/college relationship is not *caveat emptor,* and courts will likely respond to these situations the way reasonable parents might. Again, there is a moral responsibility to share in safety concerns. The facilitator is responsible to provide conditions of reasonable background safety in the interest of the student's educational pursuits.

A facilitator model envisions that the college is especially sensitive to the risks it creates when it aggregates students in collective situations. Placing students together in residence halls, for example, can create educational opportunities and life-long associations. With the benefit, however, comes burden. There *will* be "bad apple" students who endanger others; there *will* be off-campus predators who see dormitories as opportunities to fulfill criminal desires. Aggregation facilitates education, but it also potentially facilitates crime and danger by creating a target zone of risk.

A facilitator will use reasonable care to prevent foreseeable risks. Notice again how courts allocate risks and responsibility to students *and* colleges. When a dangerous person is specifically or readily foreseeable to the college, the college must act to reasonably prevent danger *(Nero, Skate America,* etc.); but when the risk is the undifferentiated risk that "someone" "may" attack another student, courts will be reluctant to impose liability on a college unless a pattern emerges. The *burdens* on a university to prevent random or low probability attacks would be too great and would not likely *prevent* future harm. Moreover, the actions necessary to make a college campus 100% free of peer assault or criminal intrusion would necessarily be draconian—and courts should not, and will not, require that result. Instead, courts have often suggested that after proper training and education, a student may be in the best position to avoid and protect against otherwise random violence.

The line of foreseeability will nearly always be drawn in fact-specific, case-sensitive ways. In all torts cases "duty" is an element with an air of unavoidable uncertainty. Courts can do their part by being explicit as to what is expected and what is not. Courts should be sensitive to the way in which information regarding university law is disseminated. Even the failure to advert to key cases weakens judicial guidance to colleges. As long as the dynamics of university litigation are in place, courts must remain sensitive to the possibility that the messages they send are at risk of distortion. Opinions like *Rabel,* which fail to seriously discuss significant precedent regarding the duty of the university as landlord, contribute to the distortion of legal rules that define the proper parameters of duty with respect to the security of the learning environment.

Now consider off-campus danger that does not arise from any university-sponsored activity or action. Courts are more likely to determine that a college has no legal responsibility for these kinds of harm. For one thing, there are a plethora of risks out there that are more or less equally foreseeable to a student and a college. There is also often a lack of *closeness* between off-campus danger and the college: without a doubt, the more *remote* a danger is—in time, space, and relation to college activities—the less likely a university is legally responsible for the resulting harm if it occurs. When injuries occur off campus, courts have often been unsympathetic—but not always.

Thus, the facilitator does not think strictly in terms of *on-/off*-campus liability as such but in terms of closeness, burden, the nature of risks to be prevented, foreseeability, shared responsibility, and what could reasonably and realistically be done to prevent harm in a riskscape. For example, when a university assigns an intern to an off-campus facility owned by another agency and she is attacked there, the issue of the university's duty to her should not turn exclusively on the fact that she was off campus. The boundaries of a campus are more conceptual, even digital, than geographical. Commentators and colleges often look for a magic bright line to draw around the campus like a moat. The law recognizes a functional, factor-driven equivalent, but there is not a chalk-line of liability as such. Statements like "the injury occurred off campus," or "students are adults," or "the university/student relationship is not special," *beg the question of how these factors weigh, on balance, in a given context.*

The *Tarasoff* Seven Factors are extremely useful in guiding university case law (keeping in mind that many courts use a different, but recognizable set of general policy factors). However, courts attempting to consider the wide range of factors affecting higher education safety case law should consider the following additional factors:

(1) The relationships among common law responsibilities, contract, and regulatory compliance;
(2) The extent to which courts should defer to sound educational judgment and autonomy;
(3) The potential incentives created by imposing or not imposing duty;
(4) Relevant and proactive prevention science and scientific theory regarding questions of student safety;

(5) Good faith of administrators and a college;
(6) Differential impact, if any, of the application of common law rules to colleges in comparison to similarly situated entities in society;
(7) Costs of compliance with the law and costs of litigation.

These seven factors are "the Facilitator Seven" and should be balanced and weighed explicitly in any college litigation. Like *Tarasoff* factors, no factor is dominant, and some may not be in play in certain cases. Let's consider them in order.

Factor One asks courts to consider the relationship between differential systems of compliance. For instance, the application of timely warning requirements under federal Clery Act regulations may well call for a different set of compliance maneuvers than common law reasonable care directives. It is unfair to ask colleges to come into compliance in inconsistent ways; and it is immensely helpful for colleges to have courts guide them in putting the pieces of compliance together. A major compliance dilemma for colleges is making sense of the patchwork quilt of legal compliance directives.

Factor Two recognizes that the use of academic judgment broadly conceived is a major factor in creating a safe campus. The Supreme Court in the recent *Christian Legal Society* case has said administrators are owed "decent respect" in their decision-making, echoing a common theme in Supreme Court jurisprudence since higher education entered the judicial world after World War II. Courts should explicitly consider the uniqueness of the college experience, and managing a college environment. There is danger in some instances in supplanting litigation and lawyers for college administrators. Implicitly, courts in the duty era have accepted and worked with this factor. This factor is used explicitly in civil rights litigation and deserves equal treatment in common law cases. This factor is connected to Factor Five.

Factor Three is the *Pawlowski* factor. Bravo to *Pawlowski* for explicitly considering the incentives created by the imposition, *vel non*, of duty. Interestingly, this factor even has roots in the bystander era in cases like *Bradshaw*, which implicitly feared that the application of duty rules might cause a return of Dean Wormer. Critically, over-reliance on "rescue" rules incentivizes college administrators to fear "assuming duties." Is this the incentive a court seeks? It is time to consider incentivization explicitly.

Factor Four encourages courts and litigants to consult relevant science, within parameters already set for the use of science in courtrooms. At the time of the bystander era, much of what was "known" about higher education and learning was anecdotal, and courts were quick to take judicial notice of "facts." However, there has been a novation in higher education science, including the rush to identify "best practices" even before science can identify them. Courts must help higher education weed out charlatans selling snake oil from quality science-based initiatives. Courts should encourage the use of science to support duty analysis. We are long past the "judicial notice" world of *Bradshaw*.

Factor Five is already present in many cases lodged against public college administrators, and arises under governmental immunity categories. However, good faith should be considered in a broader range of situations—certainly juries will do so even if they are the decision-makers. Indeed in a wide range of college cases—essentially calling for application of a duty to anticipate the need for a rescue—colleges are unfairly treated vis-à-vis other putative rescuers, who typically enjoy "good faith" immunities. If a college can demonstrate good faith proactively—being a facilitator—this should factor into the calculus of whether to impose a duty.

Under Factor Six courts should explicitly consider the differential impact of the application of common law rules to colleges. In many instances there are none, as *Gross* essentially stated. However, colleges often have open campuses and deliberately eschew big box construction for educational reasons. There is educational motive in some forms of architecture not extant in other businesses. This is just one difference. There are many others.

Factor Seven considers the unfunded mandate problem. Public and private colleges are heavily dependent on governmental funding directly and indirectly. Mandates are fair game. However, mandates to higher education should be carefully assessed with respect of costs of compliance. Administrators now spend more and more time and energy trying to come into compliance with the law—taking energy and resources away from educational goals.

The Facilitator Seven Factors seek to blend the concept of the facilitator university with doctrinal duty analysis. These factors represent an approximation of what courts in the duty era actually see themselves doing, and provide a more explicit structure for courts to explain what they are doing. The value to college administrators lies in the compliance guidance that explicit factor balancing gives to them.

IV. The Facilitator Model: Contract Law, Tort Law, and Law as a Positive Tool

Universities still face legal challenges regarding the processes afforded students: students increasingly assert contractual rights. One of the paradoxes of the duty era has been the strange use of tort/duty and contract rules simultaneously.

The facilitator college recognizes, however, that in balancing the rights and responsibilities of students and college, the legal system apportions remedies into contract and tort categories. Rights of economic, dignitary, and civil varieties are typically and appropriately allocated to contract-style analysis; rights involving physical safety and injury are allocated to the tort (duty) system. It is true that ultimately even tort responsibilities are heavily influenced by the quasi-contract, voluntary association nature of the college contexts, but in general there are and will be divergences in the treatment of contract and tort cases. Truly, college is unique and requires an adaptation of basic tort and contract rules to the legal role of a facilitator. Under the facilitator model, courts will see the roots of college law in tort and contract law.

The facilitator model is, then, tailoring of basic rules of tort and contract that courts use generally in other contexts. The duty era has been a powerful time of *mainstreaming* university law while simultaneously adapting non-university legal paradigms to the context of higher education. The danger that a facilitator model addresses is that in mainstreaming college law courts will lose the "uniqueness" of college and university life.

In particular, colleges often believe that courts should protect them from burdensome financial responsibility. As a mature industry, the courts are less likely to provide special protections for a college (during the 1970s, with the enormous growth of the higher education industry, such protection was granted *de facto* under bystander rules). Yet, we do ask colleges to do more than ever today, and in some cases the strain on personnel and financial resources is acute. The burdens we place on colleges may reflect in diminished student educational opportunities. Colleges are concerned—in many cases legitimately—that duty rules will mean that they will experience heightened litigation and liability exposure like other businesses. But overstated fears of the costs of doing business should not lead colleges to avoid responsibility for student safety.

Fundamentally, facilitators are not litigators and do not seek courts primarily to redress grievances. However, facilitators will embrace law as a *positive* tool of bringing fair and reasonable solutions to campus. A facilitator college recognizes that legal scrutiny is inevitable and opts for legal involvement on its own terms in cases that can clarify the definitive legal rules needed to co-create safer campuses. No doubt, courts will continue to show deference to colleges by deciding cases as a matter of law (averting jury questions) and relying on visions of college reality that favor no-liability rules. Even these protections will, however, erode over time. The protections may erode even faster in a *regulatory* world. To the extent that colleges lose these last bastions of legal protection, questions regarding protection from damaging legal judgments will continue to arise from the college community.

The deeply rooted belief that the law should *protect* colleges by *immunities* or other special legal rules that block lawsuits is a vestige of the era of insularity in which law was seen negatively as the enemy on campus. It is easy to underestimate how deeply ingrained negativism towards law lies in the psyche of the university. Law remains—to many—"other," bad, negative, dangerous, something to be resisted, and potentially costly. Law is like muggles trying to regulate Hogwarts. There is much less recognition that law is an integral part of a college campus, a positive tool to reduce danger that can promote campus safety and order, and a way to ultimately reduce costs, including litigation costs.

The perception that there is a need for *immunity* or *protection* arises from *negative* views of law. The facilitator college sees law through a different, *positive* lens. Laws can be the conditions under which true freedom and safety can exist. A well-ordered college community—using law as an ally—can obviate the need for special legal protections by cutting off the danger and disorder before it manifests into costly student injuries and expensive lawsuits. The best protection is to do what is reasonable and to continue to seek and to devise proactive strategies that prevent injury. Law can be empowering in the search for safety on campus.

The facilitator model then, unlike its predecessors, does take one important leap forward. The facilitator college imagines law as a positive tool of empowerment in its efforts to increase safety and promote an educational environment.

Facilitators embrace law and the opportunities it provides. The facilitator college, then, in one important sense is a critical evolutionary step away from colleges of yesteryear. College is no longer an entity outside the law or above it. Colleges today should work *with* law to meet the safety and educational challenges of this transitional period and beyond. The phoenix of the facilitator university can rise from the fall of insularly and complexities of duty law. The facilitator college is a hopeful and positive place that does not look backwards to see what is lost but forward to see what is gained.

V. The Compliance University

The rise of law and a judicial culture on campus has created a scary Kafkaesque spectre for the future—the compliance university. In this potential future colleges lack autonomy and academic freedom to the grinding application of compliance steps, the fear of creating litigation, in costly arbitral litigation and pre-litigation disputes, and in a culture of the fear of application of rules of law that are only made explicit in moments of accountability and condemnation. This is the compliance university in the worst form, and in this form it is the greatest threat to a facilitator university. The facilitator model, coupled with a vision of students as visitors, is a model of academic freedom and autonomy in action. Colleges must find a way to *embrace* responsibility in a juridical world and reclaim true academic powers lost (or never claimed). The rise of the compliance university could spell the death of truly remarkable features of the American higher education experience.

One of the most common critiques of the facilitator model is that it is an "ideal" and not "operational." These criticisms come from the compliance university; the facilitator university has a different vision of *compliance* with legal "mandates."

The facilitator model is indeed an ideal—like health—something pursued. The model deliberately eschews specific "operationalizing" as such—as with "model" policies or "best practices." Just like "reasonable care," facilitation is known in context and is a *process*, not a point. Facilitator is an orientation—a way of approaching student affairs and litigation—it does not reduce to a single set of rules or compliance maneuvers. Facilitators attempt to capture the concept of academic freedom as applied to interactions with students in an educational environment with respect to issues of safety and wellbeing.

Facilitation is immensely proactive, even if it offers a vision of compliance that differs from a compliance university. The spirit of a facilitator animates every decision and every interaction with a student. For certain, every job features its share of soul-numbing tasks. However, we have opportunities every day to *choose*, and to *guide*. Facilitators are constantly searching for ways to unleash potential academic energy—to be like Neo in the Matrix—both working within a system of compliance and acting beyond it.

The compliance university dismisses the *process* of coming into compliance as not being *in* compliance. Ironically, courts and juries see the exact opposite. It is not always what you do, but *why* and *how* that matters most. A compliance university rushes to formulate rules and policies and implement "best" practices. A facilitator university respects the process of rectitude and accepts the fact that there will be answers, but there may not be *all* the answers right *now*. Many times the best practice is recognizing that there are not any right now. The lesson of the cave in *Star Wars*—all in good time.

A facilitator deeply believes in the power of one—one student and one administrator. A facilitator does not need everyone "to be on board." Facilitators are wizards, and there will always be muggles who do not believe in the magic and alchemy of education, or who are too afraid to do so. The fear of litigation is at root a fear of being judged—the mortal enemy of educational energy and the toxic mimic of real accountability. As a facilitator you will always work in non-ideal conditions seeking an ideal. You will find that even within yourself you will feel the dark side of the educational force. Fear of losing a job that may bait you into acting to keep the job as opposed to doing it; the quest for grades over learning; the desire to deflect responsibility. However, it is truly amazing what can be accomplished when the spirit of the facilitator flows through you. In the end you operationalize the facilitator model in the motivation for your work.

Facilitators will find themselves in situations where superiors do not accept facilitator concepts. There are heroes of facilitation—like Liviu Librescu[73]—but you need not pick a hill to die on to be a facilitator. Facilitation also thrives in Monday morning staff meetings—snooze—when someone has the temerity to ask, "Why are we doing this?" and in court when our lawyers argue duty theories to protect us in our core mission. A facilitator understands that motivation and belief precede "compliance" and animate it.

The great risk of the modern university is not high-risk alcohol use or plaintiffs lawyers. The compliance university could consume the very thing we try to protect. Facilitators believe in educational communities that foster growth, responsibility, and choice. College hell, if there is such a place, is where there are teams of administrators deploying best practices in a super-safe environment where all the forms are neatly filed and lawyers and regulators direct every decision. It is not hard to imagine a college that is different from that: one where we work to create reasonable conditions under which students can make responsible choices for themselves. There is always the choice to facilitate. When you encounter the compliance university—and you will—remind it that the desire to protect higher education is a laudable goal, but no one is truly safe when we ignore a power greater than law—the power of education.

---

73. Liviu Librescu was awarded the Facilitator Award in 2009 at the Stetson University College of Law's 30th Annual National Conference on Law and Higher Education, for his heroic actions during the Virginia Tech shooting on April 16, 2007. *See* http://www.law.stetson.edu/conferences/highered/2009/facilitator-awards.php (last visited Oct. 10, 2011).

VII

Conclusion

The modern American university has gradually emerged from legal insularity into a world of law. A recurring theme in this evolution has been how to balance university authority with student freedom to achieve a proper and fair allocation of legal rights and responsibilities—that maximizes student safety and promotes the educational mission of the modern college. For a society in transition out of an industrial age, finding the right balance has not been easy: colleges have had to redefine themselves in terms of their social roles and in terms of legal image simultaneously. Since World War II, and particularly since the 1960s, colleges have experienced dramatic and sometimes extreme swings in both legal image and social mission. Facilitator colleges search for the moderate and reasonable middle roads. The facilitator model is both an adaptable social vision for modern universities and a legal model for courts and college administrators to work with. The facilitator university empowers campus administrators to do their jobs and promotes shared responsibility for safety on campus. The facilitator university turns to law for positive tools and solutions regarding campus safety.

I. The Fall of Legal Insularity: Resistance to Law

Until the 1960s, the American university operated almost entirely free from legal scrutiny regarding issues of student safety and regulation. This freedom—also once given to certain other major social institutions of the industrial age—was the product of the combination of insulating legal doctrines. Colleges were considered legally immune from lawsuits by way of family, charitable, and/or governmental immunities. Legal insularity was also augmented by specialized legal doctrines of proximate causation (whereby a college drinker, or a person who did an intentional, deliberate violent act, were considered the sole causes of harm), by all-or-nothing defenses based on student fault (and assumed risk), and by liberal rules regarding responsibility for alcohol use. Commentators often look to this period to try to define the legal image of the university. What is most striking is the absence of such an image. It is common to refer to this period of insularity as the era of *in loco parentis,* as shorthand. Yet the law of this period only defined the boundaries of protection for colleges and typically avoided the positive imagination of college life. The university formed a powerful image of itself then as a non-legal, non-juristic community—a community entitled, like other hallowed social institutions once were, to be free in the large from legal scrutiny. As such, there was only a small corpus of "higher education law," even into the 1950s.

In the 1960s, students at public universities began to protest to end *de jure* racial discrimination. In many instances, students were met with suppression by public universities, particularly in the Deep South. In shameful abuses of the protections granted to them, some colleges expelled and suspended students—often with little to no process—when those students sought to exercise basic constitutional rights of speech, association, etc., for the purpose of protesting against segregationist laws and policies. Courts reacted strongly against the abuses of the privileges granted to colleges under law and revoked significant university insularity in the civil rights era.

The loss of an important type of insularity in the form of the fall of protective immunities came close in time when other protective legal doctrines were falling within law generally. Charitable immunities were largely abolished; governmental immunities were substantially reduced. In personal injury cases, rules of proximate causation were relaxed to reflect more modern ideas of shared responsibility, and comparative fault replaced all-or-nothing defenses. In short, partly due to abuses of power by certain colleges and partly due to exogenous social changes, the walls of university legal protection began to crumble.

The sense of loss of privilege and protection from law permeates higher education and higher education law even today. Attachment to insularity has led many American colleges to resist law and to view law in negative terms. Instead of facilitating the creation of a new image of the modern college under law, universities resisted the formation of an appropriate new image (other than perhaps the bystander image or the new "compliance university"), creating confusion, some bad cases, and disempowering campus administrators. At the same time, American college campuses began to experience more incivility, disorder, and crime than ever before. The combination of increasing disorder, danger, and disempowerment led to disastrous consequences on campus.

In response to the civil rights cases of the 1960s, colleges began to refashion their relationship to students and in many instances endeavored to fight legal responsibility for student safety at every turn. In the immediate period following the civil rights cases—the bystander era—universities fought to defend and re-create privileges lost. In a prominent series of no-duty-to-student cases (*Bradshaw* et al.), courts created a new set of protections for colleges based upon rescue law and doctrine, purported lack of (custodial) control over students, and the increasing distance between students and college administration. Universities actually convinced several courts that they could no longer manage student affairs and protect student safety. In cases involving alcohol use especially, universities were successful in casting students as uncontrollable "strangers." American courts of the bystander period were still sympathetic to institutions where alcohol was used. The bystander era first arose when the "social host" was broadly construed and largely protected. Universities, in search of protection from law, found some assistance recreating insularity in libertarian legal attitudes towards social drinking.

Yet, even in the bystander period, powerful crosscurrents in the case law were present. When student safety issues did not involve alcohol, courts began to question whether colleges deserved any special legal protections. Courts began to treat universities like other institutions, particularly businesses. Many cases during the bystander era began to cast students in more commercial roles vis-a-vis the college—as consumer or tenant. In particular, the role of legal duty became prominent, and that role has only solidified since the mid 1980s.

Even recently, as courts have increasingly mainstreamed college affairs into the legal world, universities have resisted the loss of privilege and legal insularity. For example, colleges have litigated for the right not to fix broken locks in dormitory entrances and have defended placing dangerous sexual predators in dormitories without warnings or other protections in place.

Since the fall of *in loco parentis* and the era of insularity, messages to campus law enforcement and campus administrators sometimes have been dangerously ambiguous. The no-duty case law of the bystander era resulted in admonitions against "assuming duties" to students for fear of legal liability. The law sent some messages to college campuses that the best legal strategy to avoid liability for student injury was distance, disengagement, and bifurcation of functions into academic/student affairs; bystanders who got involved could be sued, so avoiding assumption of duty was a paramount objective. Confusingly, the law also sent messages that there were new legal responsibilities for residential life, student activities, etc. College administrators and campus law enforcement officers became motivated by fear of triggering legal liability and were encouraged to pursue strategies in their jobs that would minimize the risk of lawsuits but not necessarily reduce risk or injury. In short, the law encouraged the destruction of much of the student/university relationship outside the classroom. (It is too early to tell if the new onset of the compliance university will have the same effect—it might.)

In the current duty era, resistance to law is increasingly futile (as well as a wasted opportunity) as a college legal strategy. In light of teetering legal protections for social hosts and new social attitudes about college-aged drinking, the bystander era protections for student alcohol use are in danger of being lost. Recent events send a clear signal of public frustration over abusive, predatory, and high-risk college-aged drinking. Regulators are also losing patience with high-risk alcohol culture.

The resistance to law and negative, avoid-legal-scrutiny strategies are typical of adolescent industries that are in transition. However, it is increasingly clear that such strategies are dangerous, counterproductive, and inconsistent with realities and missions of modern universities. Distance, of the kind Boyer described, facilitates danger. As a community grows apart and distant from its officials and police forces, disorder and danger grows. A loss of community efficacy hurt our cities; a similar phenomenon has occurred on our college campuses. Fostering a sense of shared responsibility is essential to campus safety. Legal strategies that seek to turn students into uncontrollable strangers work against safer models based upon shared community responsibility.

Strategies of resistance to law are also counterproductive. If boards of trustees and college presidents believe that there is no duty regarding many student safety issues, there will be a tendency to allocate resources away from residence halls, campus law enforcement, and other departments that can impact safety. More resources to fix broken locks can prevent injuries that could result in large dollar litigation. Loss avoidance is often the best litigation avoidance strategy. Energies spent resisting legal scrutiny can be better directed to educational solutions and to fixing problems that create disorder and danger on campus. Moreover, a campus that fails to adequately address danger and disorder is less educationally sound. Colleges and universities that spend their time resisting student litigation on the grounds that their students are beyond their control, spend money on lawyers and lawsuits that might be better spent remedying danger and disorder and preventing student injury. A college or university is often better off demonstrating that it exercised reasonable care under the circumstances than to assert that it had no duty to a student regarding her safety on campus.

The resistance to law and the desire to avoid assumed duties to students is also inconsistent with realities in modern universities. Student affairs administrators study and are trained to be managers of student life and direct housing, student activities, etc. Many campus administrators are professional counselors. Many campus law enforcement officers are specially trained to maintain order and reduce risks of criminal intrusion. Campus police easily understand that many strategies that involve far less than custodial control are highly effective for managing danger and criminality. Administrators and campus security officers have the professional training, experience, and judgment to do their jobs. Colleges have given them their missions, but the law has all too often disempowered them by telling them that proaction can be a source of legal liability. This kind of disempowerment leads to dangerous decisions. Few college professors/administrators today would fail to provide the supervision that would have prevented the horrible injury that occurred in the *Beach* case. Campus security departments are appalled to think that broken entry door locks in dormitories would go unrepaired as in *Delaney*; a decision to let a dangerous person go on his way to kill someone, as in *Tarasoff*, was likely facilitated by fear of litigation; most campus police want *rules* to stop and question students like those fraternity hazing-bound students who roamed campus before the sad incident in *Furek*. These states of affairs are directly contrary to the missions of universities and the role of student life administrators and other teachers. The facilitator university seeks to reverse the longstanding resistance to law and overcome the danger, disempowerment, and disorder that come from unclear responsibilities and campuses where students and the college are disconnected.

II. Facilitating Shared Responsibility: Empowerment Through Positive Use of Law

To reduce danger on campus and enhance the educational program, we must facilitate shared responsibility for safety. In the rush to resist law and blame or distance themselves from students, colleges lost sight of important opportunities to build safer campus environments and close the distance between administration/faculty, students, and even college life and the law itself. In retrospect, it was bad social policy and a losing legal strategy to resist partnerships with law. The law can bring campus communities together and provide the structure in which student freedoms can flourish. Students can be free and safe and yet enjoy constitutional adulthood; students simply need structure and guidance to manage their educational and personal development opportunities in college. Some structure actually enhances the hard-won student constitutional freedoms. Lack of structure undermines those freedoms.

A principal goal of a facilitator university is to identify and manifest shared responsibility. This means that students must acknowledge their critical role in protecting their own and other students' safety. Legal rules of comparative negligence, for example, can reinforce this message. The university also shares responsibility with students for their safety. The typical college has many tools at its disposal to manage and reduce risks, including control of maintenance and security, housing assignments, and the identification of activities that are promoted or discouraged, etc. A college can establish some circumstances of campus life and engender others. Appropriately applied legal rules regarding duty can facilitate understanding of what colleges can and should do.

Campus administrators and police can be more effective with the law as an ally. The law should allow and encourage them to do their jobs as best they can, and they should be able to look to the law for assistance in how to manage new and difficult safety issues on campus. In a world of law and litigation, lawsuits are a fact of life. It is better—all the way around—for campus officials to do their jobs as they know best and not to turn their job descriptions into "litigation avoidance." Empowerment is more reasonable, much safer, and makes good legal and practical sense. Law does not facilitate the proper dynamic with no-duty rules, which discourage reasonable efforts at addressing campus safety issues. Duty rules—balanced with shared student responsibility rules—facilitate cooperative, proactive university administration.

This does not mean that colleges will no longer face lawsuits and menacing legal regulation from time to time. However, even in the face of hostile litigation a college can have the opportunity to use the legal process as a way to define parameters of safety and responsibility on campus. And viewing the law through a positive lens, the university can elect the conditions under which it will most likely encounter legal process and litigation. For example, in *Nero,* the university could have elected to eliminate the dangerous student from the summer dormitory. The attack presumably would not have occurred, thus avoiding an inevitable lawsuit from the victim or her family; the removed student may sue, and in a worst case scenario the university will learn the lawful conditions under which it may deal with the next student who arguably threatens the safety of other students. In that sense, even a losing case is a winner in that it offers guidelines for future conduct. Indeed, a college may deliberately risk one type of litigation rather than another. Sometimes only by making a court state a clear rule of decision can confusion and uncertainty about the margins of the law be cleared up. The courts have a heavy responsibility to decide cases in ways that facilitate efforts to promote student safety. The facilitator model offers courts a way to work closely with rules and procedures that are already in place so as to promote safer campuses and to recognize the uniqueness of colleges.

III. The Rise of the Compliance University and the end of the Facilitator University?

Bystanderism has baited regulatory intervention. Where courts have hesitated, regulators have become significant agents of change. In just the last few years there has been a demonstrable uptick it regulatory initiatives designed to promote safer and more responsible campuses. This marks a significant departure from both the era of insularity and the civil rights era. The notion of highly regulated college environments was foreign to the era of insularity; the civil rights era was an incomplete period of reform because it focused so heavily on political and civil liberties and not student safety or even core mission delivery (such as learning outcomes). There is the possibility that regulatory compliance will come to dominate student affairs and legal staff—to the point that facilitation becomes only something that can be, at best, a secondary task. Indeed, compliance requirements may force colleges to deliver services arising from mandates from external sources. The rise of compliance trained and oriented "educrats" may ensue; we already are observing an increase in *legalists* on campus—those who have some legal training performing tasks with legal/compliance overtones. Will a surge in regulatory activity erase the hope of a facilitator university?

Time will tell, but there is time.

The strength of the facilitator model is that it does not propose or describe a radical change in law or higher education administration—nor does it imagine an extreme relationship with the law where law is either absent or the day-to-day supervisor. The vision of the facilitator university emphasizes what is reasonable and positive in the relationships among students, universities, and the legal system. Perpetuation of extreme positions and paradigms guarantees failure. The rise of regulation of higher education should push colleges even harder to fight for reasonable, fair, and balanced solutions to the problems that vex all campuses. A legal paradigm that asks colleges to exercise reasonable care for student safety—and asks students to be accountable when they are at fault—is equitable, balanced, safer, and contributes to a sense of community. There is a historic opportunity to seize this moment in the history of higher education, to embrace this time of transition and create closer and safer campuses. We still have the choice to be facilitators. There is still time to show leadership and demonstrate to students, courts, and regulators that the best and safest solutions to the dangers of college life are those that arise from within a facilitator university.

Bibliography

Texts & Monographs

Judith Areen, *Higher Education and the Law: Cases and Materials* (Foundation Press 2009).

1 Sir William Blackstone, *Commentaries on the Laws of England* (Oxford, Clarendon Press 1765).

Ernest L. Boyer, *College: The Undergraduate Experience in America* (Harper & Row 1987).

William Bratton with Peter Knobler, *Turnaround—How America's Top Cop Reversed the Crime Epidemic* (Random House 1998).

Gene Deisinger, Marisa Randazzo, Daniel O'Neill & Jenna Savage, *The Handbook for Campus Threat Assessment & Management Teams* (Applied Risk Management 2008).

John L. Diamond, Lawrence C. Levine & M. Stuart Madden, *Understanding Torts* (2nd ed., Lexis Pub. 2000).

Edward Elliott & M.M. Chambers, *The Colleges and the Courts* (The Carnegie Foundation for the Advancement of Teaching 1936).

Amy Gajda, *The Trials of Academe: The New Era of Campus Litigation* (Harvard Univ. Press 2009).

David Halberstam, *The Children* (Random House 1998).

Charles Homer Haskins, *The Rise of Universities* (Cornell University Press 1957) (1923).

Neil Howe & William Strauss, *Millennials Rising: The Next Great Generation* (Vintage Books 2000).

Richard D. Kadison & Theresa Foy DiGeronimo, *College of the Overwhelmed: The Campus Mental Health Crisis and What to Do About It* (Jossey-Bass 2004).

William A. Kaplin & Barbara A. Lee, *The Law of Higher Education* (4th ed., Jossey-Bass 2006).

Alyssa Keehan, *Threat Assessment Teams for Troubled Students—Putting the Pieces Together* (Risk Management Counsel, United Educators 2009).

George Kelling & Catherine Coles, *Fixing Broken Windows—Restoring Order and Reducing Crime in Our Communities* (The Free Press 1996, Touchstone 1998).

Peter F. Lake, *Beyond Discipline—Managing the Modern Higher Education Environment* (Hierophant Enterprises, Inc. 2009).

Arthur Levine, *When Dreams and Heroes Died* (Jossey-Bass 1980).

Arthur Levine & Jeanette S. Cureton, *When Hope and Fear Collide: A Portrait of Today's College Student* (Jossey-Bass 1998).

William L. Prosser, *Handbook of the Law of Torts* (3d ed., West Pub. Co. 1964).

Restatement (Second) of Torts (1965).

Jean M. Twenge, *Generation Me: Why Today's Young Americans are More Confident, Assertive, Entitled—and More Miserable Than Ever Before* (Free Press 2006).

Jean M. Twenge & W. Keith Campbell, *The Narcissism Epidemic: Living in the Age of Entitlement* (Free Press 2009).

Juan Williams, *Eyes on the Prize: America's Civil Rights Years, 1954-1965* (Penguin Books 1987).

Statutes, Regulations & Laws

Federal Acts

Americans with Disabilities Act, 42 U.S.C. §§12213 (2006).

Civil Rights Act of 1964, Title VI, 42 U.S.C. §2000(d)–2000(d)(1).

Civil Rights Act of 1964, Pub. L. No. 88-352, 78 Stat. 241 (1964).

Civil Rights Act of 1968, Pub. L. No. 90-284, 82 Stat. 73 (1968).

Education Amendments of 1972, Title IX, 20 U.S.C. §1681 (2010).

Family Educational Rights and Privacy Act (FERPA), 12 U.S.C. §1232(g) (2006).

Jeanne Clery Disclosure of Campus Security Policy and Campus Crime Statistics Act (Clery Act), 20 U.S.C. §1092(f) (2006).

Rehabilitation Act of 1973, Section 504, 29 U.S.C. §794 (2006).

Safe and Drug-Free Schools and Communities Act, 20 U.S.C. §7101 (2006).

State Laws & Rules

Cal. Penal Code §245.6 (West 2007).

Fla. Stat. §1006.63(2) (2004).

Mass. Gen. Laws ch. 269 §17 (2002).

Mass. Gen. Laws ch. 269, §18 (2002).

N.Y. Penal Law §120.16 (McKinney 2004).

Ohio Rev. Code Ann. §2305.51 (2008).

Law Reviews, Law Journals & Other Journals

John M. Adler, *Relying Upon the Reasonableness of Strangers: Some Observations About the Current State of Common Law Affirmative Duties to Aid or Protect Others*, 1991 Wis. L. Rev. 867 (1991).

Hazel G. Beh, *Student Versus University: The University's Implied Obligation of Good Faith and Fair Dealing*, 59 Md. L. Rev. 183 (2000).

Robert D. Bickel, *Tort Accident Cases Involving Colleges and Universities: A Review of the 1995 Decisions*, 23 J.C. & U.L. 357 (1997).

Robert D. Bickel & Peter F. Lake, *Reconceptualizing the University's Duty to Provide a Safe Learning Environment: A Criticism of the Doctrine of In Loco Parentis and the Restatement (Second) of Torts*, 20 J.C. & U.L. 261 (1994).

Kathleen M. Burch, *Going Global: Managing Liability in International Externship Programs—A Case Study*, 36 J.C. & U.L. 455 (2010).

Kathleen C. Butler, *Shared Responsibility: The Duty to Legal Externs*, 106 W. Va. L. Rev. 51 (2003).

William Cohen, *The Private-Public Legal Aspects of Institutions of Higher Education*, 45 Denv. L.J. 643 (1968).

Comment, *Common Law Rights for Private University Students: Beyond the State Action Principle*, 84 Yale L.J. 120 (1974).

Jane A. Dall, *Determining Duty in Collegiate Tort Litigation: Shifting Paradigms of the College-Student Relationship*, 29 J.C. & U.L. 485 (2003).

Victoria J. Dodd, *The Non-Contractual Nature of the Student-University Contractual Relationship*, 33 U. Kan. L. Rev. 701 (1985).

David J. Drum, Chris Brownson, Adryon Burton Denmark & Shanna E. Smith, *New Data of the Nature of Suicidal Crises in College Students: Shifting the Paradigm*, 40 Professional Psychology: Research and Practice 3 (2009) [Drum Study].

Susan H. Duncan, *College Bullies—Precursors to Campus Violence: What Should Universities and College Administrators Know About the Law?*, 55 Vill. L. Rev. 269 (2010).

Marc Edelman & David Rosenthal, *A Sobering Conflict: The Call for Consistency in the Message Colleges Send About Alcohol*, 20 Fordham Intell. Prop. Media & Ent. L.J. 1389 (2010).

Richard Fossey, Suzanne Eckes & Todd A. DeMitchell, *Anti-Gay T-Shirt Litigation in the Seventh and Ninth Circuits: Conflicts of Outcomes, But Changing Values*, 256 Ed. Law Rep. 1 (2010).

Gerard A. Fowler, *The Legal Relationship Between the American College Student and the College: An Historical Perspective and the Renewal of a Proposal*, 13 J.L. & Educ. 401 (1984).

Alvin L. Goldman, *The University and the Liberty of Its Students—A Fiduciary Theory*, 54 Ky. L.J. 643 (1966).

Michael P. Haines & Sherilyn F. Spear, *Changing the Perception of the Norm: A Strategy to Decrease Binge Drinking Among College Students*, 45 J. Am. C. Health 134 (1996).

John C. Hogan & Mortimer Schwartz, *In Loco Parentis in the United States 1765-1985*, 8 J. Legal Hist. 260 (1987).

Wesley Newcomb Hohfeld, *Some Fundamental Legal Conceptions as Applied in Judicial Reasoning*, 23 Yale L.J. 16 (1913).

Brian Jackson, *The Lingering Legacy of In Loco Parentis: An Historical Survey and Proposal for Reform*, 44 Vand. L. Rev. 1135 (1991).

Cheryl McDonald Jones, *In Loco Parentis and Higher Education: Together Again?*, 1 Charleston L. Rev. 185 (2007).

Peter F. Lake, *Common Law Duty in Negligence Law: The Recent Consolidation of a Consensus on the Expansion of the Analysis of Duty and the New Conservative Liability Limiting Use of Policy Considerations*, 34 San Diego L. Rev. 1503 (1997).

Peter F. Lake, *Private Law Continues to Come to Campus: Rights and Responsibilities Revisited*, 31 J.C. & U.L. 621 (2005).

Peter F. Lake, *Recognizing the Importance of Remoteness to the Duty to Rescue*, 46 DePaul L. Rev. 315 (1997).

Peter F. Lake, *Revisiting Tarasoff*, 58 Alb. L. Rev. 97 (1994).

Peter F. Lake, *The Special Relationship(s) Between a College and a Student: Law and Policy Ramifications for the Post in Loco Parentis College*, 37 Idaho L. Rev. 531 (2001).

Peter F. Lake, *Still Waiting: The Slow Evolution of the Law in Light of the Ongoing Student Suicide Crisis*, 34 J.C. & U.L. 253 (2008).

Peter F. Lake, *Tort Litigation in Higher Education*, 27 J.C. & U.L. 255 (2000).

Peter F. Lake & Joel C. Epstein, *Modern Liability Rules and Policies Regarding College Student Alcohol Injuries: Reducing High-Risk Alcohol Use Through Norms of Shared Responsibility and Environmental Management*, 53 Okla. L. Rev. 611 (2000).

Peter F. Lake & Nancy Tribbensee, *The Emerging Crisis of College Student Suicide: Law and Policy Responses to Serious Forms of Self-Inflicted Injury*, 32 Stetson L. Rev. 125 (2002).

David Lisak & Paul M. Miller, *Repeat Rape and Multiple Offending Among Undetected Rapists*, 17 Violence and Victims 73 (2002).

Joseph W. Little, *Erosion of No-Duty Negligence Rules in England, the United States, and Common Law Commonwealth Nations*, 20 Hous. L. Rev. 959 (1983).

Robert B. McKay, *The Student as Private Citizen*, 45 Denv. L.J. 558 (1968).

Marcus Misinec, *When the Game Ends, the Pandemonium Begins: University Liability for Field Rushing Injuries,* 12 Sports Law J. 181 (2005).

Christopher H. Munch, *Comment*, 45 Den. L.J. 533 (1968).

Ian M. Newman et al., *Use of Policy, Education, and Enforcement to Reduce Binge Drinking Among University Students: The NU Directions Project,* 17 Int'l J. of Drug Policy 339 (2006).

H. Wesley Perkins & Henry Wechsler, *Variation in Perceived College Drinking Norms and Its Impact on Alcohol Abuse: A Nationwide Study*, 26 J. Drug Issues 961 (1996).

Kristen Peters, *Protecting the Millennial College Student,* 16 S. Cal. Rev. L. & Soc. Just. 431 (2007).

Gary T. Schwartz, *The Beginning and the Possible End of the Rise of Modern American Tort Law,* 26 Ga. L. Rev. 601 (1992).

Warren A. Seavey, *Dismissal of Students: "Due Process,"* 70 Harv. L. Rev. 1406 (1957).

Theodore C. Stamatakos, *The Doctrine of In Loco Parentis, Tort Liability and the Student-College Relationship,* 65 Ind. L.J. 471 (1990).

Joshua A. Sussberg, Note, *Shattered Dreams: Hazing in College Athletics*, 24 Cardozo L. Rev. 1421 (2003).

Christopher Jayson Swartz, *The Revivification of In Loco Parentis Behavioral Regulation in Public Institutions of Higher Education to Combat the Obesity Epidemic*, 45 New Eng. L. Rev. 101 (2010).

James J. Szablewicz & Annette Gibbs, *Colleges' Increasing Exposure to Liability: The New In Loco Parentis,* 16 J.L. & Educ. 453 (1987).

Nancy Tribbensee, *Tort Litigation in Higher Education: A Review of Cases Decided in Year 2001*, 29 J.C. & U.L. 249 (2003).

Melissa Weberman, *University Hate Speech Policies and the Captive Audience Doctrine*, 36 Ohio N.U. L. Rev. 553 (2010).

Kent Weeks & Rich Haglund, *Fiduciary Duties of College and University Faculty and Administrators*, 29 J.C. & U.L. 153 (2002).

Charles A. Wright, *The Constitution on the Campus,* 22 Vand. L. Rev. 1027 (1969).

Perry A. Zirkel & Henry F. Reichner, *Is the "In Loco Parentis" Doctrine Dead?,* 15 J.L. & Educ. 271 (1986).

Other Authority

Animal House (Universal Pictures 1978).

Elyse Ashburn, *Education Dept. Tells 2 Colleges to Revamp Sexual-Harassment Policies*, Chron. of Higher Educ. (Dec. 10, 2010), *available at* http://chronicle.com/article/Education-Dept-Tells-2/125704/.

Association of Governing Boards & United Educators, *State of Enterprise Risk Management at Colleges and Universities Today* (2009), *available at* http://agb.org/sites/agb.org/files/u3/AGBUE_FINAL.pdf.

Elizabeth Bernstein, *Colleges Move Boldly on Student Drinking*, Wall St. J. (Dec. 6, 2007), *available at* http://online.wsj.com/article/SB119690910535115405.html.

Correcting Misperceptions of Norms on Seven Campuses, 4 Catalyst No. 1, 6 (Summer/Fall 1998), *available at* http://www.higheredcenter.org/files/product/catalyst11.pdf.

Will Creeley, *Why the Tyler Clementi Act Threatens Free Speech on Campuses*, Chron. Higher Educ. (Apr. 10, 2011), *available at* http://chronicle.com/article/Why-the-Tyler-Clementi-Act/127062/.

Crisis Reality Training, *Lockdown Development and Implementation*, https://www.crisisrealitytraining.com/conference_list.php?sid=14 (last visited October 5, 2011).

William DeJong et al., Higher Educ. Ctr. for Alcohol and Other Drug Prevention, *Environmental Management: A Comprehensive Strategy for Reducing Alcohol and Other Drug Use on College Campuses* (1998), *available at* http://www.higheredcenter.org/services/publications/environmental-management-comprehensive-strategy-reducing-alcohol-and-other-drug.

Felton J. Earls, *Project on Human Development in Chicago Neighborhoods: Longitudinal Cohort Study, 1994-2001* (2002), *available at* http://dvn.iq.harvard.edu/dvn/dv/isq/faces/study/StudyPage.xhtml?studyId=380&tab=catalog.

Kelly Field & Goldie Blumenstyk, *What the 'Gainful Employment' Rule Means for Colleges*, Chron. Higher Educ. (June 2, 2011), *available at* http://chronicle.com/article/Audio-What-the-Gainful/127750/.

Lisa W. Foderaro, *3 Plead Guilty in Inquiry into Fatal College Hazing*, N.Y. Times (Oct. 11, 2003), *available at* http://www.nytimes.com/2003/10/11/nyregion/3-plead-guilty-in-inquiry-into-fatal-college-hazing.html.

Trip Gabriel, *Mental Health Needs Seen Growing at Colleges*, N.Y. Times (Dec. 19, 2010), *available at* http://www.nytimes.com/2010/12/20/health/20campus.html?pagewanted=all&_r=0.

Jordi Gasso, *Yale Not Alone in Title IX Probe*, Yale Daily News (Apr. 15, 2011), *available at* http://www.yaledailynews.com/news/2011/apr/15/yale-not-alone-in-title-ix-probe/Gavan Gideon & Caroline Tan, *Department of Education Ends Title IX Investigation*, Yale Daily News (June 15, 2012), *available at* http://www.yaledailynews.com/news/2012/jun/15/department-education-ends-title-ix-investigation/.

Michael P. Haines, *U.S. Dep't of Educ., A Social Norms Approach to Preventing Binge Drinking at Colleges and Universities* (1996), *available at* http://www.higheredcenter.org/files/product/socnorms.pdf.

Terry W. Hartle, *A Federal Outrage Against Virginia Tech*, Chron. Higher Educ. (April 10, 2011), *available at* http://chronicle.com/article/A-Federal-Outrage-Against/127055/.

J.J. Hermes, *Virginia's Governor Signs Laws Responding to Shootings at Virginia Tech*, Chron. Higher Educ. (April 10, 2008), *available at* http://chronicle.com/article/New-Virginia-Laws-Respond-to/675.

Higher Education Mental Health Alliance and The Jed Foundation, *Balancing Safety and Support on Campus: A Guide for Campus Teams* (2012), *available at* http://www.jedfoundation.org/campus_teams_guide.pdf.

Eric Hoover, *The Millennial Muddle: How Stereotyping Students Became a Thriving Industry and a Bundle of Contradictions*, Chron. Higher Educ. (Oct. 11, 2009), *available at* http://chronicle.com/article/The-Millennial-Muddle-How/48772/.

The International Association of Campus Law Enforcement Administrators (IACLEA), http://www.IACLEA.org (last visited May 17, 2012).

JED Foundation, *Student Mental Health and the Law: A Resource for Institutions of Higher Education* (2008), *available at* https://www.jedfoundation.org/assets/Programs/Program_downloads/StudentMentalHealth_Law_2008.pdf.

Judge Overturns Findings and Fines Against Virginia Tech Under Clery Act, Chron. of Higher Educ. (Mar. 30, 2012), http://chronicle.com/blogs/ticker/education-department-judge-overturns-findings-and-fines-against-virginia-tech-under-clery-act/41849.

Judge Upholds Negligence Verdict from Va. Tech Shootings but Reduces Damages, Chron. of Higher Educ. (June 20, 2012), http://chronicle.com/blogs/ticker/judge-upholds-negligence-verdict-from-va-tech-shootings-but-reduces-damages/44651.

Juno (Fox Searchlight Pictures 2007).

Eric Kelderman, *Most Colleges Avoid Risk Management, Report Says*, Chron. Higher Educ. (June 25, 2009), *available at* http://chronicle.com/article/Most-Colleges-Avoid-Risk/47806.

Kick-Ass (Lionsgate 2010).

Peter F. Lake, *Student-Privacy Rules Show a Renewed Trust in Colleges*, Chron. Higher Educ. (Feb. 6, 2009), *available at* http://chronicle.com/article/Student-Privacy-Rules-Show-a/20332.

Peter F. Lake, *What's Next for Private Universities? Accountability*, Chron. of Higher Educ. (Dec. 5, 2010), *available at* http://chronicle.com/article/Whats-Next-for-Private/125599/.

Linda Langford, *Preventing Violence and Promoting Safety in Higher Education Settings: Overview of a Comprehensive Approach*, http://searchpubs.higheredcenter.org/files/product/violence.pdf (last visited June 16, 2011).

Sara Lipka, *Allowing More Guns on Campuses is a Bad Idea, Administrators Argue*, Chron. Higher Educ. (Feb. 19, 2008), *available at* http://chronicle.com/article/More-Guns-Wont-Make-Campuses/519.

Sara Lipka, *Colleges Face Conflicting Pressures in Dealing with Cases of Sexual Assault*, Chron. Higher Educ. (March 20, 2011), *available at* http://chronicle.com/article/Colleges-Face-Conflicting/126818/.

Sara Lipka, *U. of Virginia President Meets with Governor to Push for Access to Law-Enforcement Records*, Chron. Higher Educ. (May 12, 2010), *available at* http://chronicle.com/article/A-Call-for-Access-to-Students/65482/.

Linda Major & Thomas Workman, *Organizing a Community Coalition: Lessons Learned from Lincoln, Nebraska*, http://bcm.academia.edu/ThomasWorkman/Papers/125408/Organizing_a_Campus_Community_Coalition (last visited Sept. 22, 2011).

National Institute on Alcohol Abuse and Alcoholism (NIAAA), *A Call to Action: Changing the Culture of Drinking at U.S. Colleges* (2002), *available at* http://www.collegedrinkingprevention.gov/niaaacollegematerials/taskforce/taskforce_toc.aspx.

Gary Pavela, 7 Synthesis: Law and Policy in Higher Education (1992).

Elia Powers, *Testing an Anti-Hazing Law*, Inside Higher Ed. (Jan. 31, 2007), *available at* http://insidehighered.com/layout/set/print/news/2007/01/31/hazing.

The Real World: New Orleans (MTV television broadcast 2010).

Molly Redden, *Supreme Court Decision on Arbitration May Have Eroded For-Profit Students' Right to Sue*, Chron. Higher Educ. (June 21, 2011), *available at* http://chronicle.com/article/Supreme-Court-Decision-May/127964/.

Leo Reisberg, *MIT Pays $6-Million to Settle Lawsuit over a Student's Death*, Chron. Higher Educ. (Sept. 29, 2000), *available at* http://chronicle.com/article/MIT-Pays-6-Million-to-Sett/32171/.

Secretary Duncan Will Have Final Word on Virginia Tech, Chron. Higher Educ. (May 6, 2012), http://chronicle.com/blogs/ticker/secretary-duncan-will-have-final-word-on-virginia-tech/43080.

Security on Campus, http://www.securityoncampus.org (last visited May 17, 2012).

Lauren Sieben, *Education Dept. Issues New Guidelines for Sexual Assault Investigations*, Chron. Higher Educ. (Apr. 4, 2011), *available at* http://chronicle.com/article/Education-Dept-Issues-New/127004/.

Joseph A. Slobodzian, *Penn Students Guilty in '05 Hazing Incident*, Philly.com (Nov. 21, 2006), http://www.insidehazing.com/ headline.php?id=344.

Some Student Bullying May Violate Federal Law, Education Department Says, Chron. Higher Educ. (Oct. 25, 2010), http://chronicle.com/blogs/ticker/some-student-bullying-may-violate-federal-law-education-department-says/27906.

Something Borrowed (Warner Bros. 2011).

Stetson University College of Law, *Facilitator Awards*, http://www.law.stetson.edu/conferences/highered/2009/facilitator-awards.php (last visited Oct. 10, 2011).

Beckie Supiano & Elyse Ashburn (Eric Hoover, contributing), *With New Lists, Federal Government Moves to Help Consumers and Prod Colleges to Limit Price In-*

creases, Chron. Higher Educ. (June 30, 2011), *available at* http://chronicle.com/article/Governments-New-Lists-on/128092/.

Caroline Tan, *UP CLOSE: Title IX, One Year Later*, Yale Daily News (Apr. 9, 2012), *available at* http://www.yaledailynews.com/news/2012/apr/09/up-close-title-ix-one-year-later/.

Nancy L. Thomas, *The Attorney's Role on Campus—Options for Colleges and Universities,* 30 Change: The Magazine of Higher Learning 34 (May/June 1998).

The Truman Show (Paramount Pictures 1998).

Twilight (Summit Entertainment 2008).

Robynn Tysver, *Ex-Student Settles with UNL in Fall from Fraternity House*, Omaha World Herald, Aug. 9, 2000, at 15.

United Educators, *Managing Liability,* (2008), http://www.unh.edu/cie/pdf/risk-ue-understanding-risks.pdf (last visited May 17, 2012).

University of Nebraska—Lincoln, *College Drinking Data*, http://www.nudirections.org/drinkingData.php (last visited Sept. 22, 2011).

U.S. Department of Education's Higher Education Center for Alcohol and Other Drug Prevention, http://www.higheredcenter.org (last visited Sept. 22, 2011).

U.S. Department of Education's Higher Education Center for Alcohol and Other Drug Prevention, *MIT Settlement Makes Other Colleges and Universities Take Notice* (Sept. 15, 2000), *available at* http://www.higheredcenter.org/files/thisweek/tw000915.html.

U.S. Department of Education's Office for Civil Rights, *Dear Colleague Letter* (Apr. 4, 2011), *available at* http://www2.ed.gov/about/offices/list/ocr/letters/colleague-201104.pdf.

U.S. Department of Education's Office for Civil Rights, Region 1, *Resolution Letter to Yale University* (June 15, 2012), *available at* http://www2.ed.gov/documents/press-releases/yale-letter.pdf.

U.S. Department of Education's Office for Civil Rights, Region 1, *Voluntary Resolution Agreement for Yale University* (June 11, 2012), *available at* http://www2.ed.gov/documents/press-releases/yale-agreement.pdf.

Wookieepedia, *Padawan*, http://starwars.wikia.com/wiki/Padawan (last visited Oct. 4, 2011).

Robert Zimmerman, *U.S. Dep't of Educ., Social Marketing Strategies for Campus Prevention of Alcohol and Other Drug Problems* (1997), *available at* http://www.higheredcenter.org/services/publications/social-marketing-strategies-campus-prevention-alcohol-and-other-drug-problems.

Table of Cases

Pages in bold font indicate substantial discussion of the case.

N

O

P

Index

D

M

N

O

P

V

W

Y